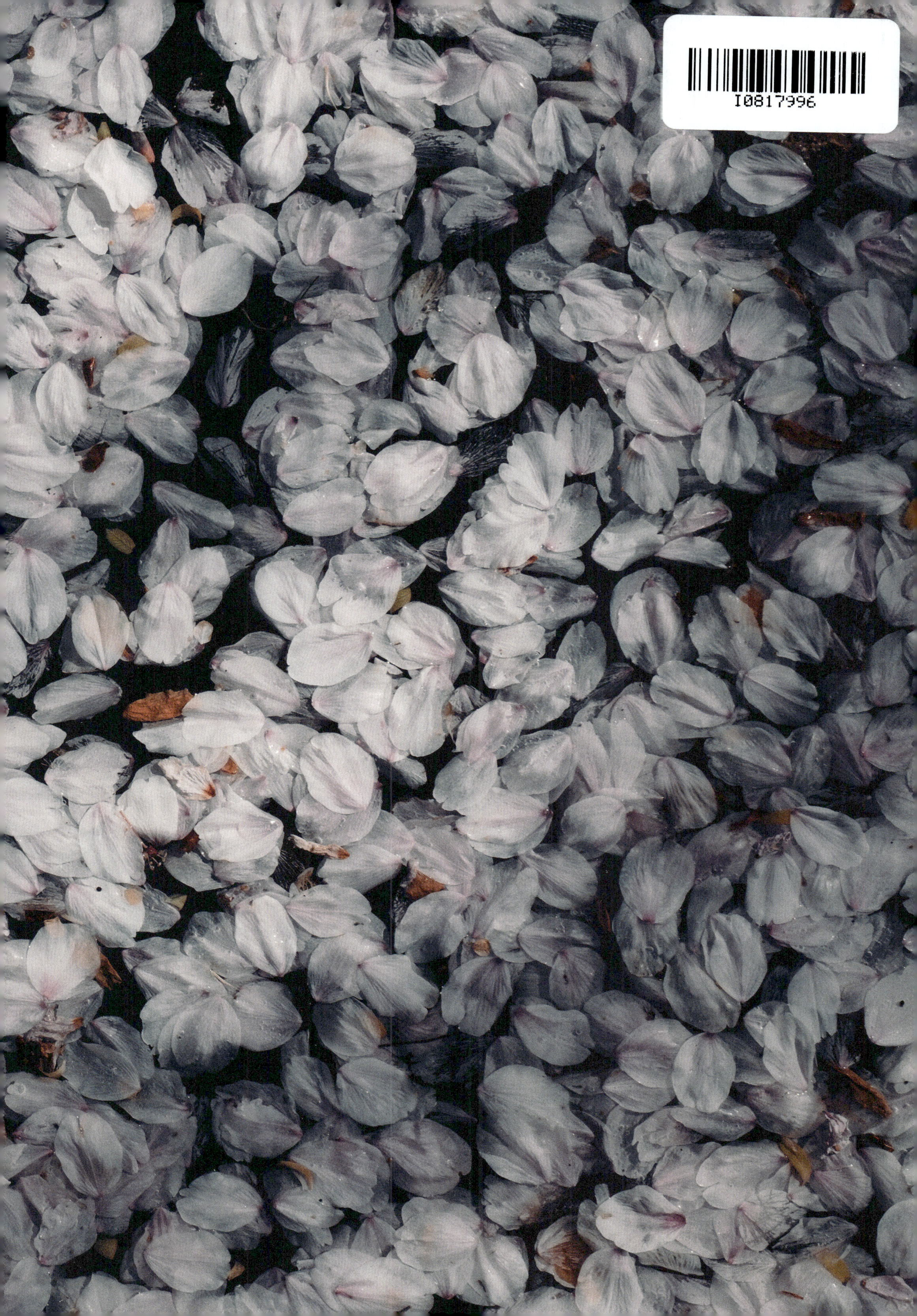
I0817996

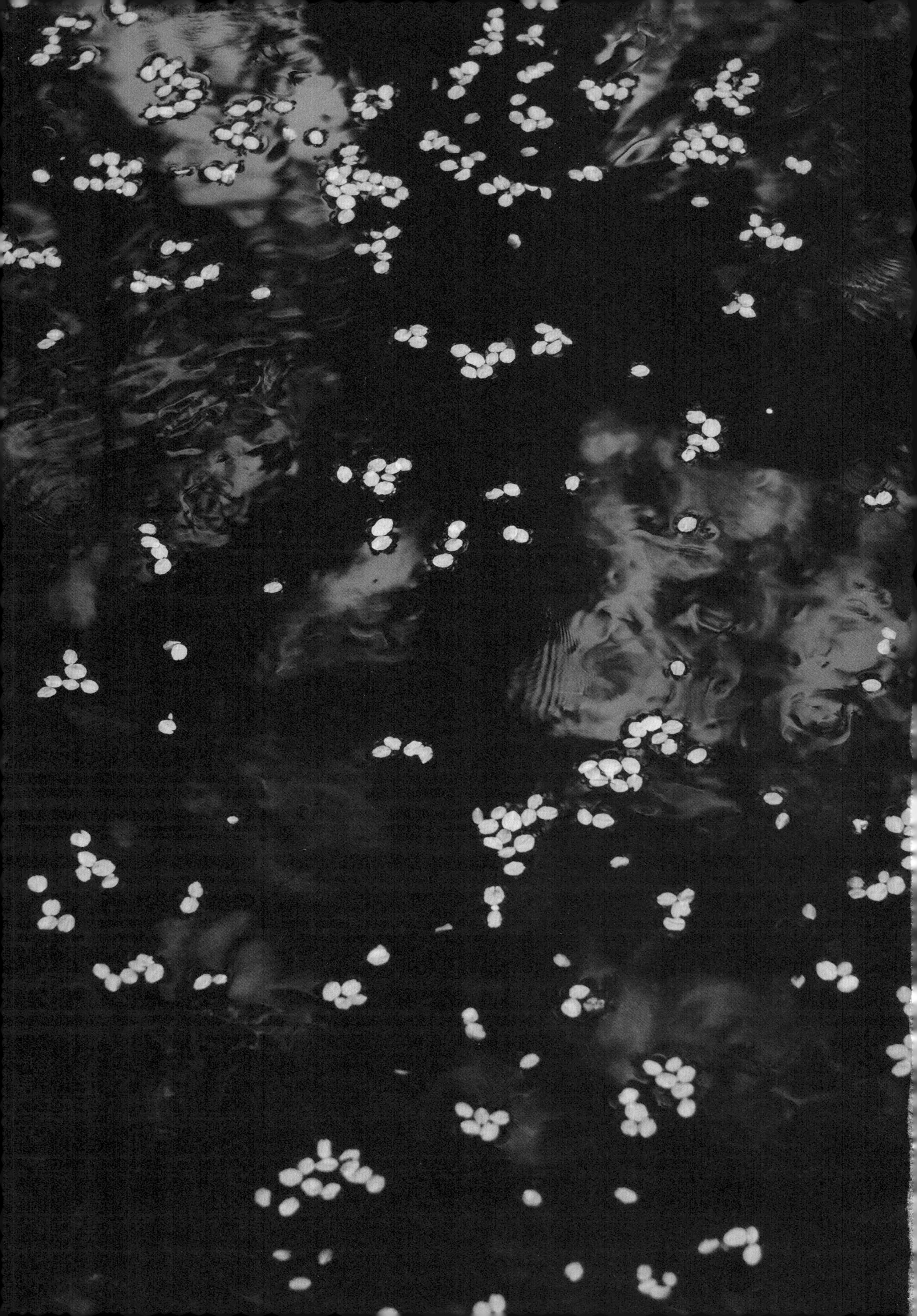

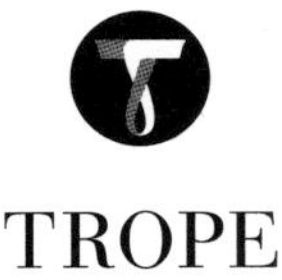

TROPE PUBLISHING Co.

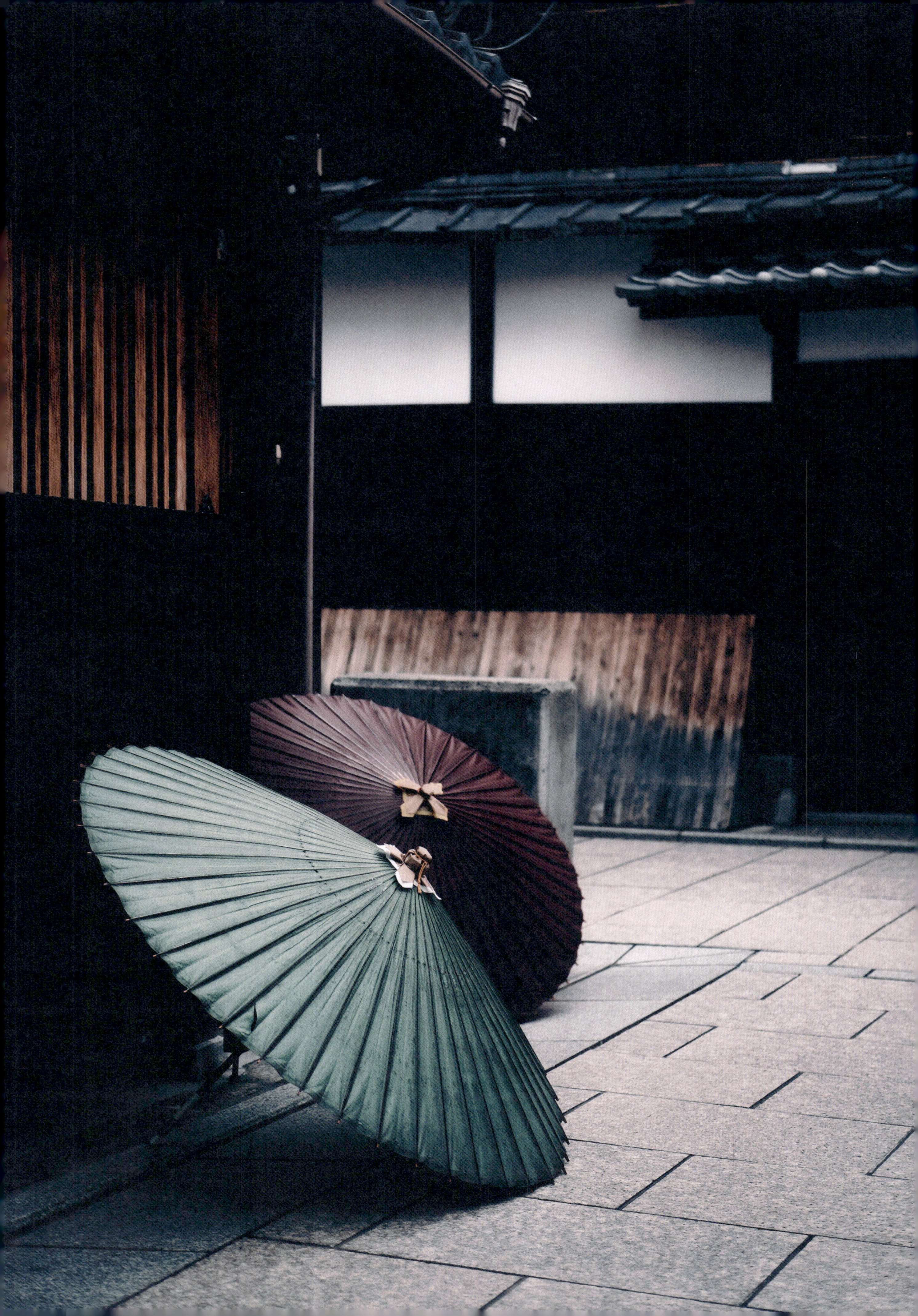

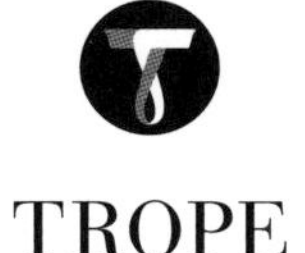

TROPE

KYOTO DREAMING

TARO MOBERLY

TROPE PUBLISHING Co.

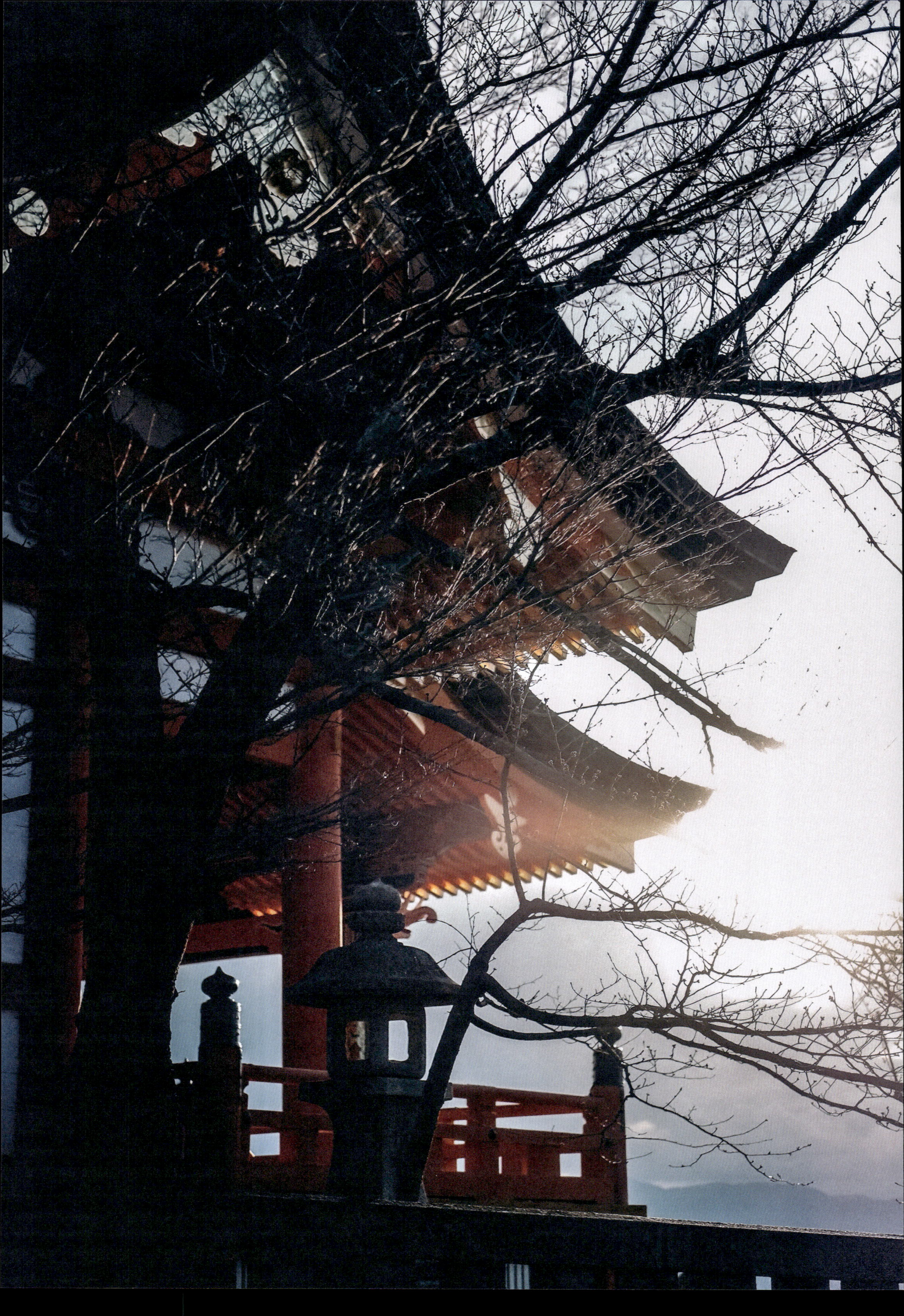

INTRODUCTION

Kyoto has countless stories to tell. It is a city deeply rooted in culture, holding true to traditions—some of which have lasted for centuries. It is a city that cherishes the peace and tranquility of nature, embracing the four seasons and the change that comes with them. It is a city that has grown prosperous over its history of more than a thousand years, developing into the urban center of activity it is today.

Though I grew up in the United States, I have felt a deep connection to Kyoto my entire life. My mother was born and raised in its outskirts, her ancestry rooted in the city. My parents met for the first time in the area around Kyoto Station. I have plenty of memories of visiting Kyoto as a young child to see my grandmother and grandfather: being amazed by the grandness and scale of the then-new Kyoto Station building, trying to make my way through Nijo Castle without making the floorboards squeak, watching the giant *omikoshi* make their way through the streets for the Gion Matsuri (though mostly I remember being enamored with the toy train shop on the top floor of the Daimaru department store on Shijo Street).

This connection has long given me a desire to further understand my heritage, in Kyoto and in Japan. This hunger to learn more was a factor in my move to Kyoto from my home in California in 2015. In the following years, I discovered so much about the unique and fascinating culture of my adopted homeland. Even more keenly, this journey of being immersed in the Japanese culture gave me incredible insight into myself—giving me an even greater curiosity about the world around me, driving me further to explore all Kyoto has to offer. Kyoto has changed how I see the world and helped me become the person I am today.

I left Kyoto to return to my native California in 2023, but within myself I still see Kyoto as a major part of my identity. The city, the culture, and the people of Kyoto have left a profound impact, and I will be forever grateful for the lessons and character taught to me by what now feels like my second home.

This book you hold in your hands is a culmination of eight years of my life in Kyoto, the exploration of this city that I hold so close to my heart and the stories that it has to tell. I'm glad to bring you along with me on this journey.

TARO MOBERLY

@taromoberly

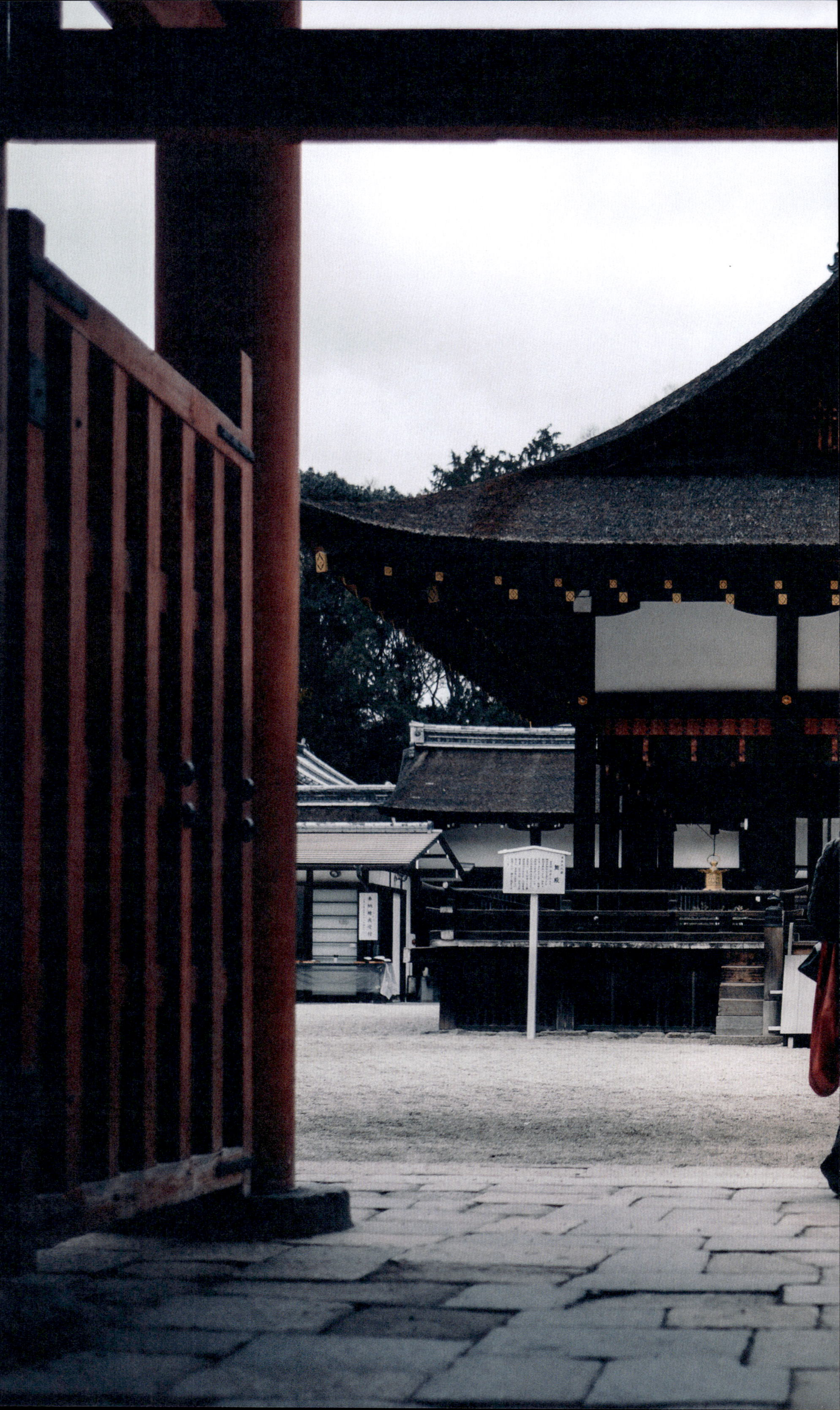

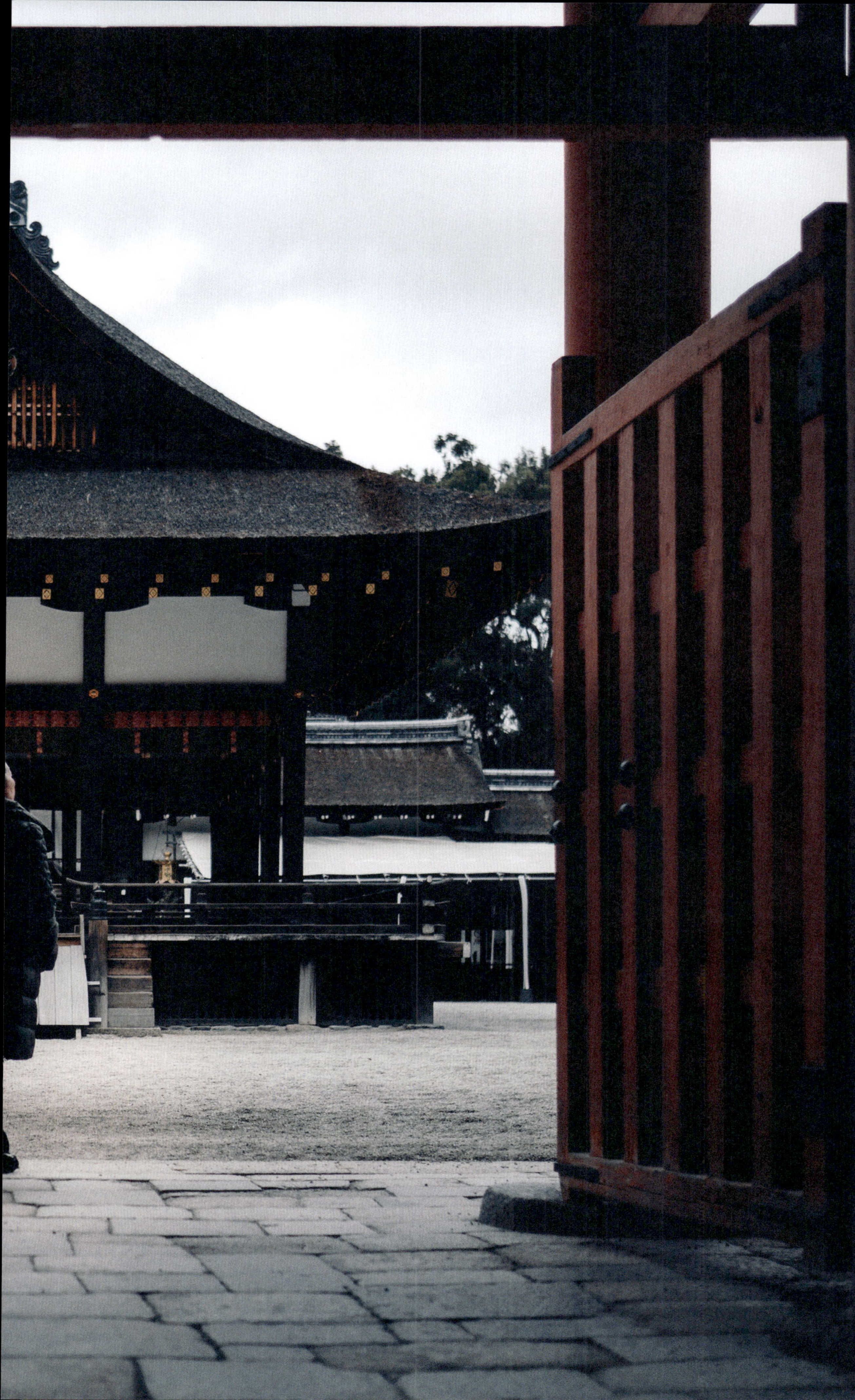

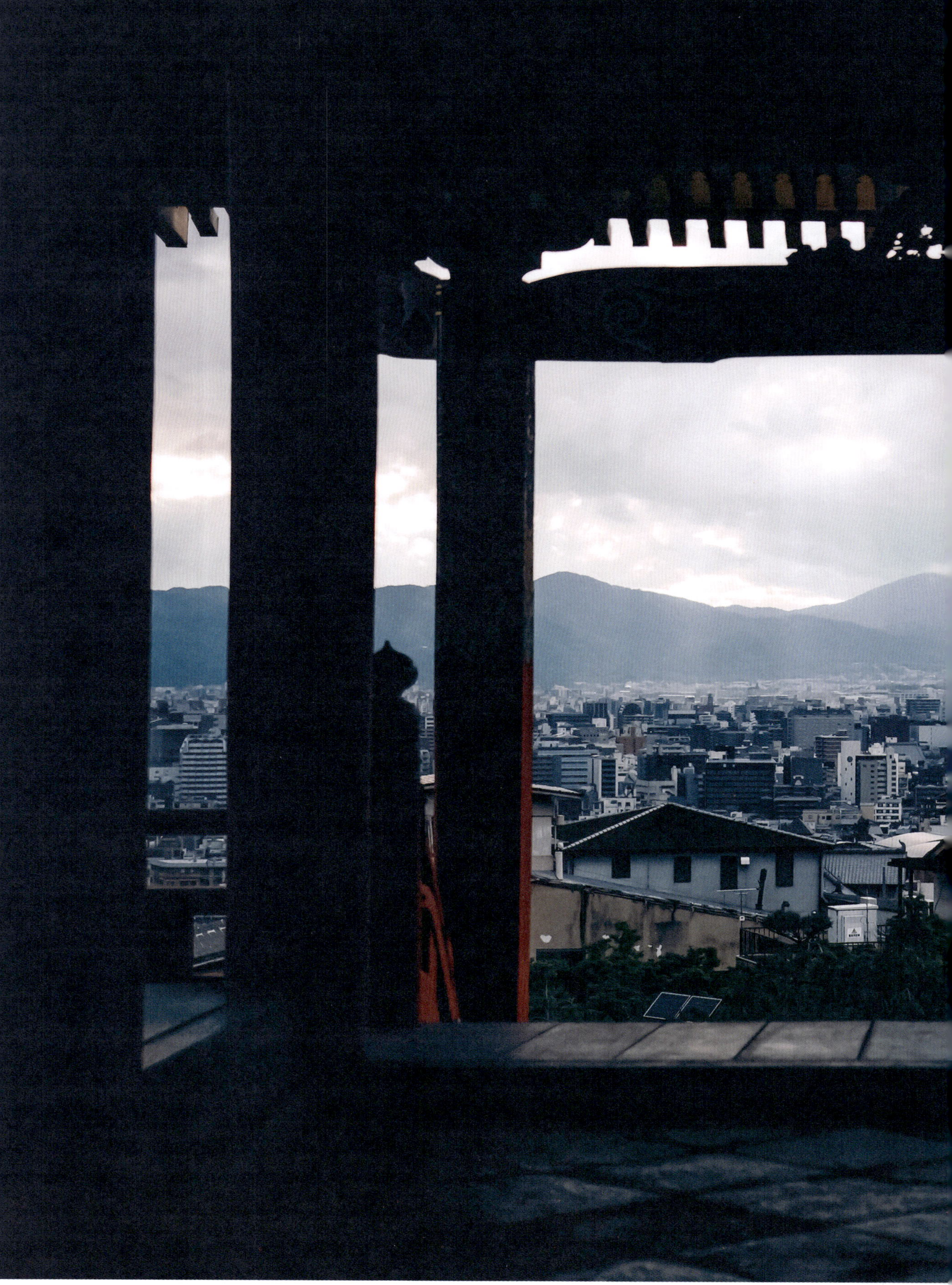

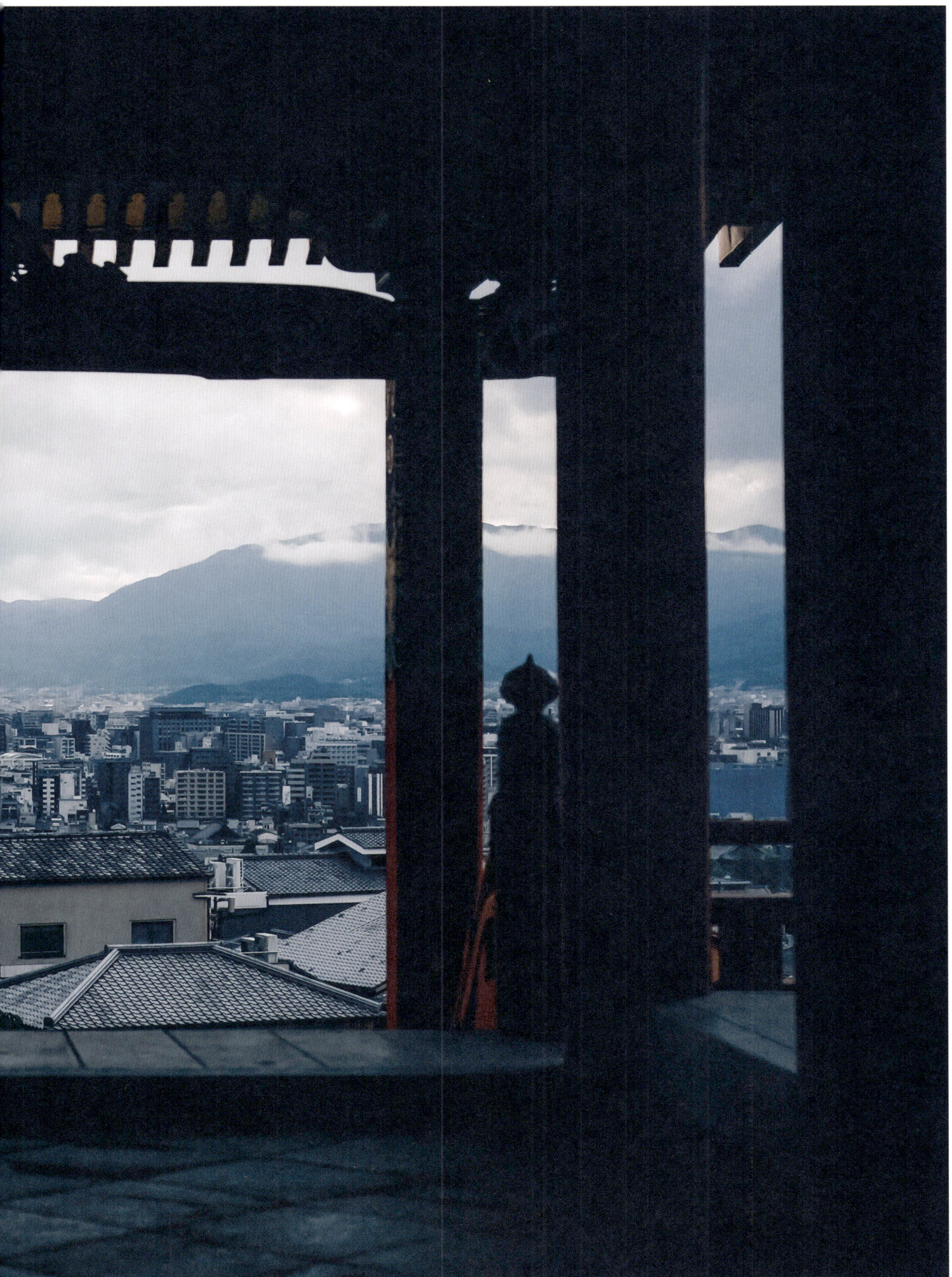

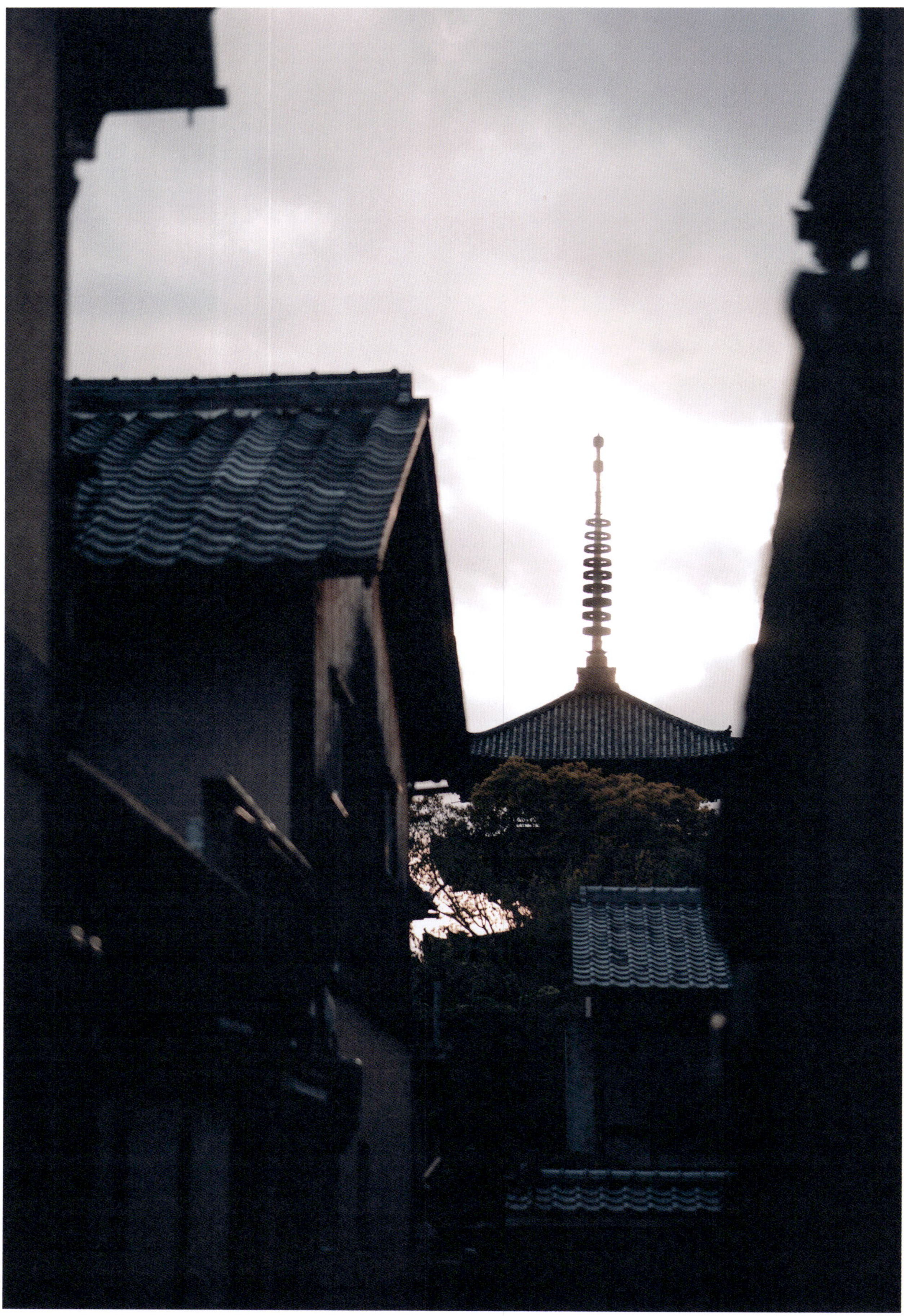

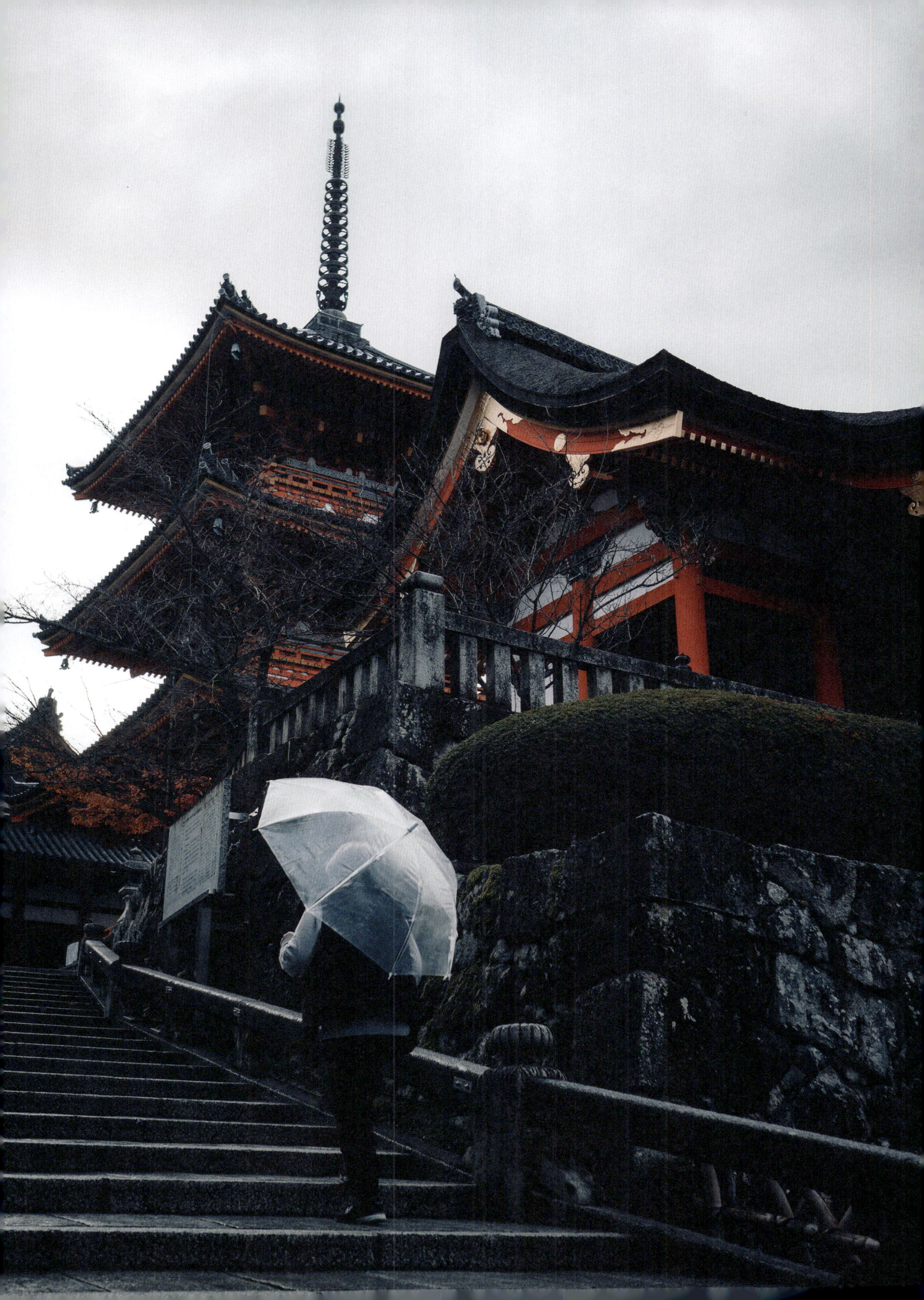

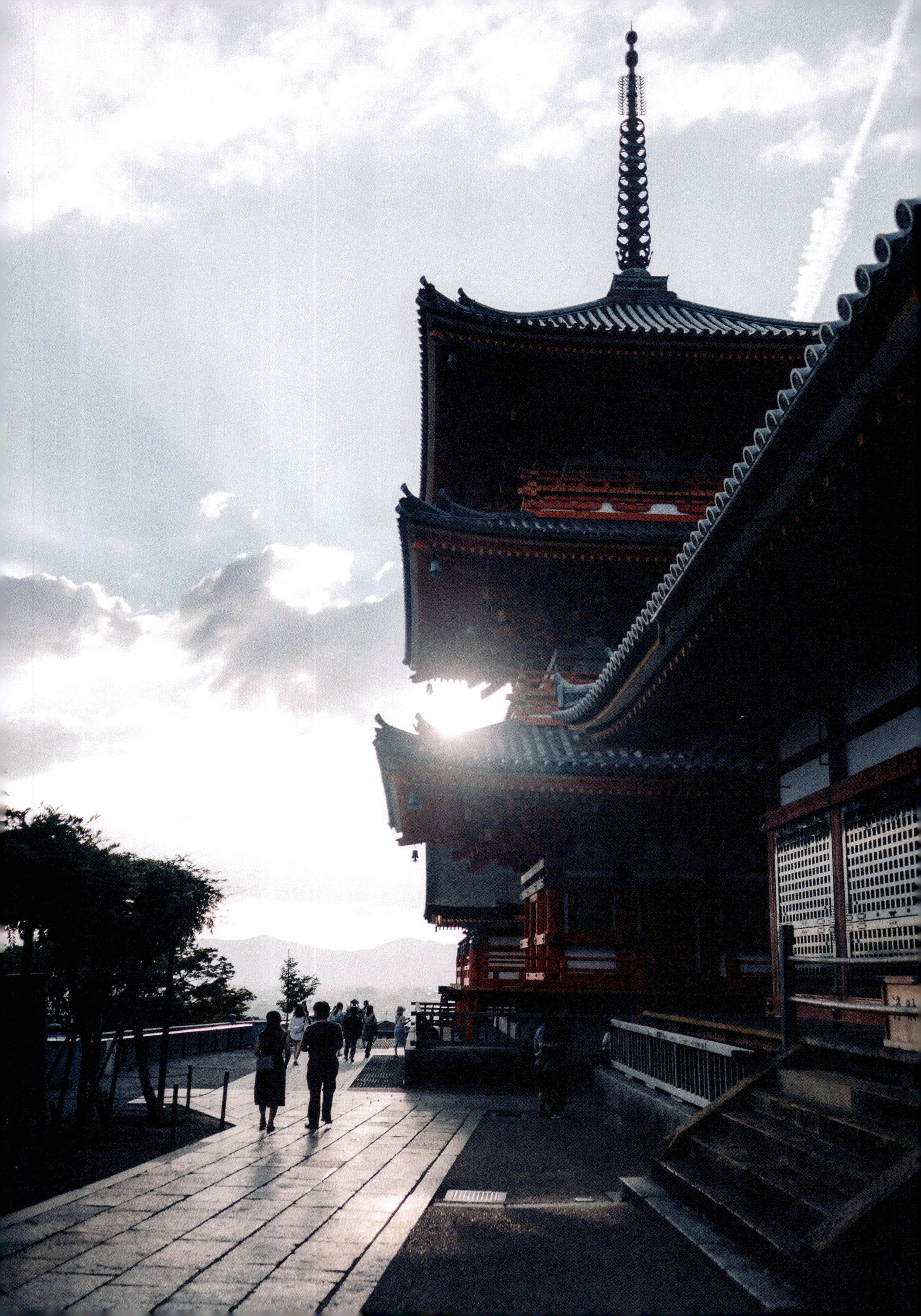

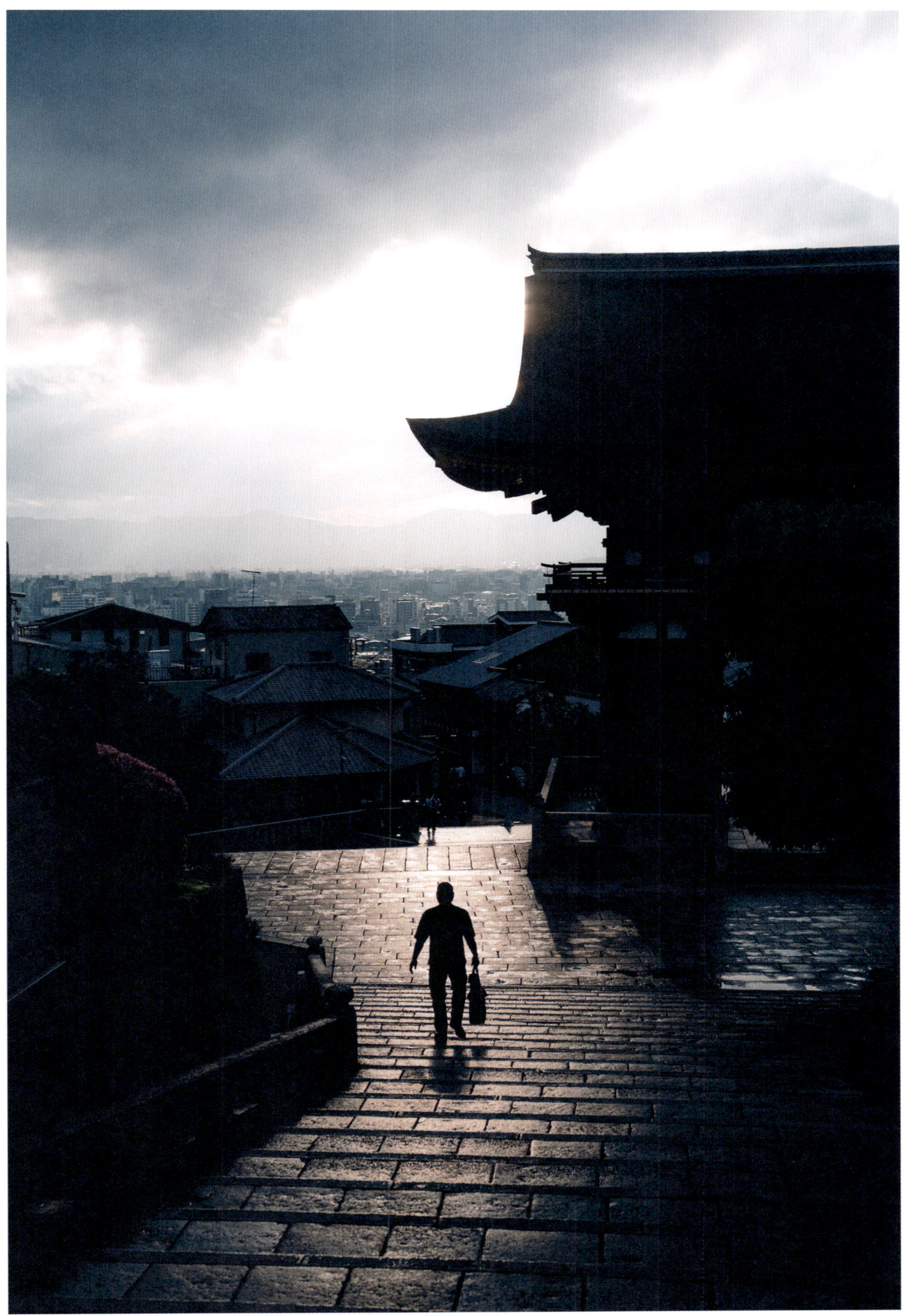

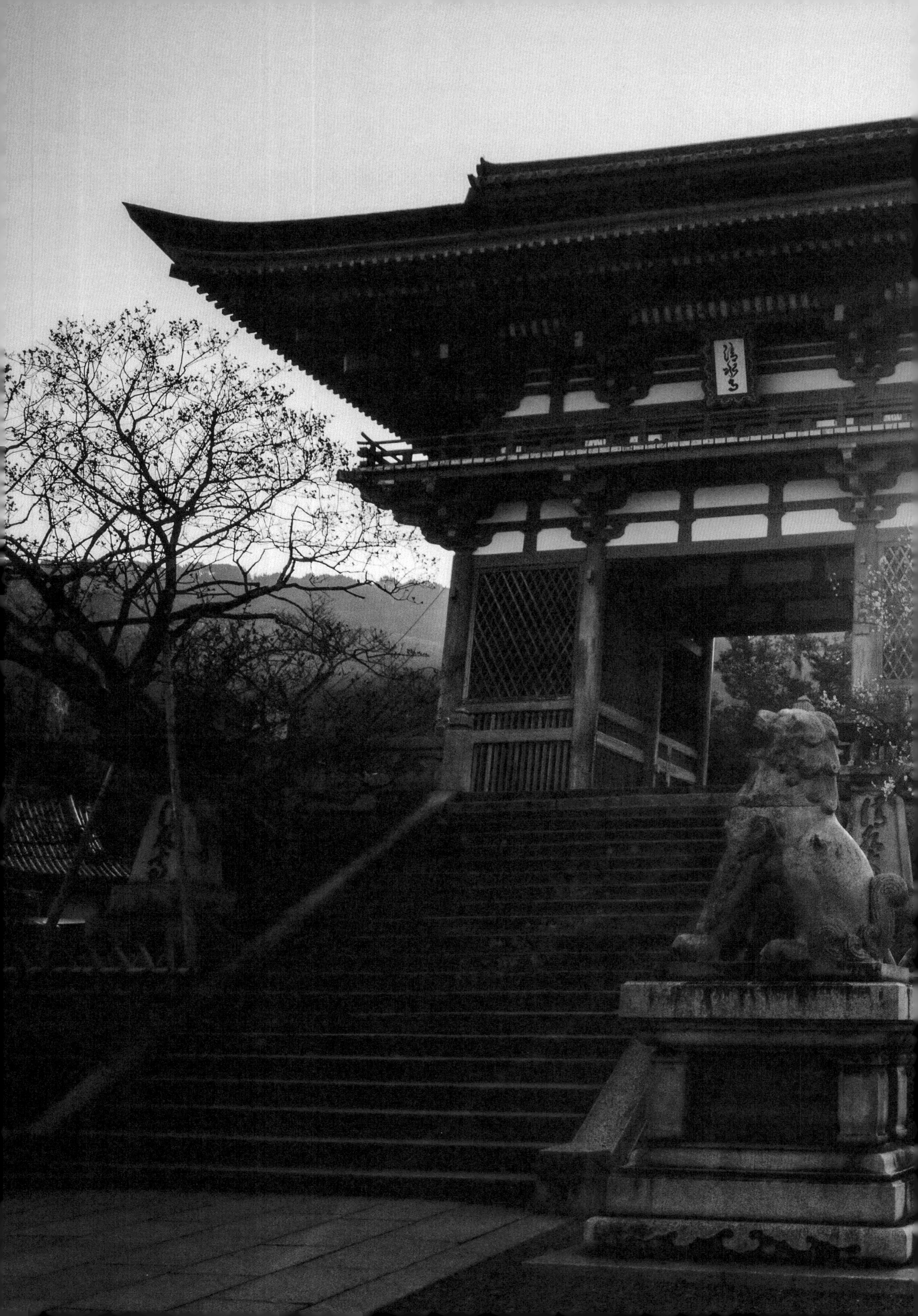

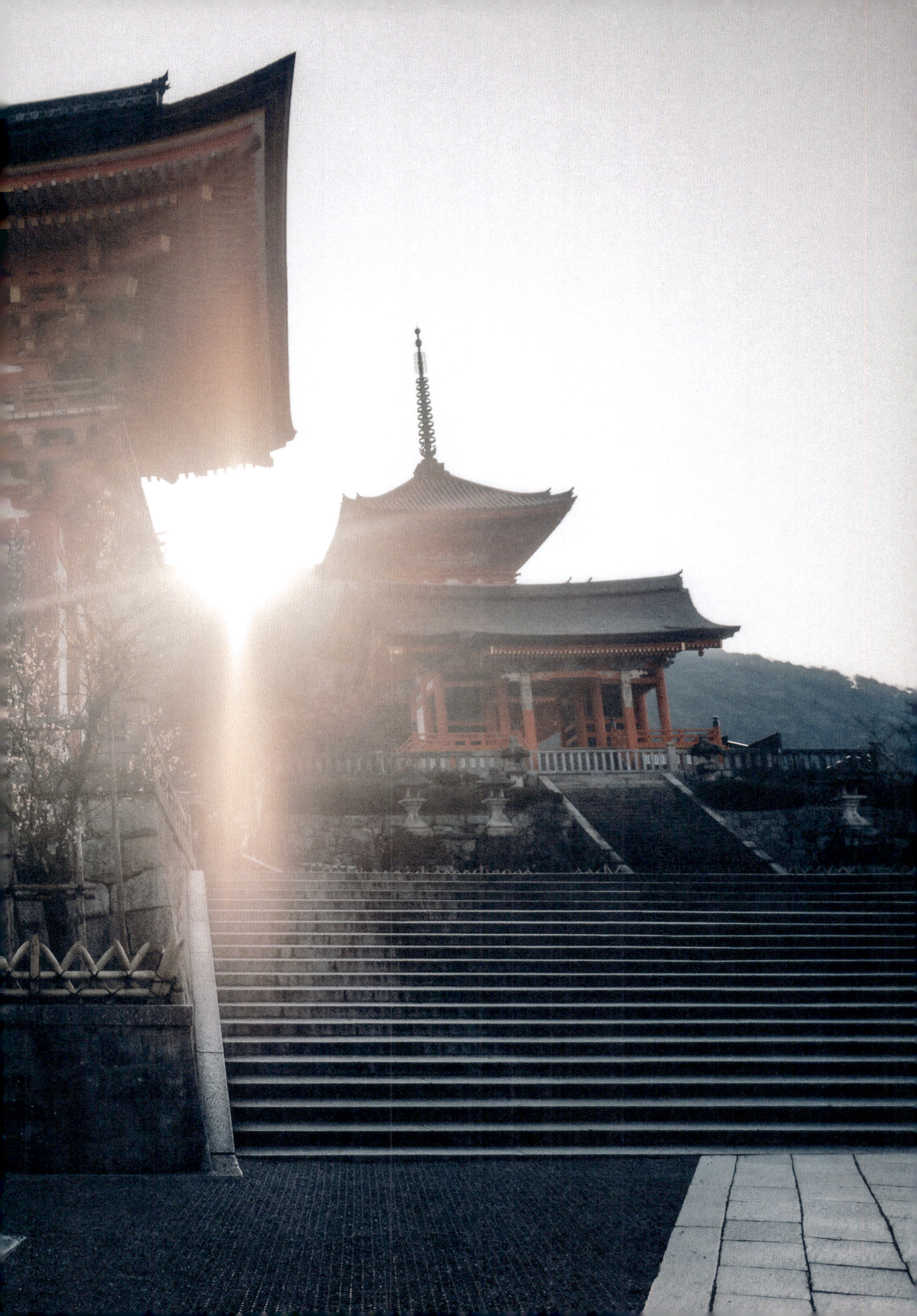

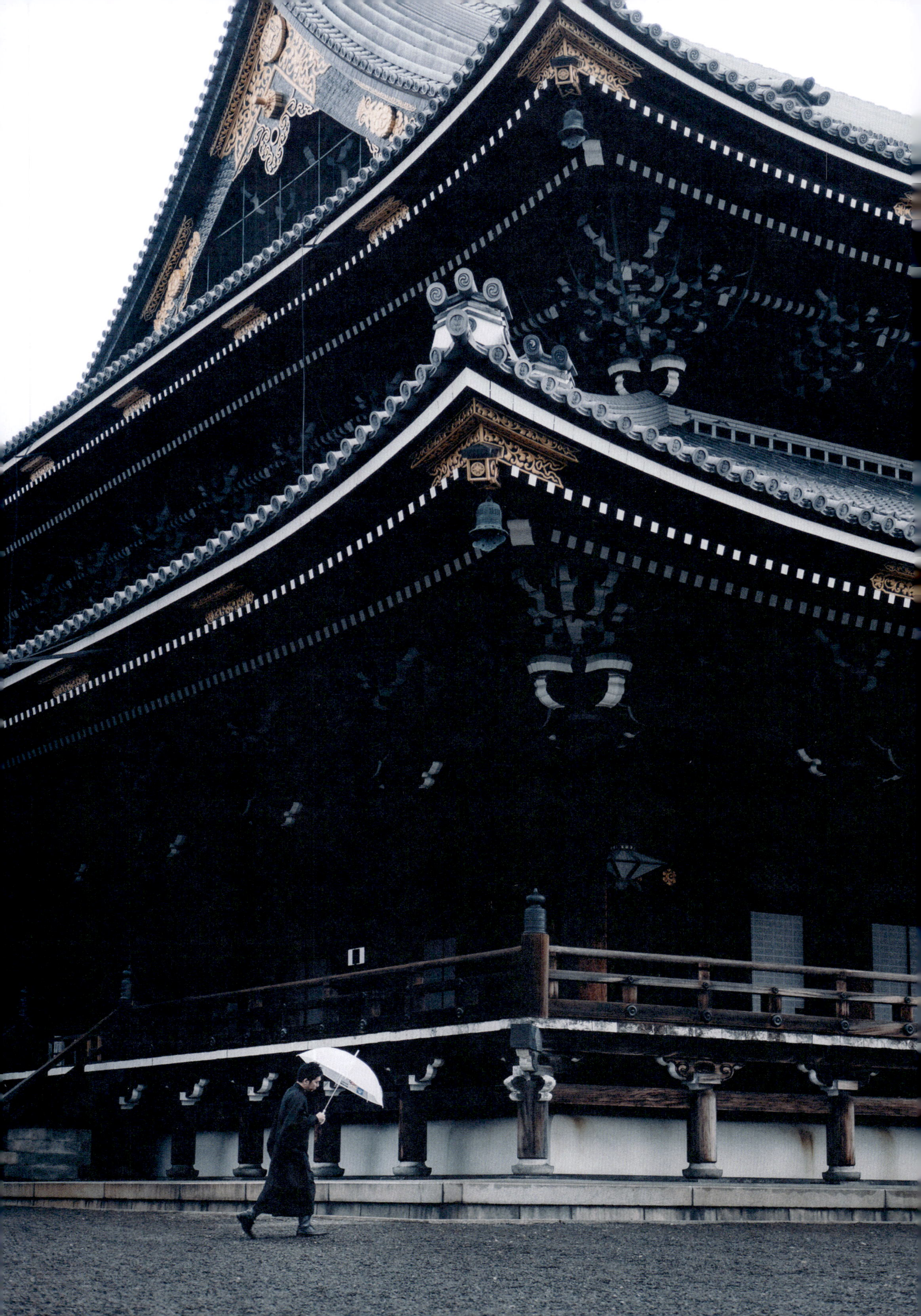

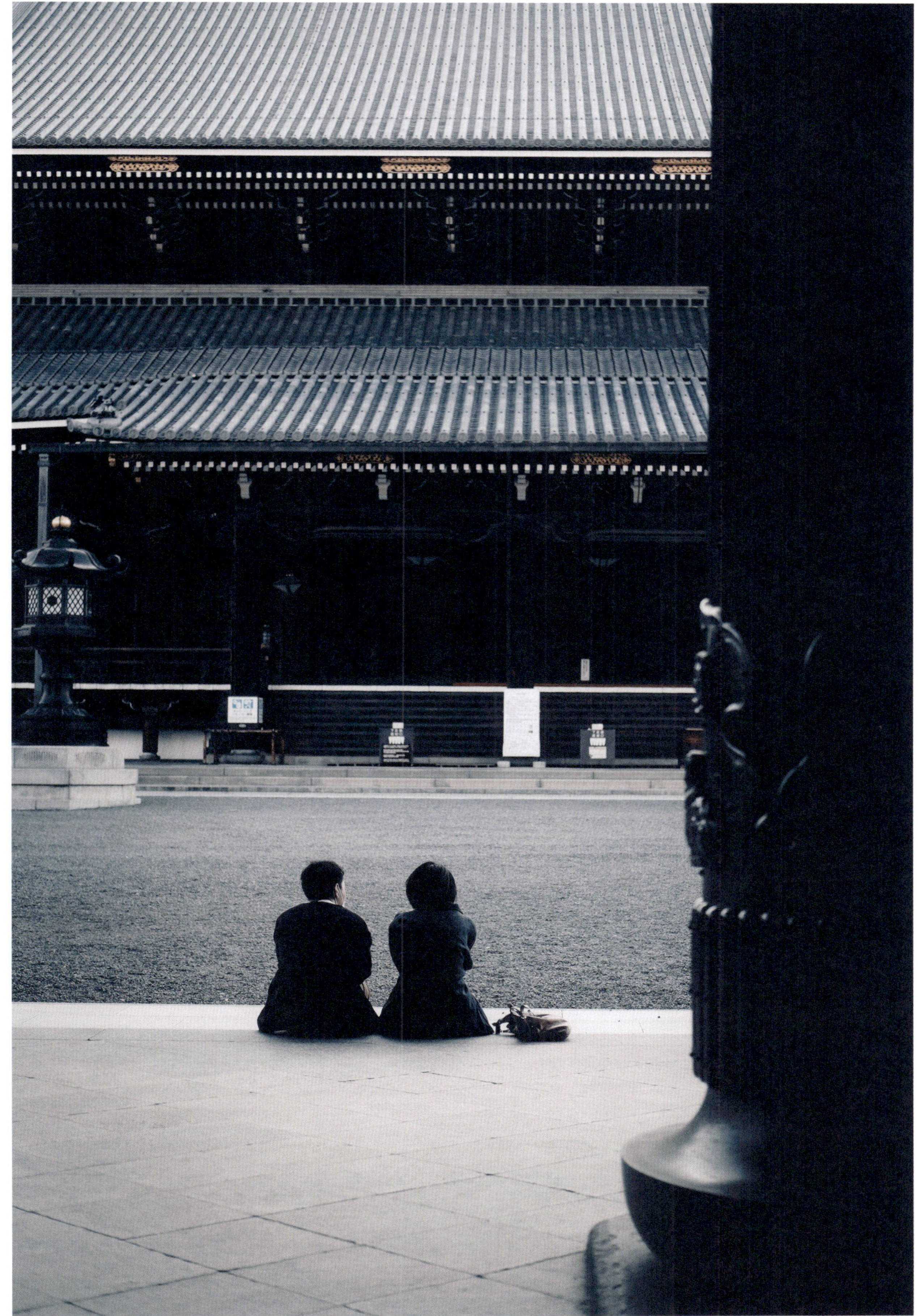

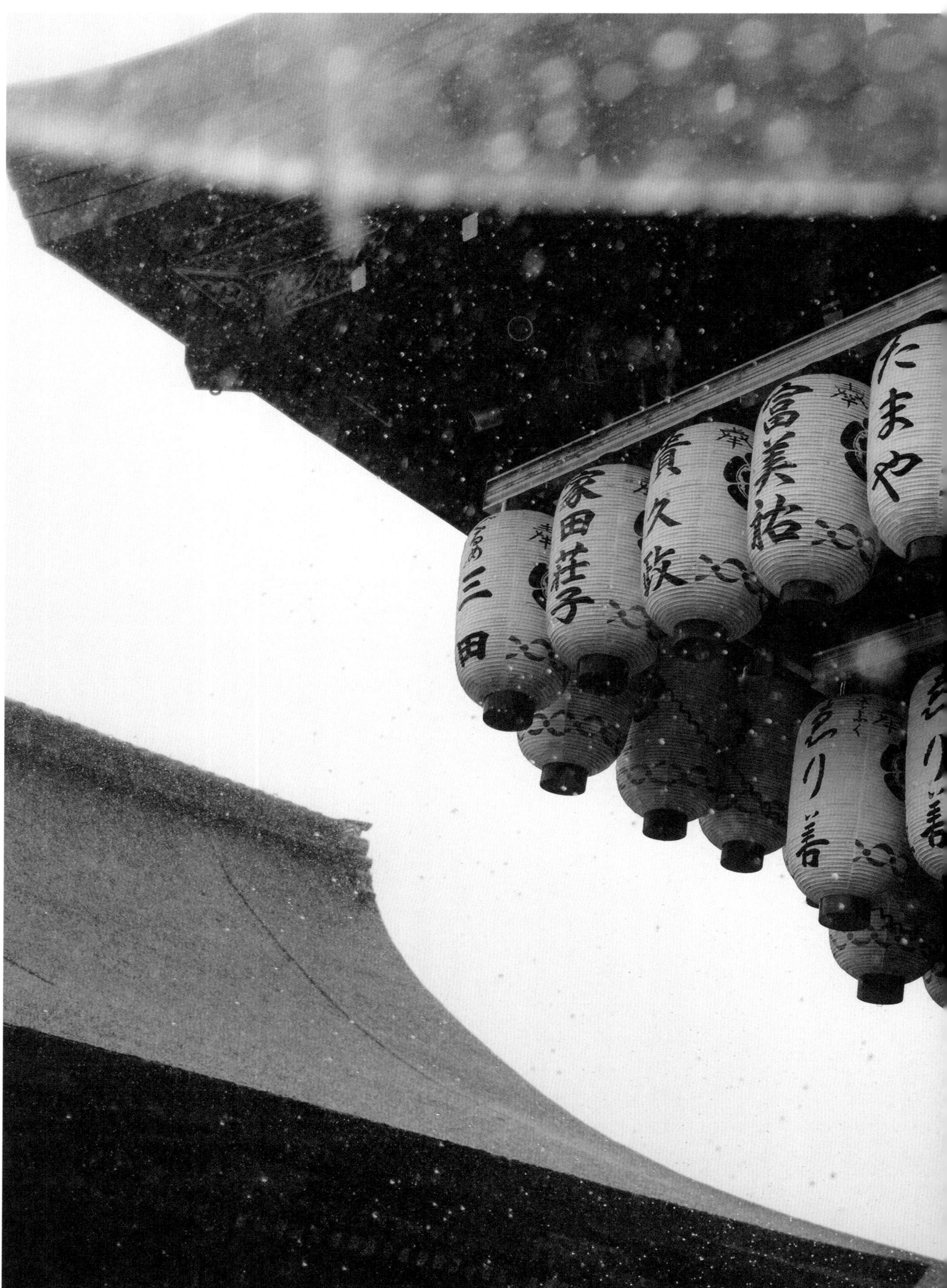
たまや
家田荘子

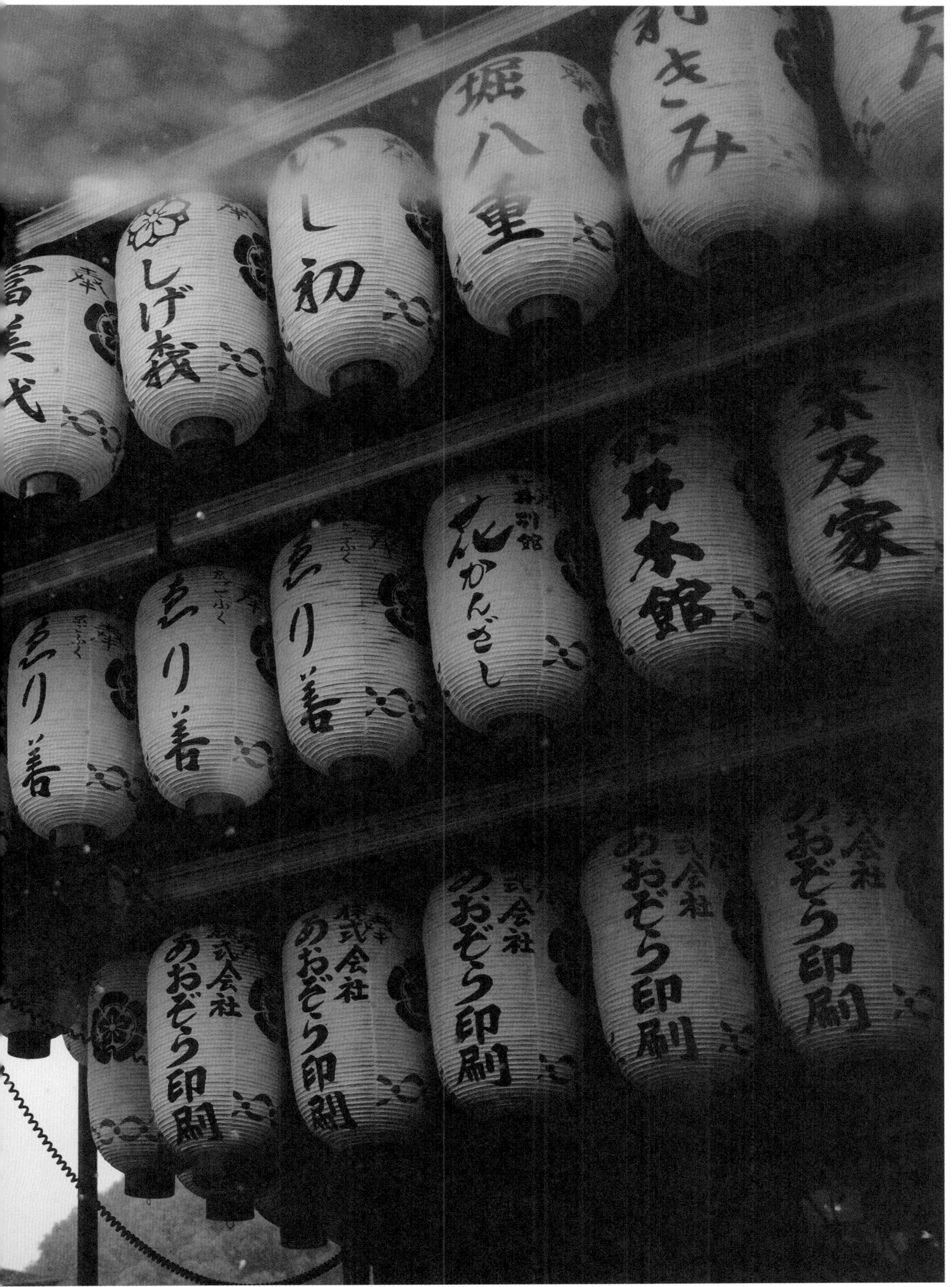
富美代
花かんざし
あおぞら印刷
あおぞら印刷
あおぞら印刷
あおぞら印刷
あおぞら印刷

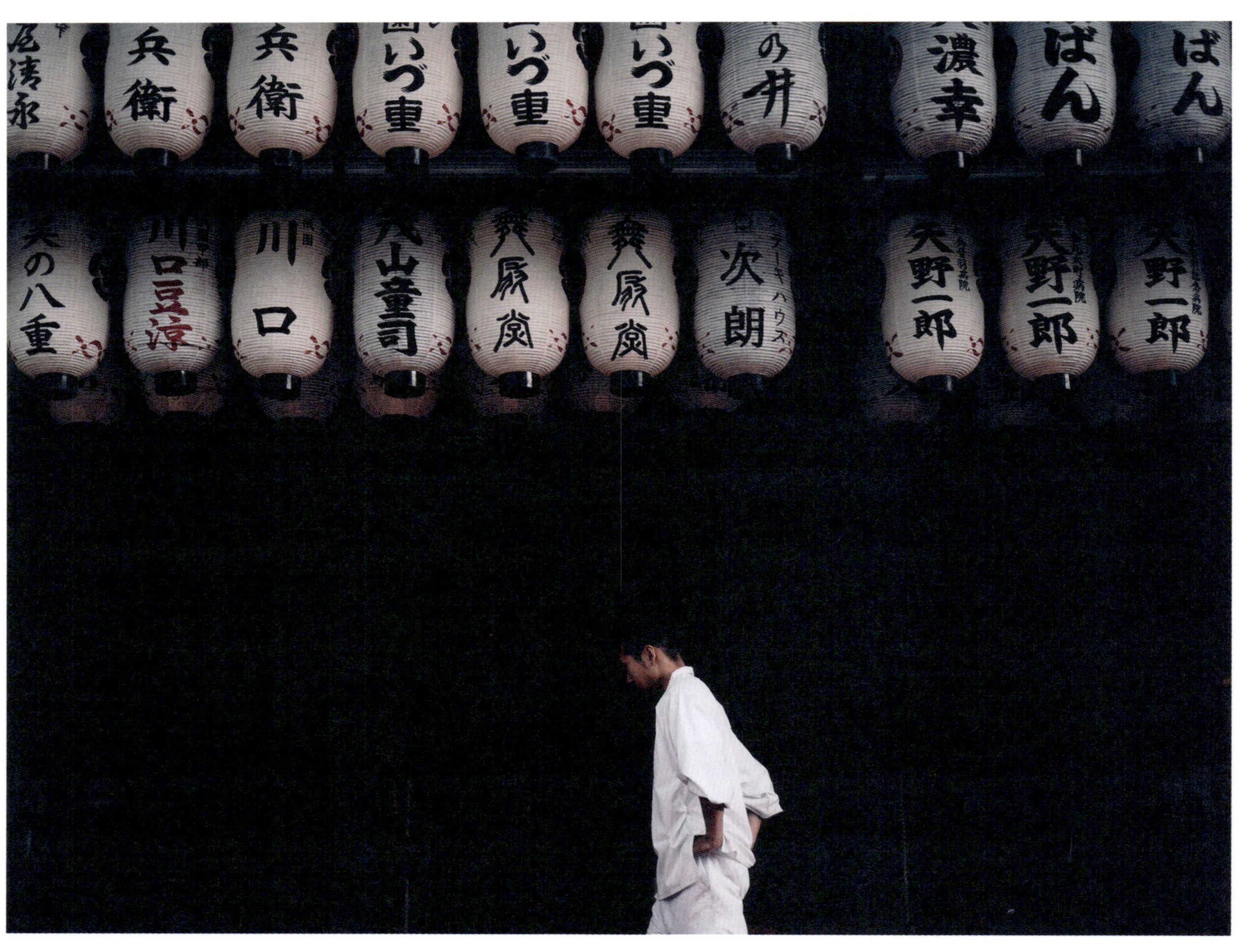
兵衛
兵衛
いづ重
いづ重
いづ重
の井
濃幸
ばん
ばん
の八重
川口
山童司
次朗
野一郎
野一郎
野一郎

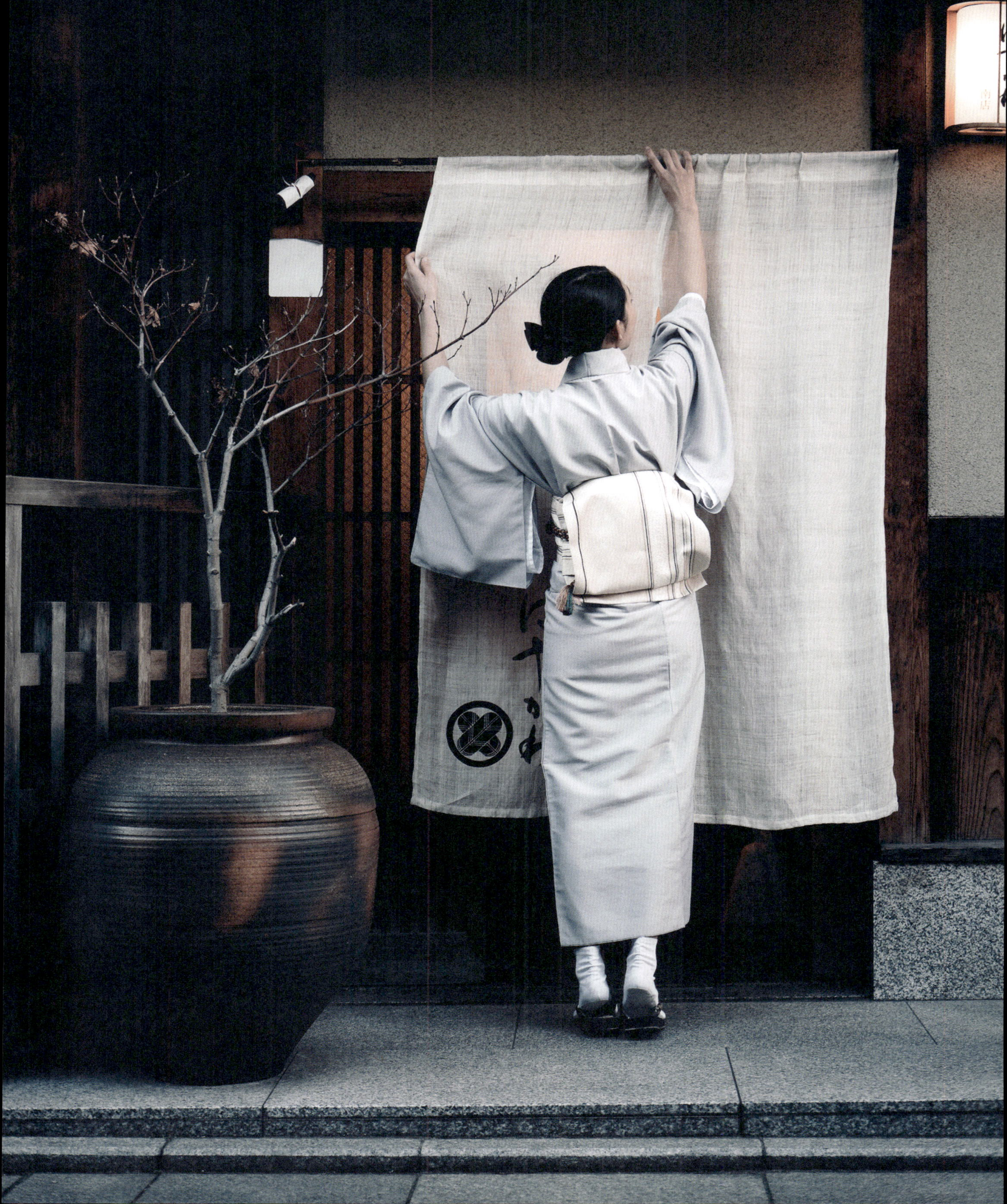

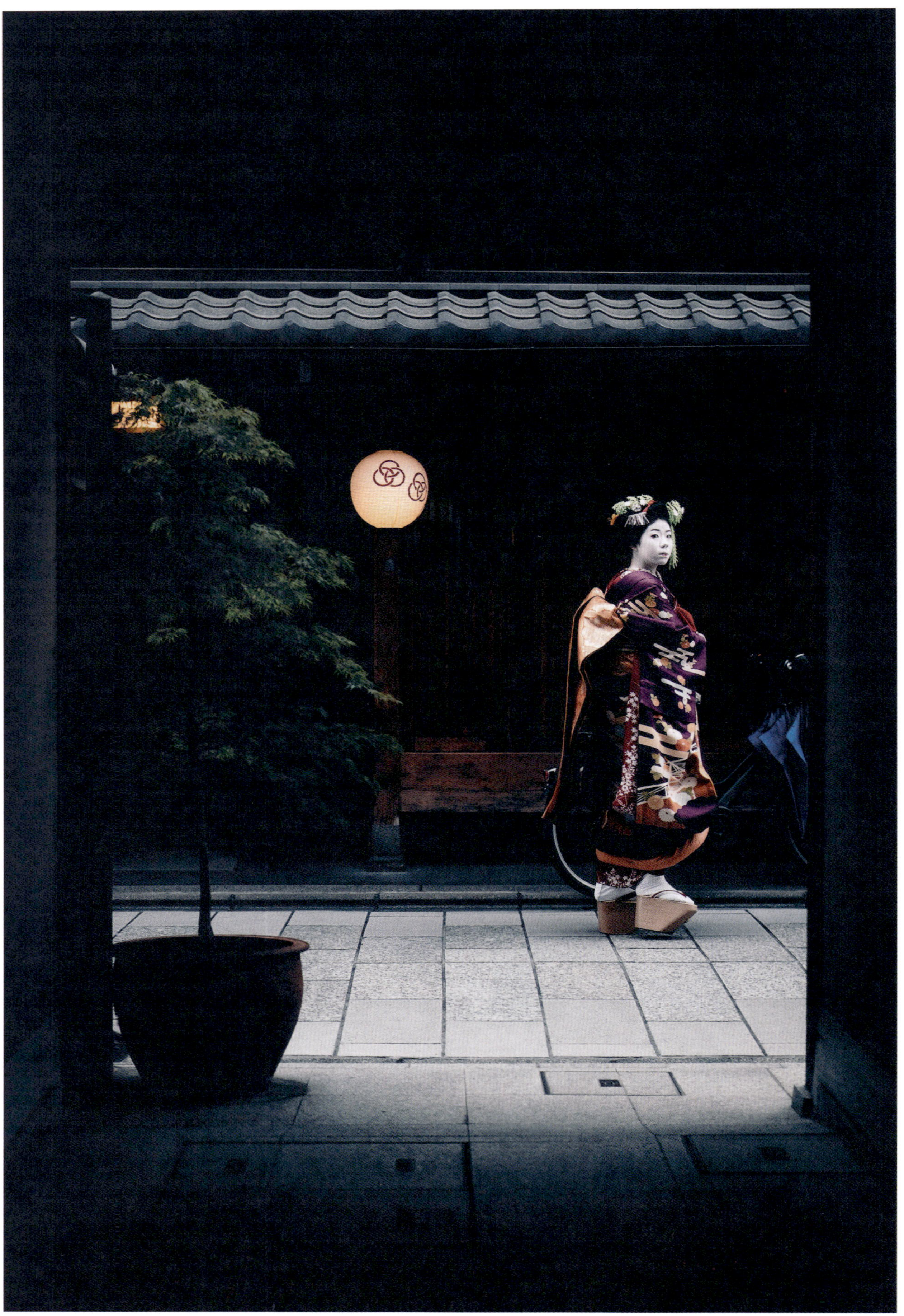

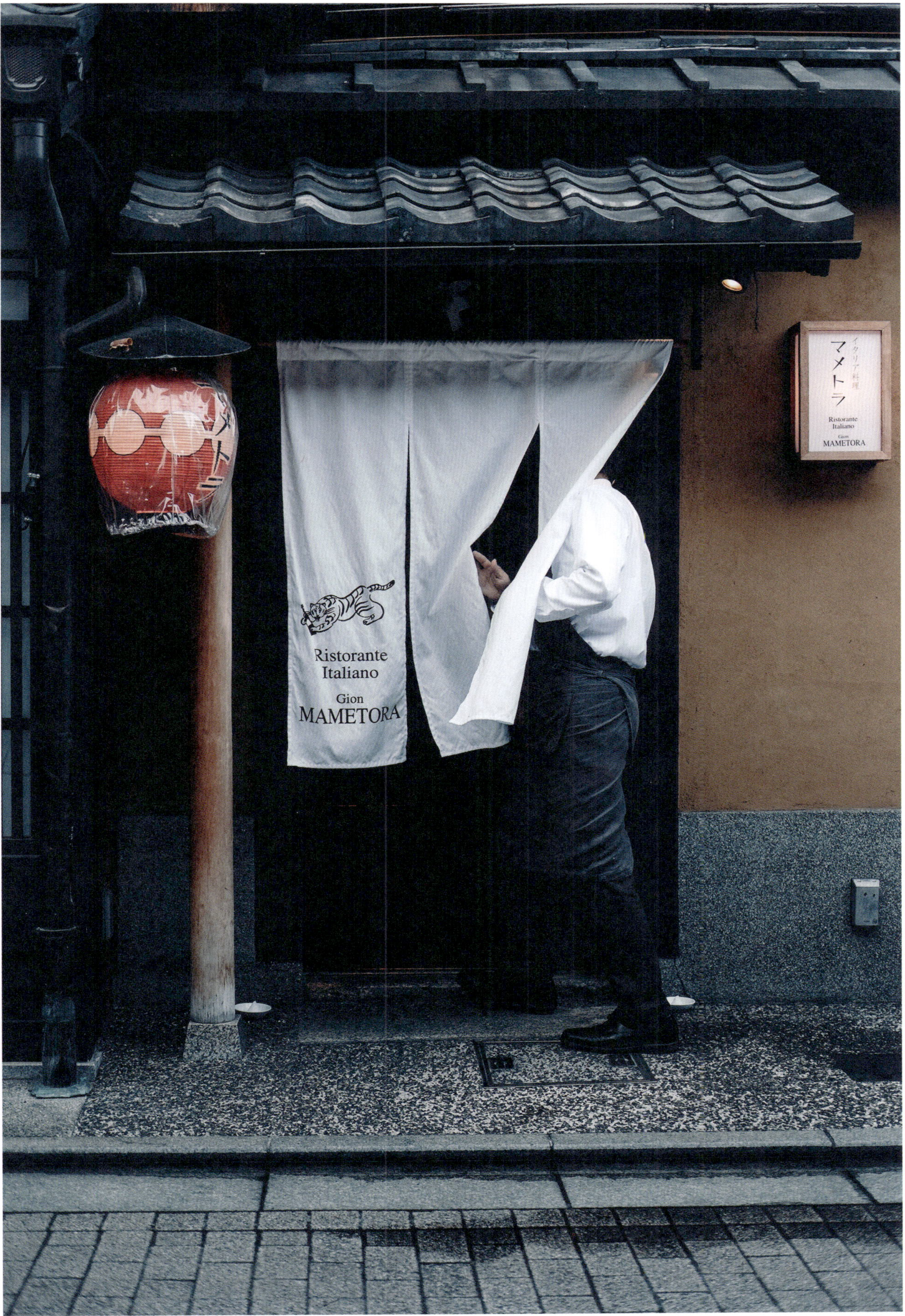
Ristorante
Italiano
Gion
MAMETORA
イタリア料理
マメトラ
Ristorante
Italiano
Gion
MAMETORA

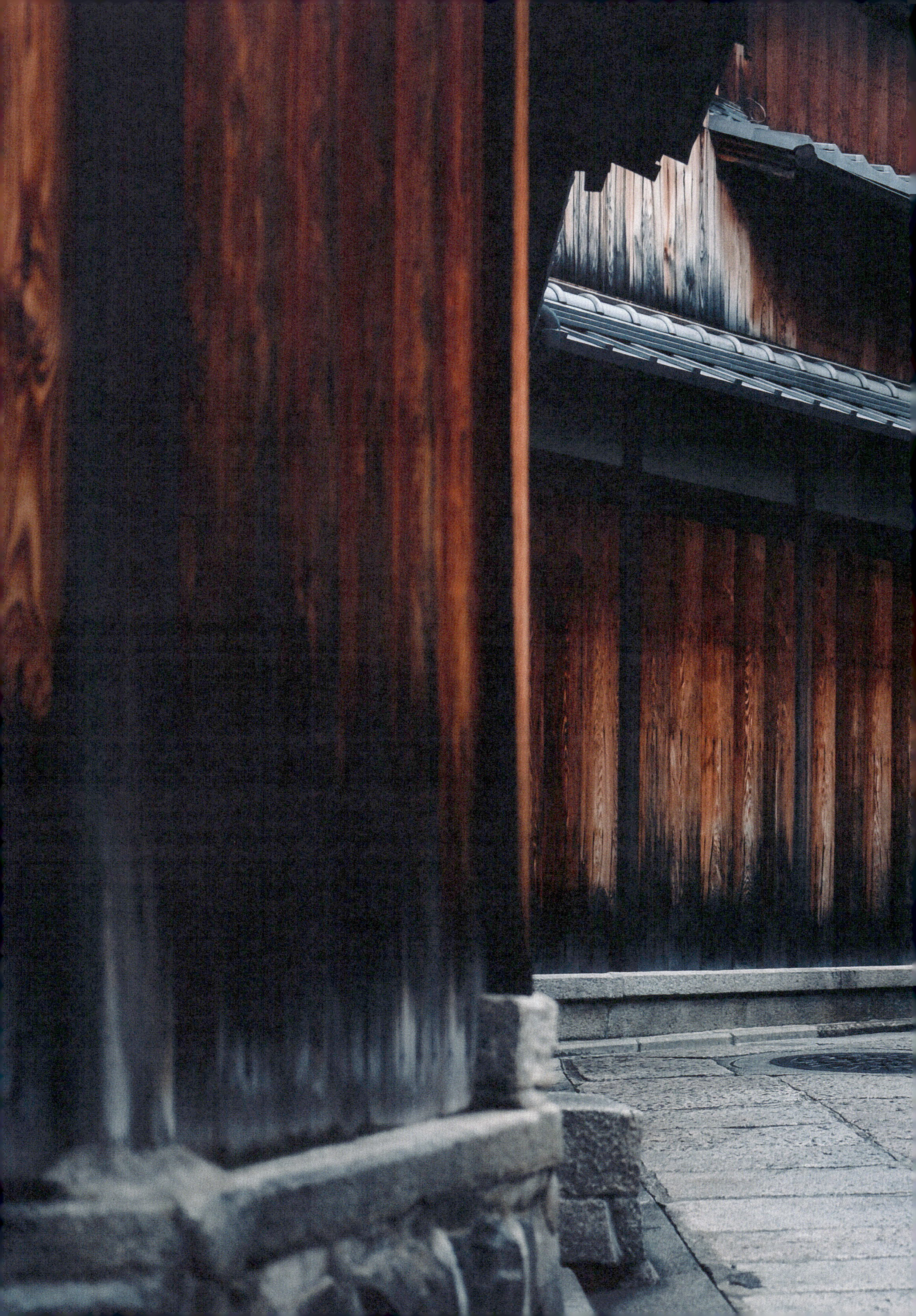

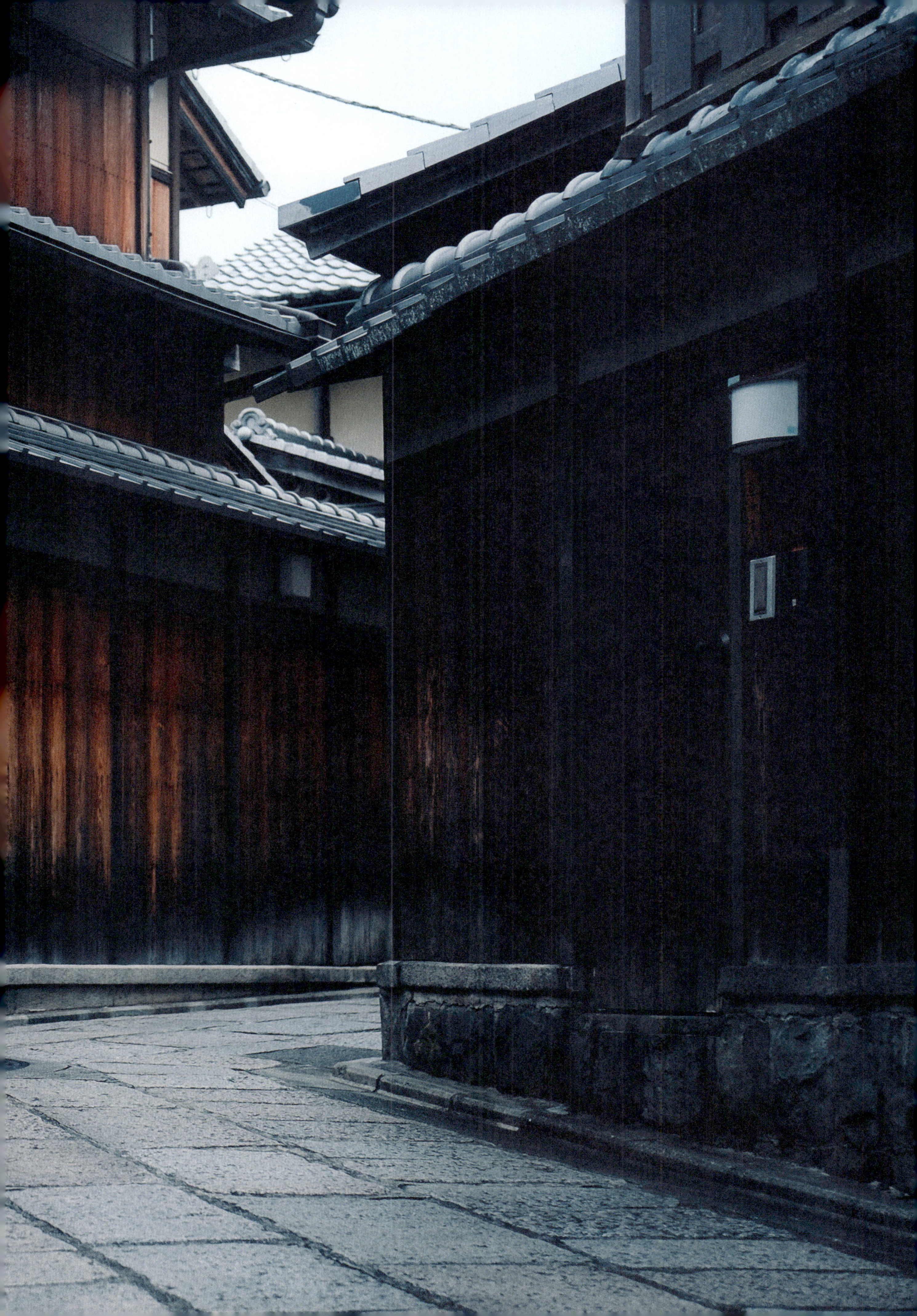

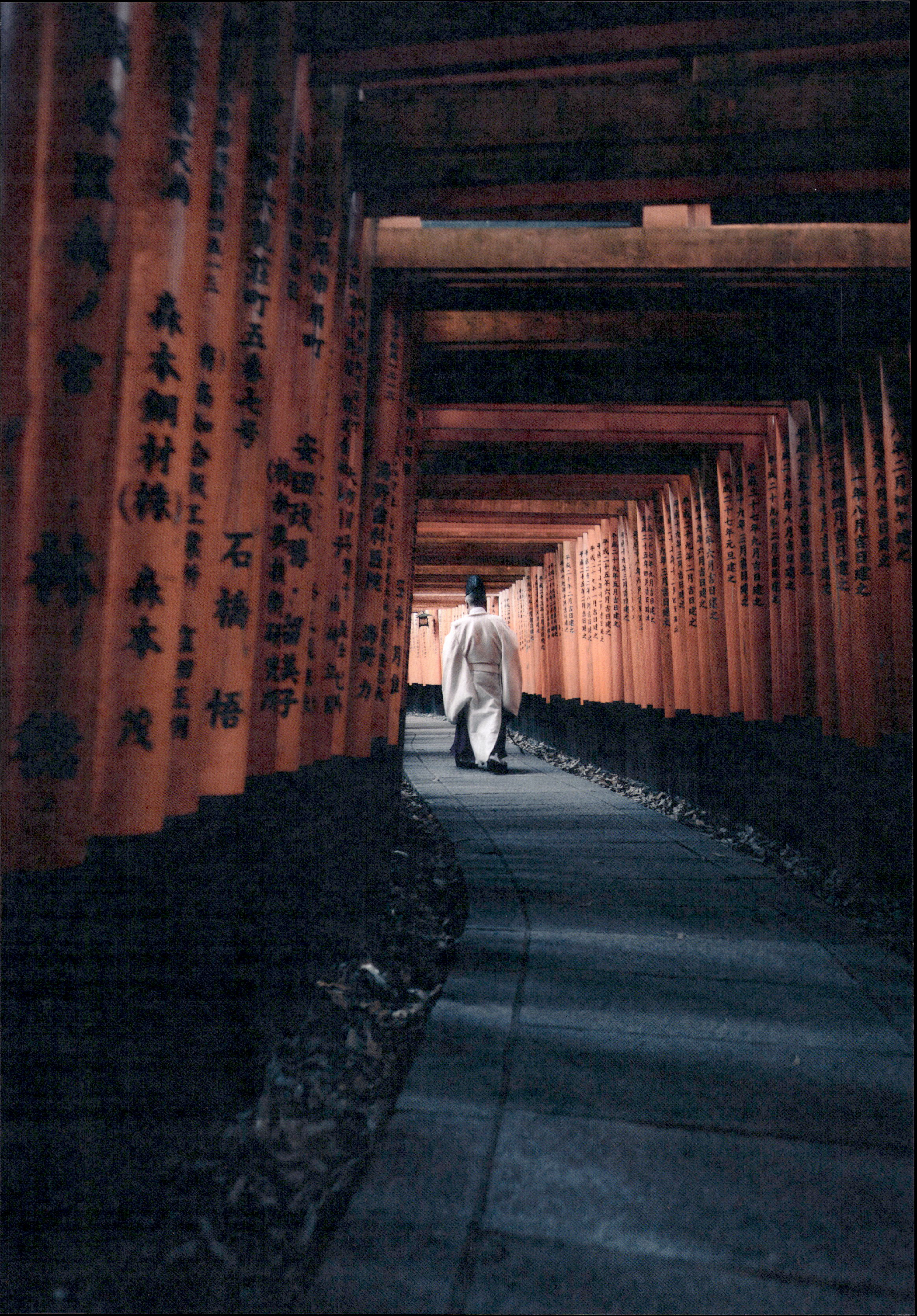
森本鋼材(株) 森本茂
石橋 悟

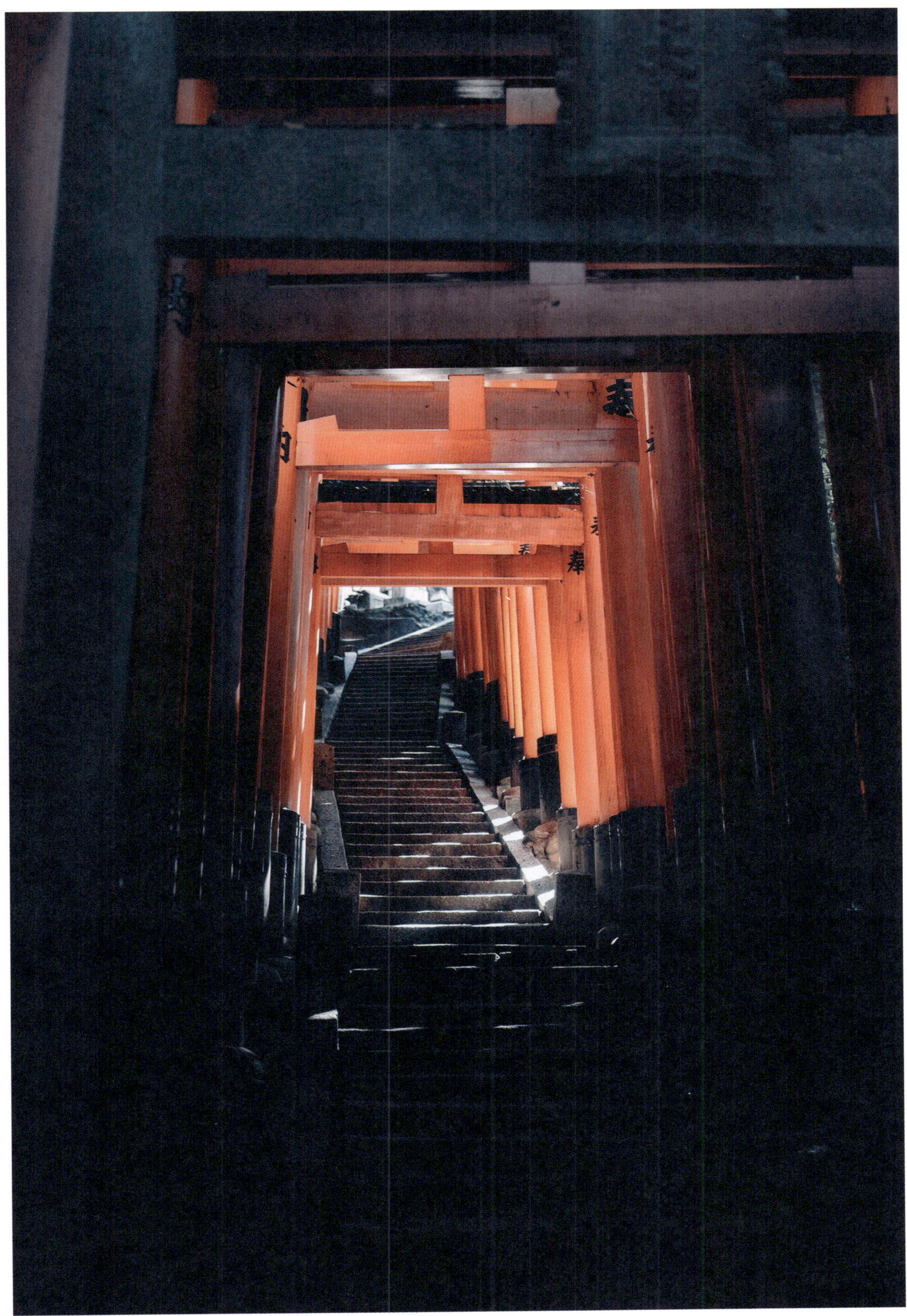

文ならぬ
いろはもかきて
火中哉

松尾　芭蕉

Though not words of
Passion, these matching colours are swept up
And consigned to the flames.

Bashō

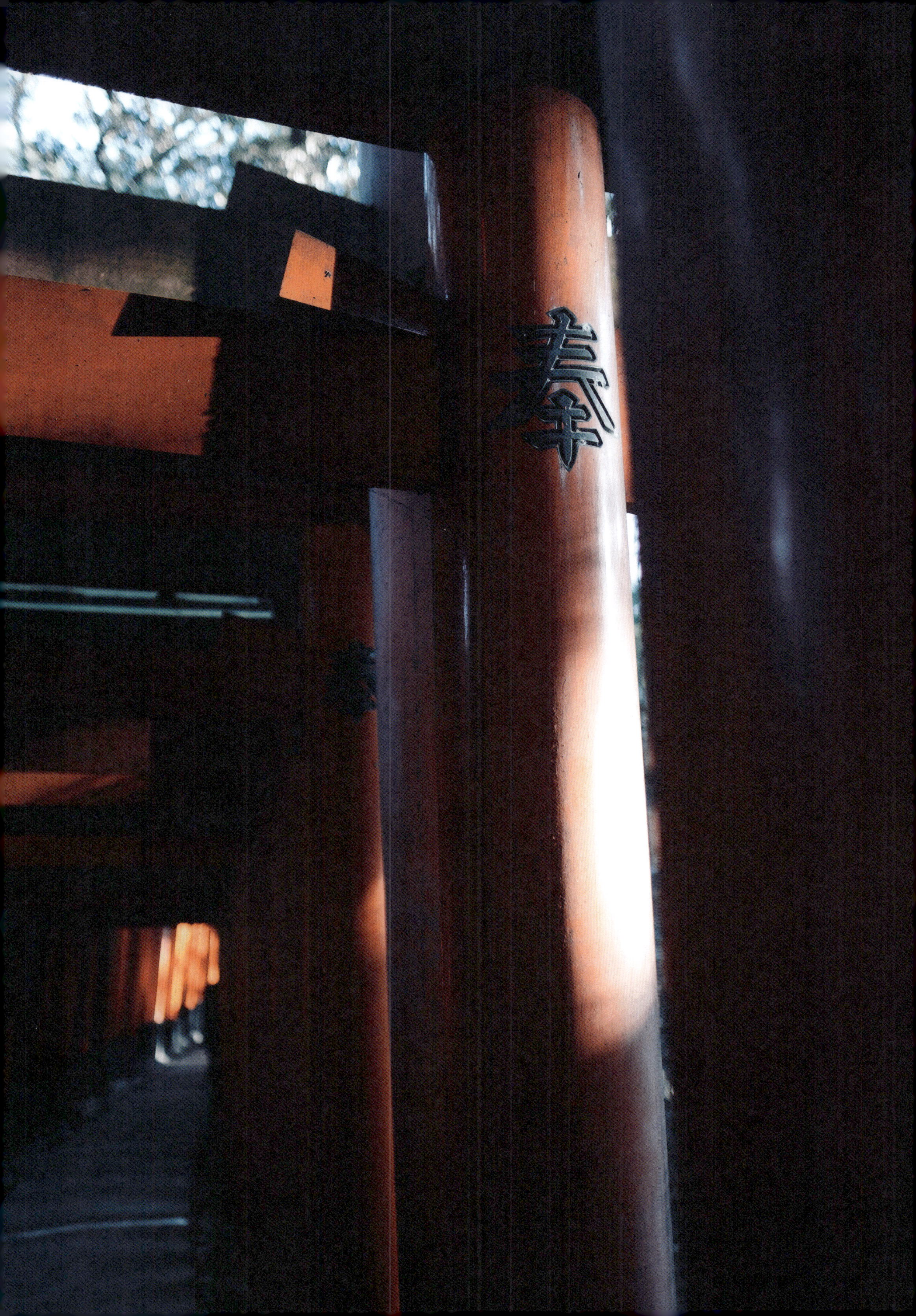
奉

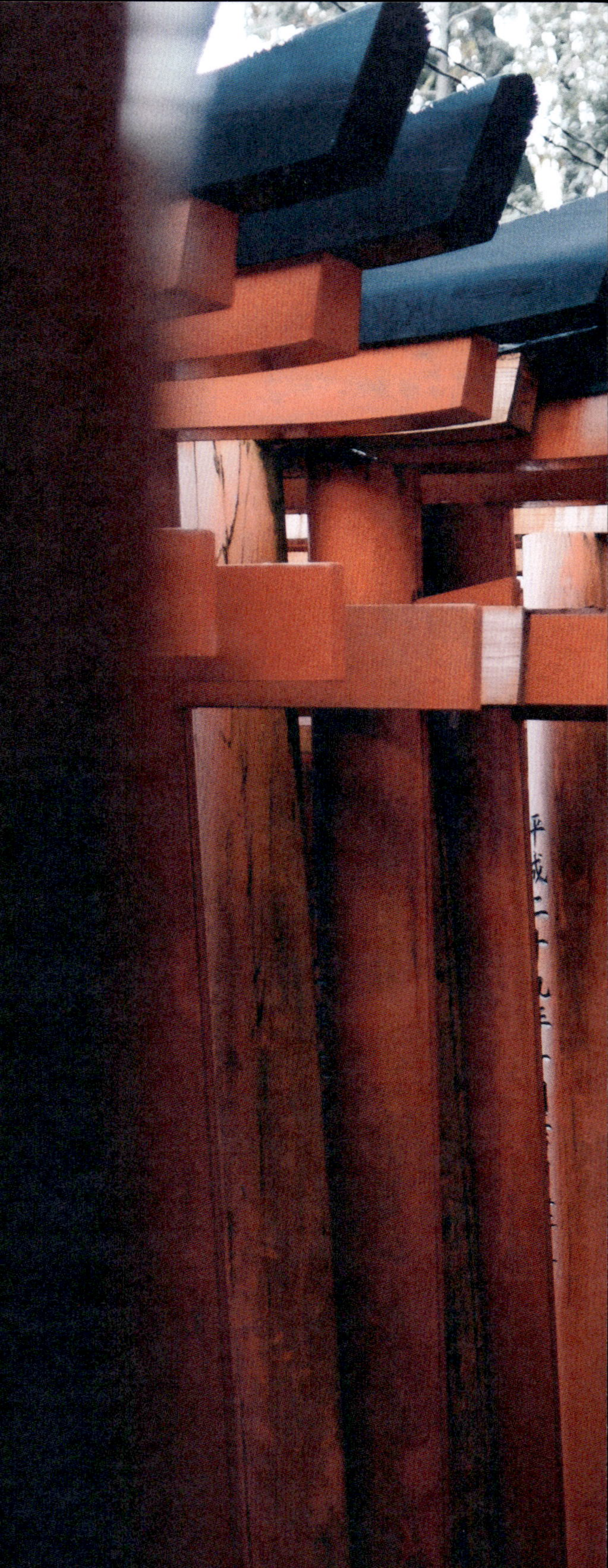
平成二

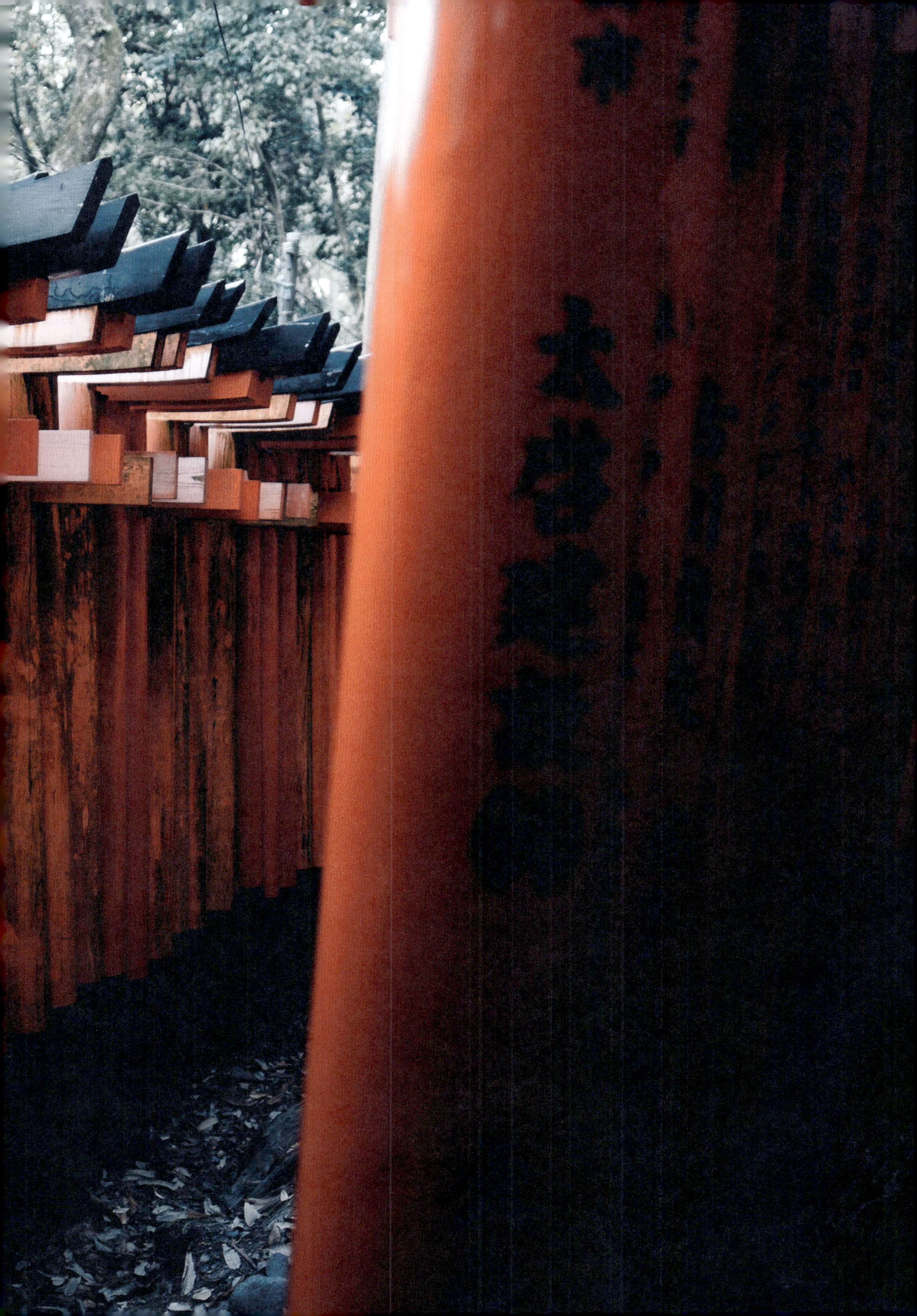

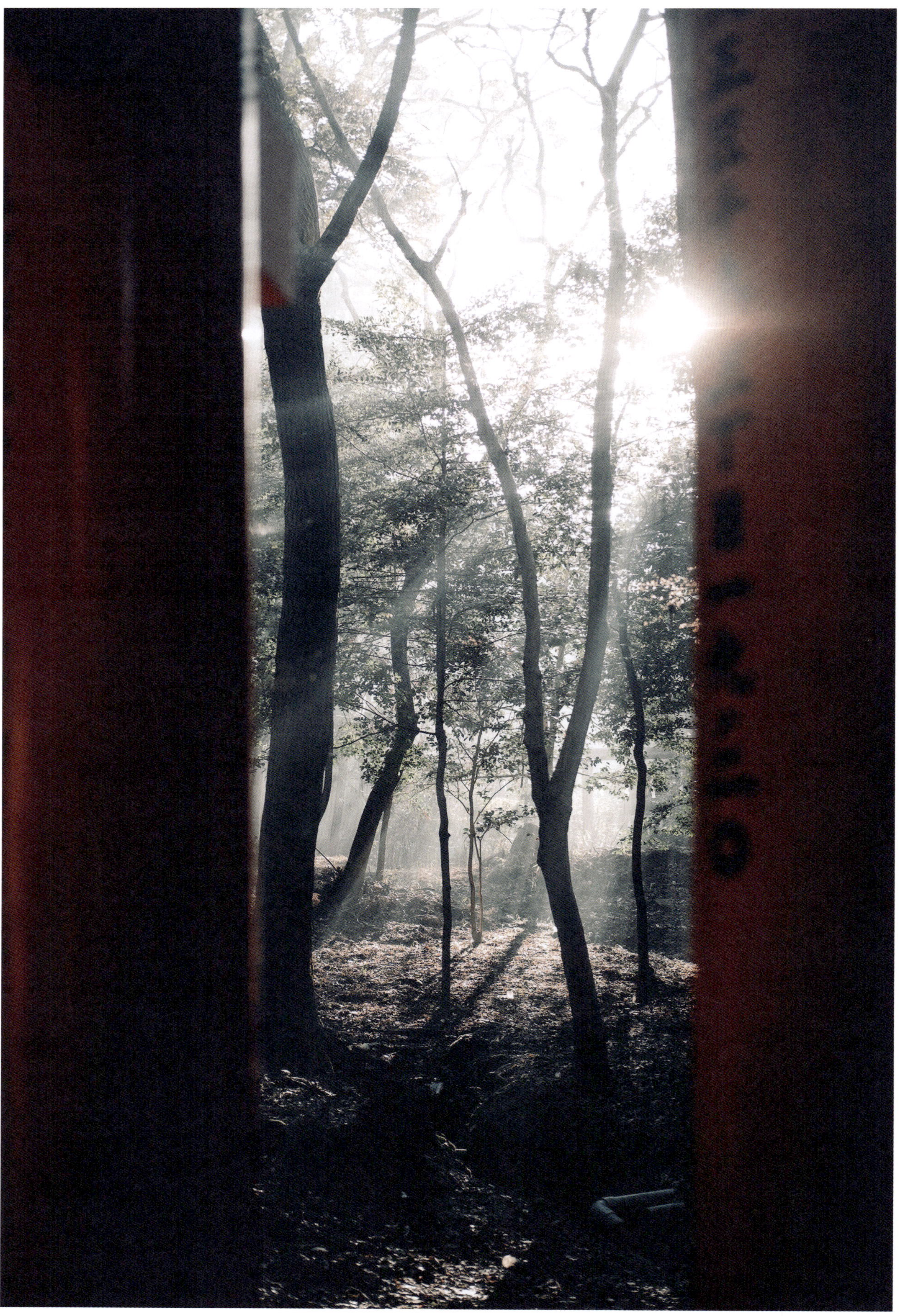

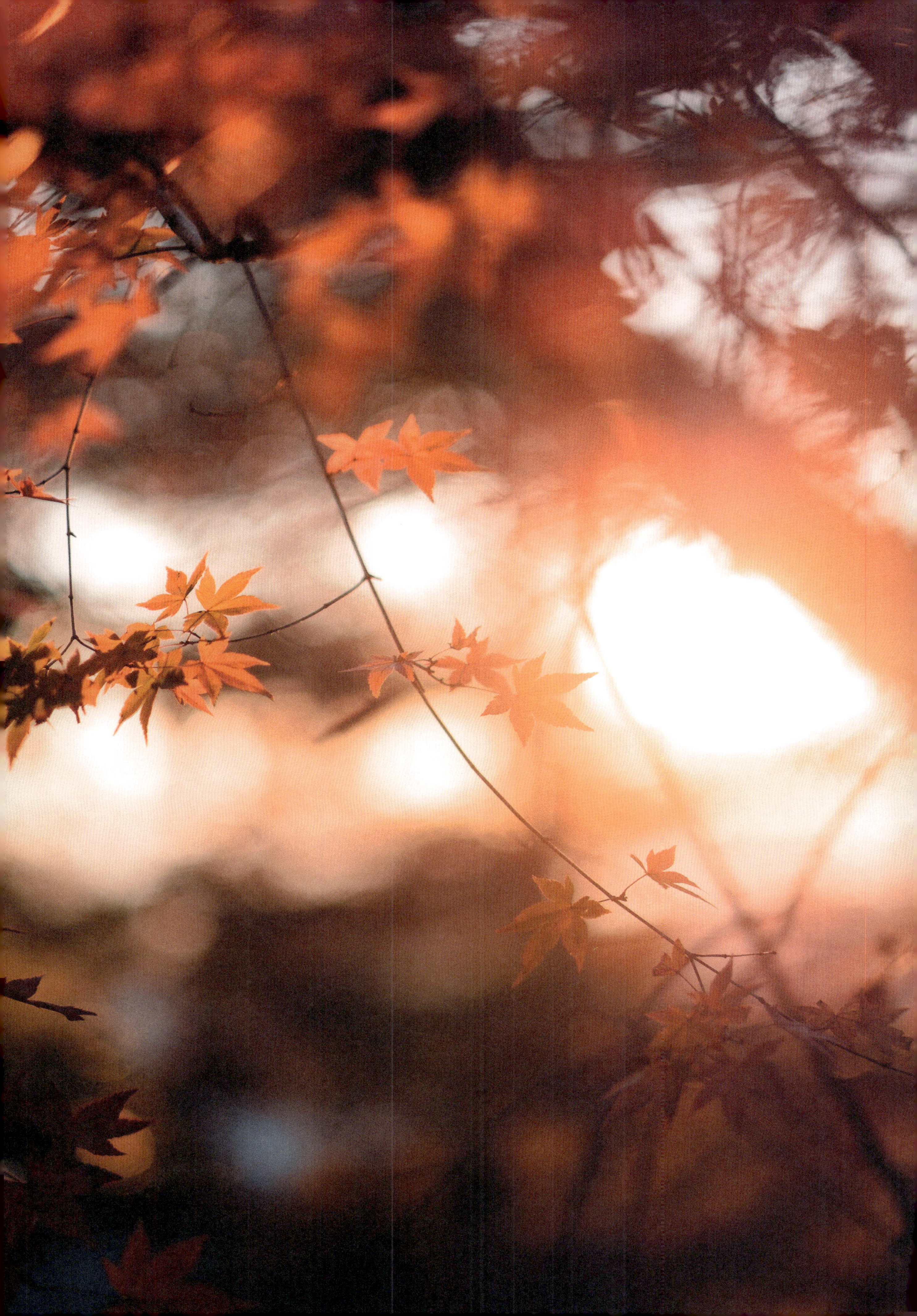

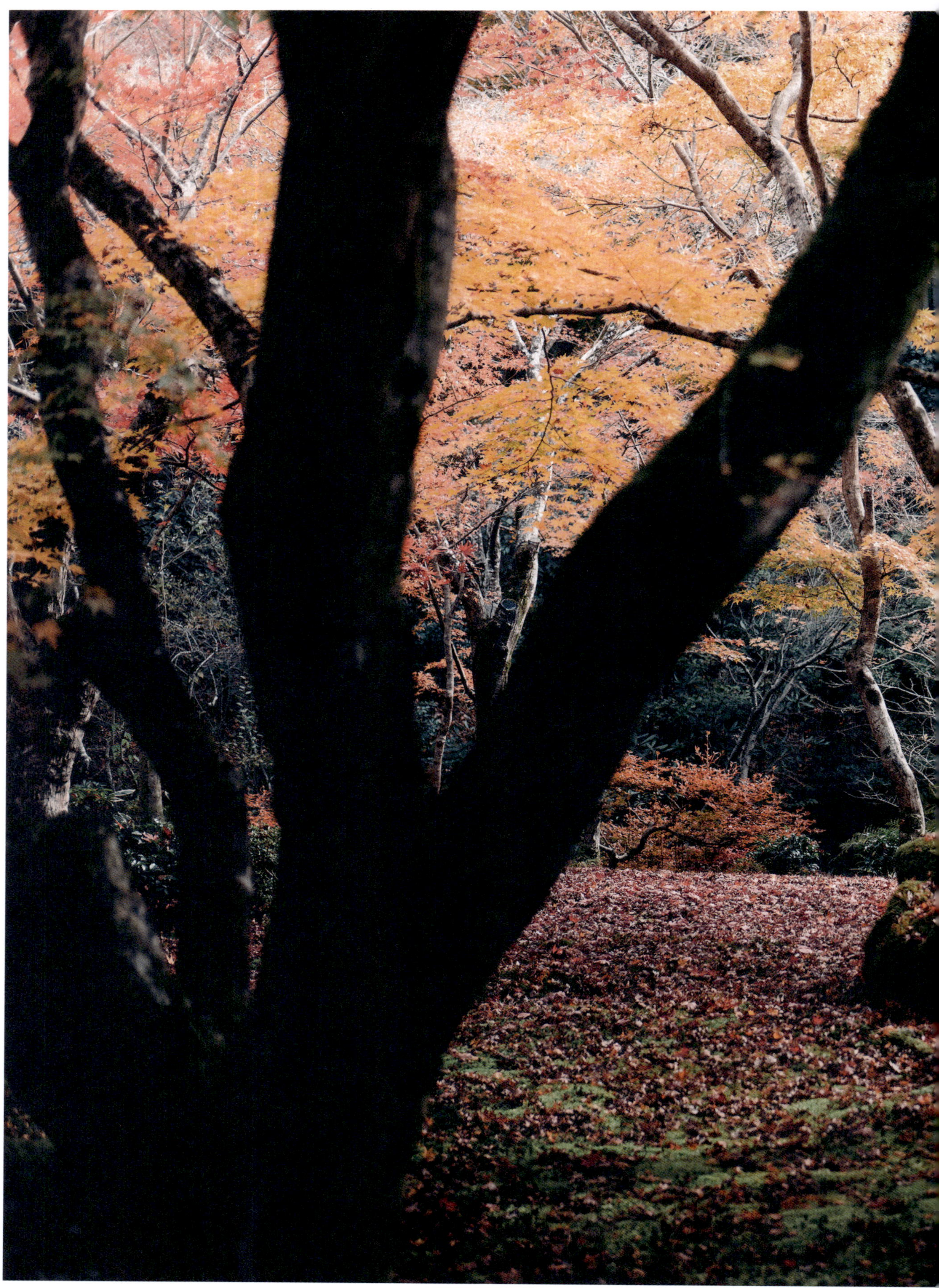

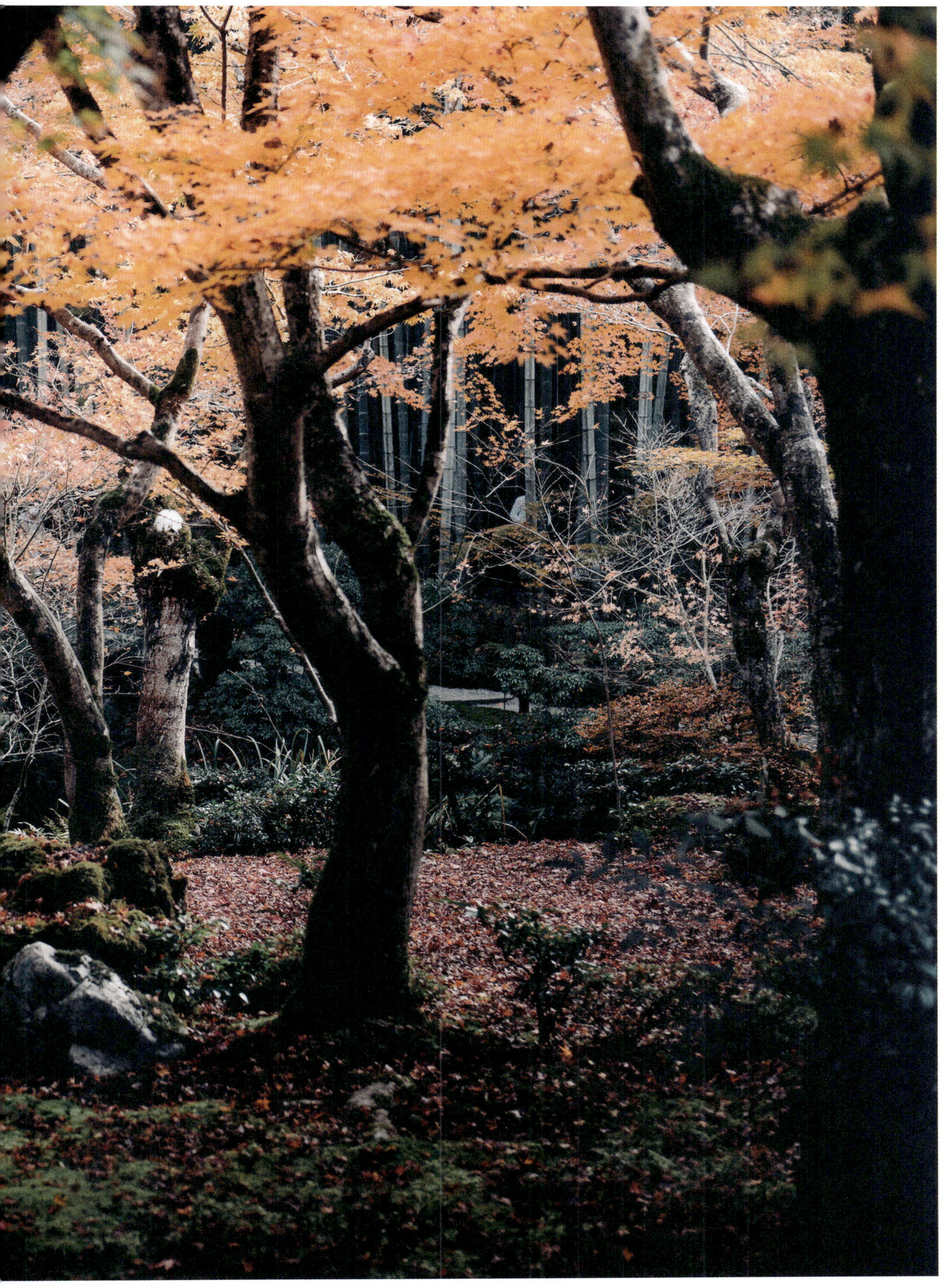

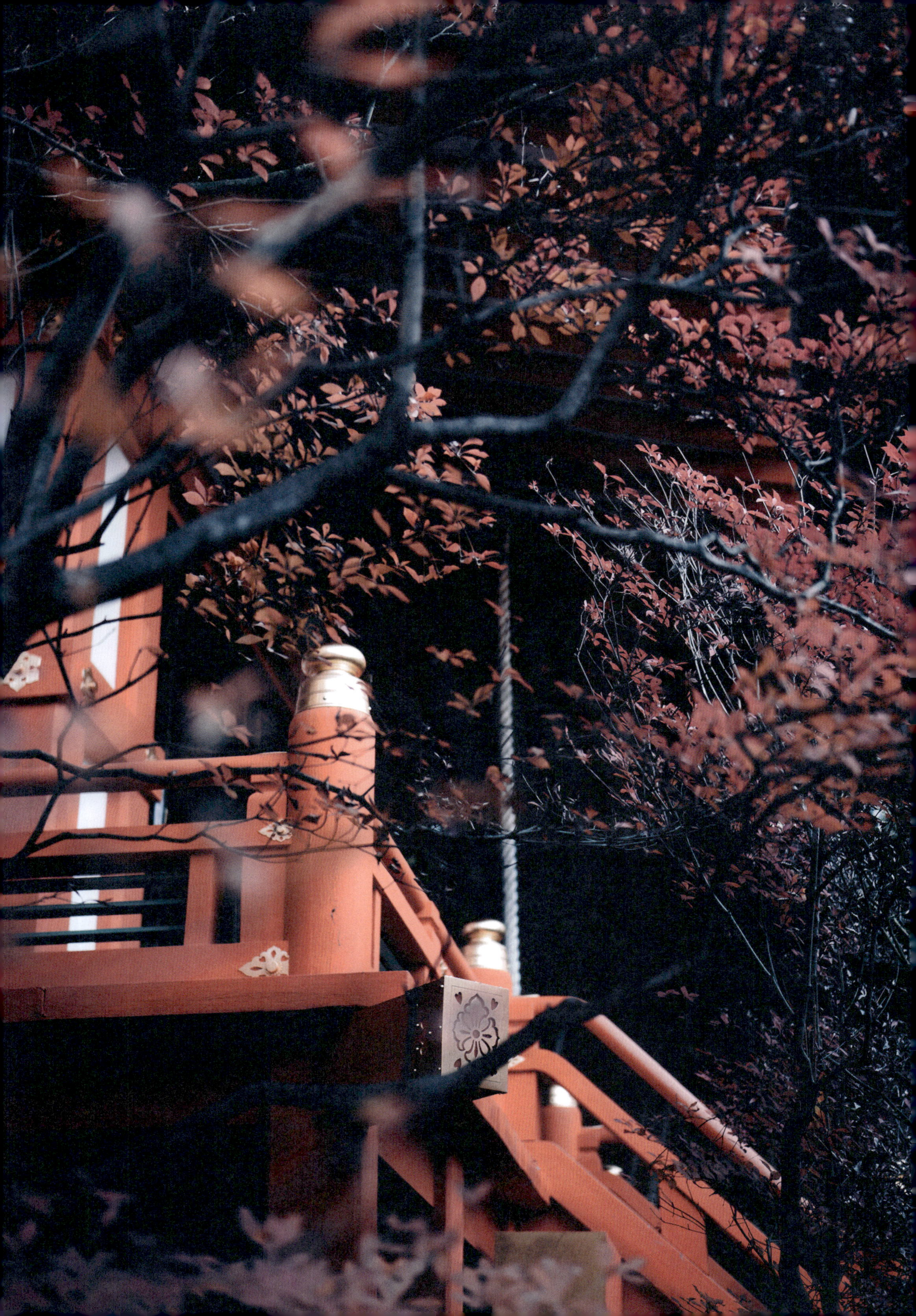

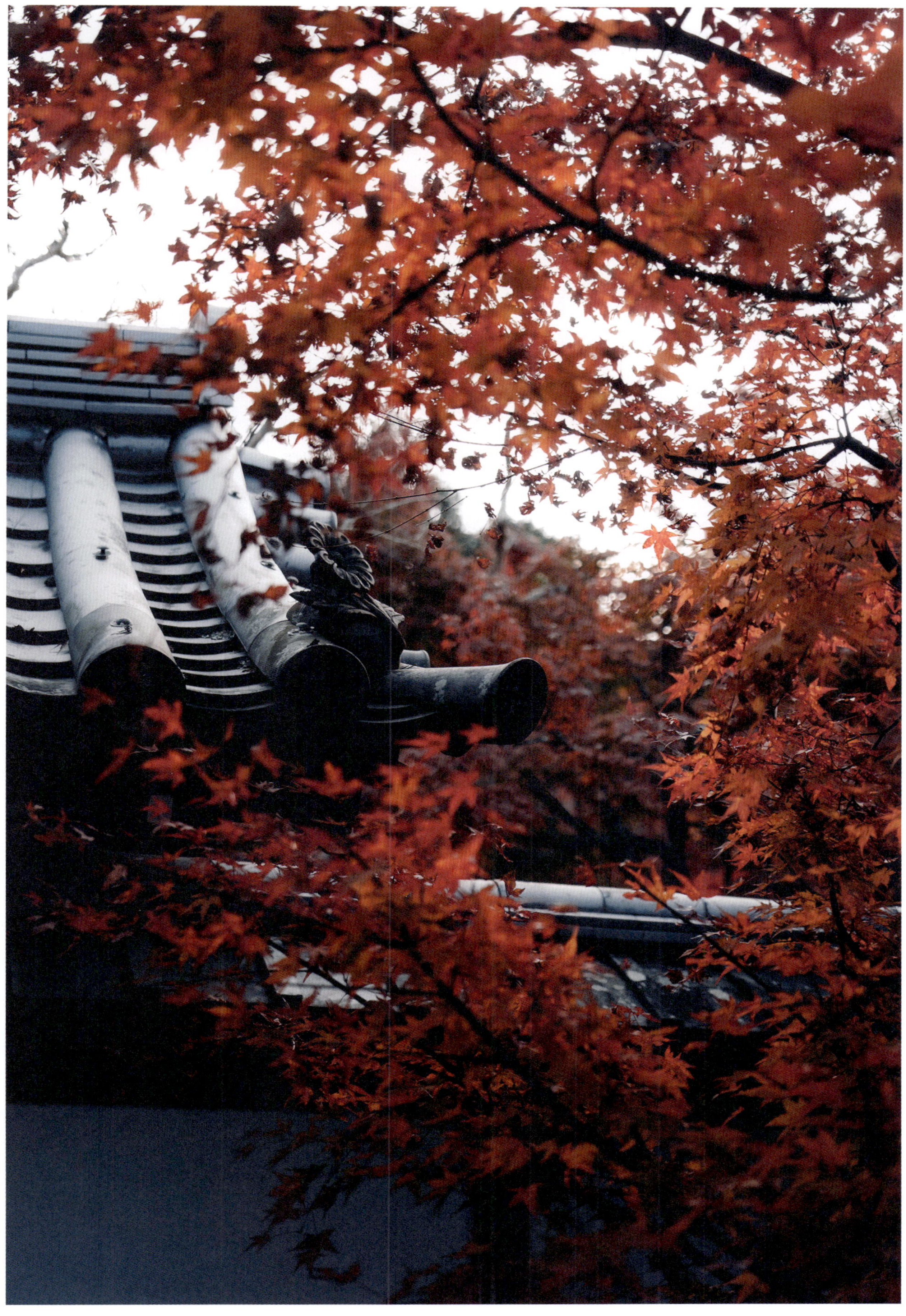

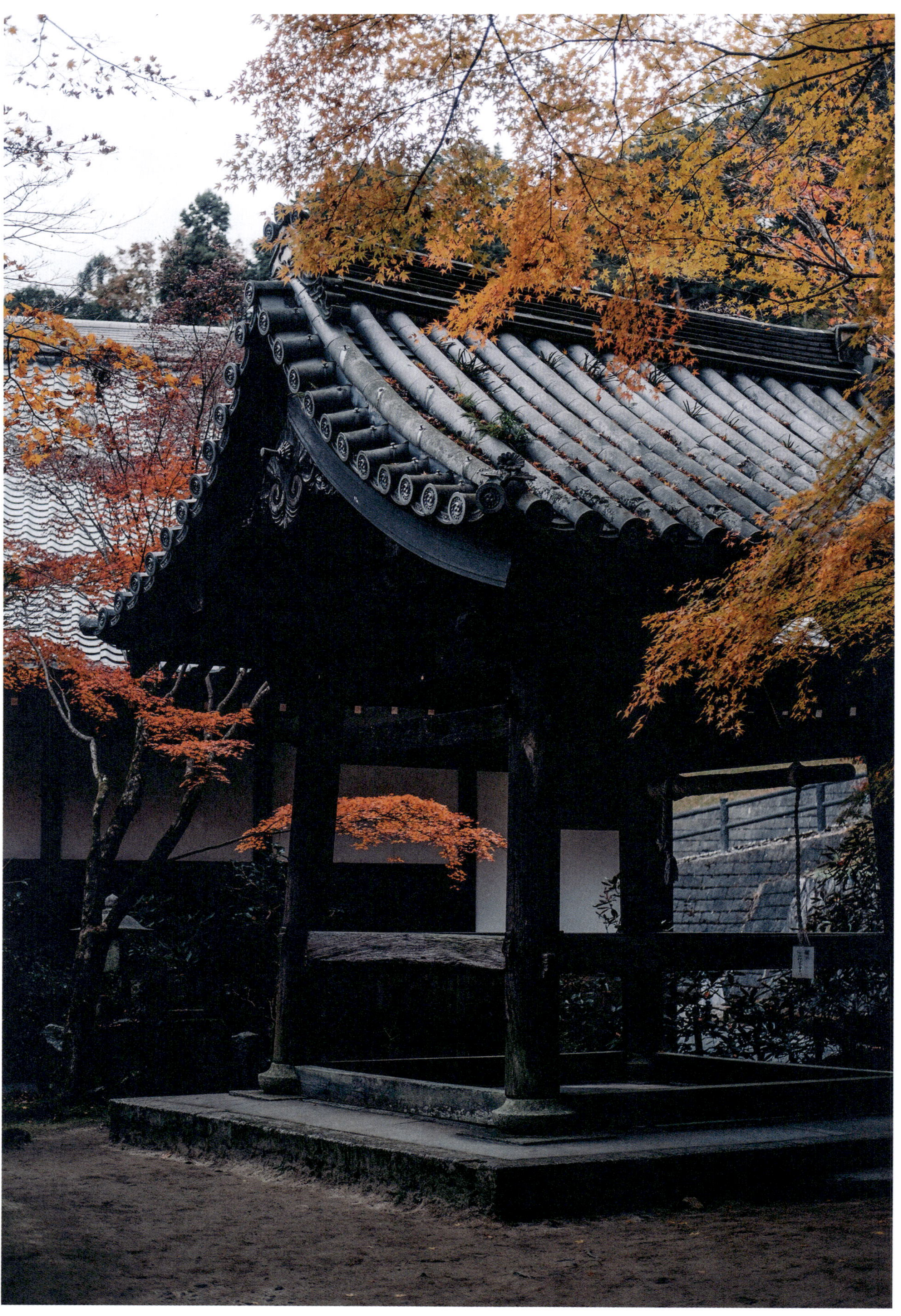

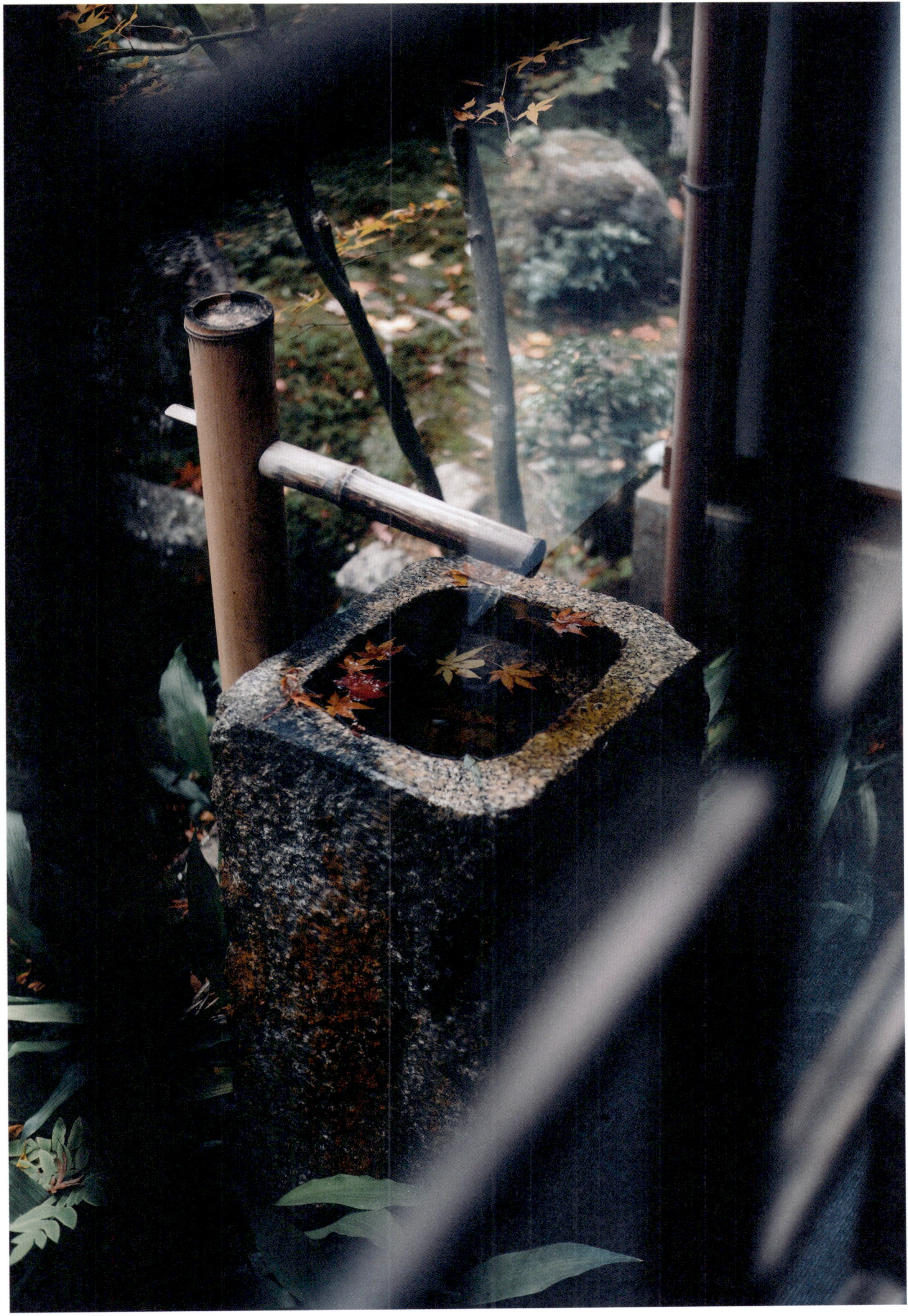

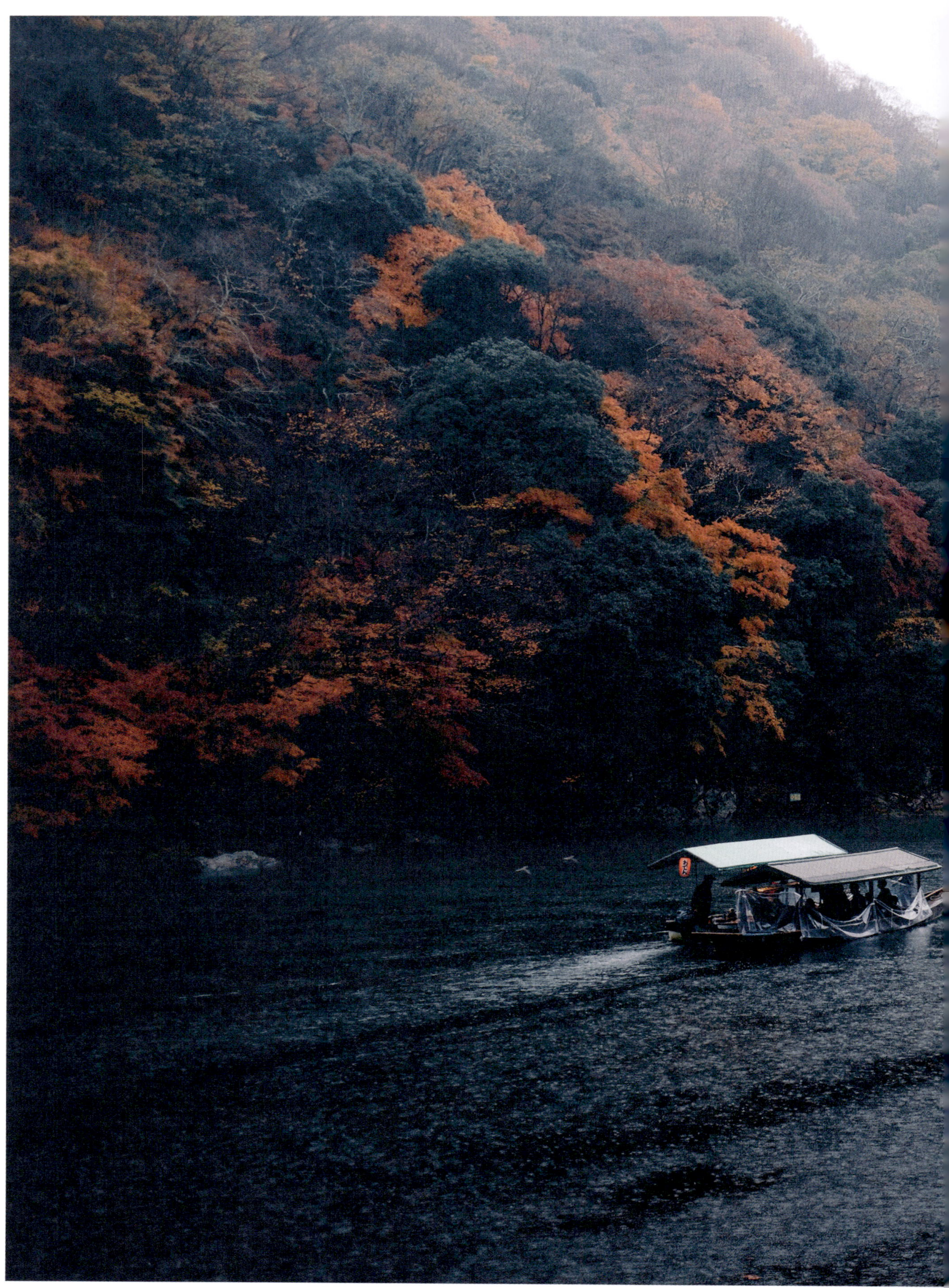

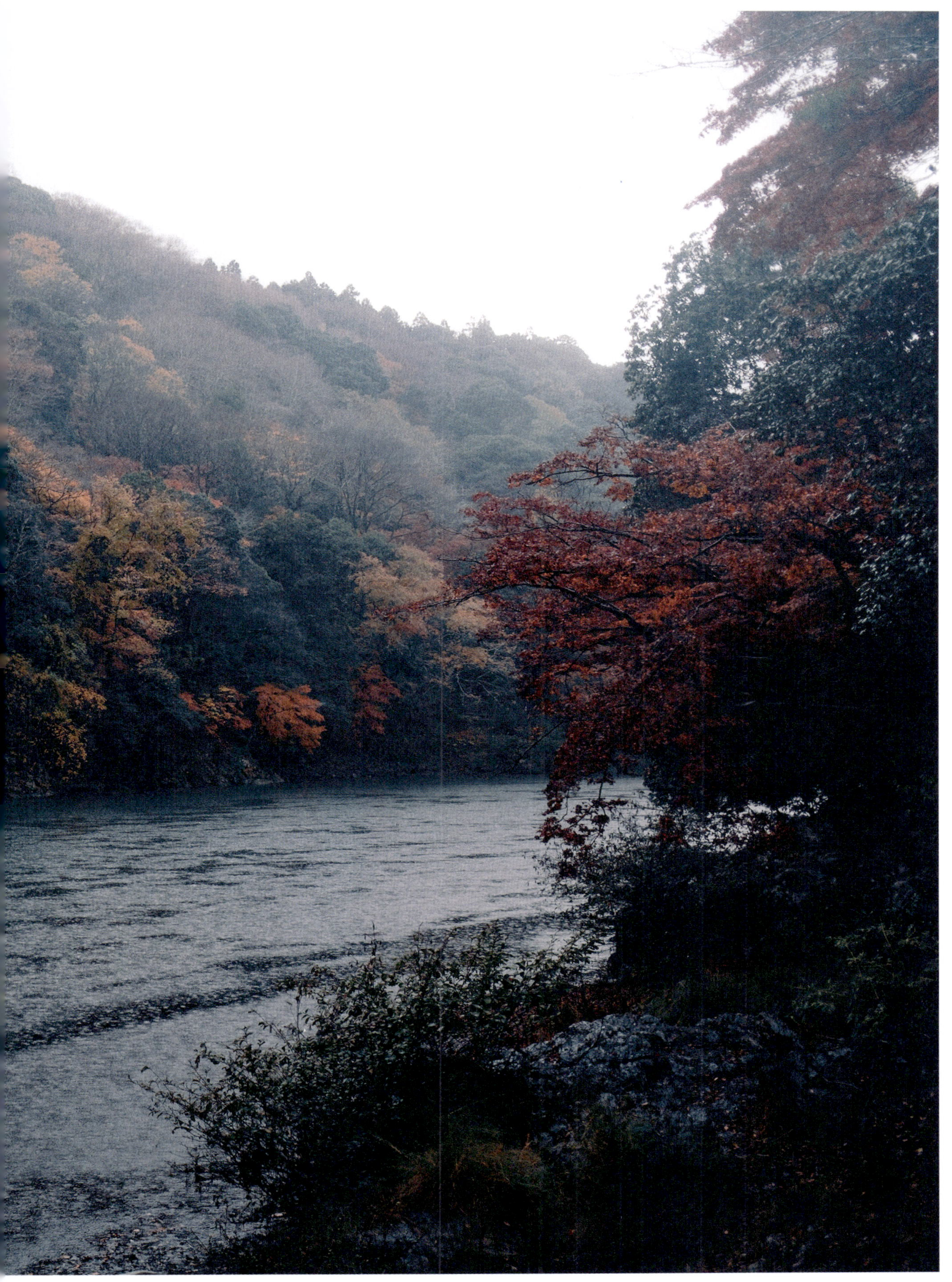

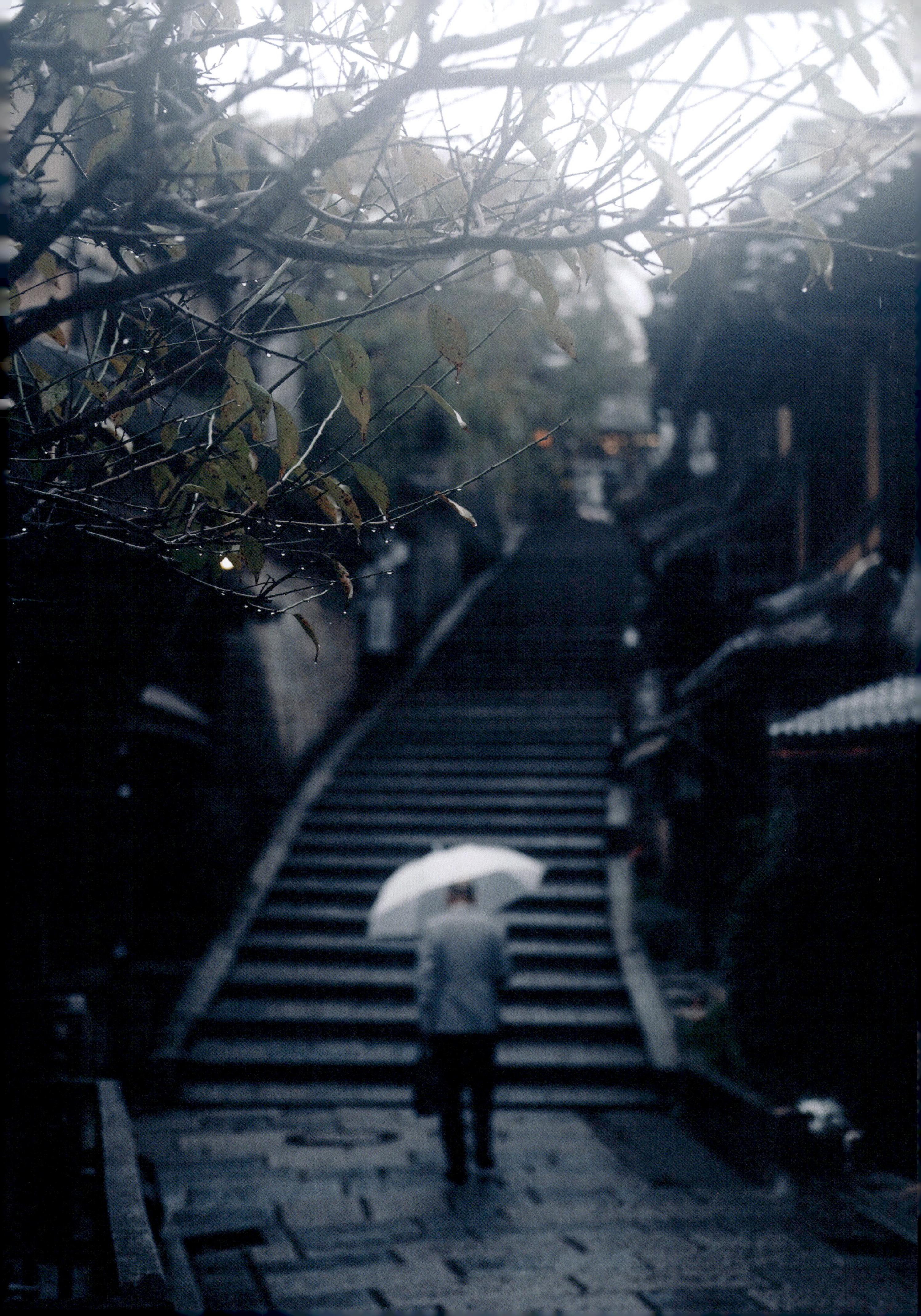

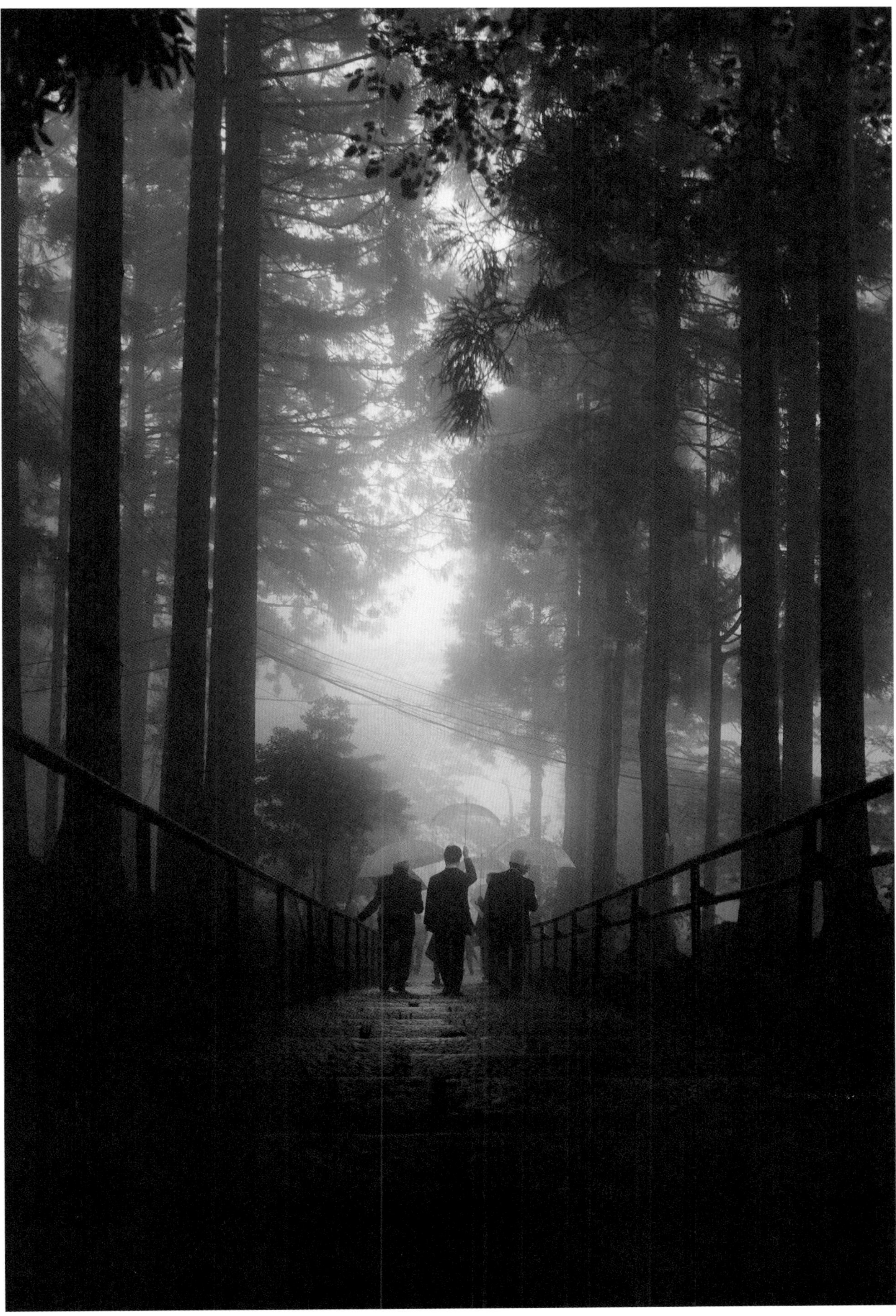

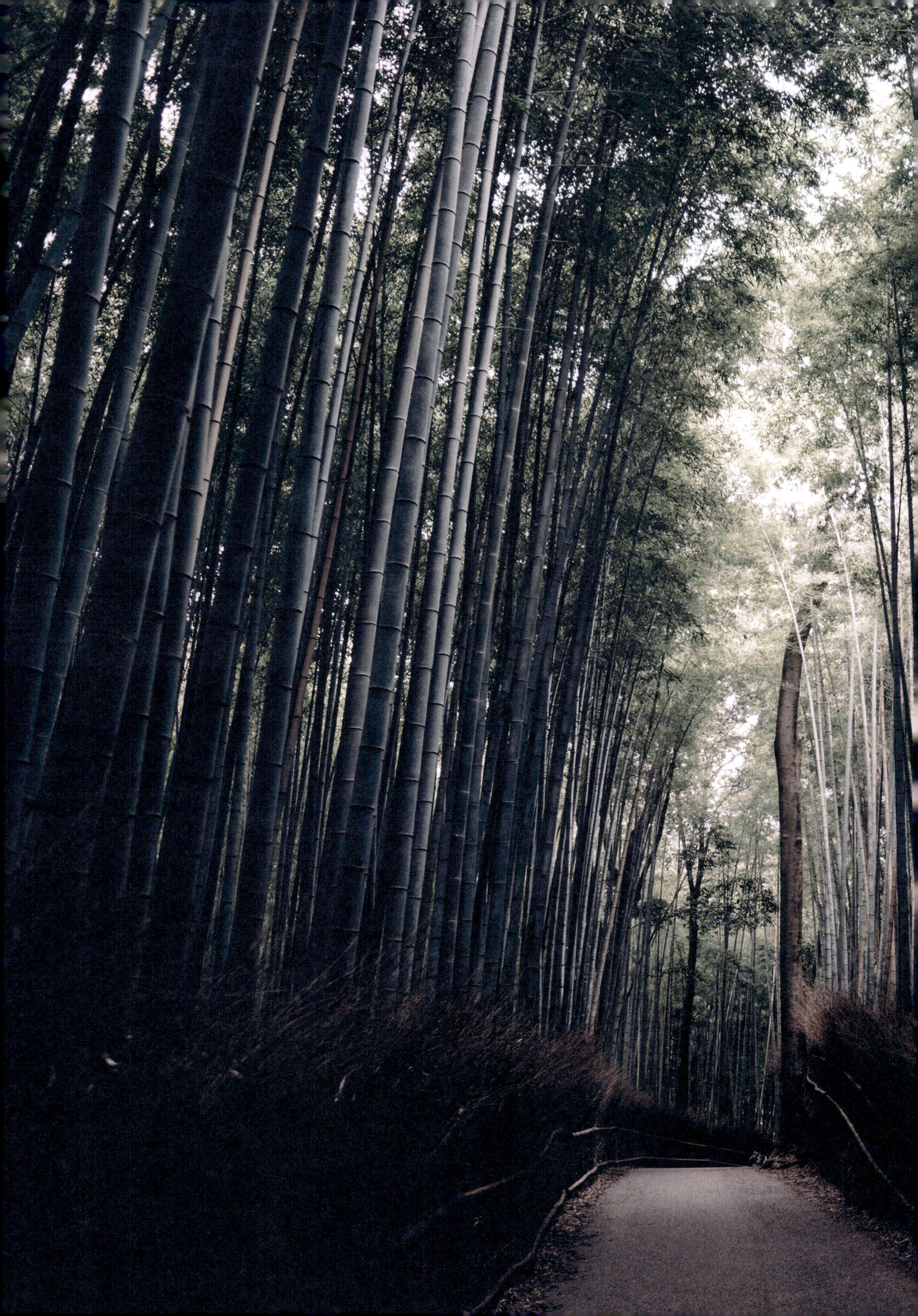

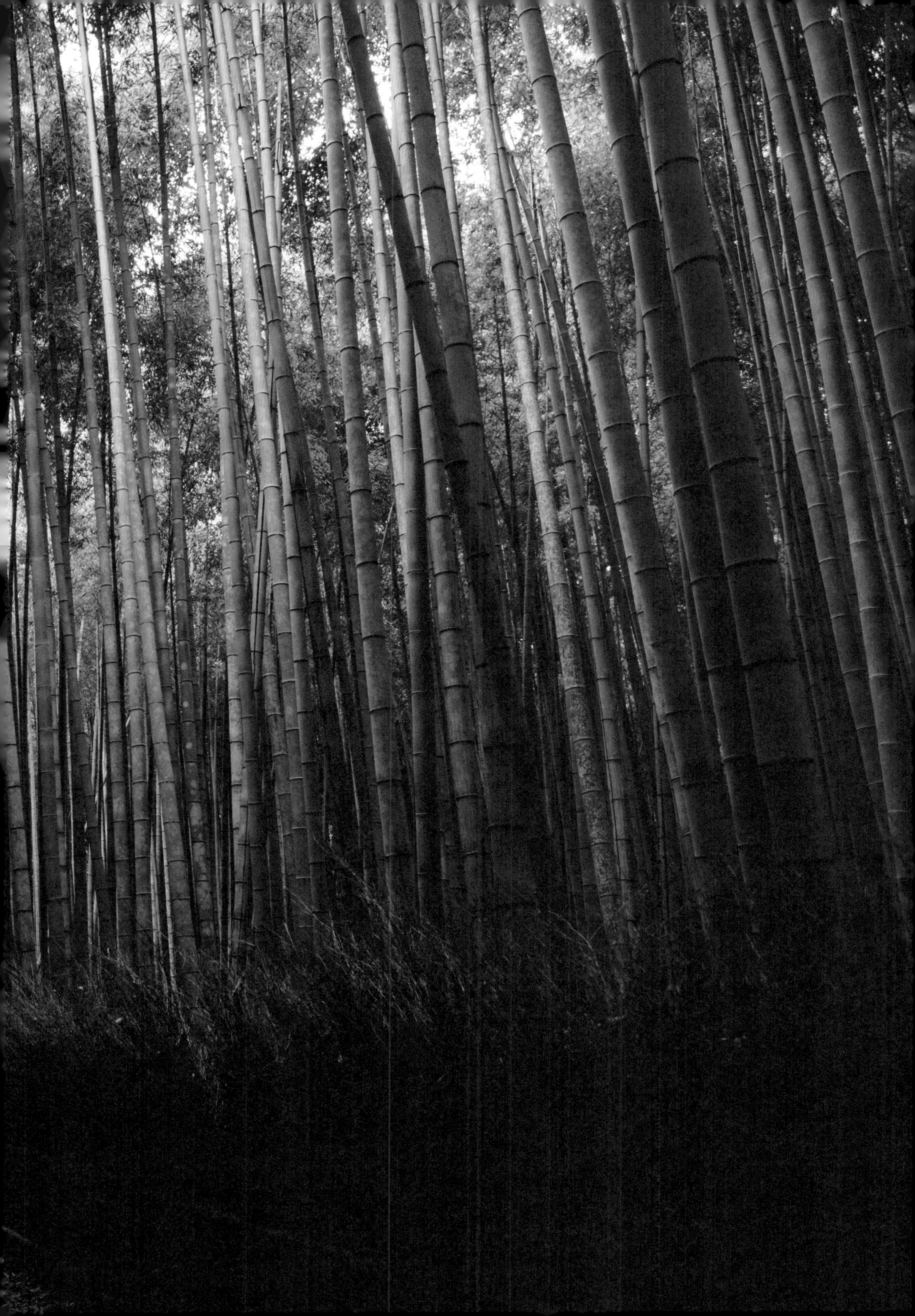

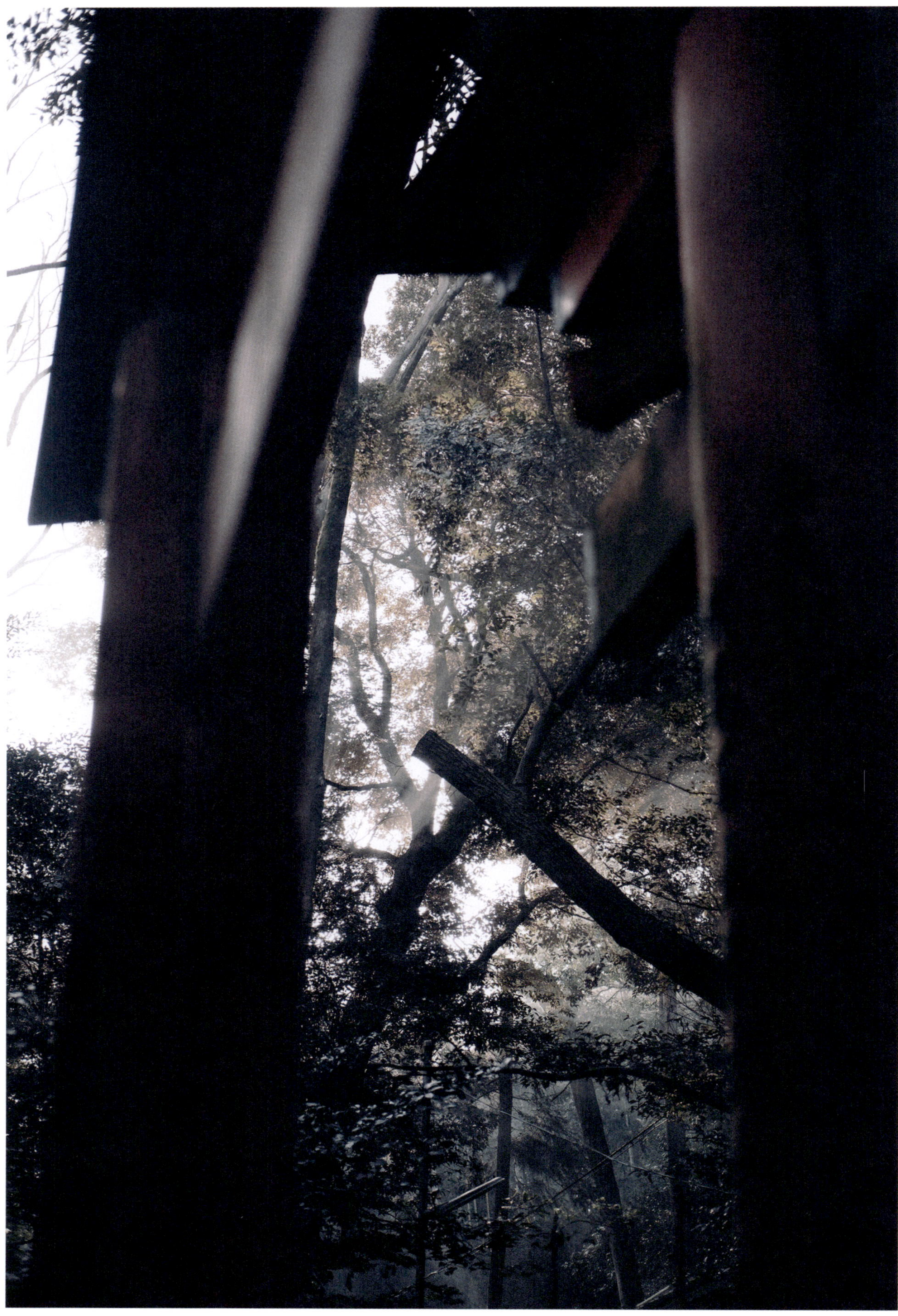

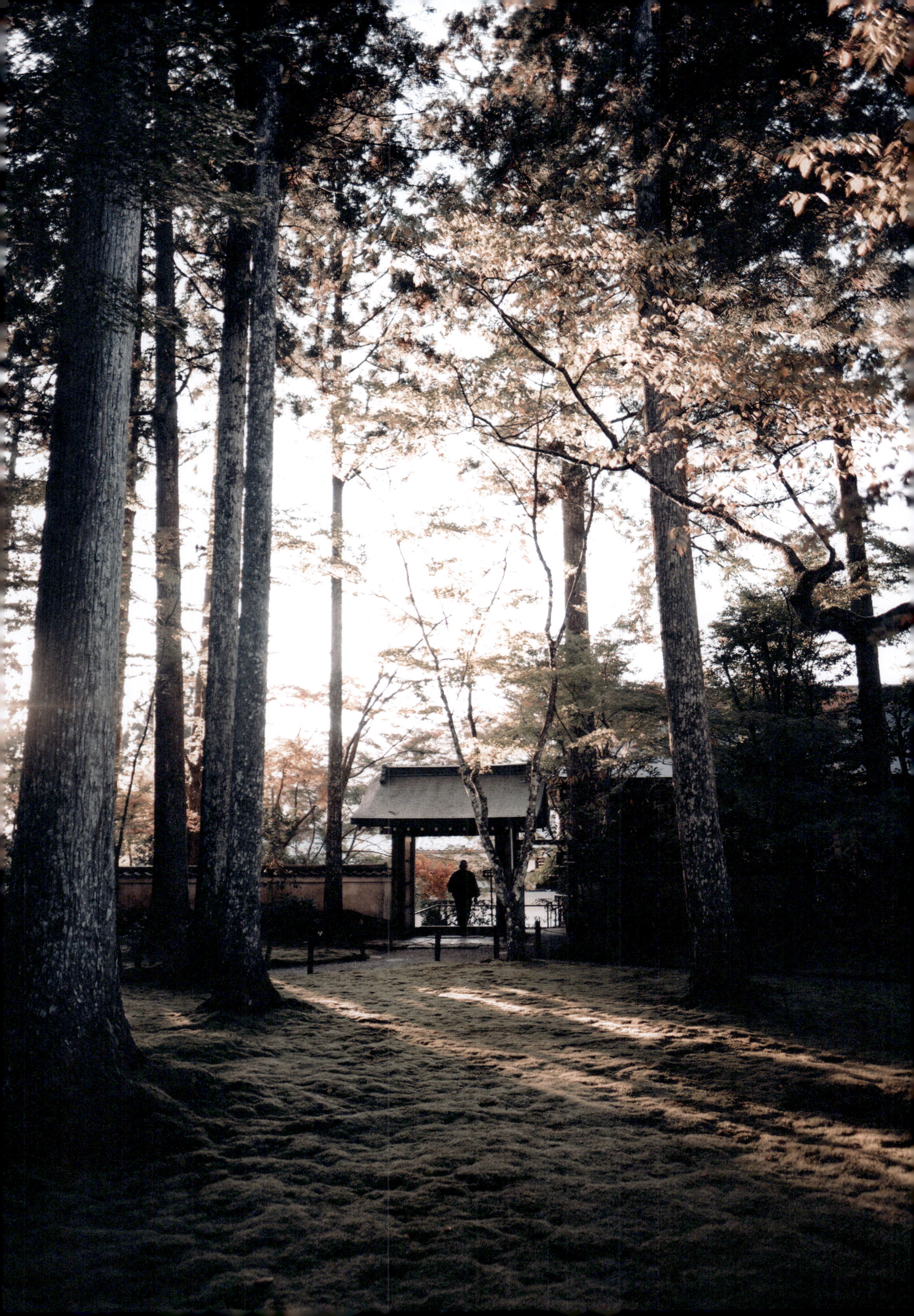

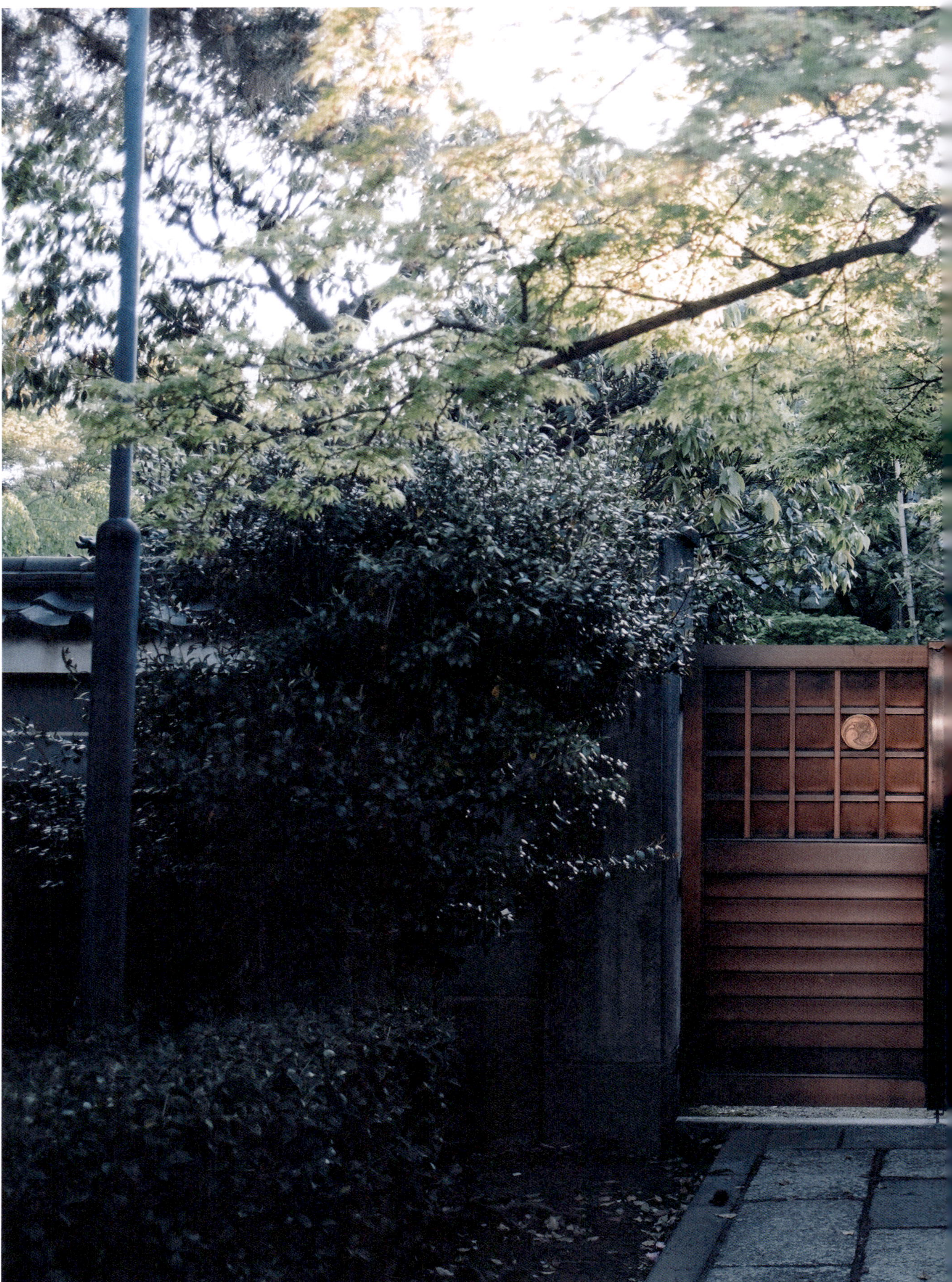

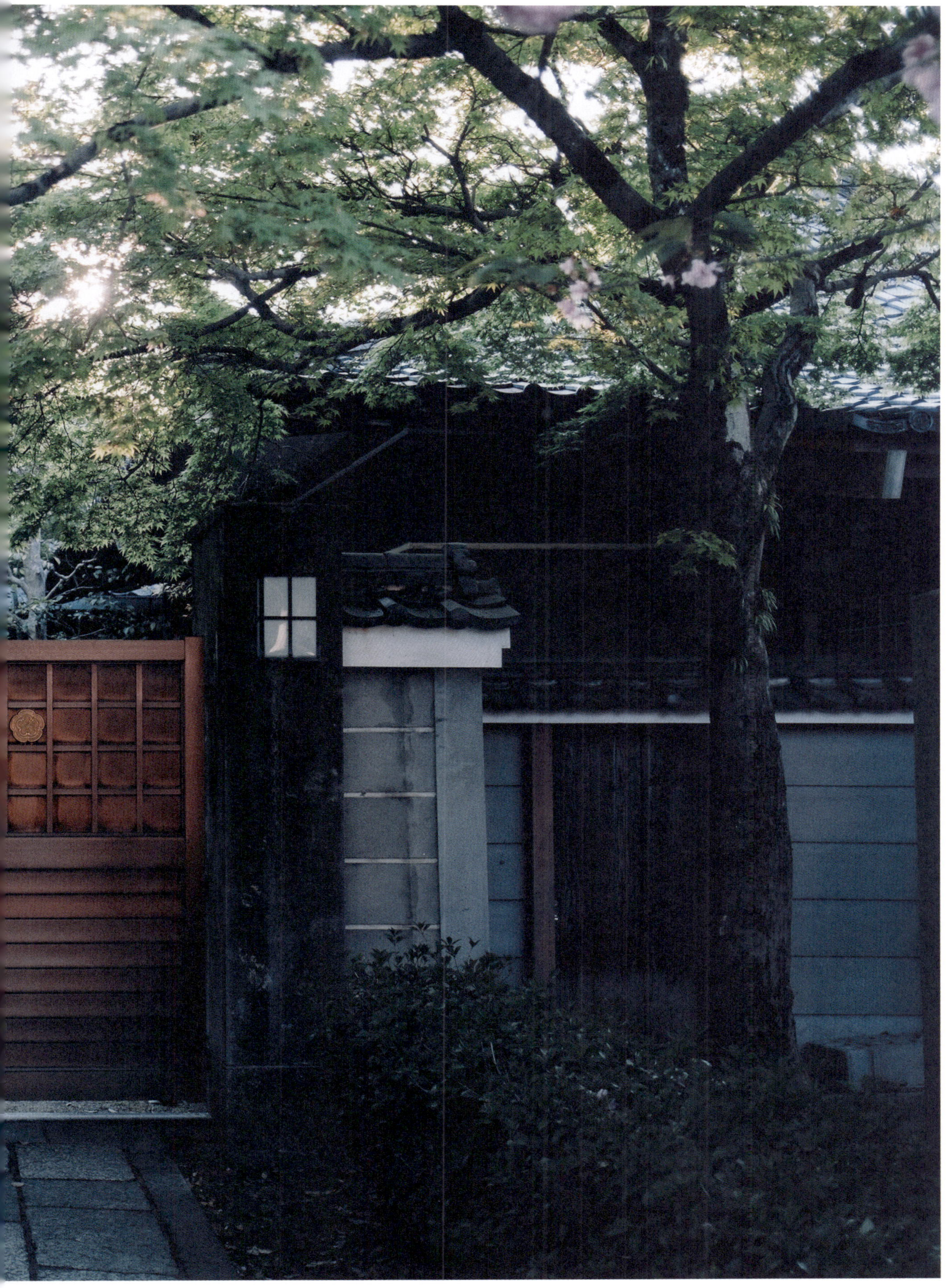

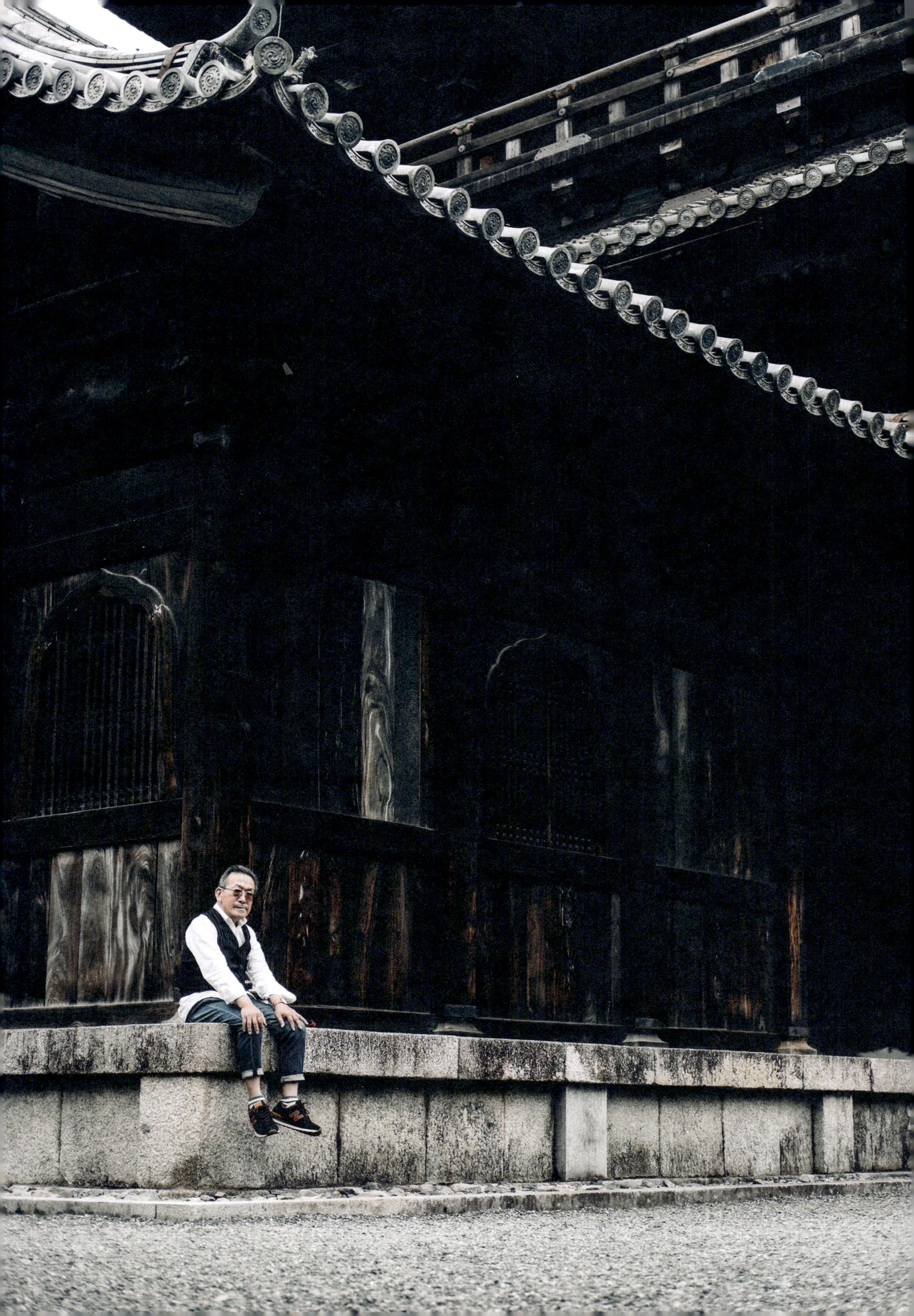

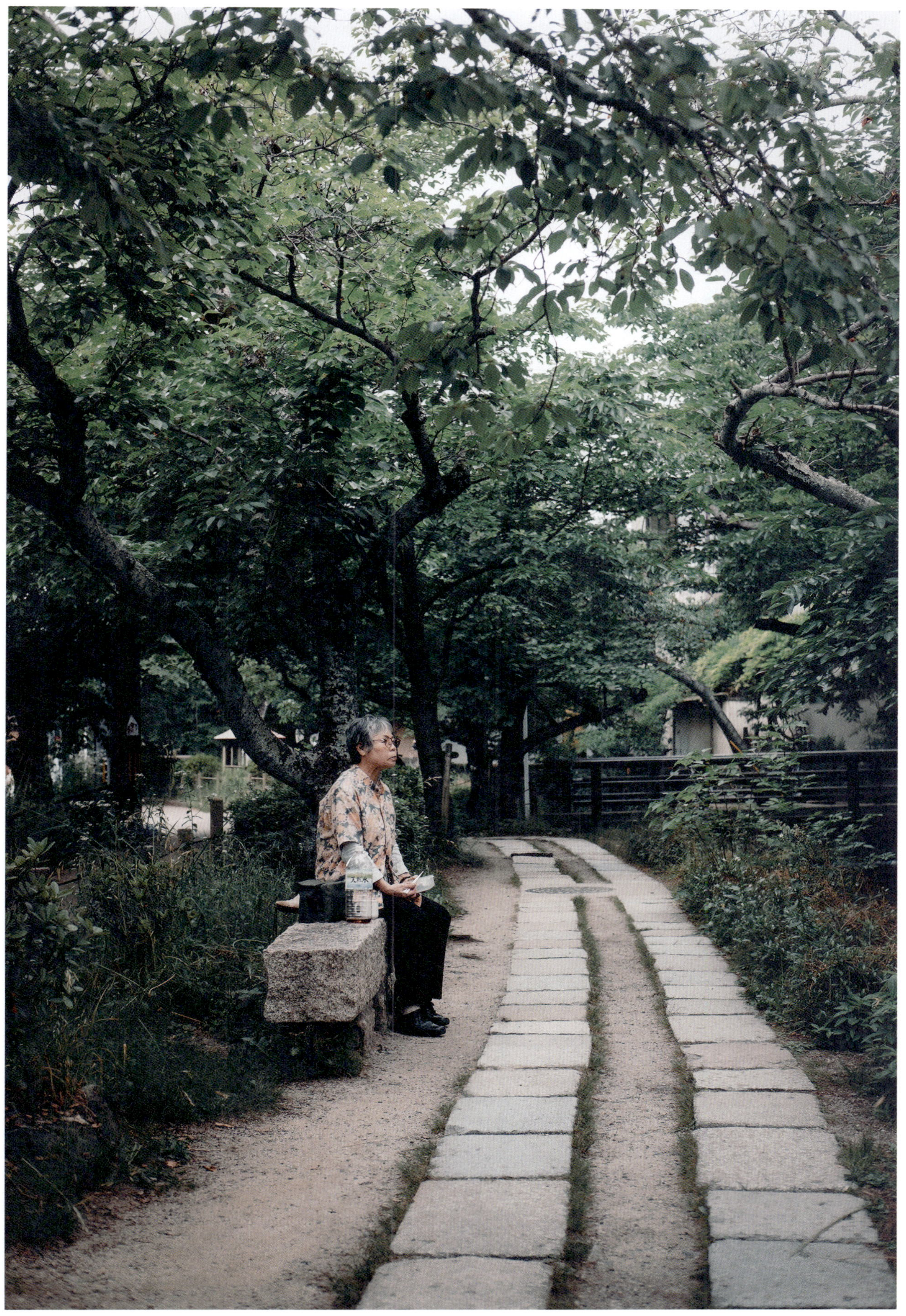

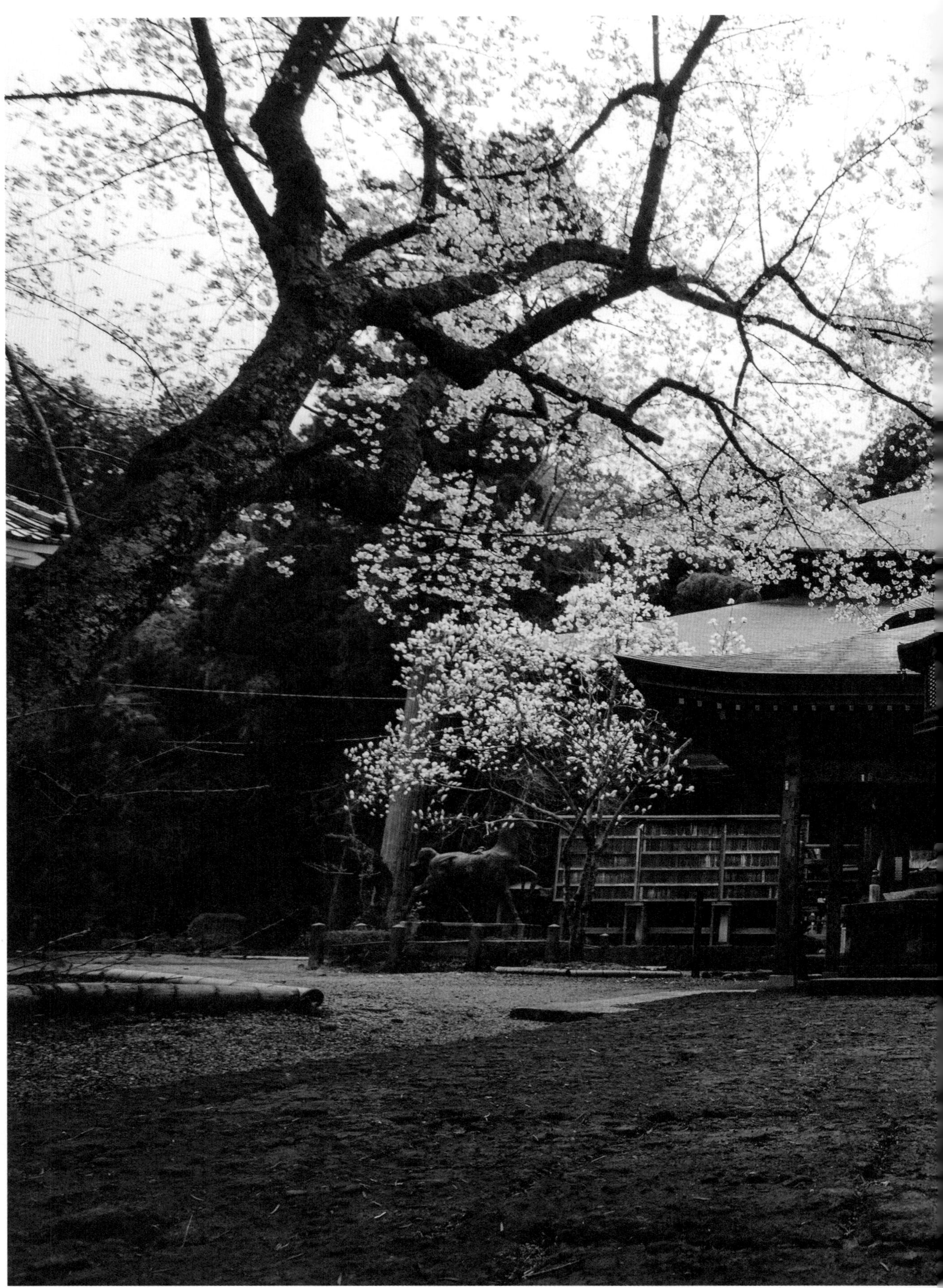

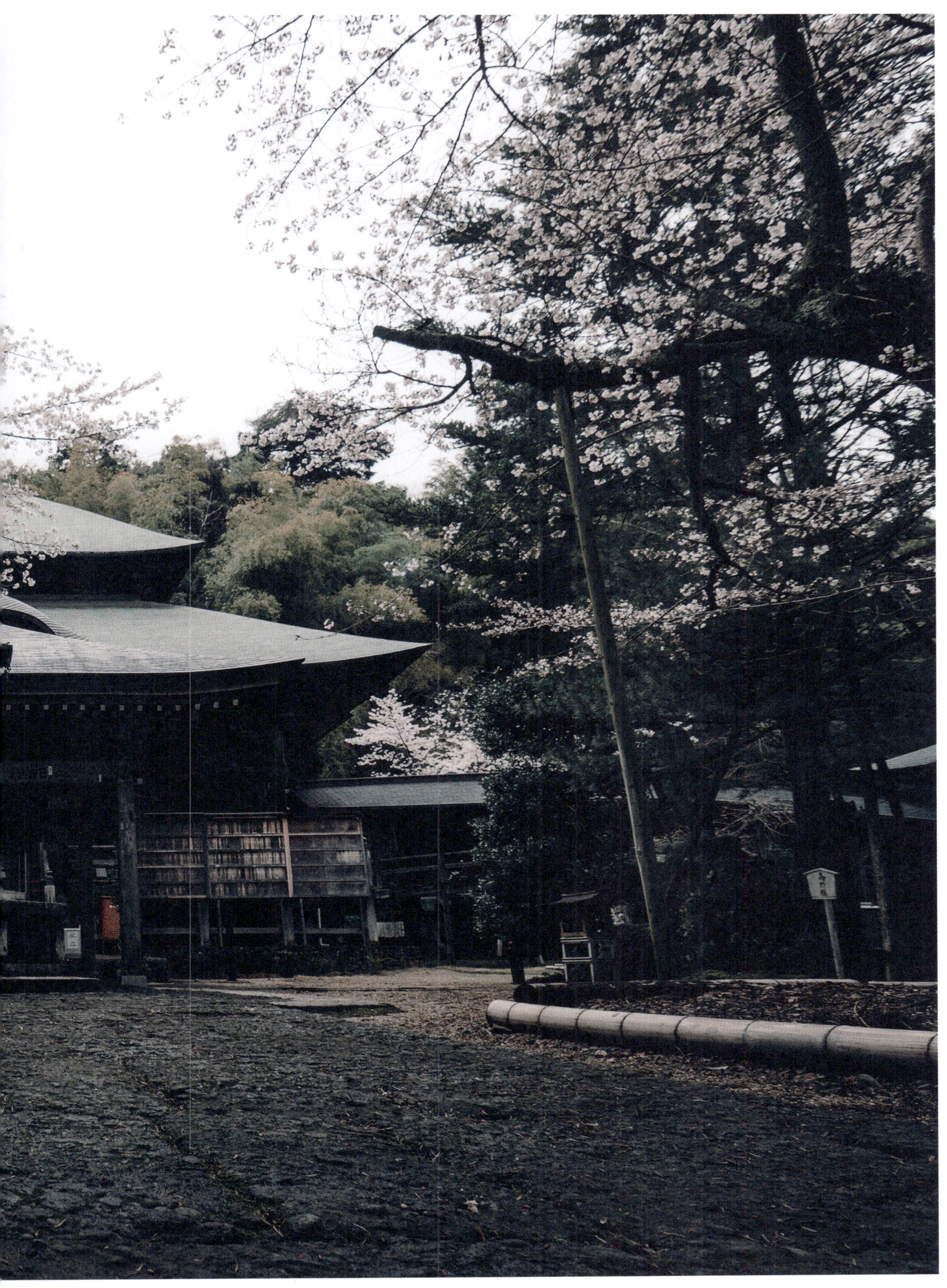

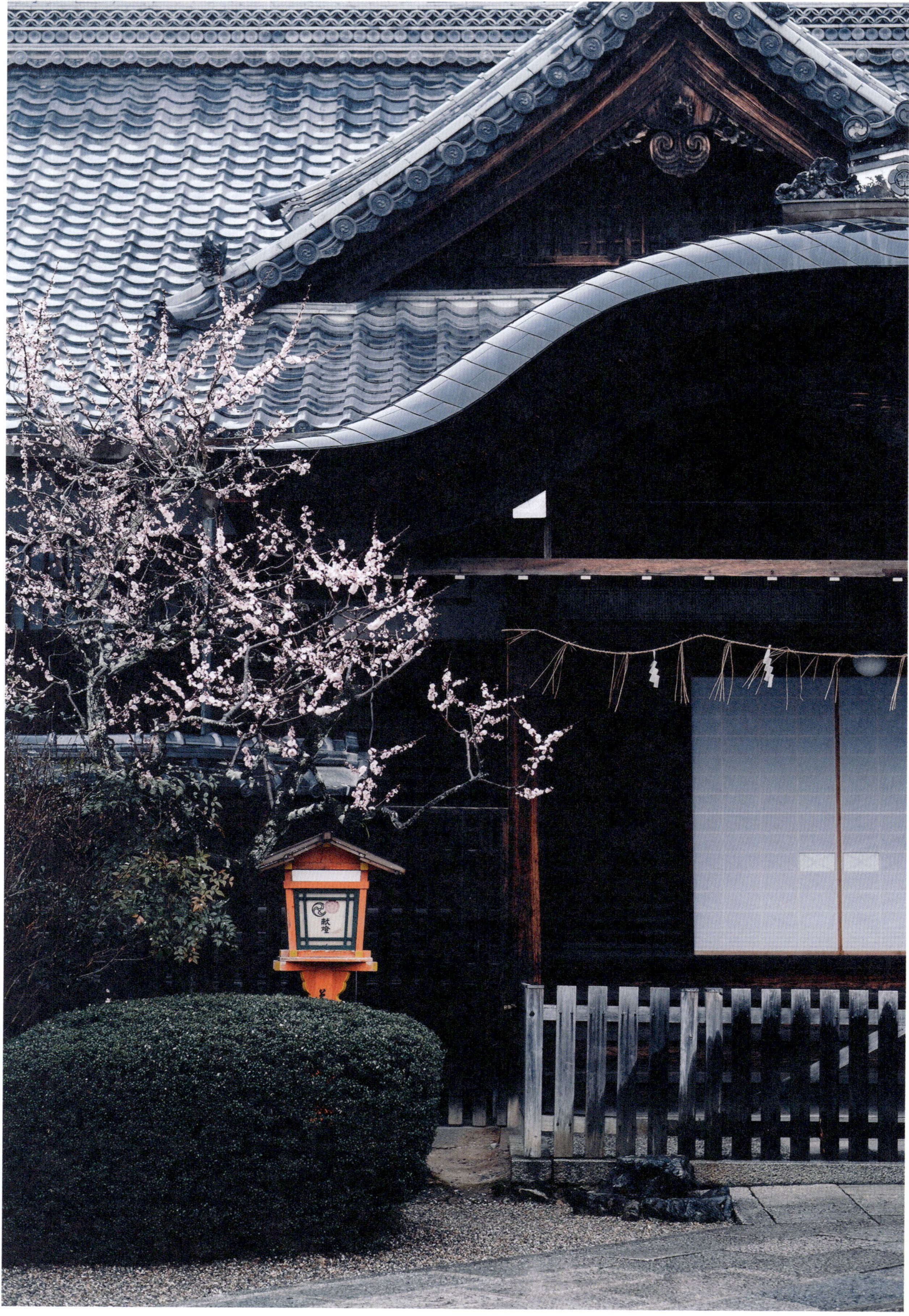

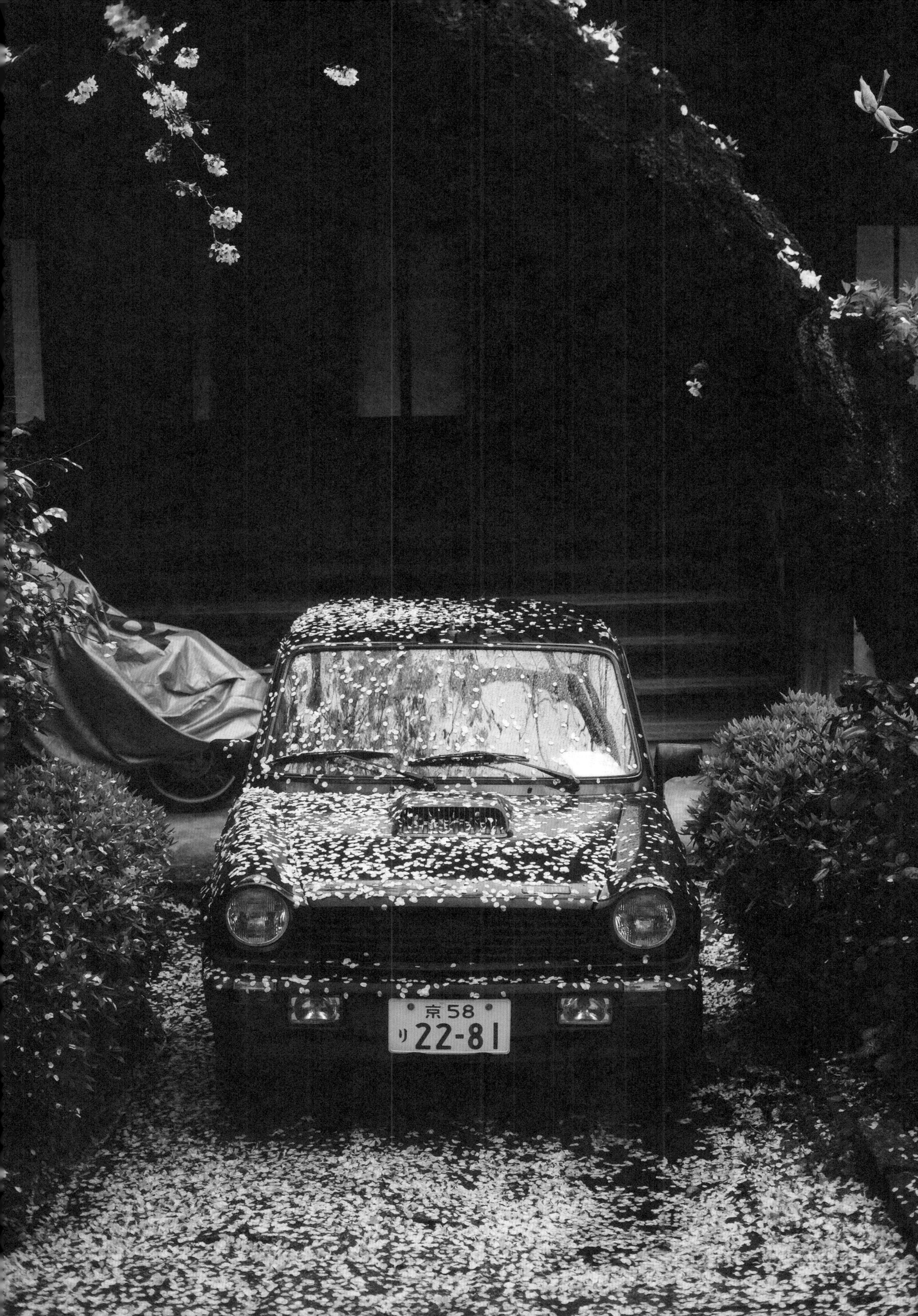
京58
り22-81

咲きてとく散るは
憂けれど行く
はる花の都を
たちかへりみよ

紫式部

Petals bloom then scatter

a sorrowful spring parting

but you will surely come again

to view the flowering capital

Murasaki Shikibu

excerpt from *The Tale of Genji*

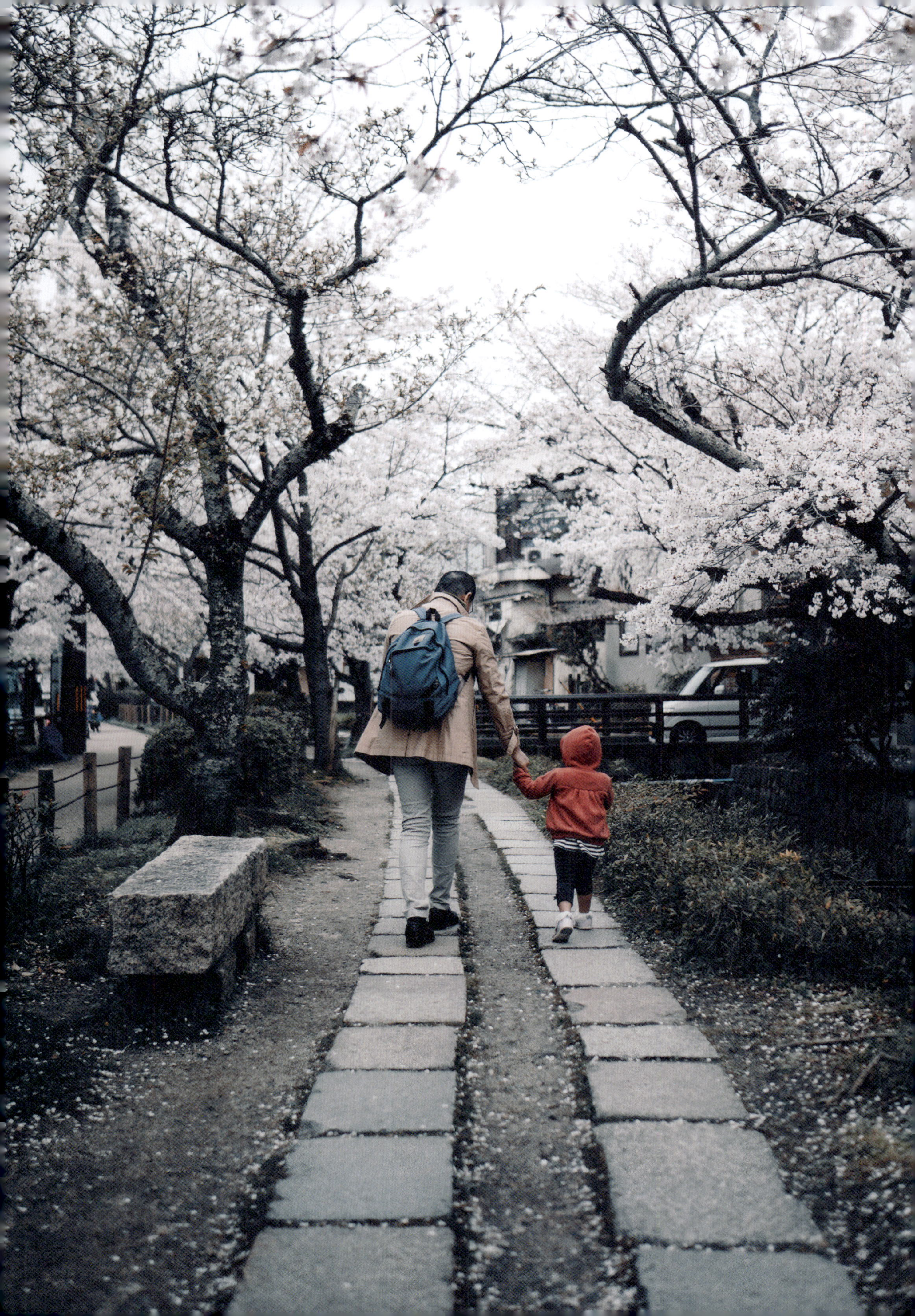

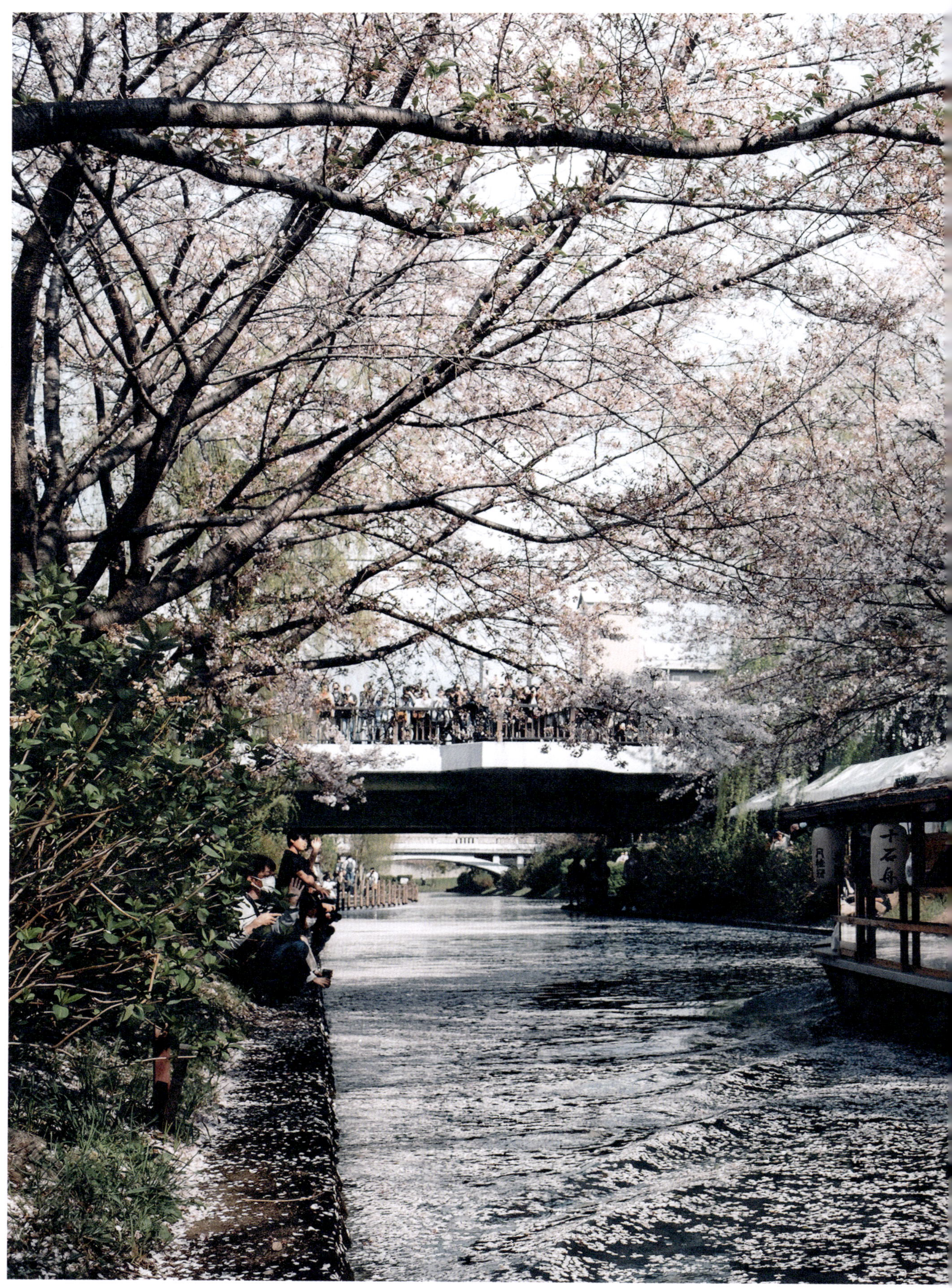
十石舟

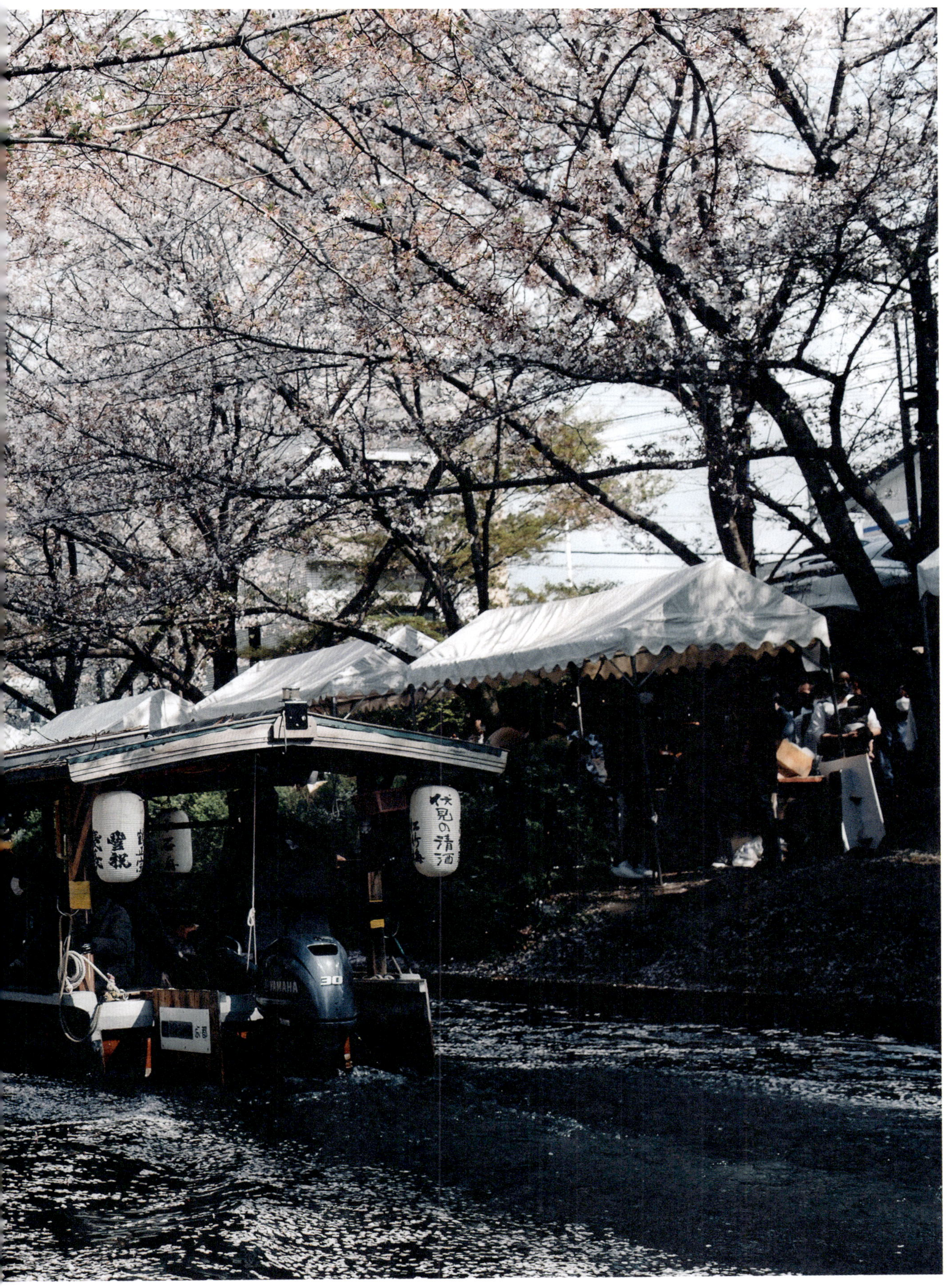
伏見の清酒
YAMAHA
30

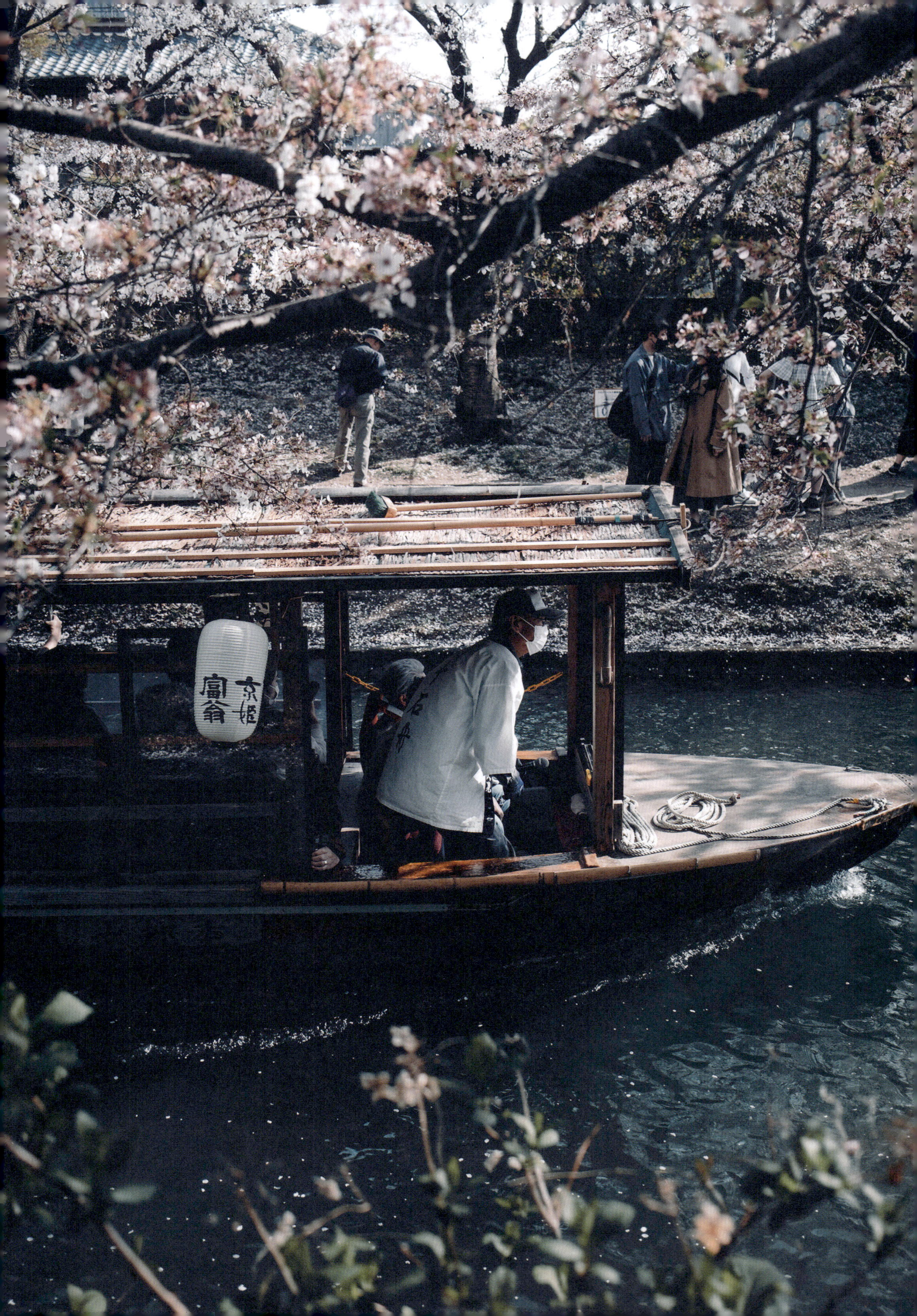
京姫
富翁

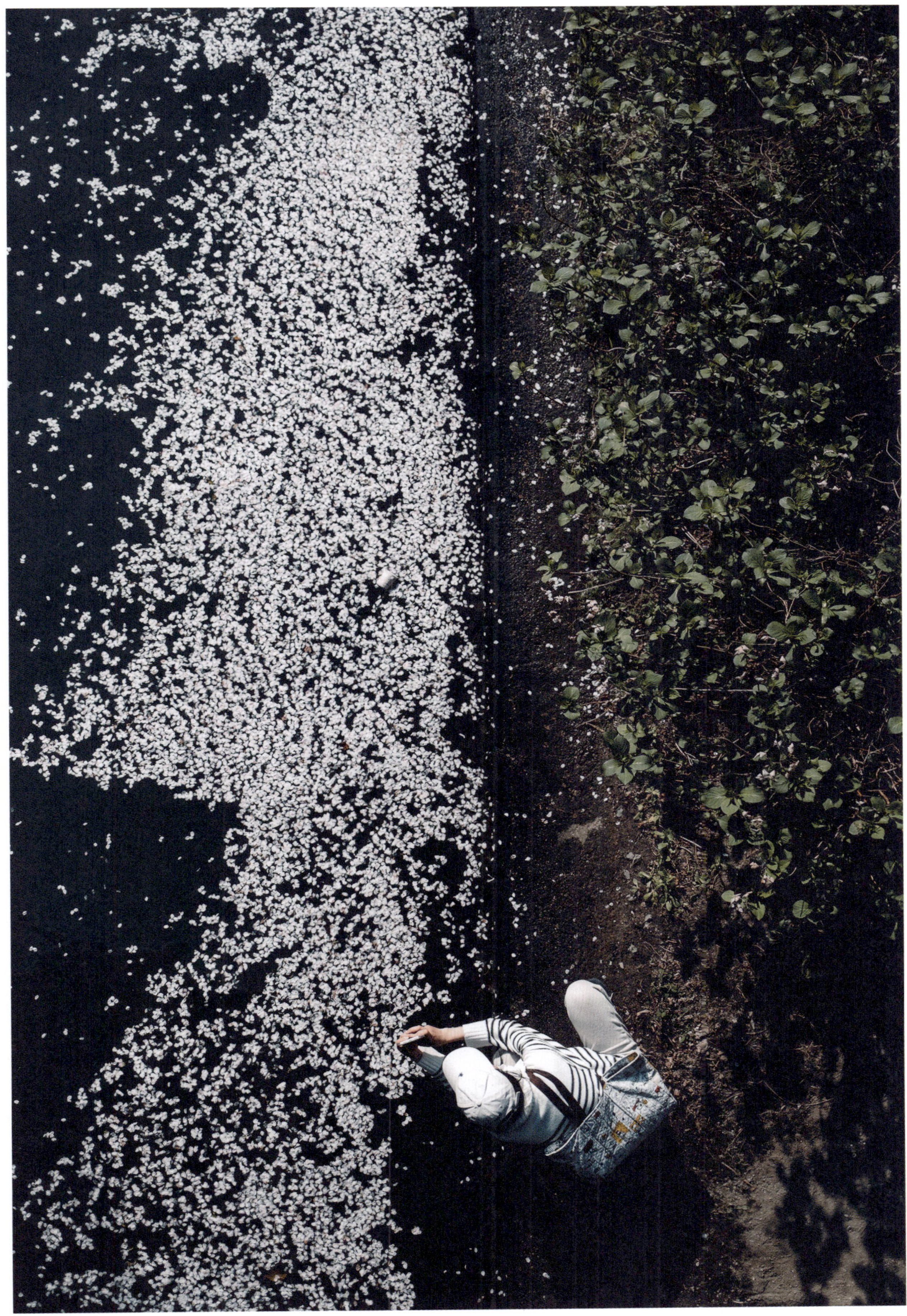

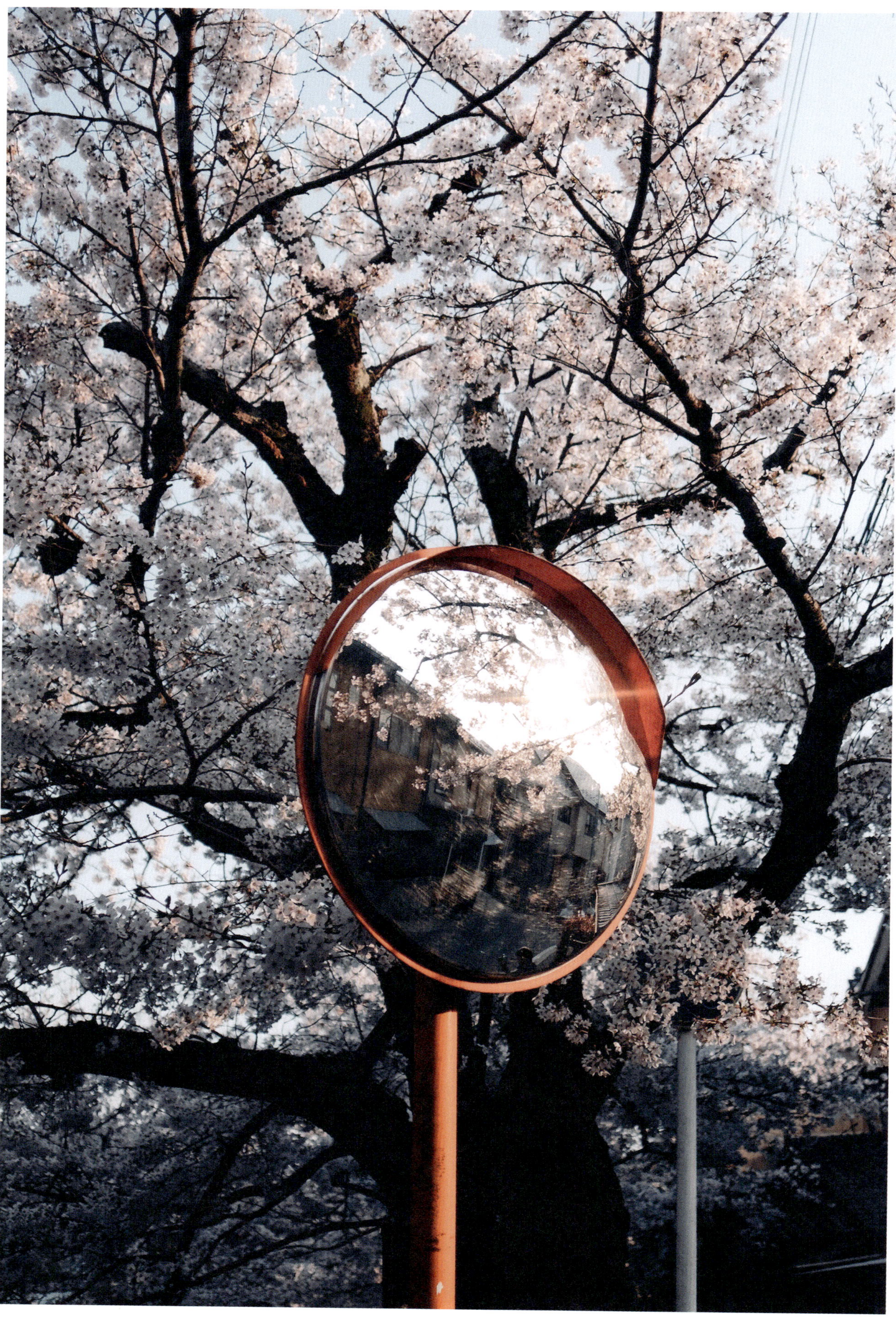

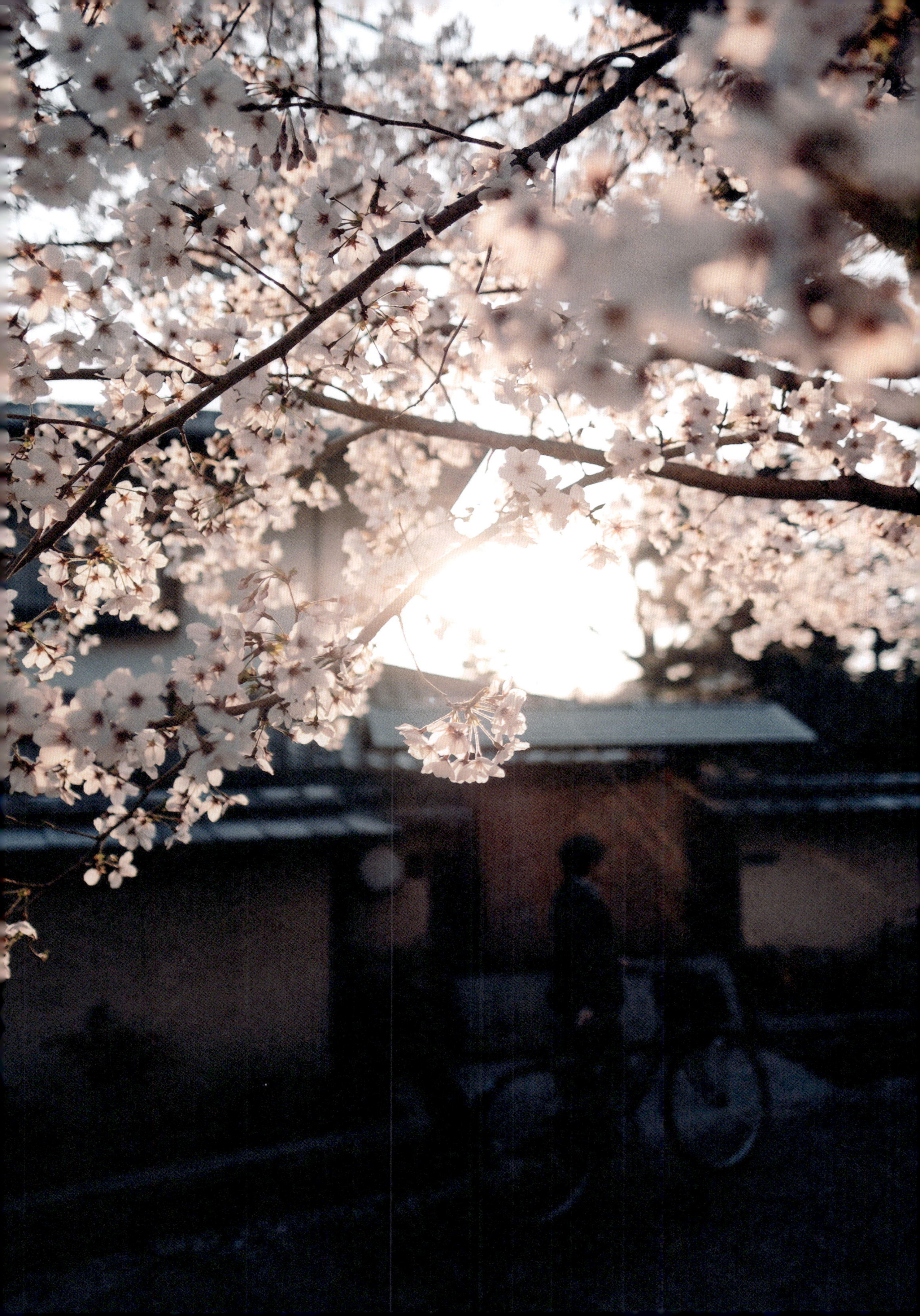

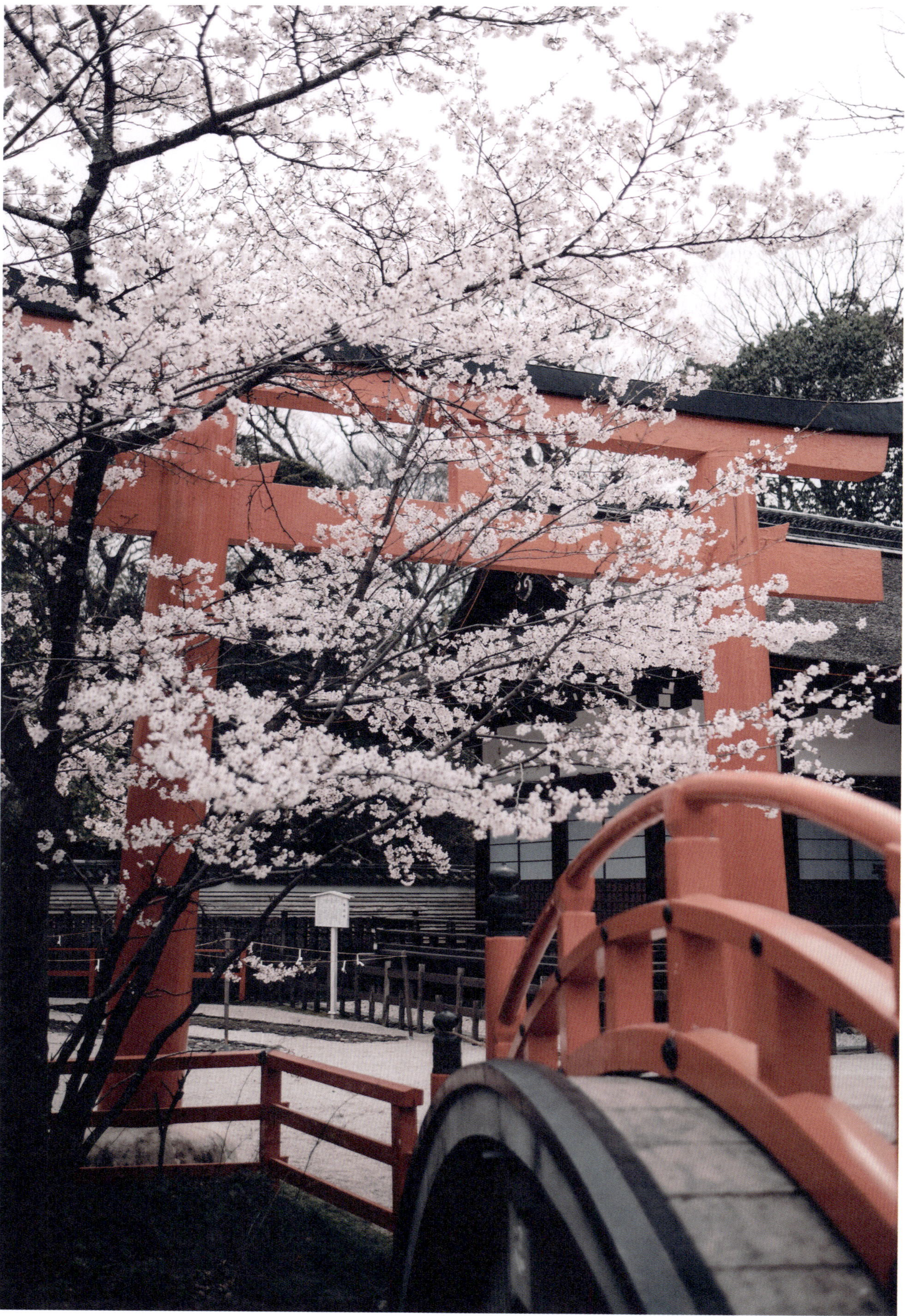

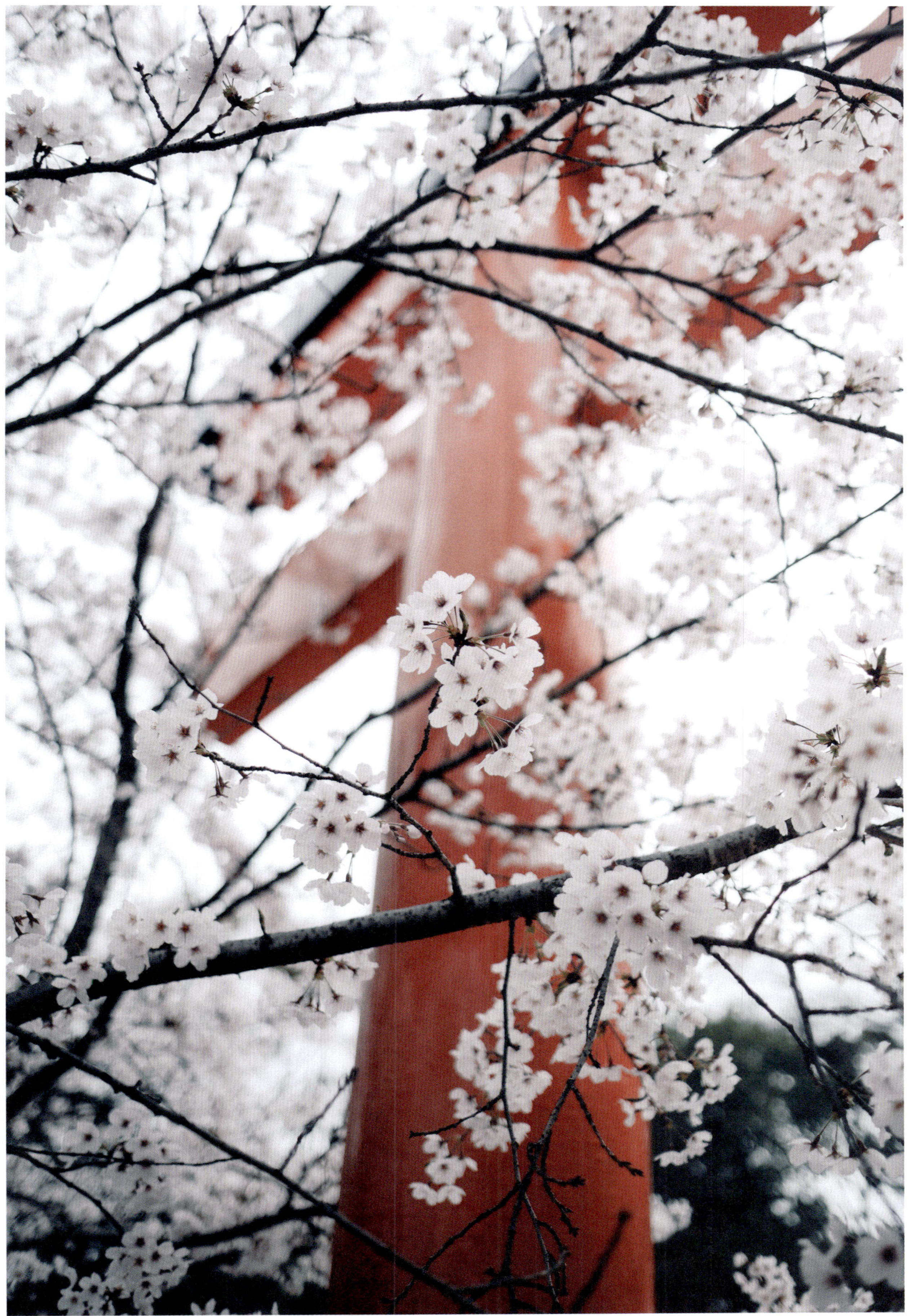

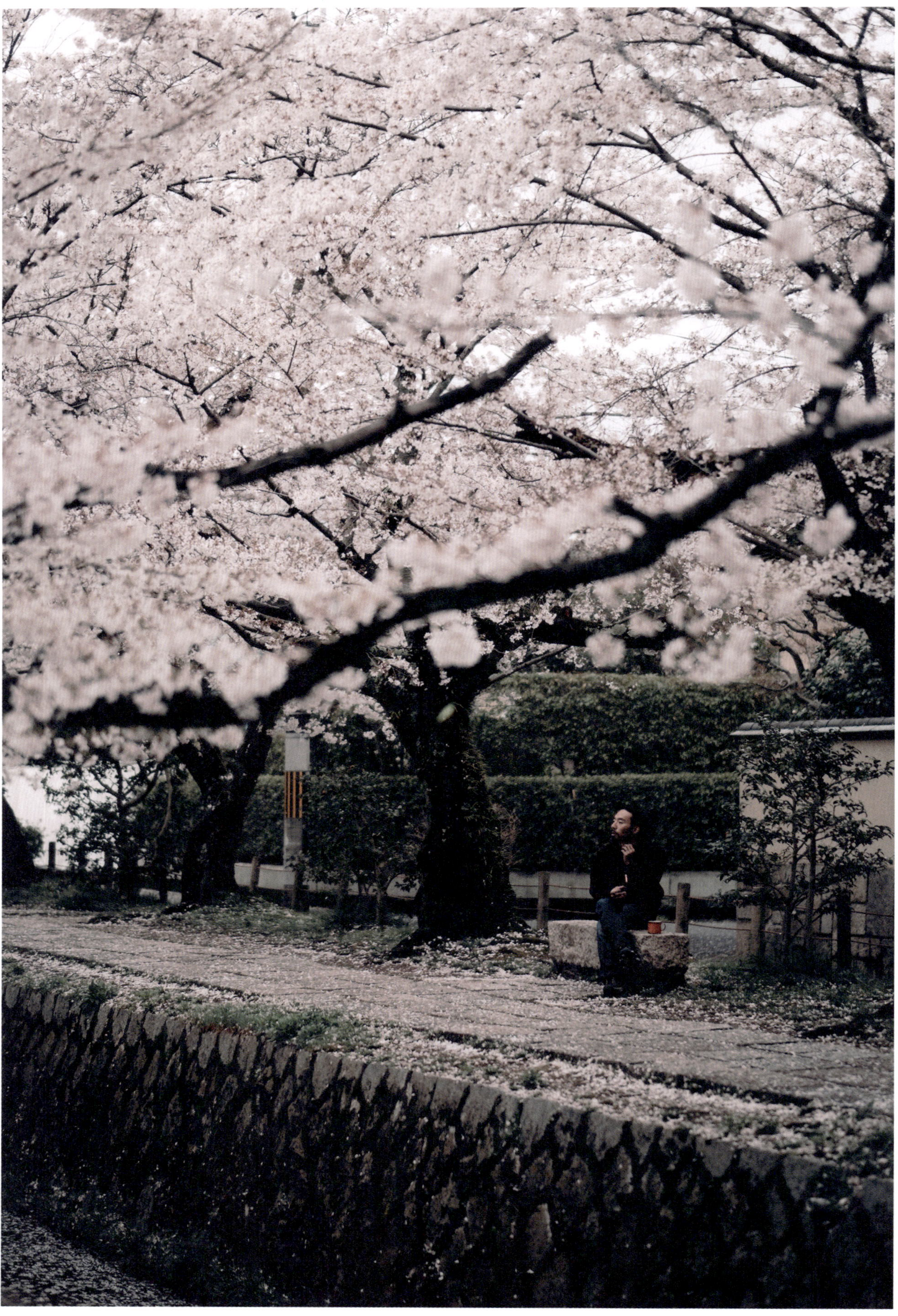

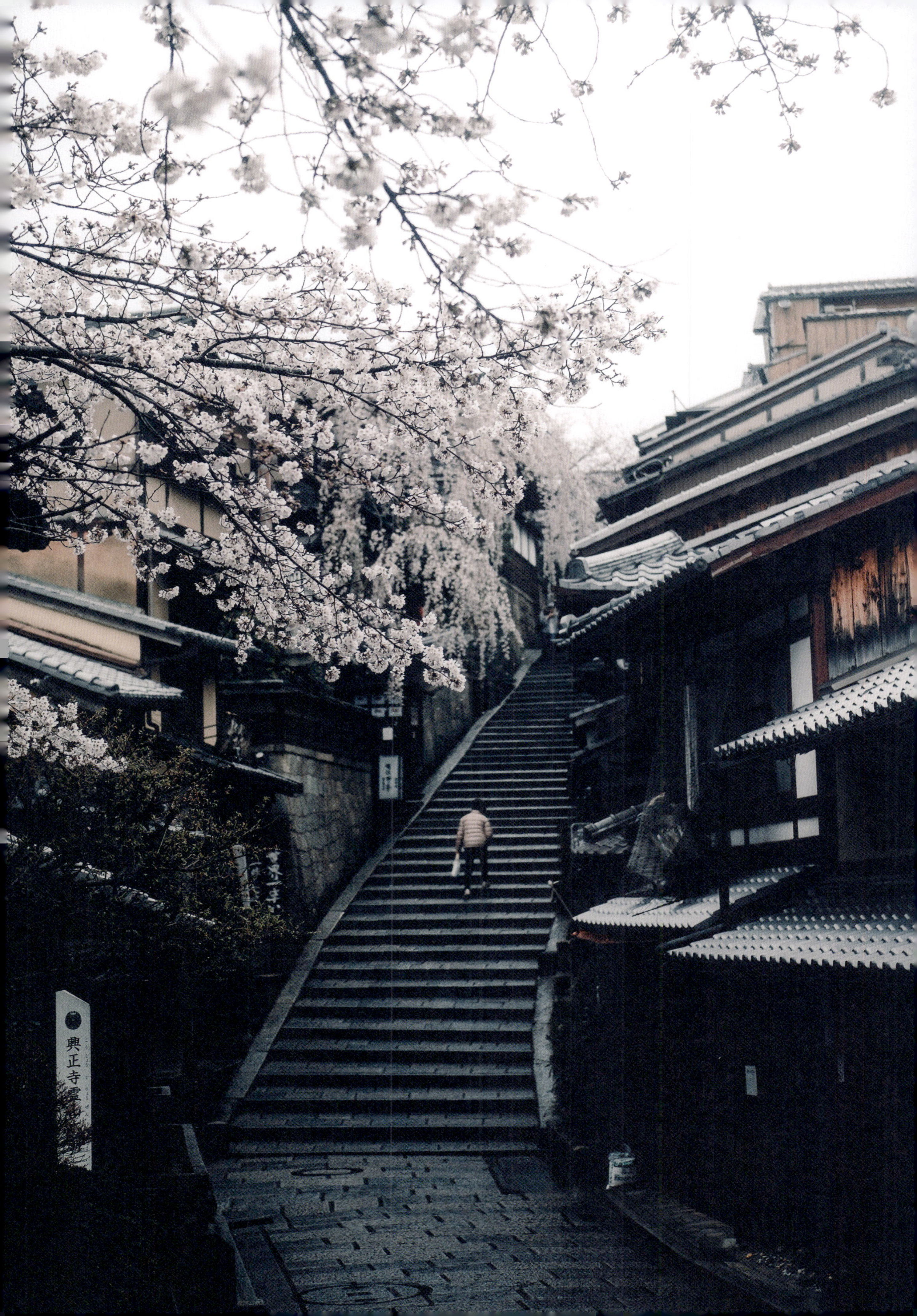

興正寺霊

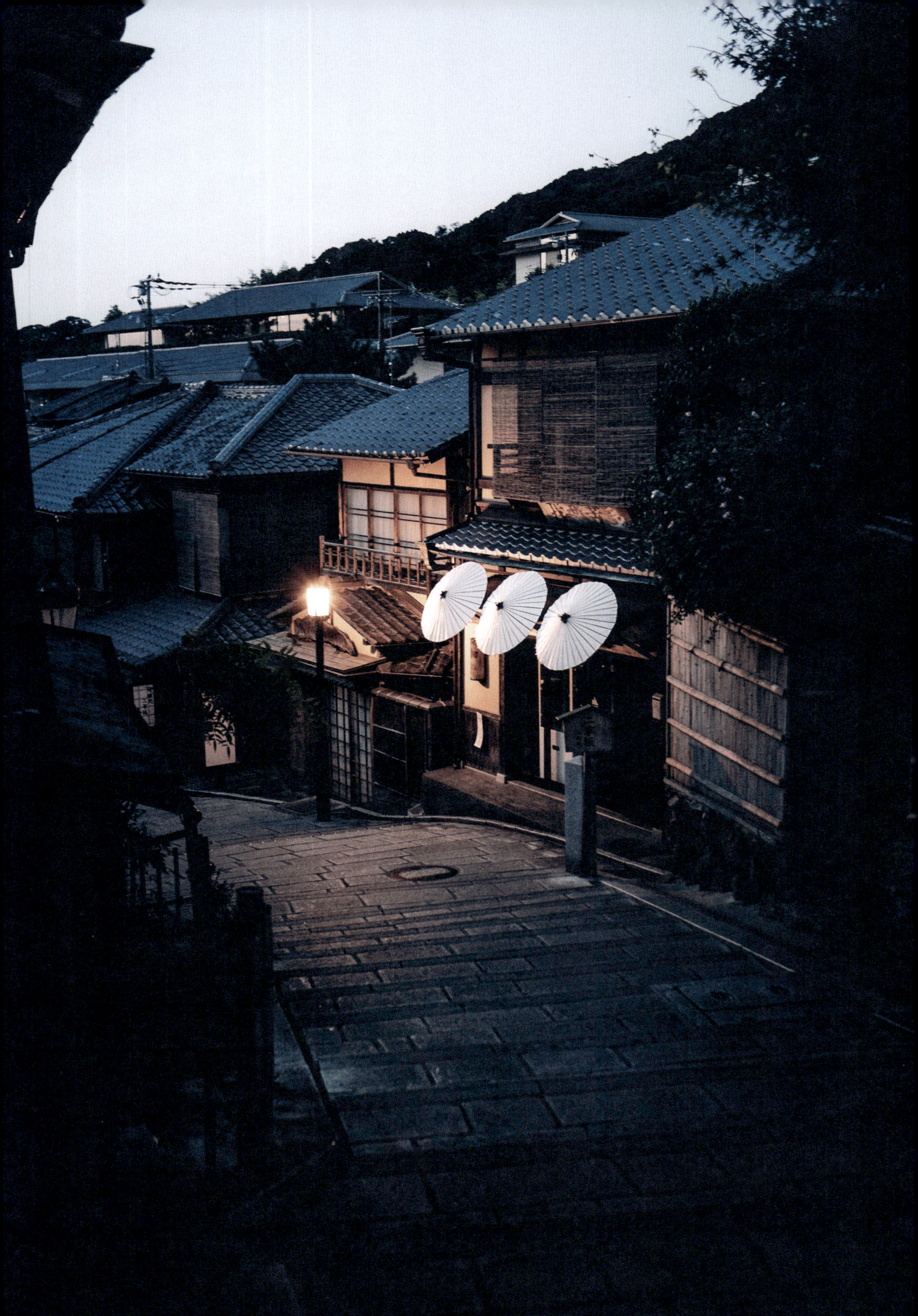

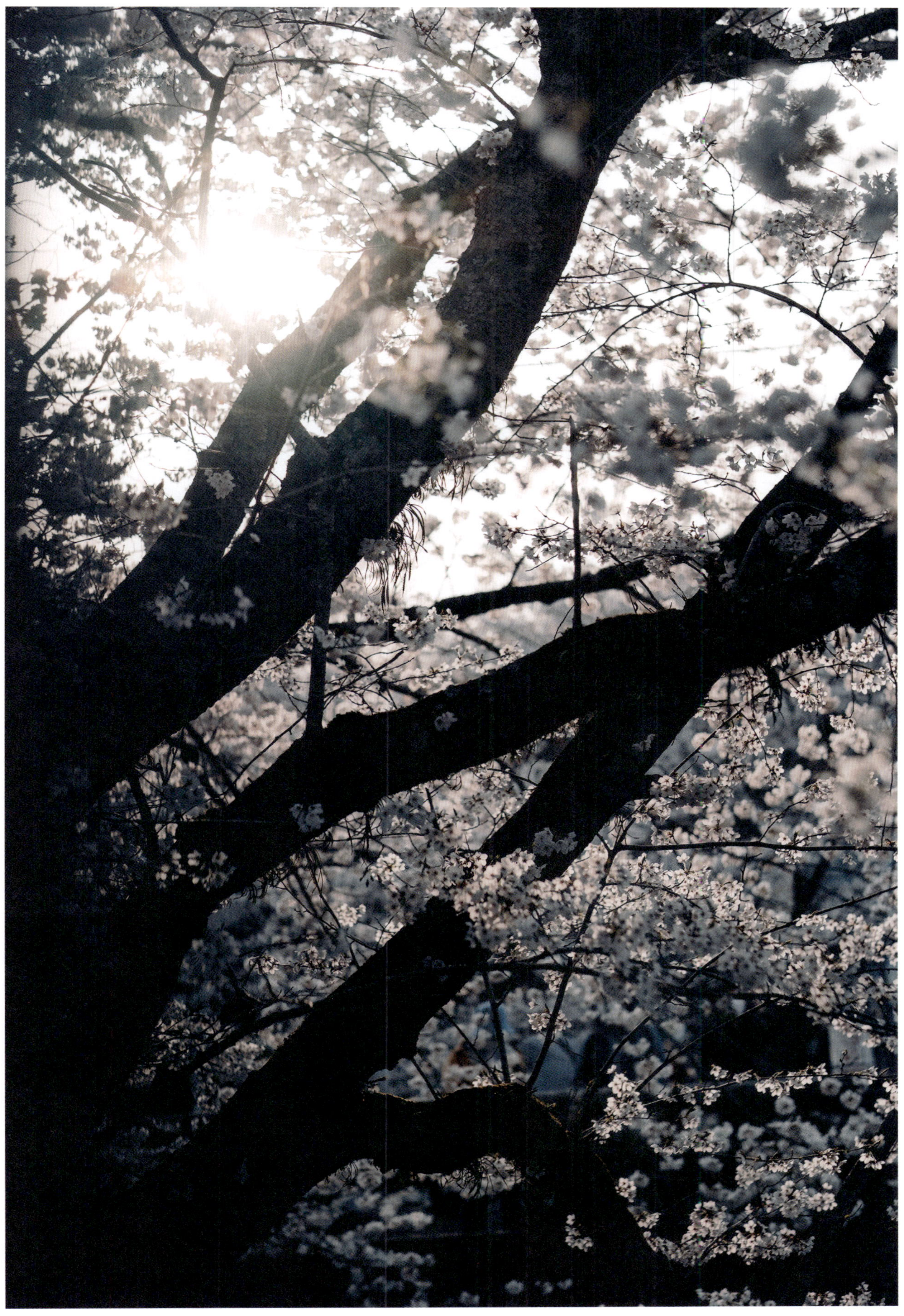

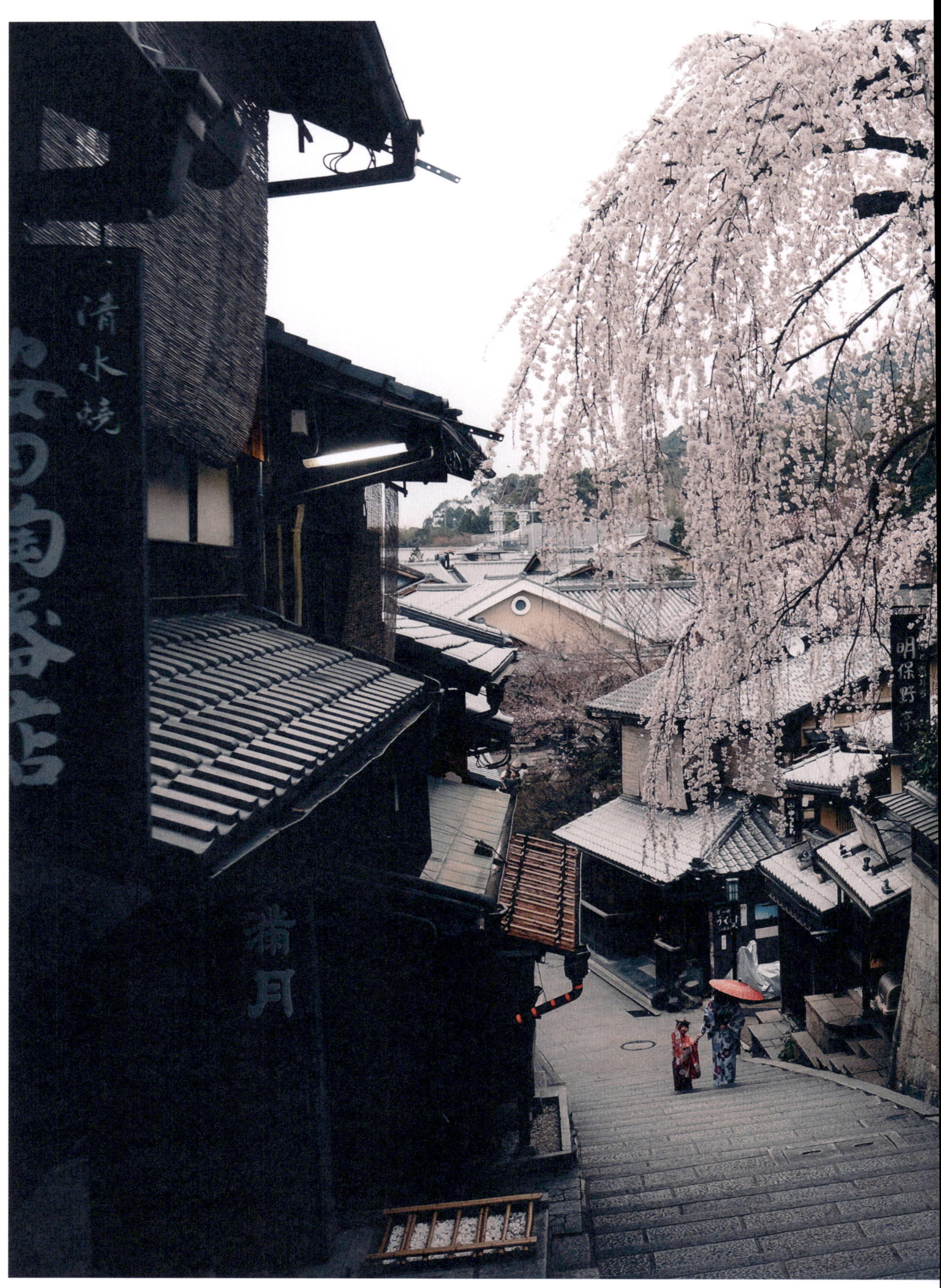

清水焼
満月
明保野亭

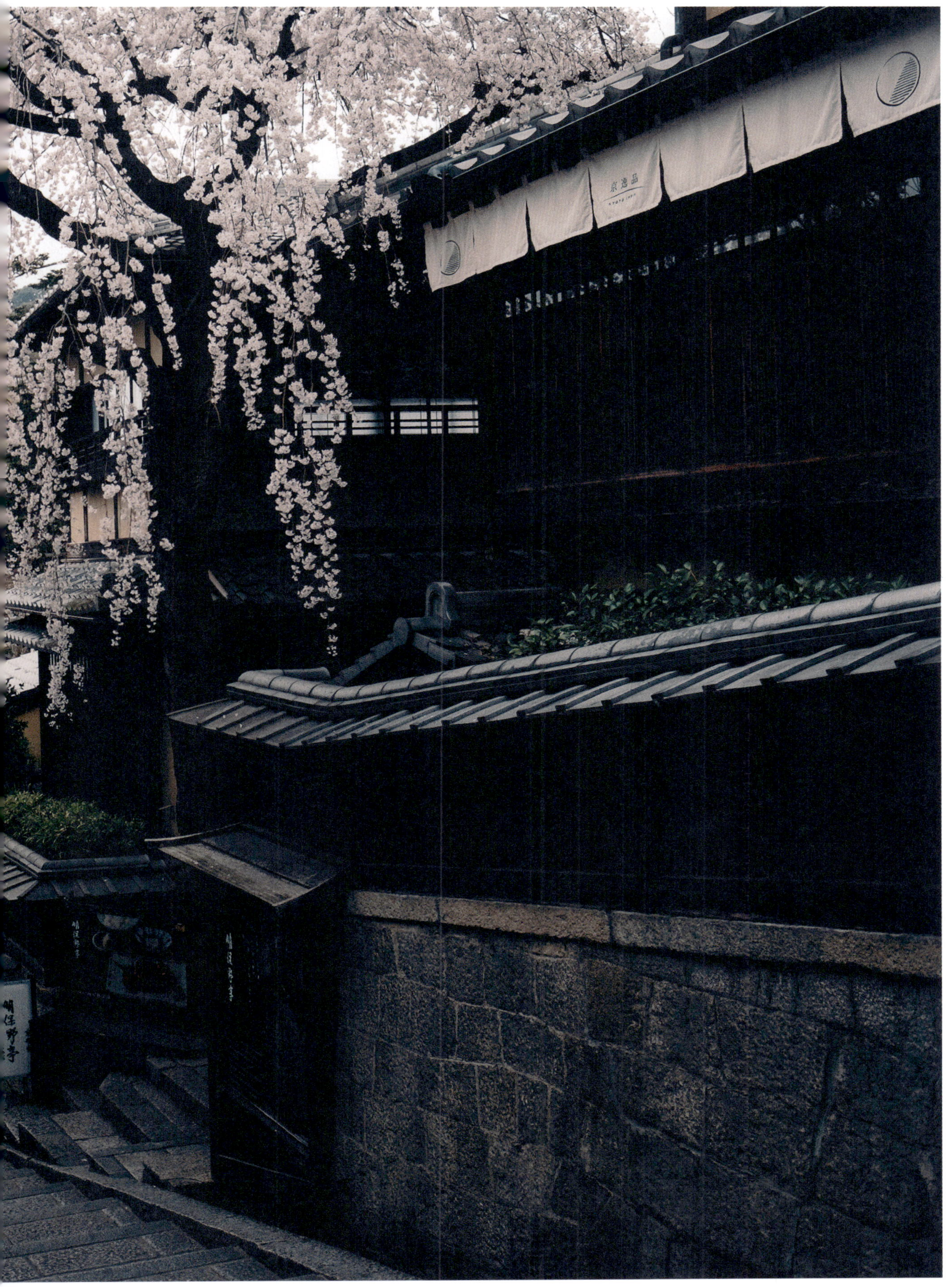
京逸品
明保野亭

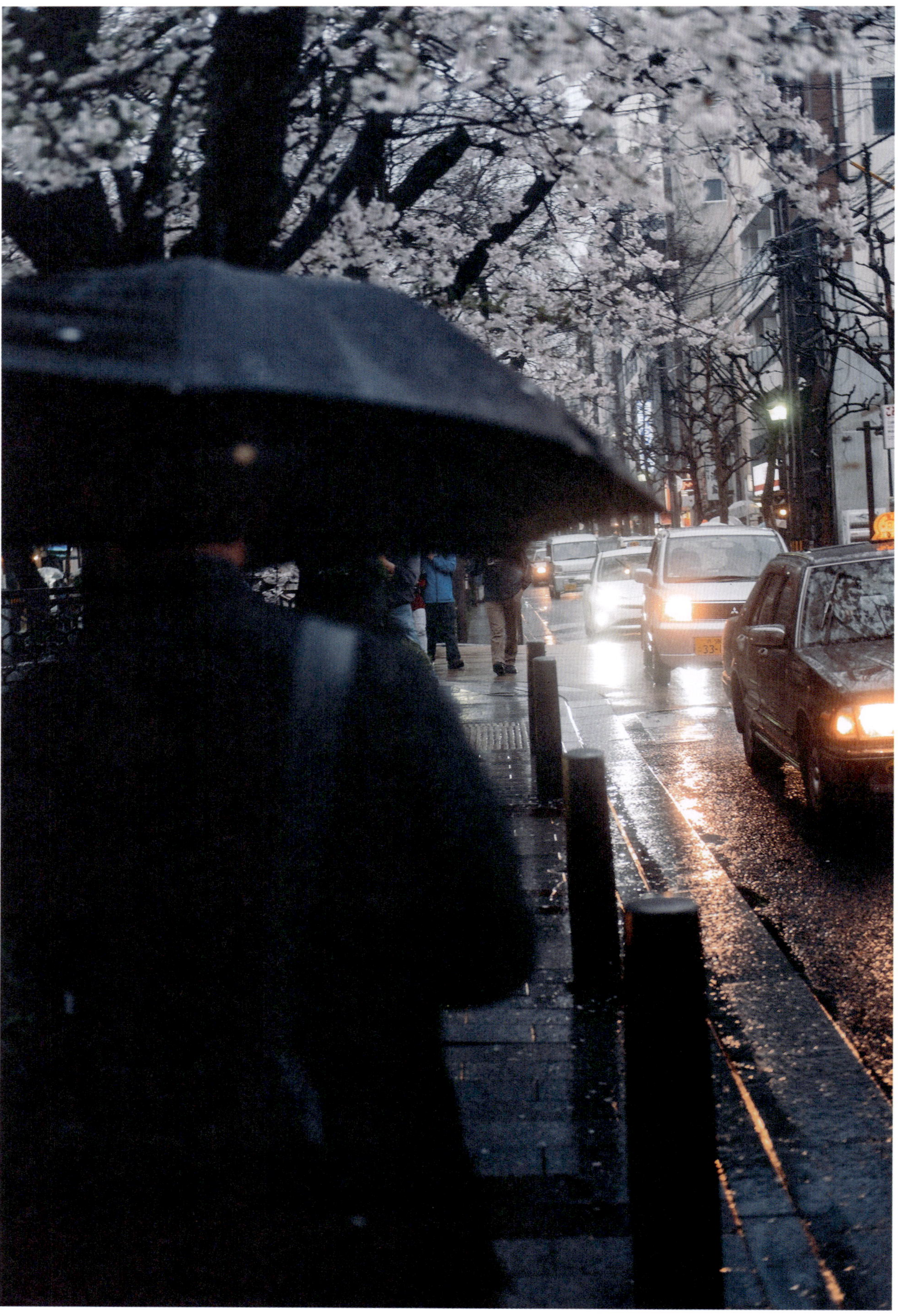

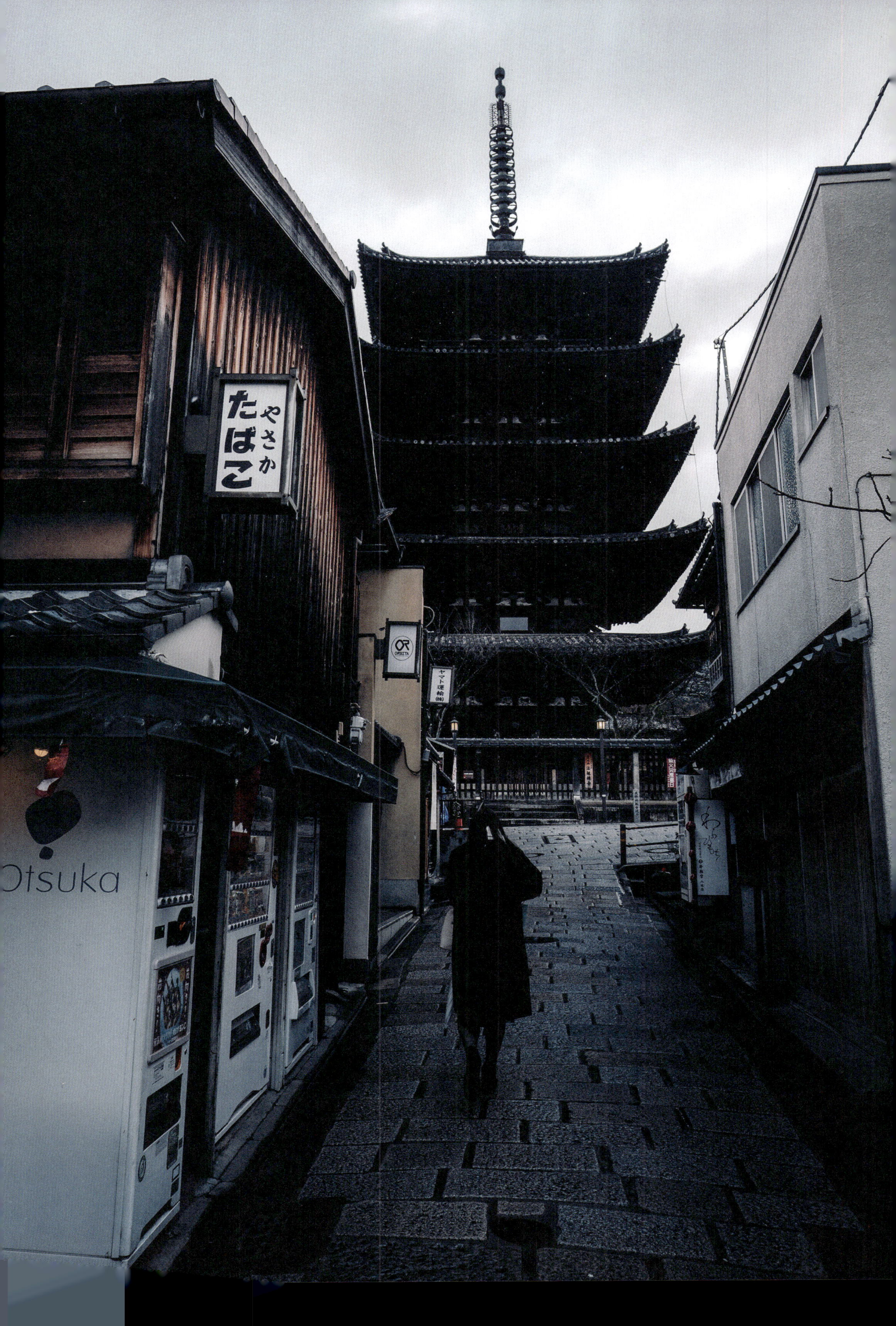
やさか
たばこ
ORBITA
ヤマト運輸(株)
Otsuka

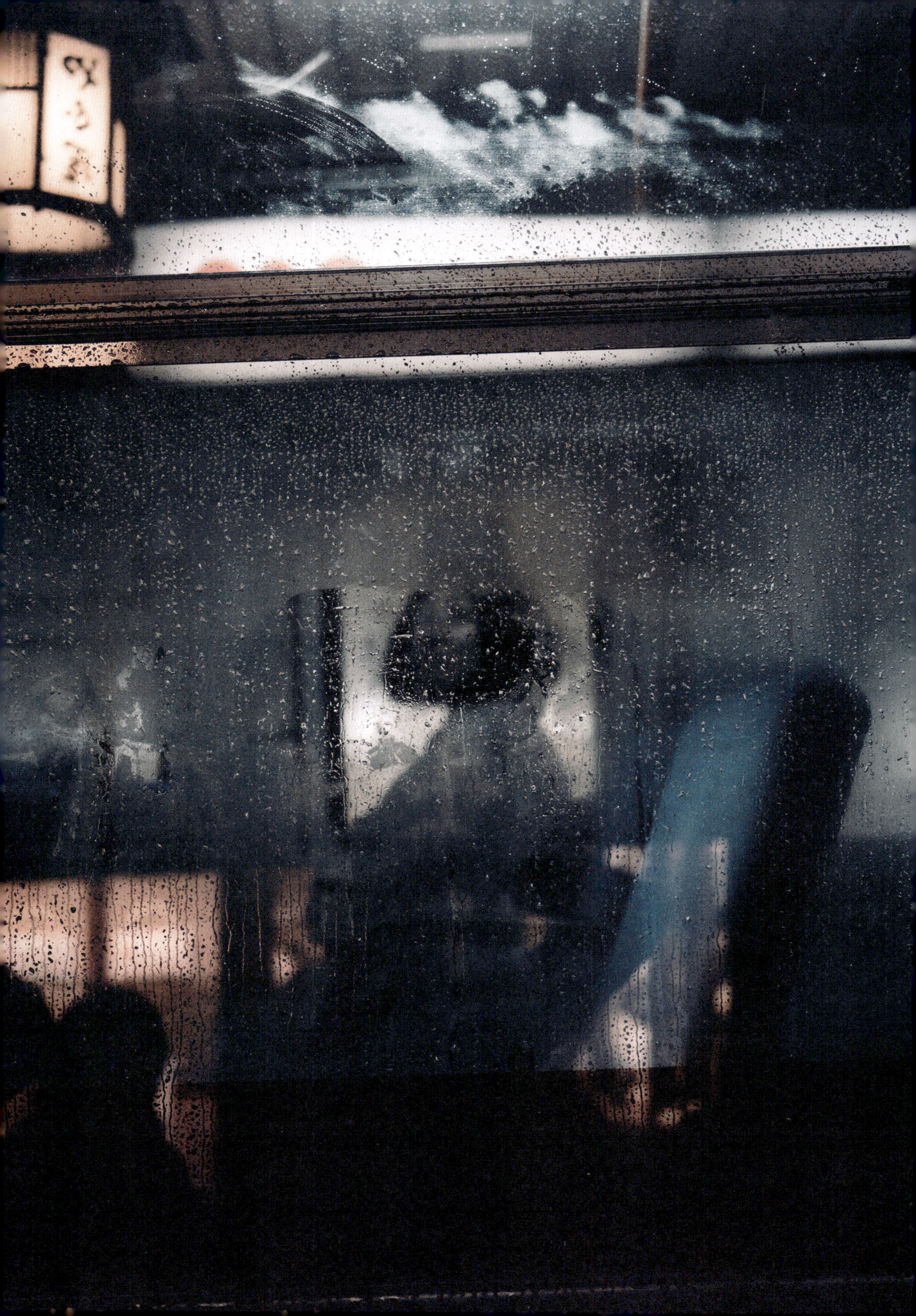

一夜さに
櫻はさゝら
ほさら哉

小林一茶

Within but a single night
The cherry blossoms vanish
And are completely gone.

Kobayashi Issa

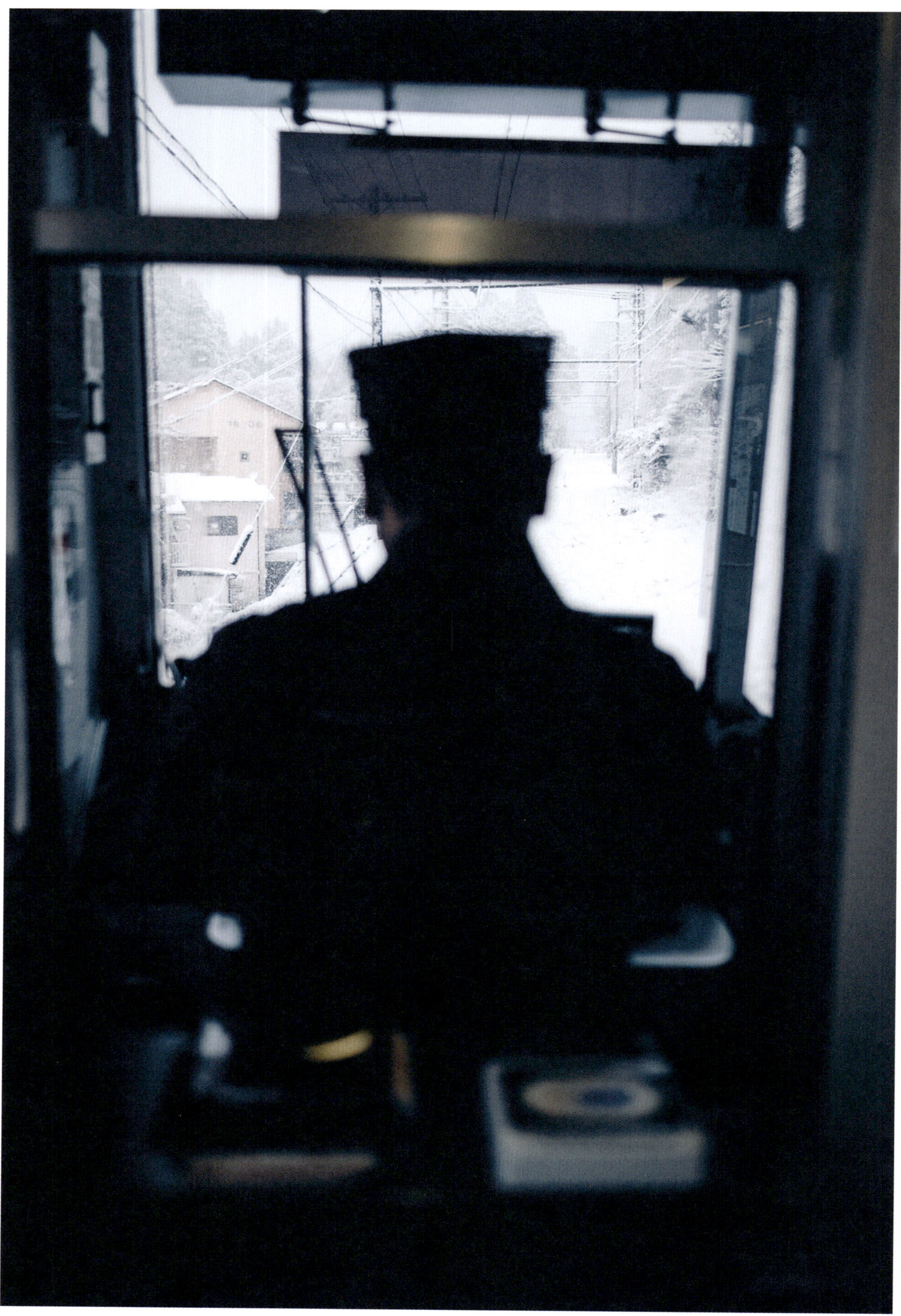

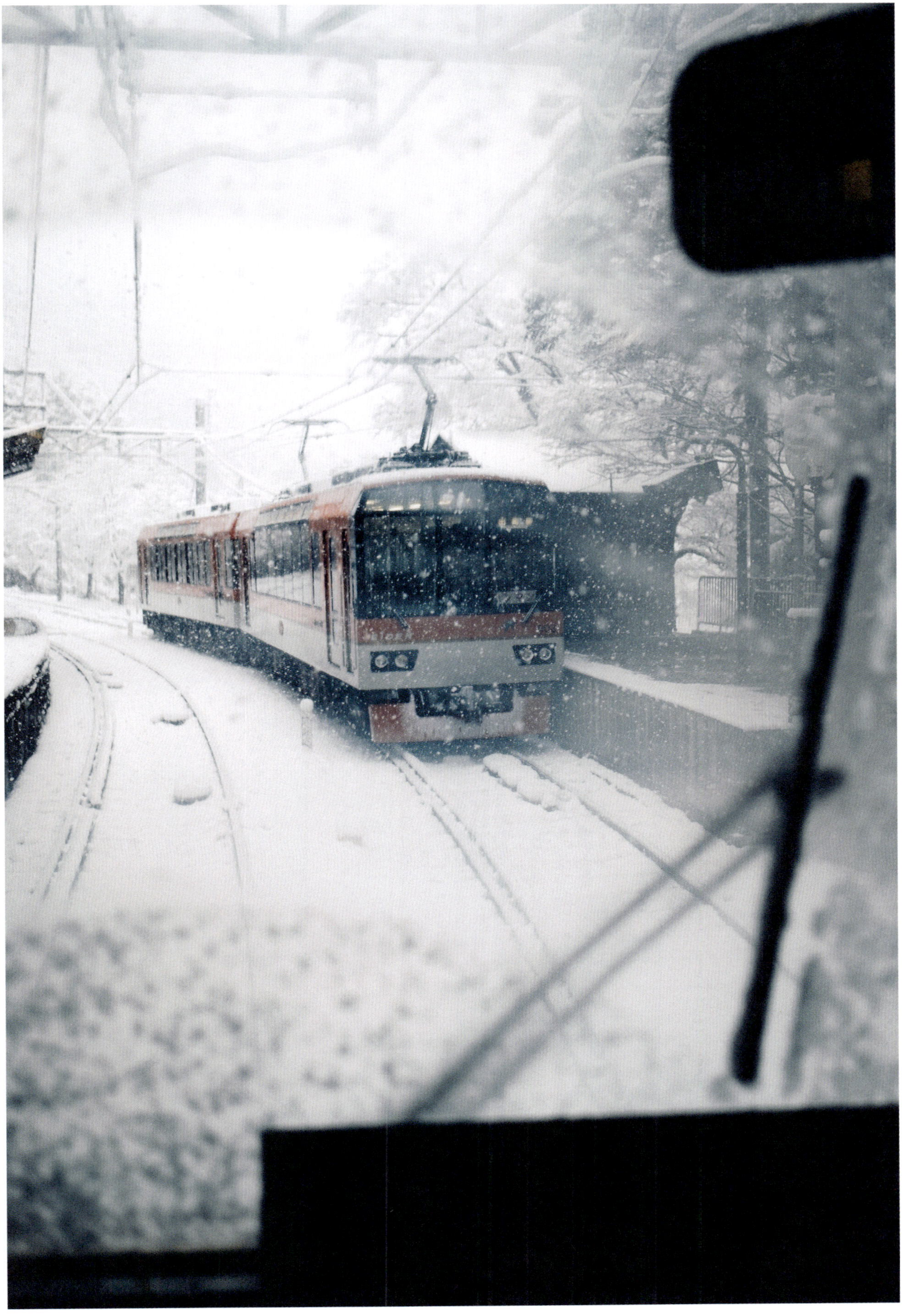

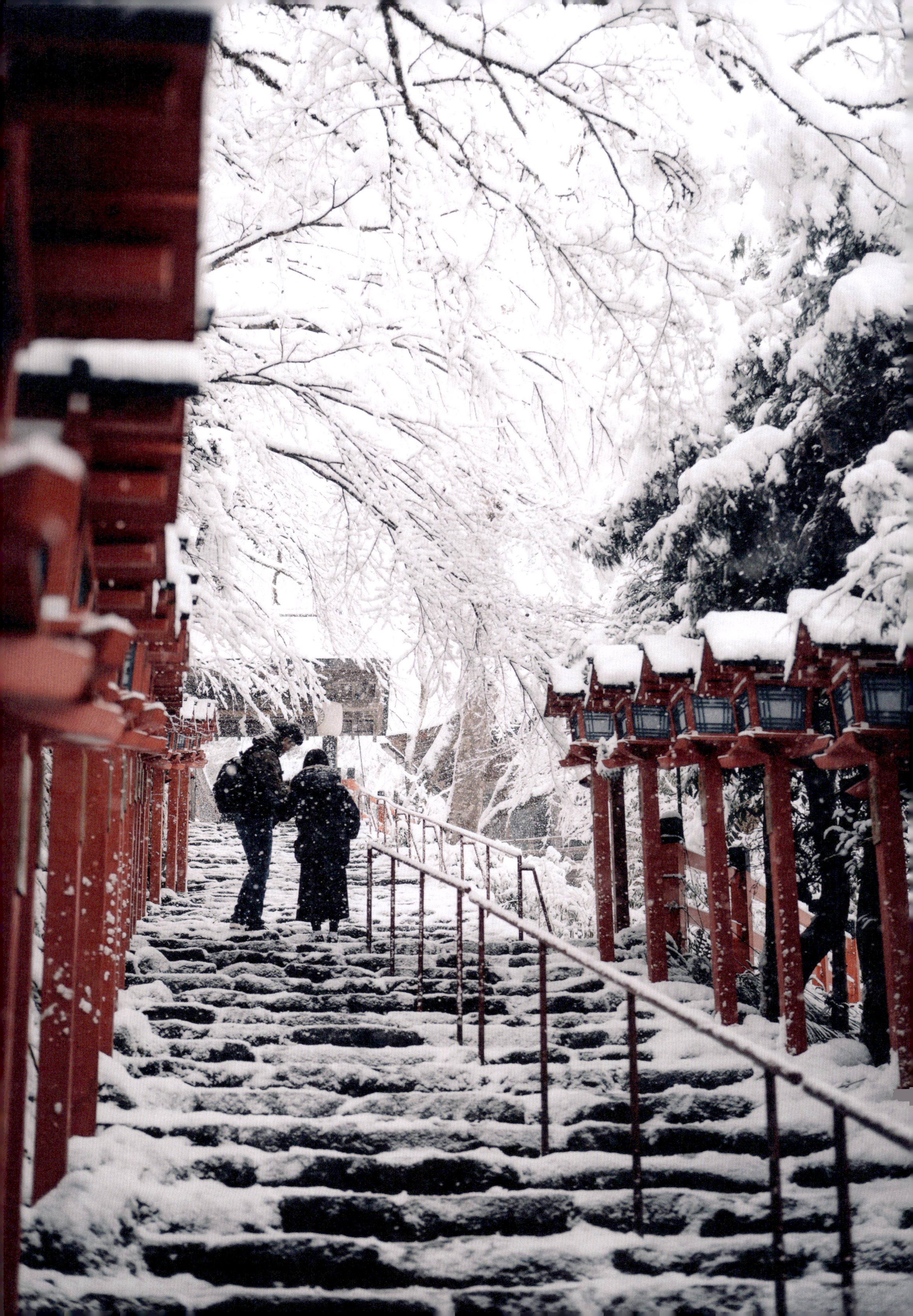

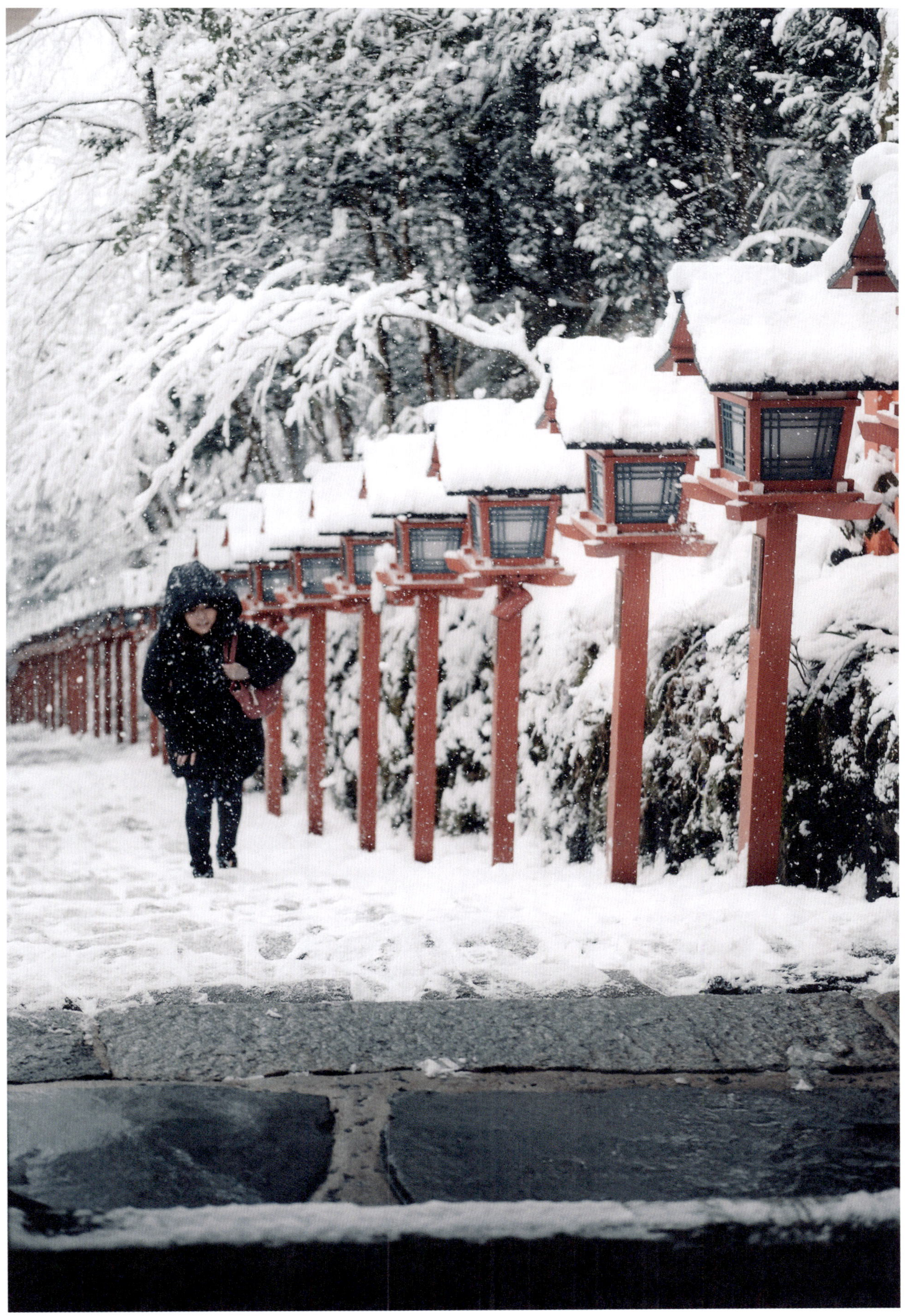

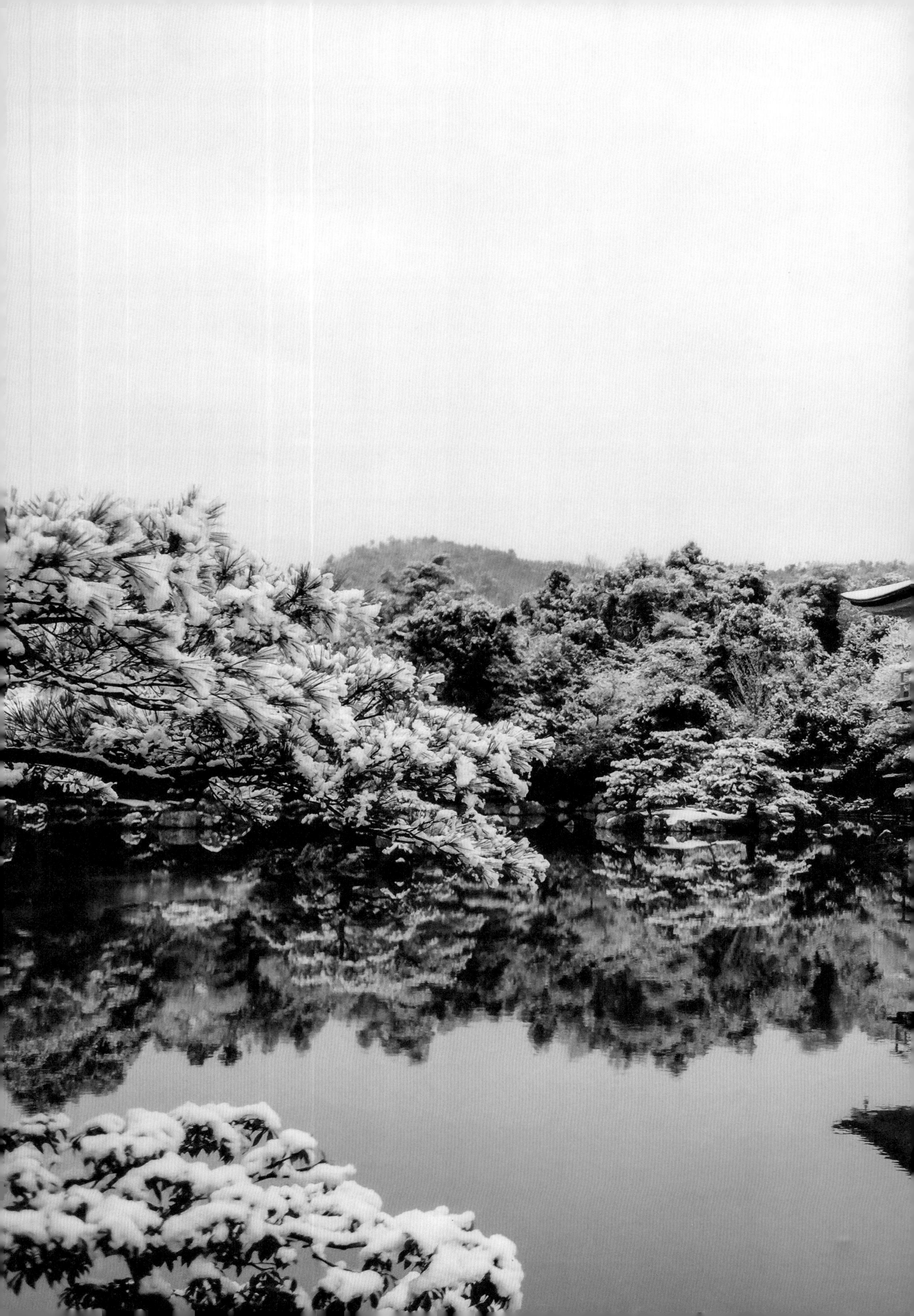

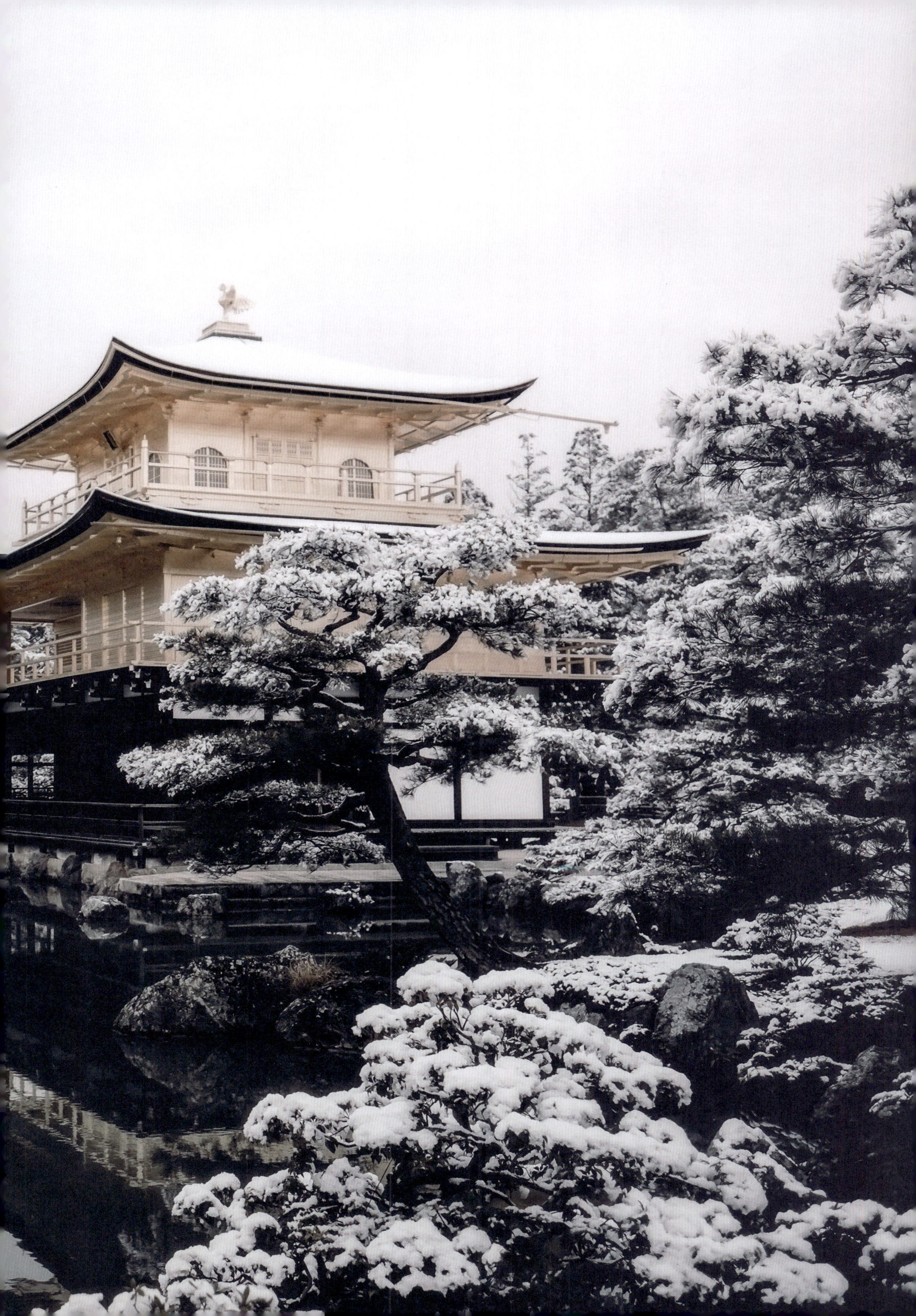

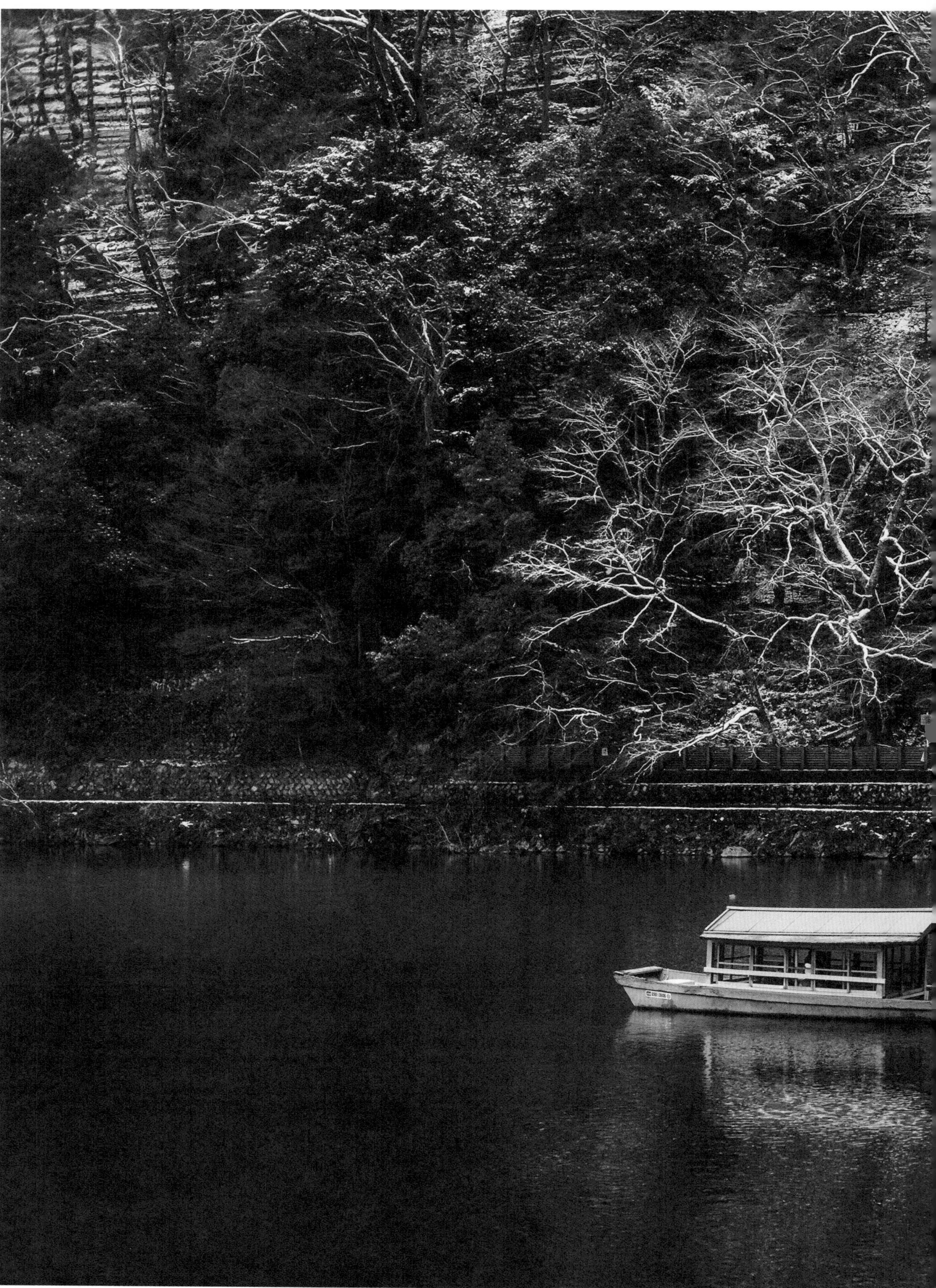

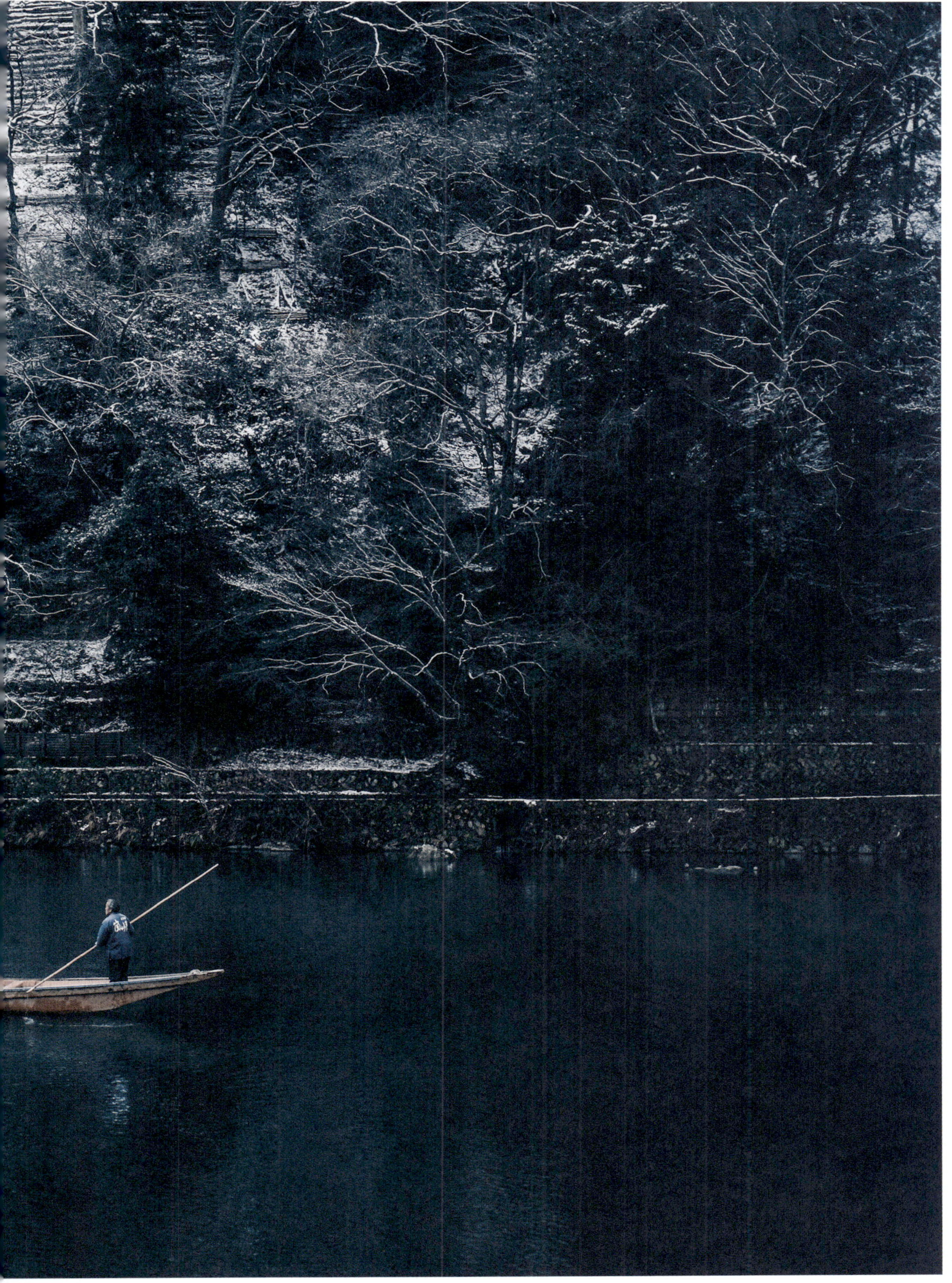

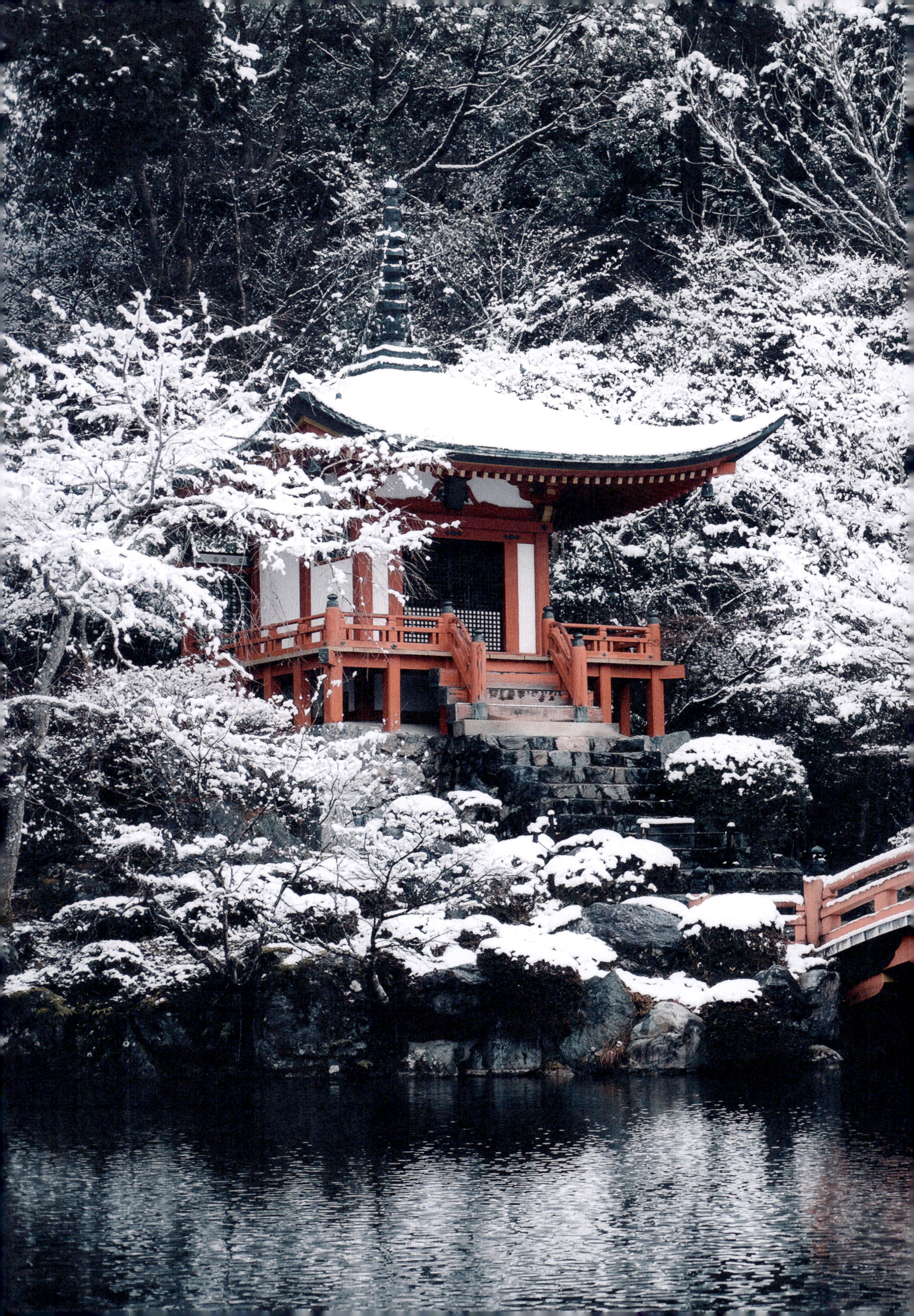

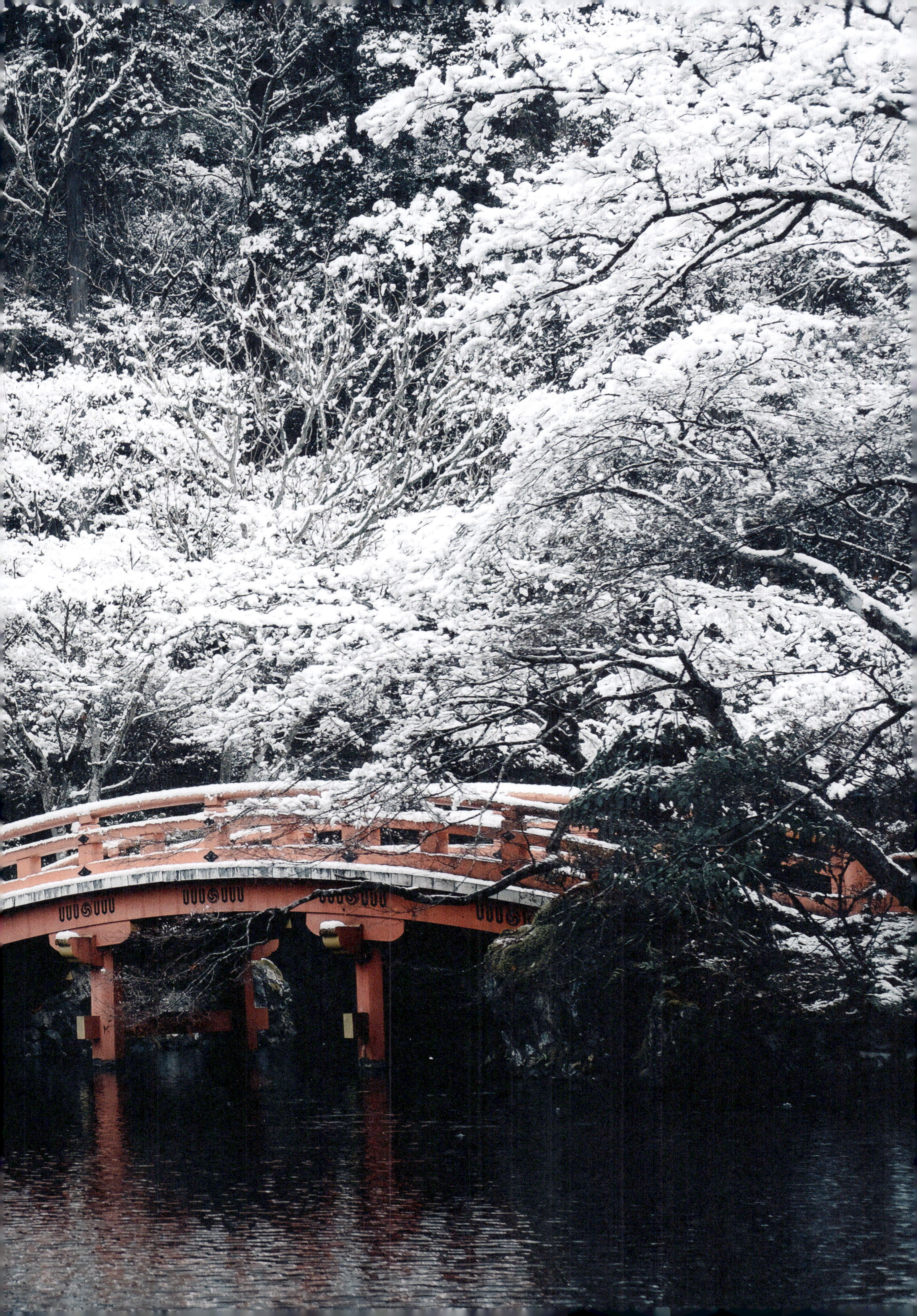

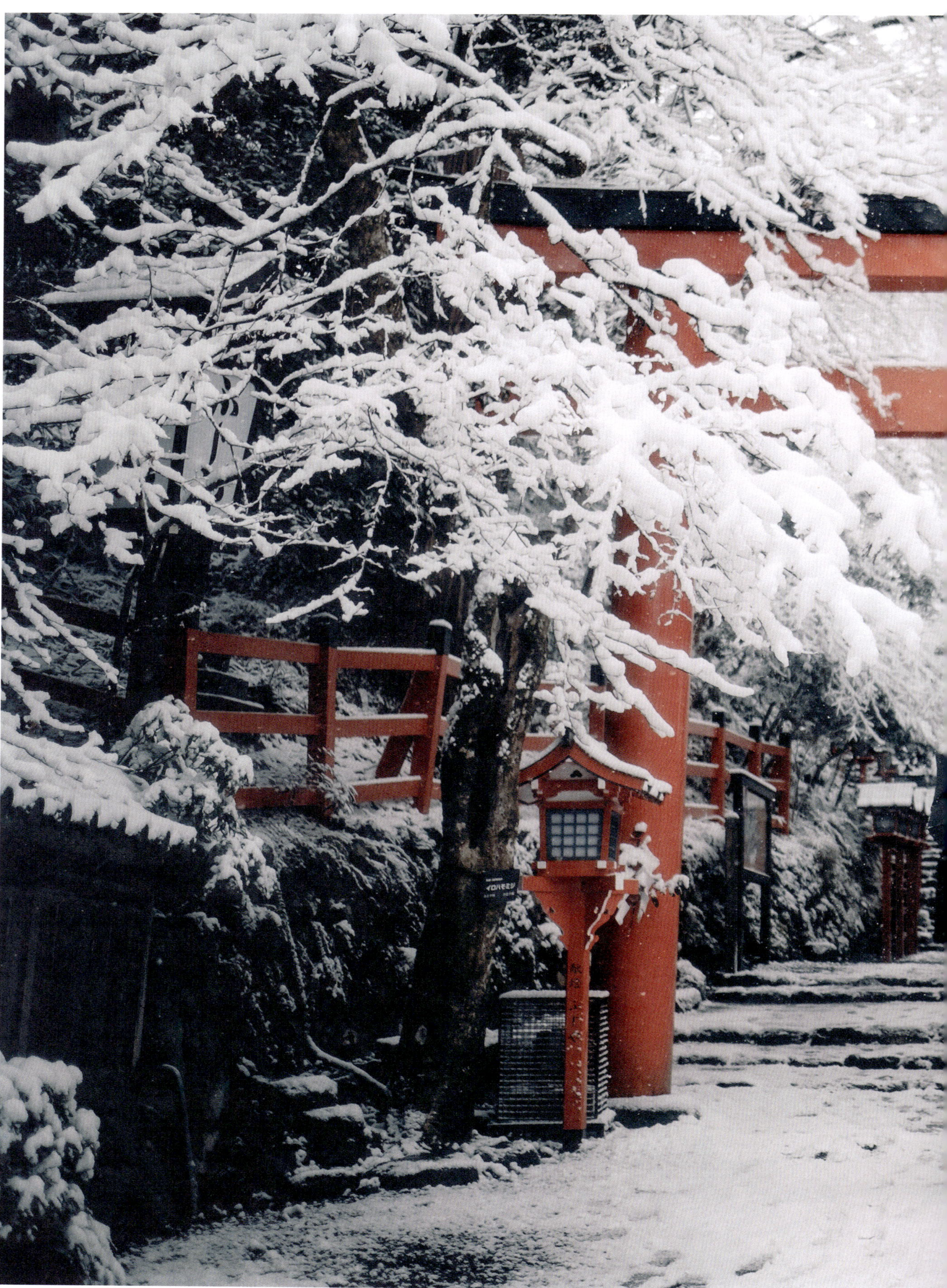

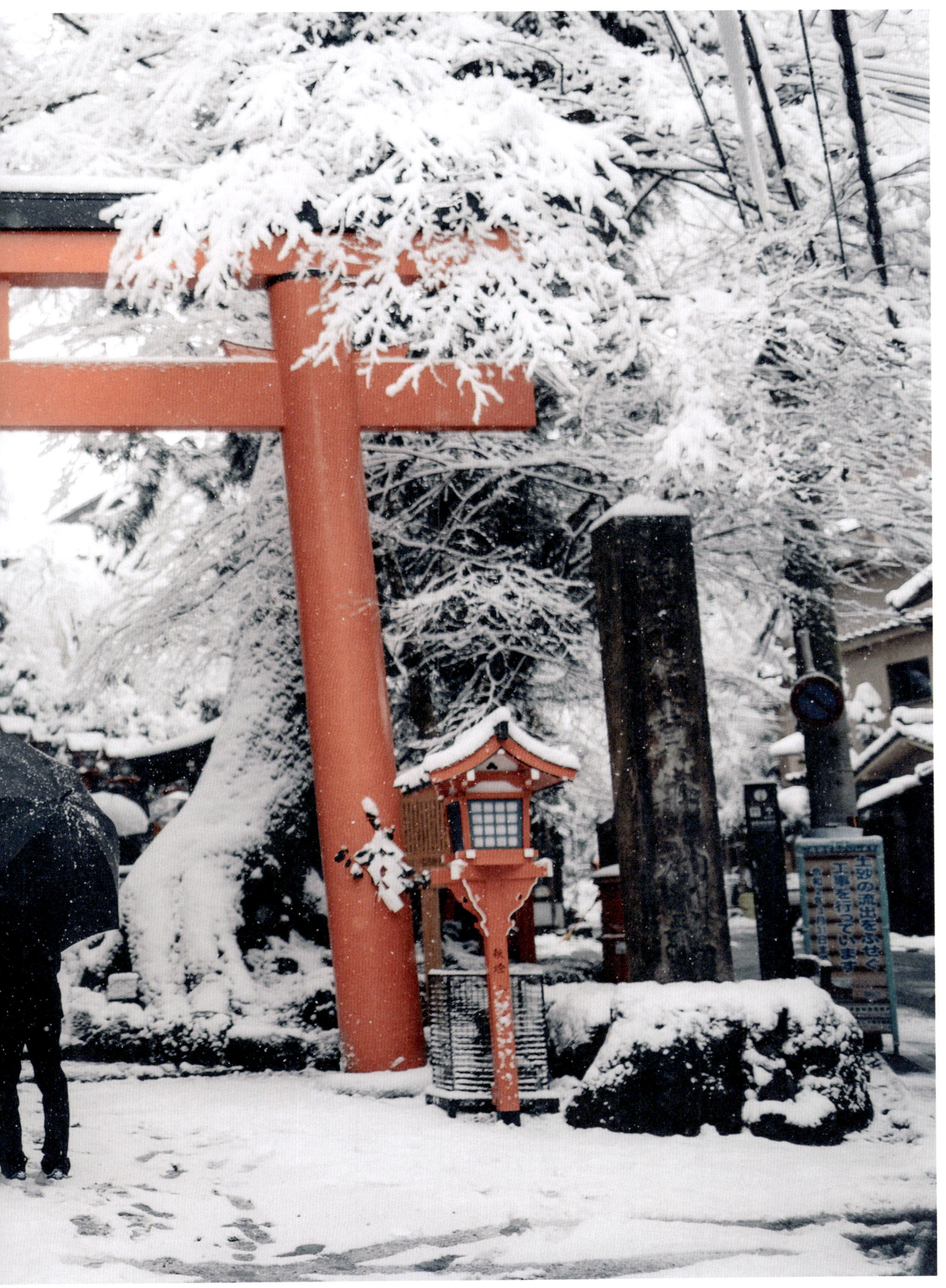
土砂の流出をふせぐ
工事を行っています

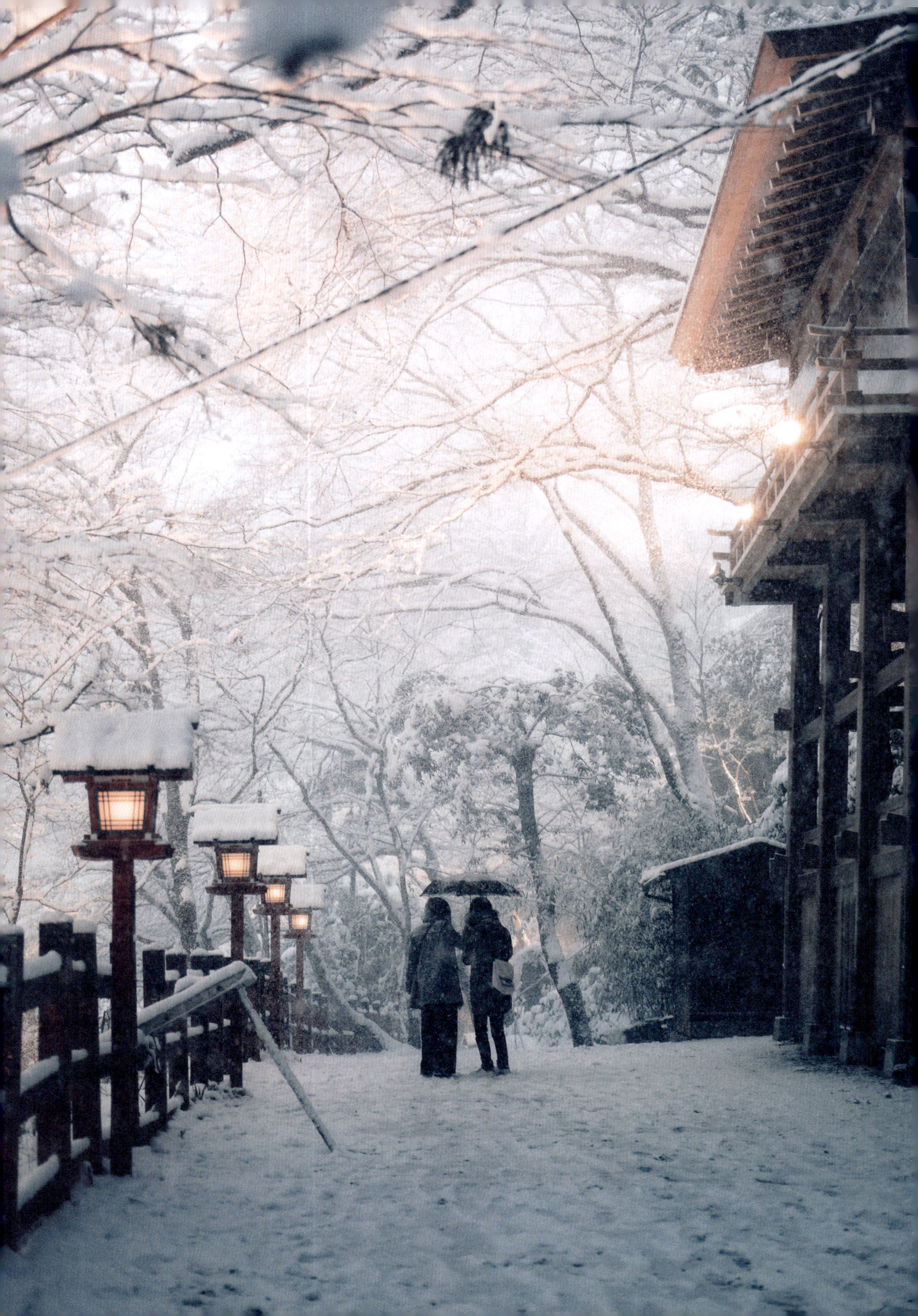

ひごろ
にくき鳥も
雪の朝哉

松尾　芭蕉

Most days they're hateful, yet
Even the crows, against the snow
This morning seem fine.

Bashō

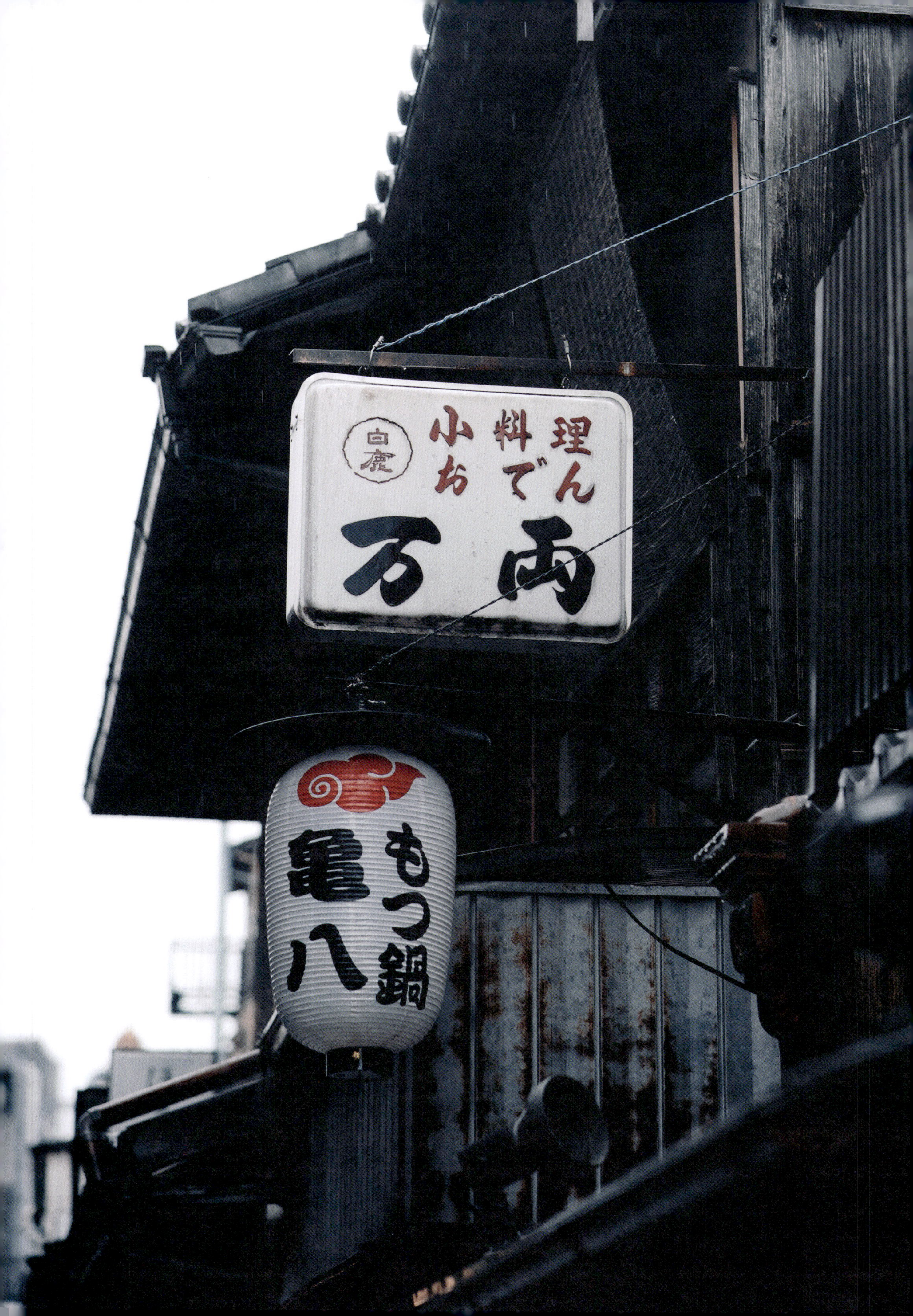
白鹿
小料理
おでん
万両
もつ鍋
亀八

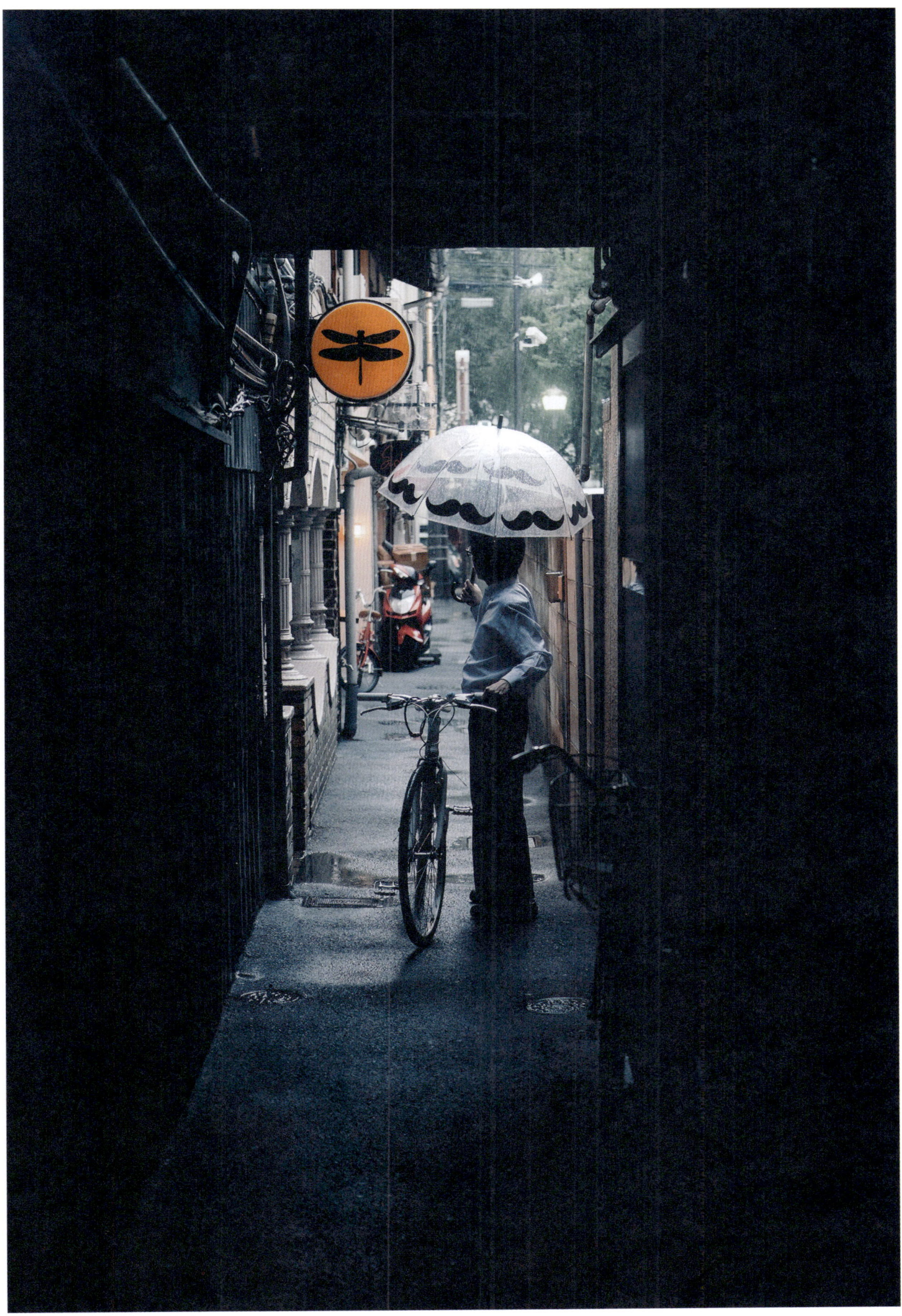

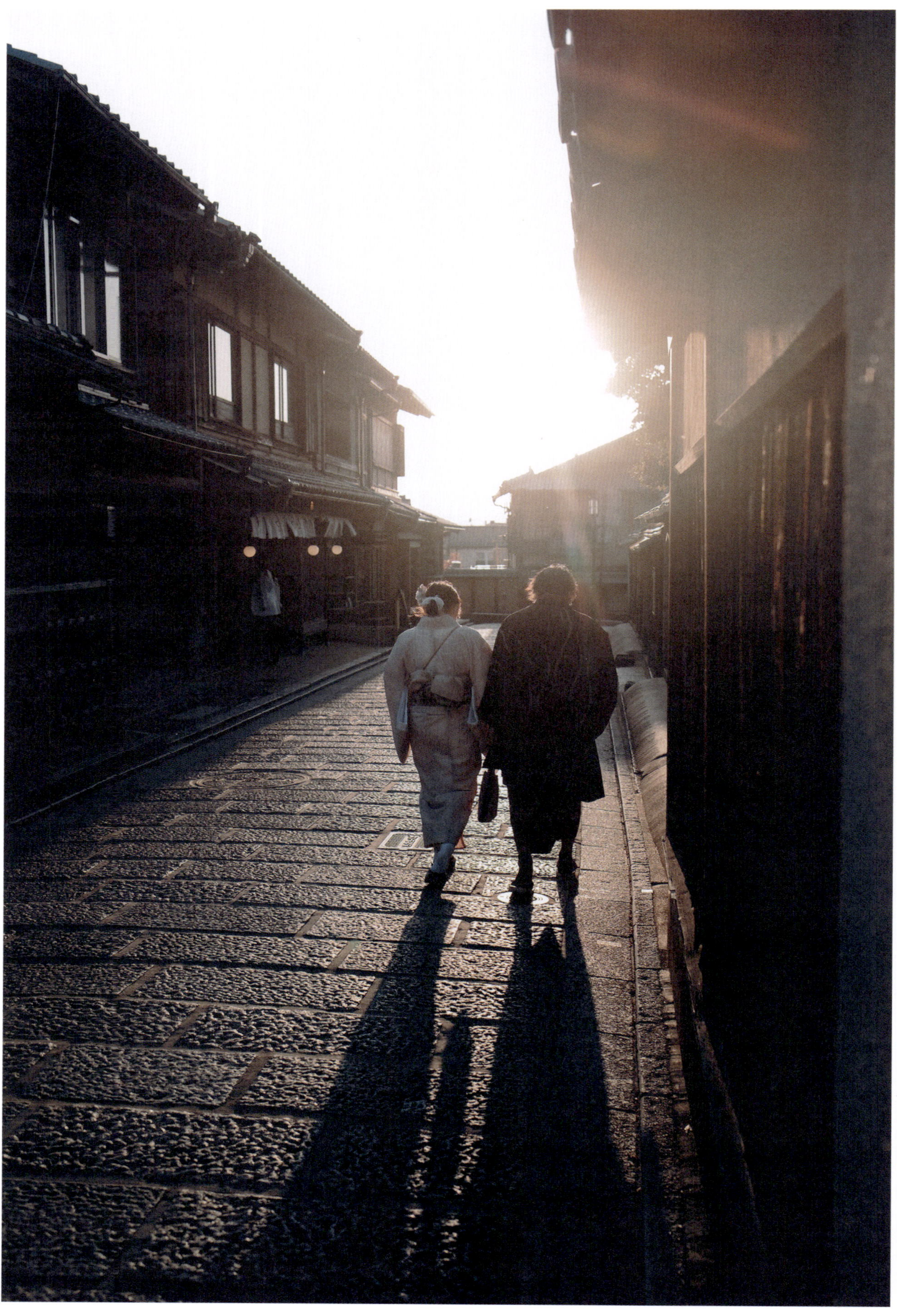

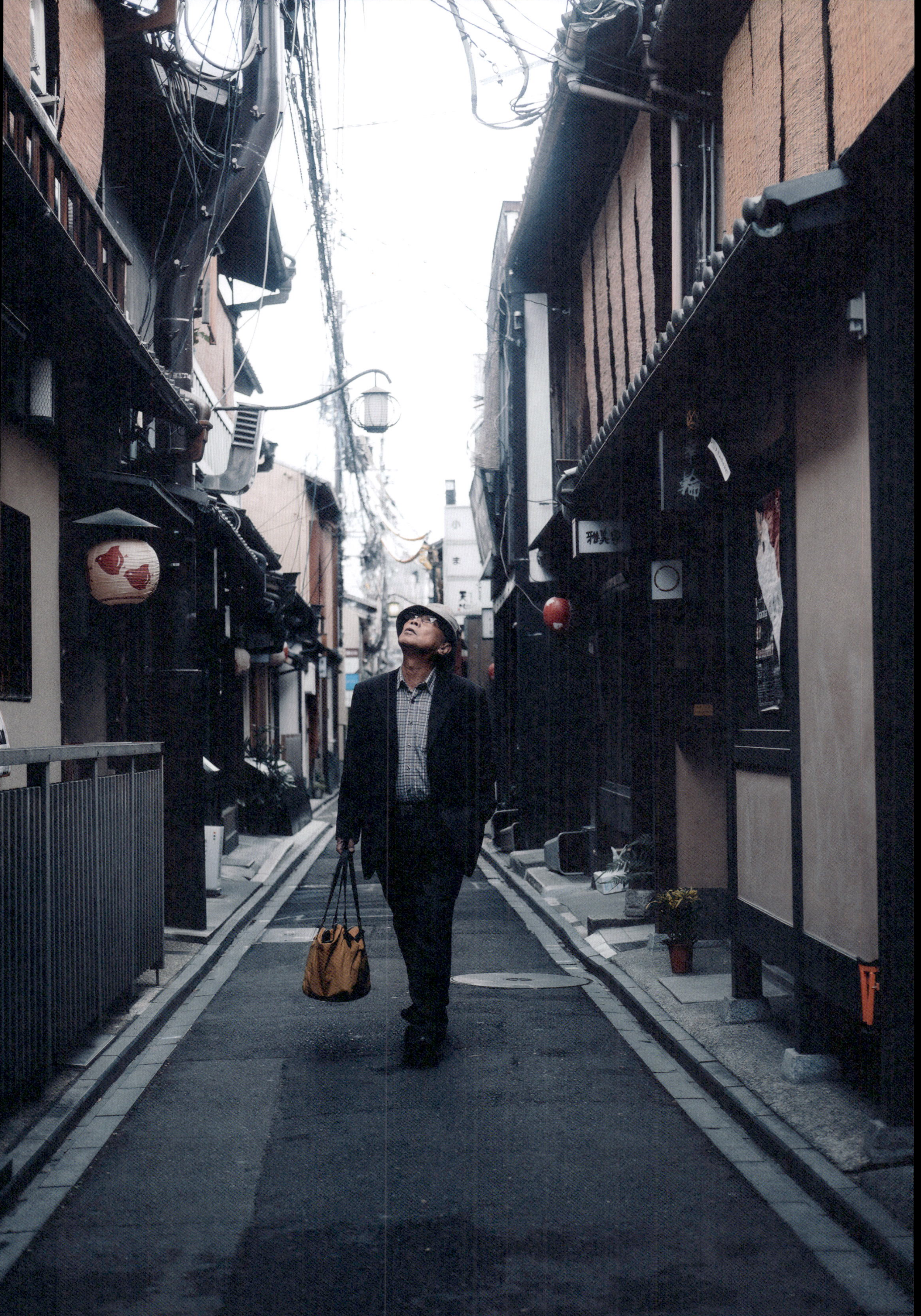

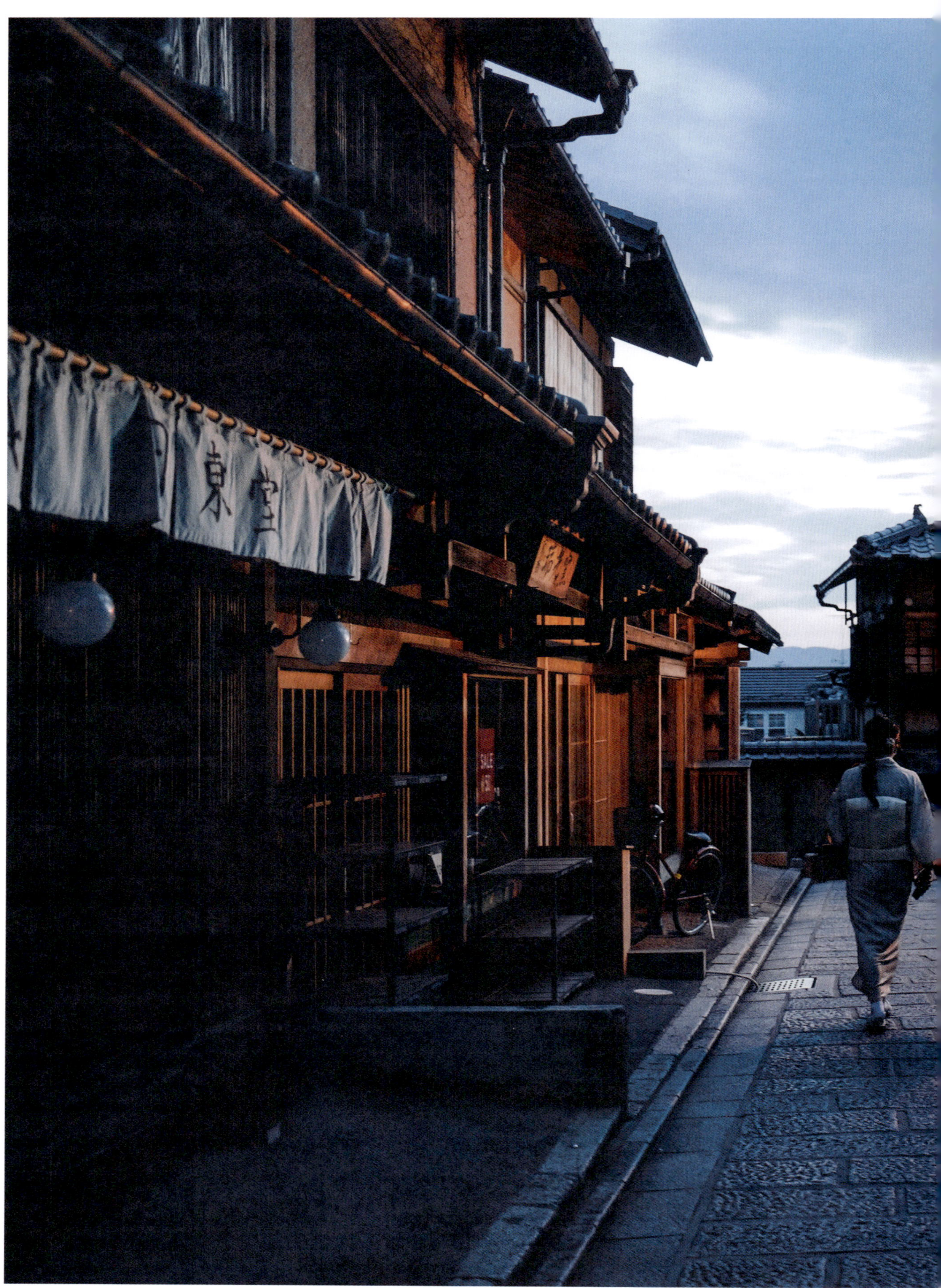
東
SALE

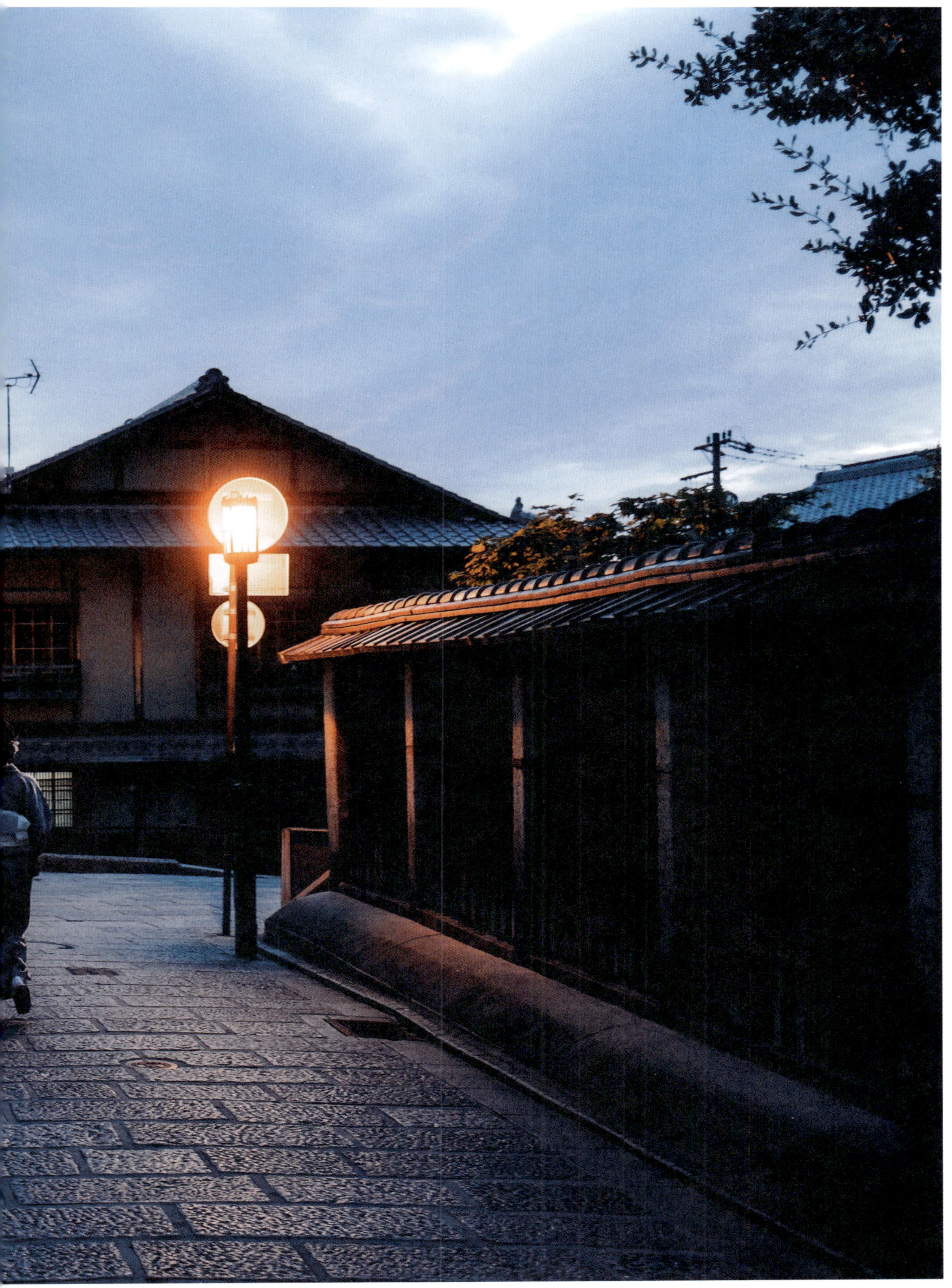

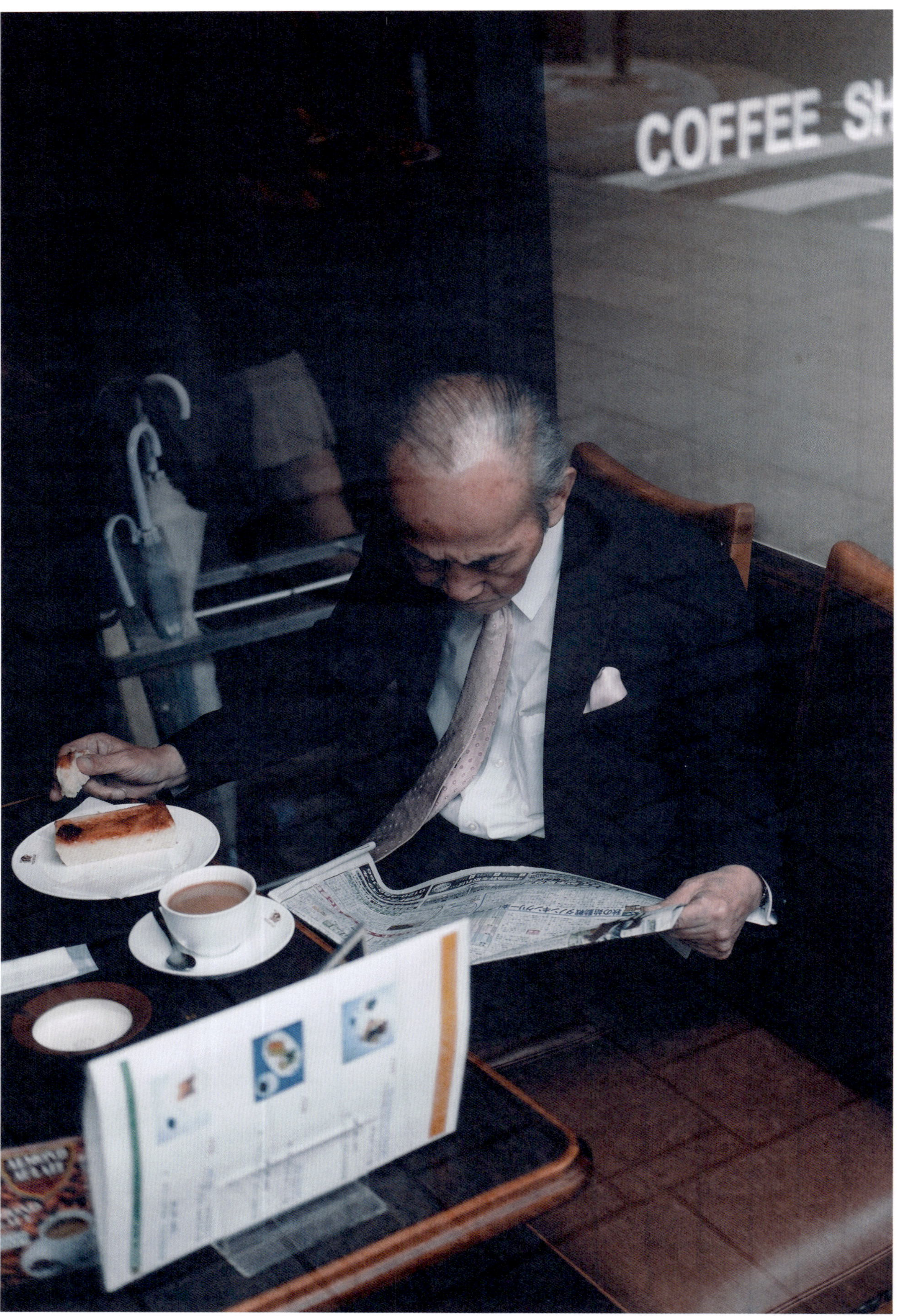
COFFEE SH

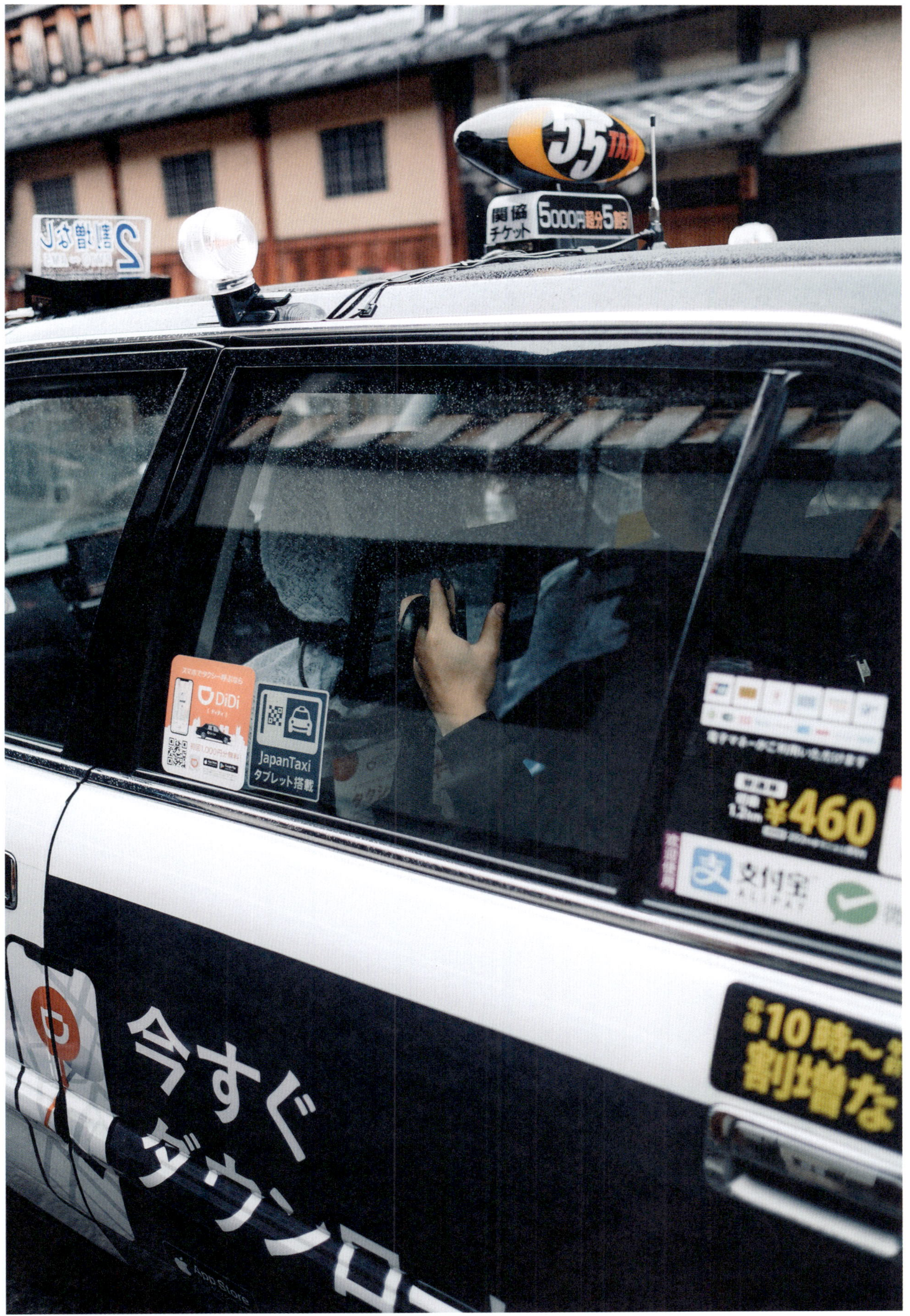
55 TAXI
関協 チケット
5000円超分5割引
DiDi
JapanTaxi
タブレット搭載
¥460
支付宝
ALIPAY
10時〜
割増な
今すぐ
ダウンロ
App Store

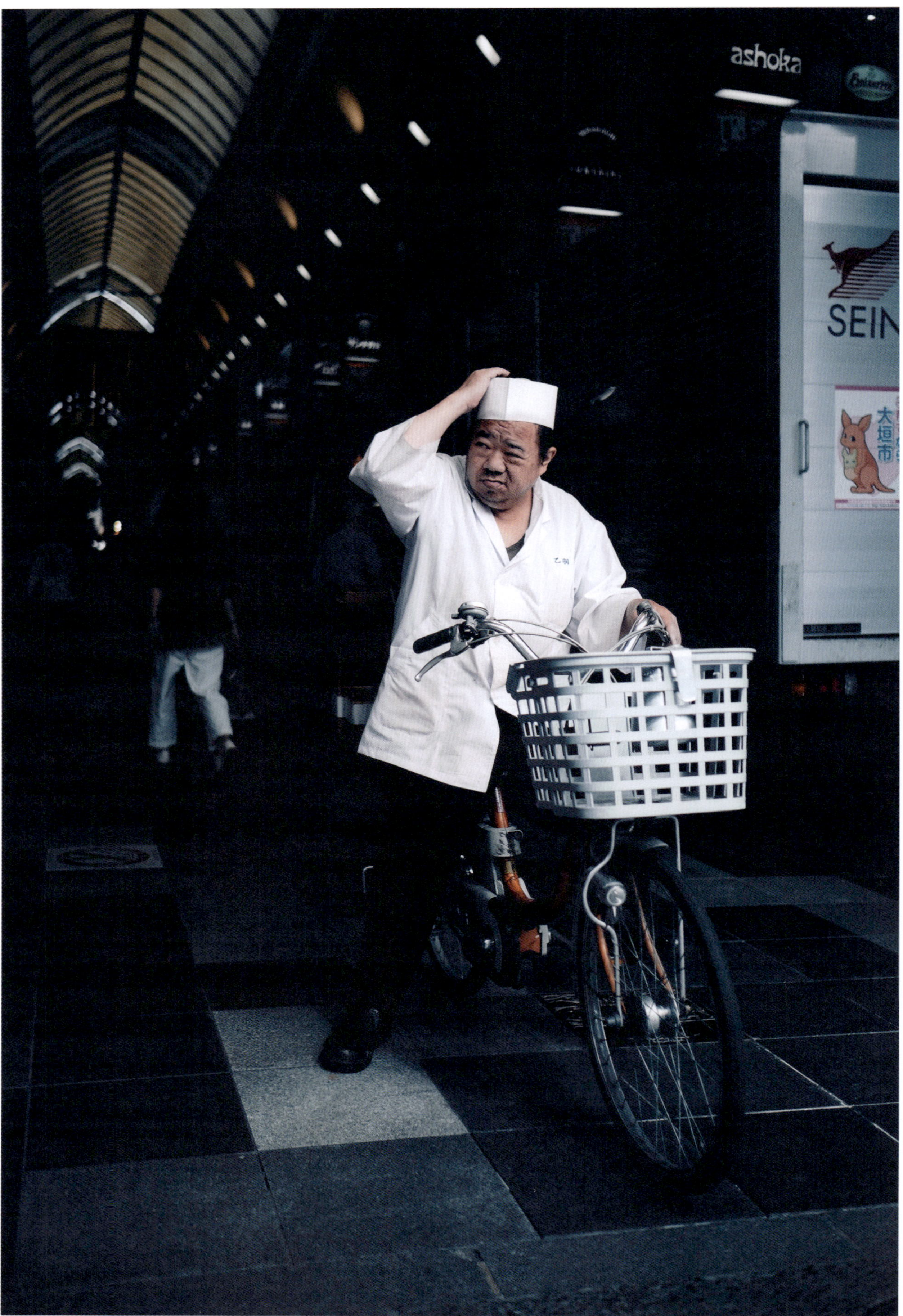
ashoka
SEIN
大垣市

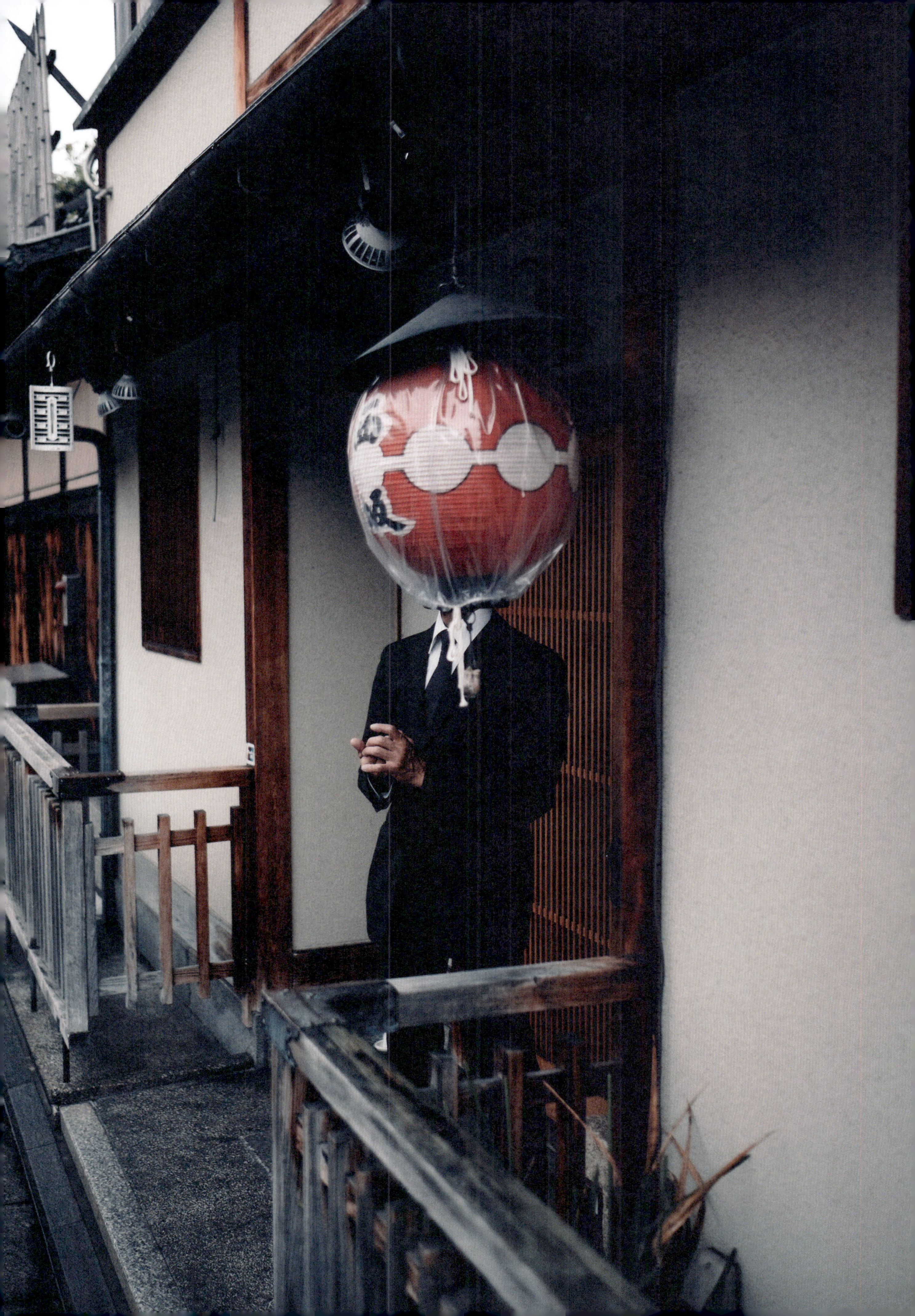

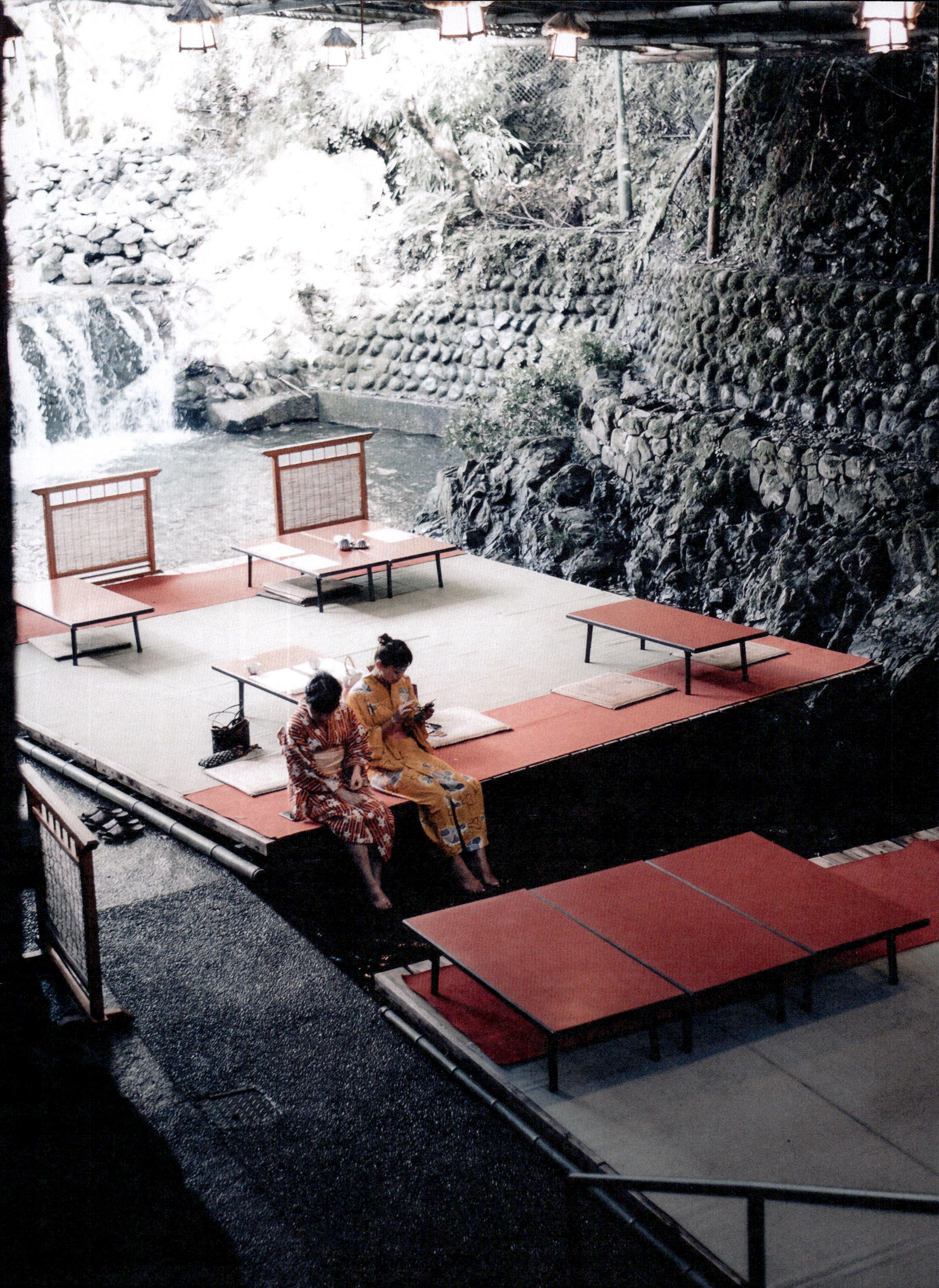

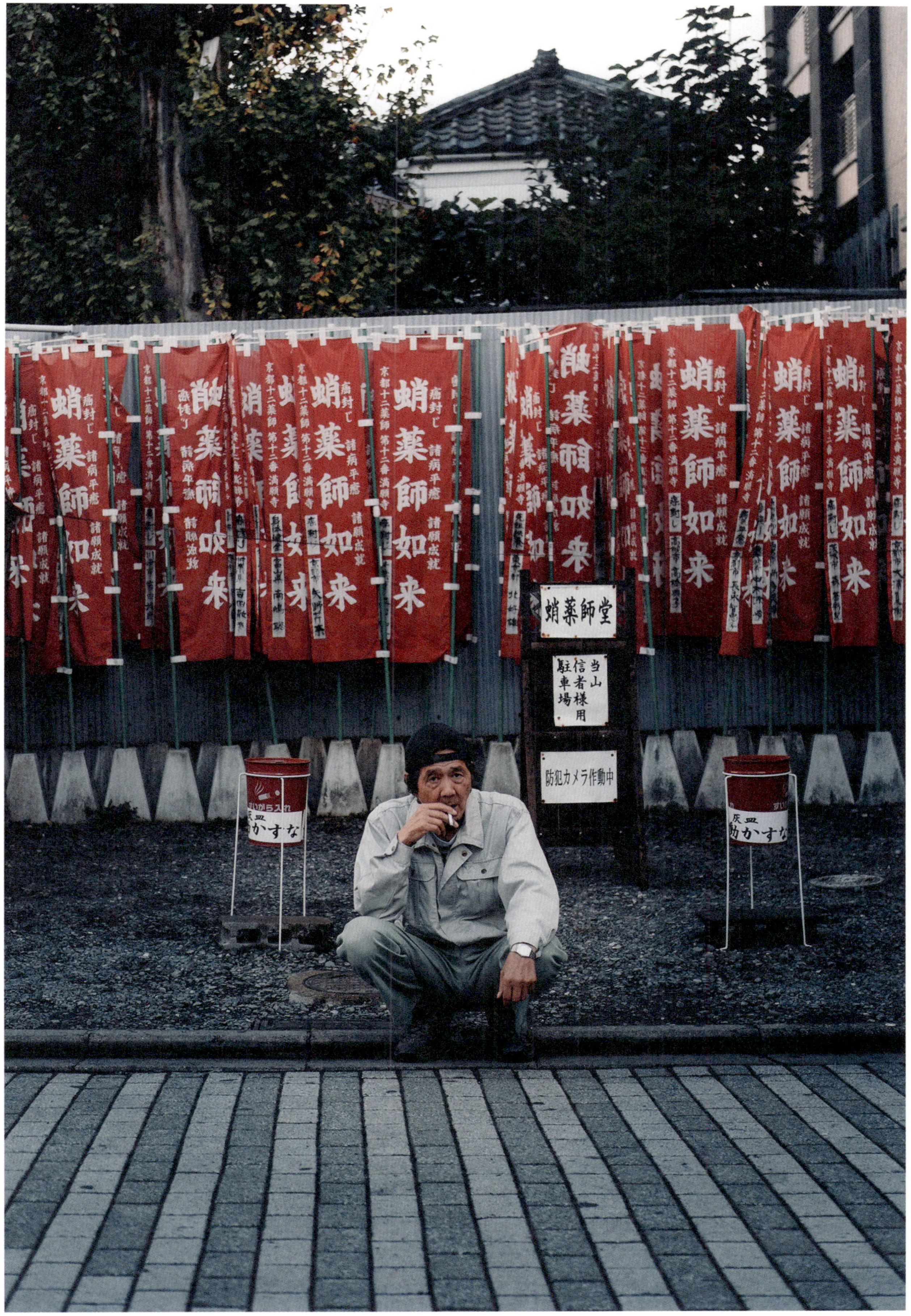

蛸薬師如来
病封じ
諸病平癒
諸願成就
蛸薬師堂
当山信者様用駐車場
防犯カメラ作動中
灰皿

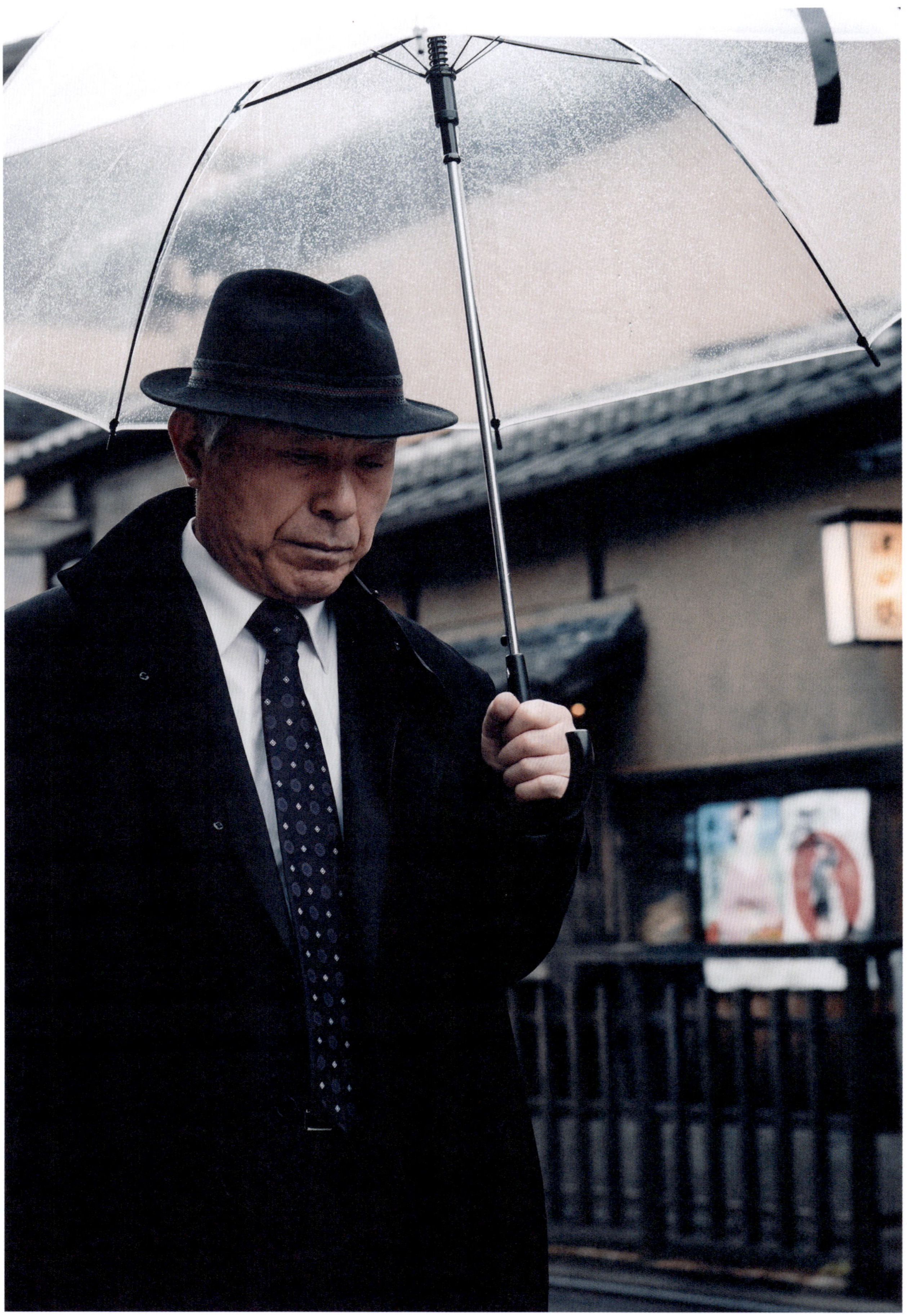

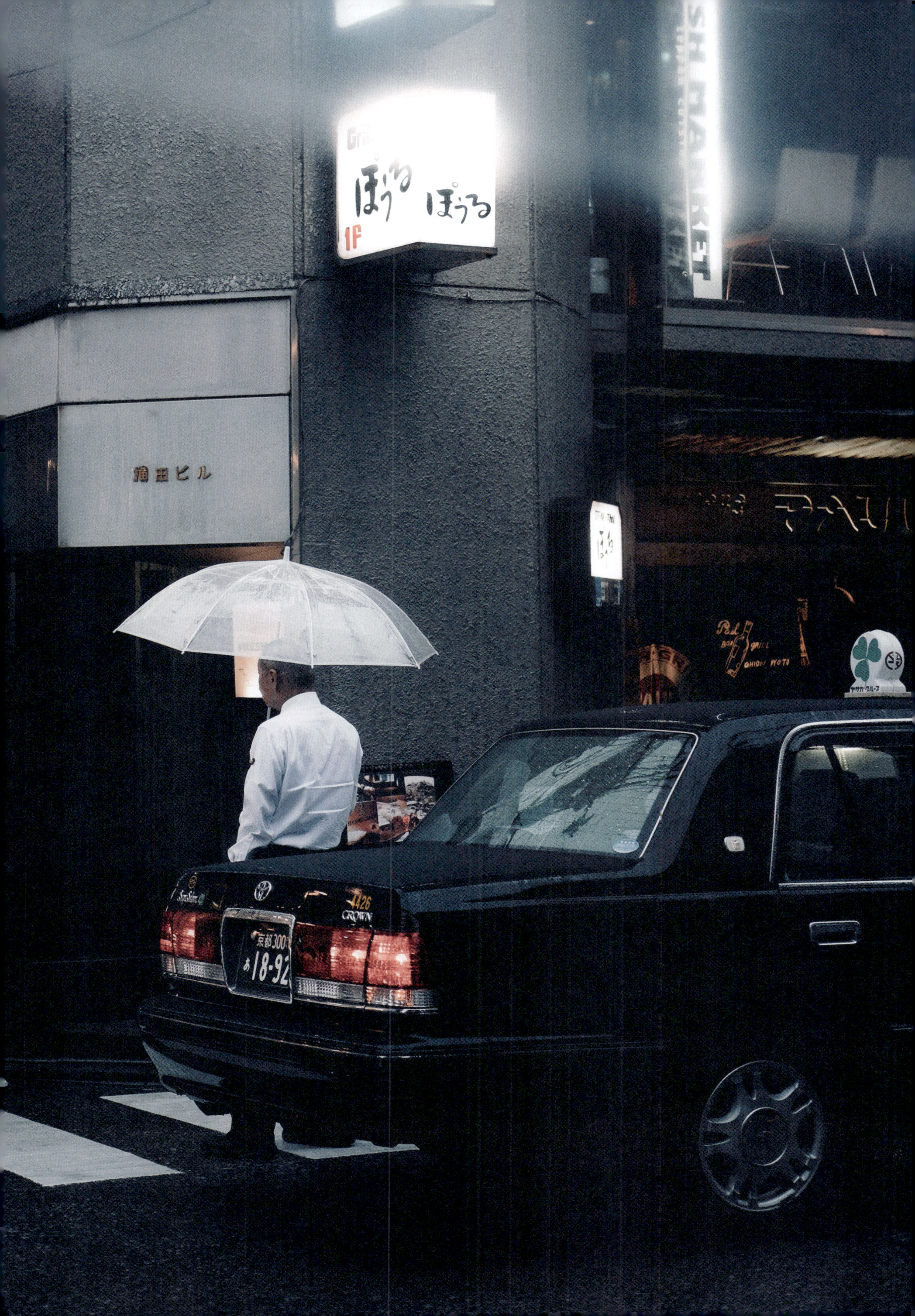
ぽうる
ぽうる
1F
CROWN
京都300
あ18-92

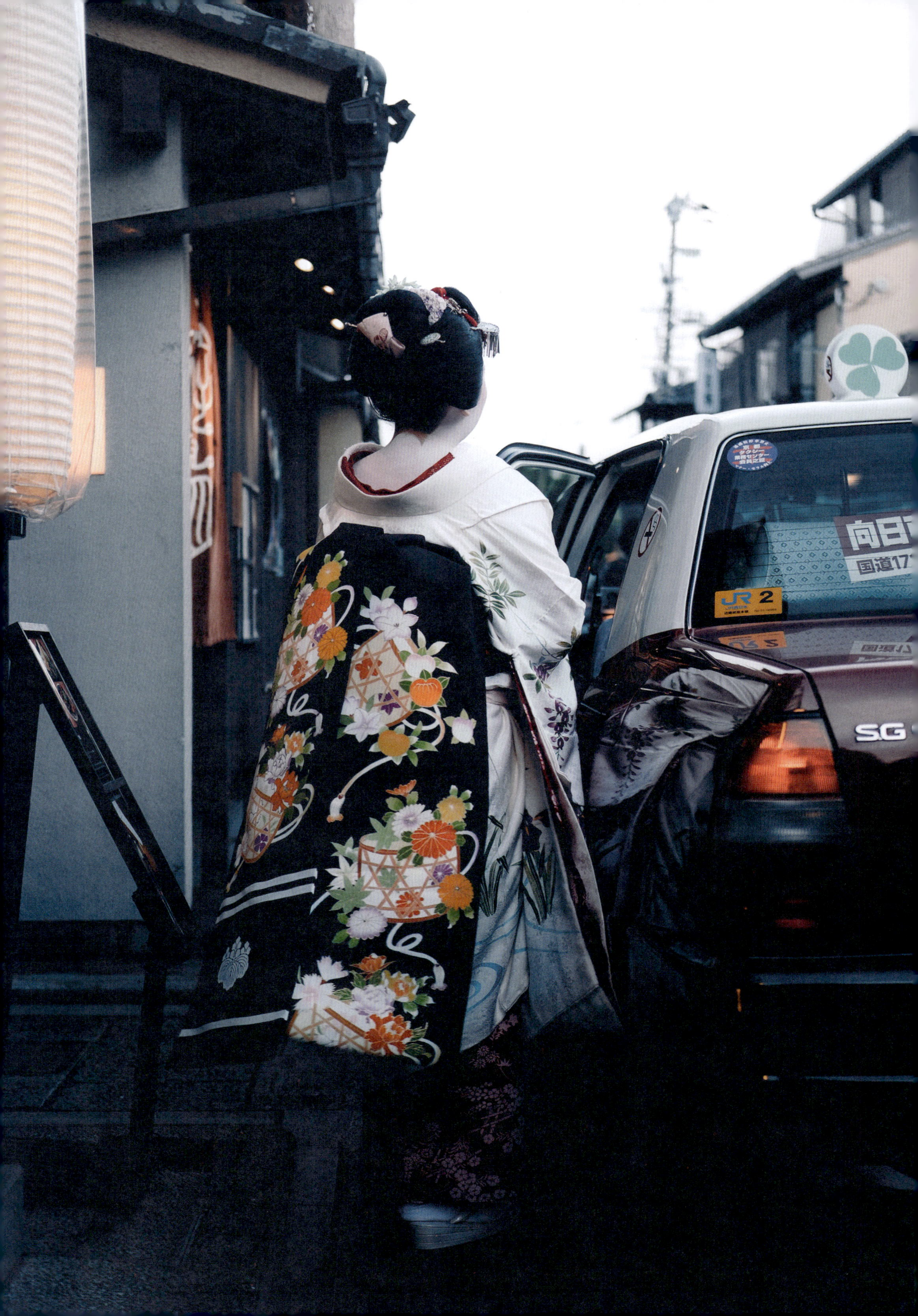

向日
国道17
JR 2
S.G

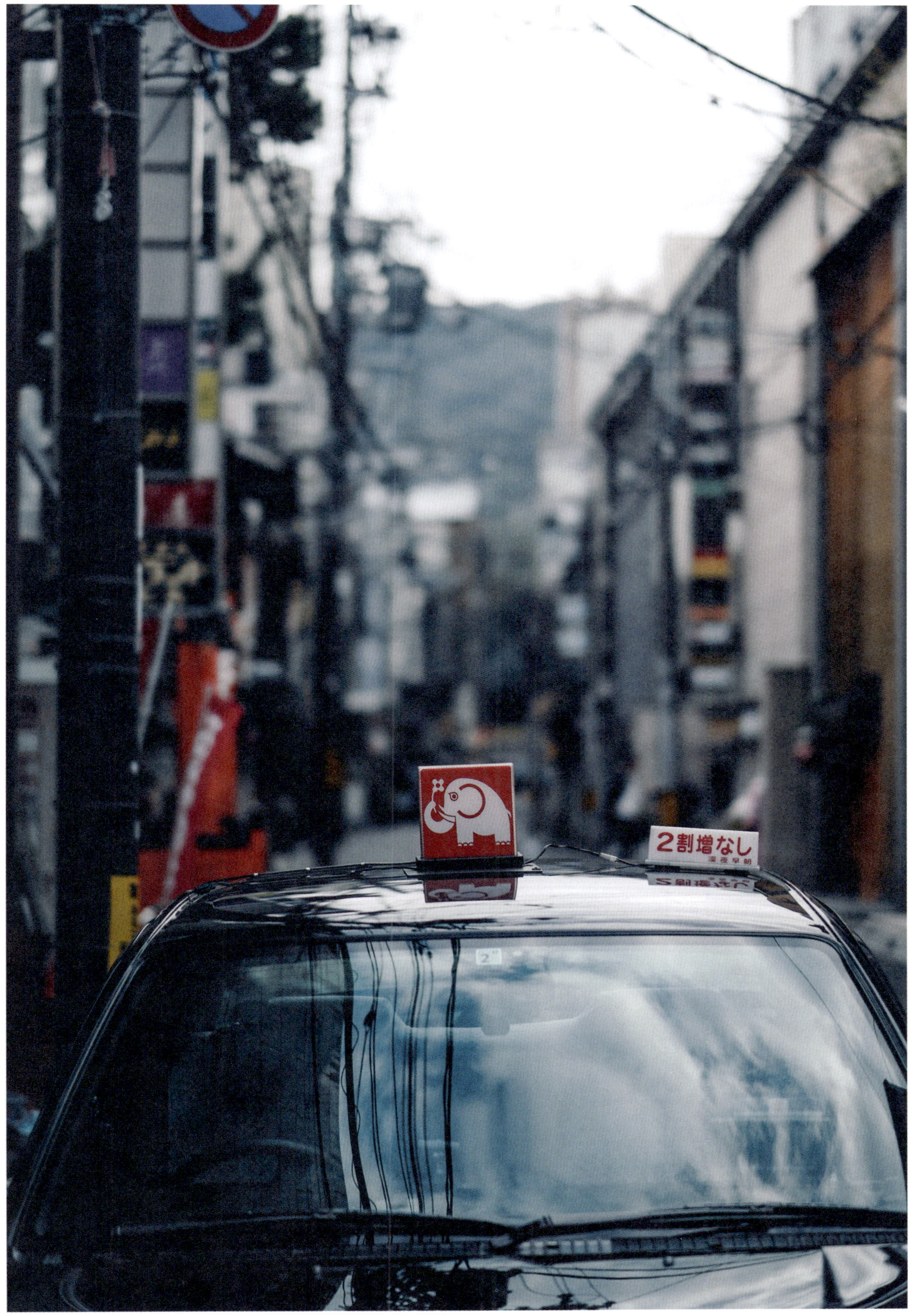
2割増なし
深夜早朝

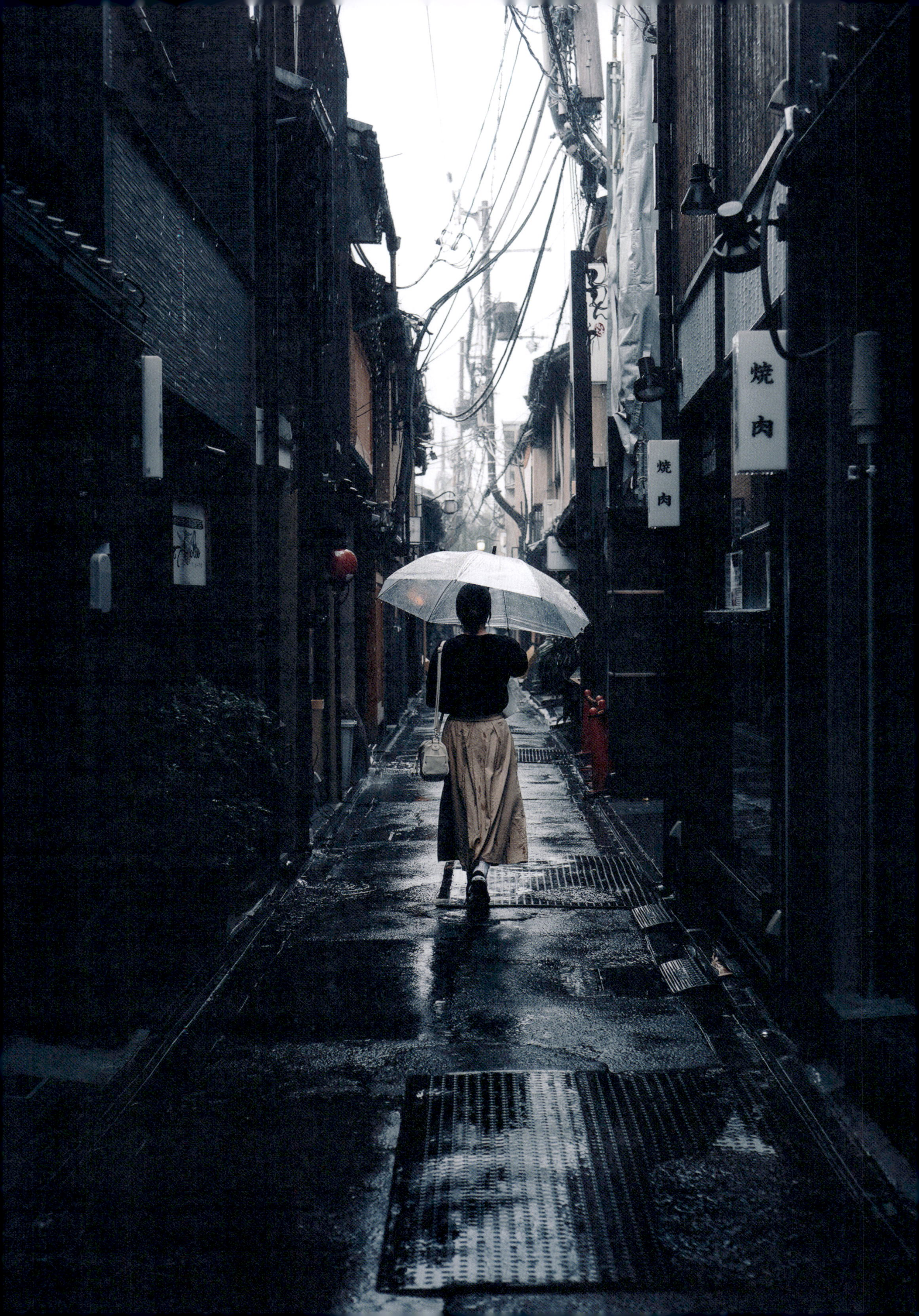
焼肉
焼肉

古傘の
婆さと月夜の
時雨哉

与謝　蕪村

Old umbrellas
Spring up by the score on a moonlit night
When the rain comes down.

Yosa Buson

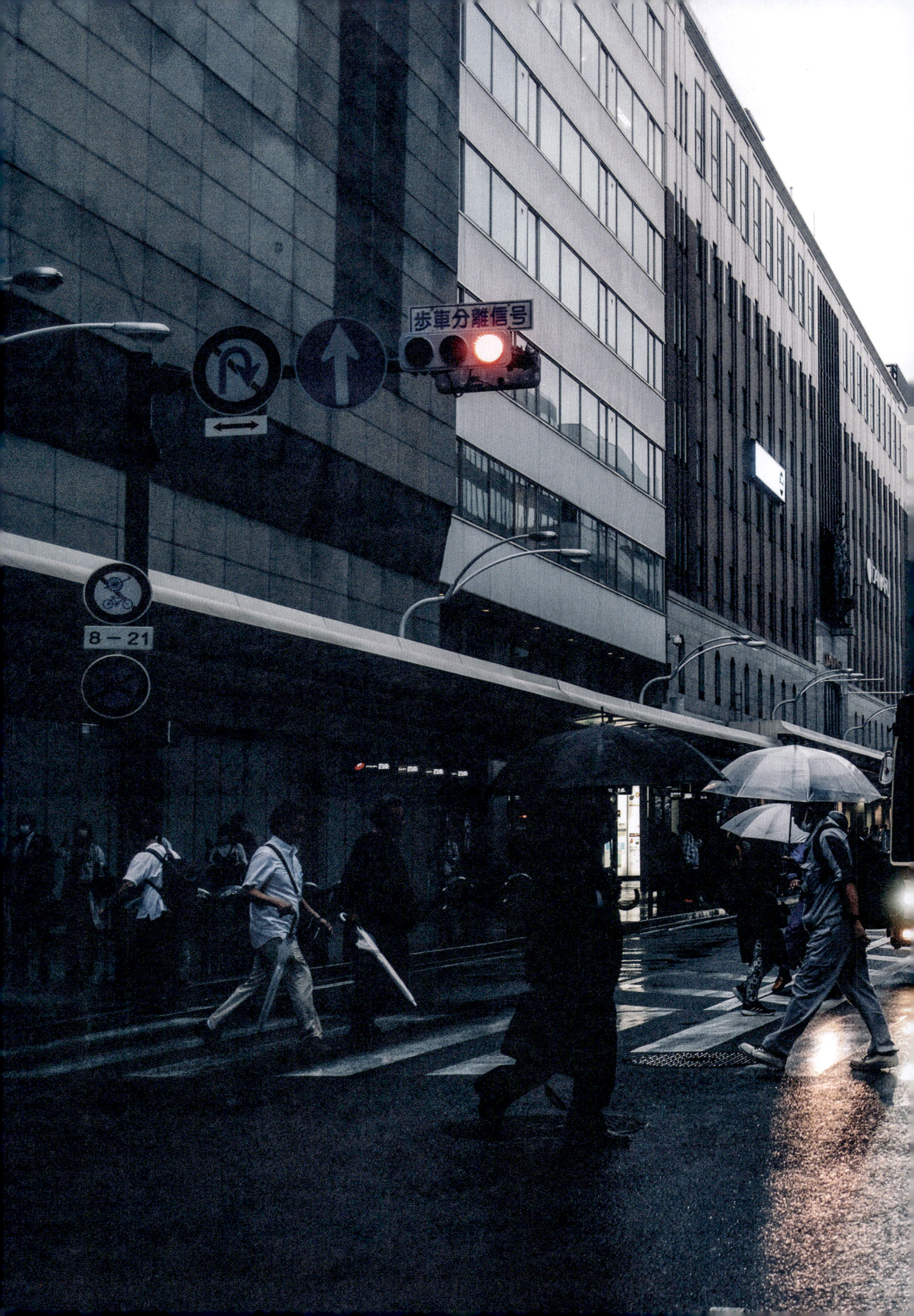
歩車分離信号
8－21

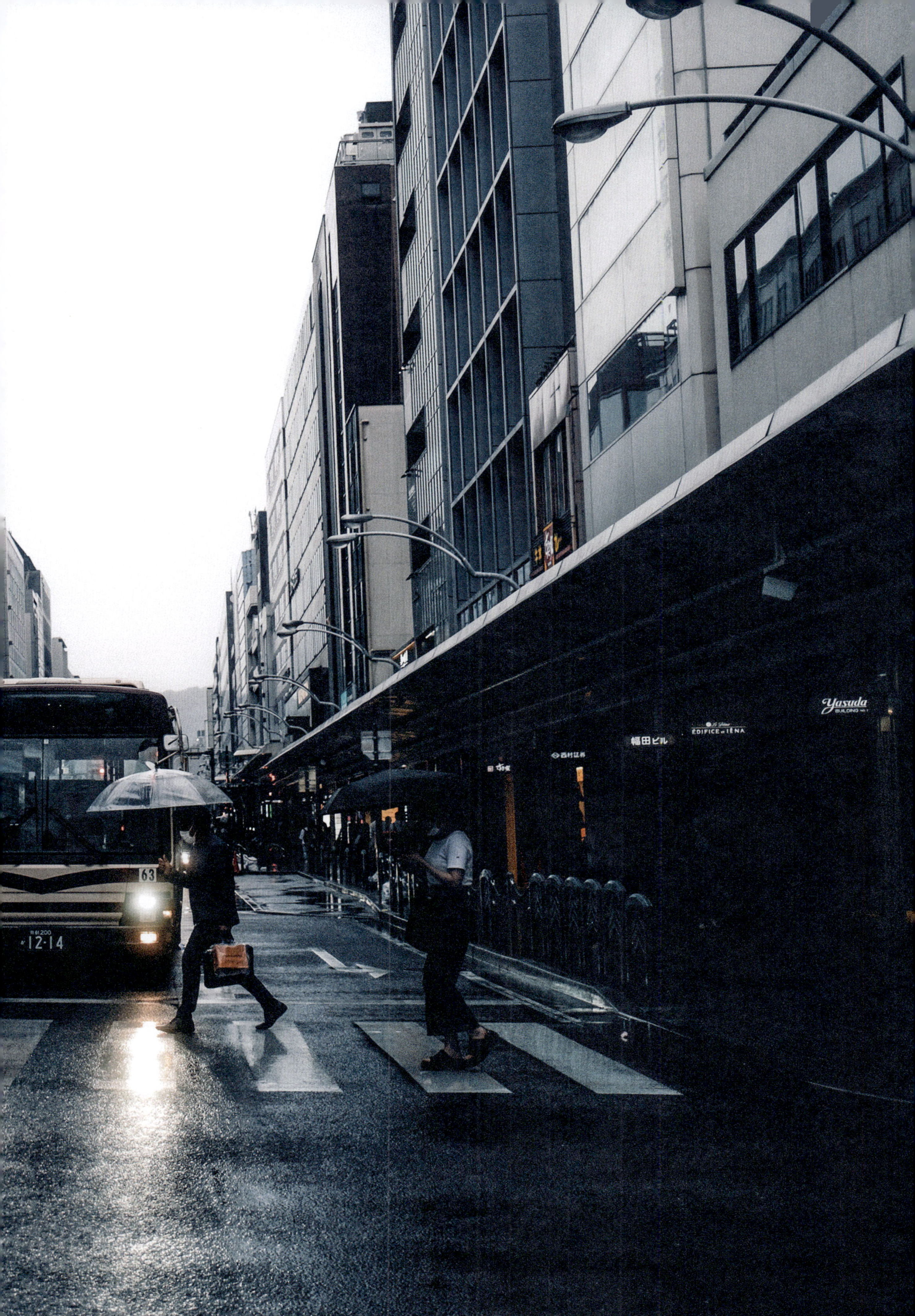
Yasuda
BUILDING No. 1
ÉDIFICE et IÉNA
幅田ビル
西村証券
63
12-14

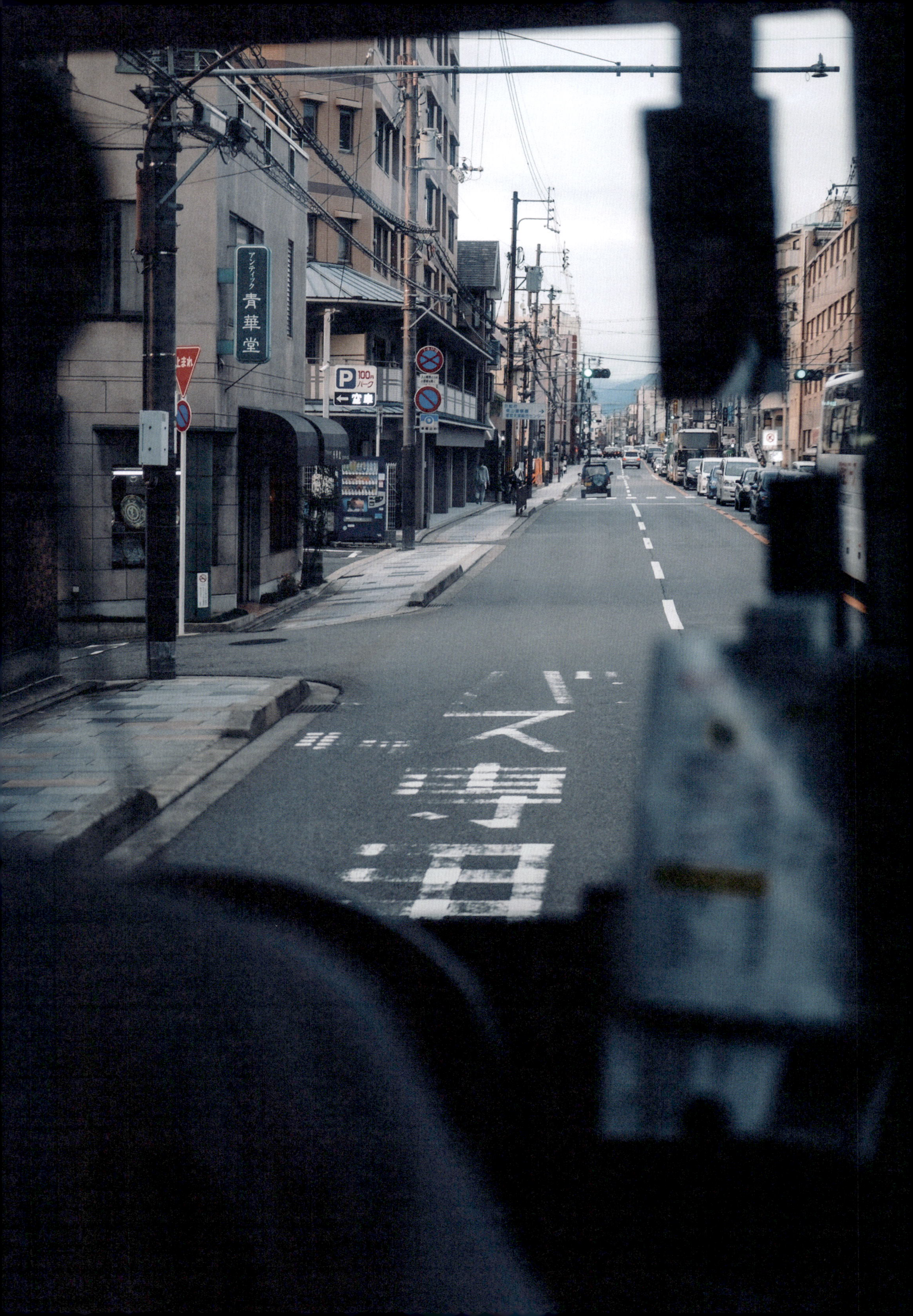
アンティック
青華堂
P 100円 パーク
← 空車

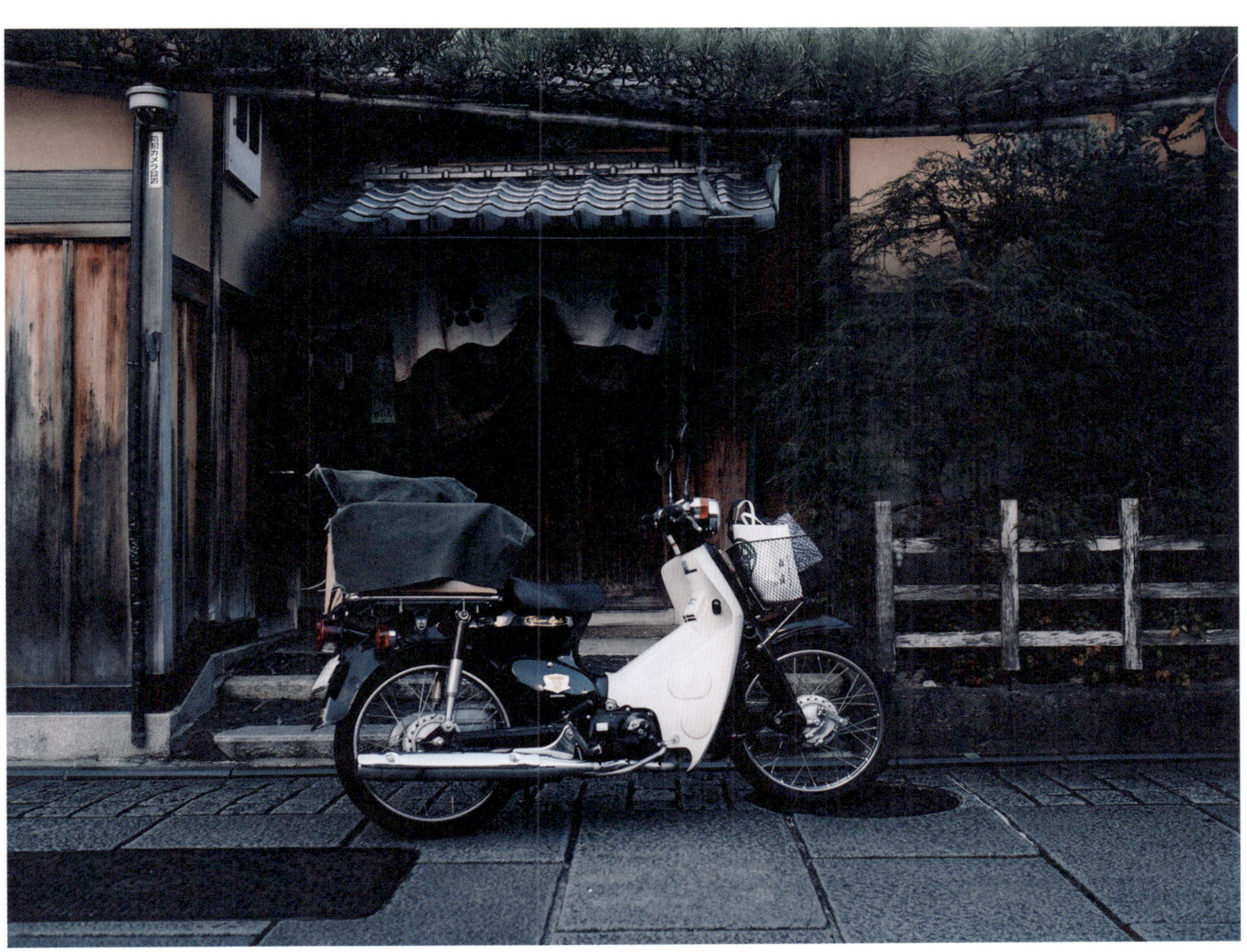
防犯カメラ設置

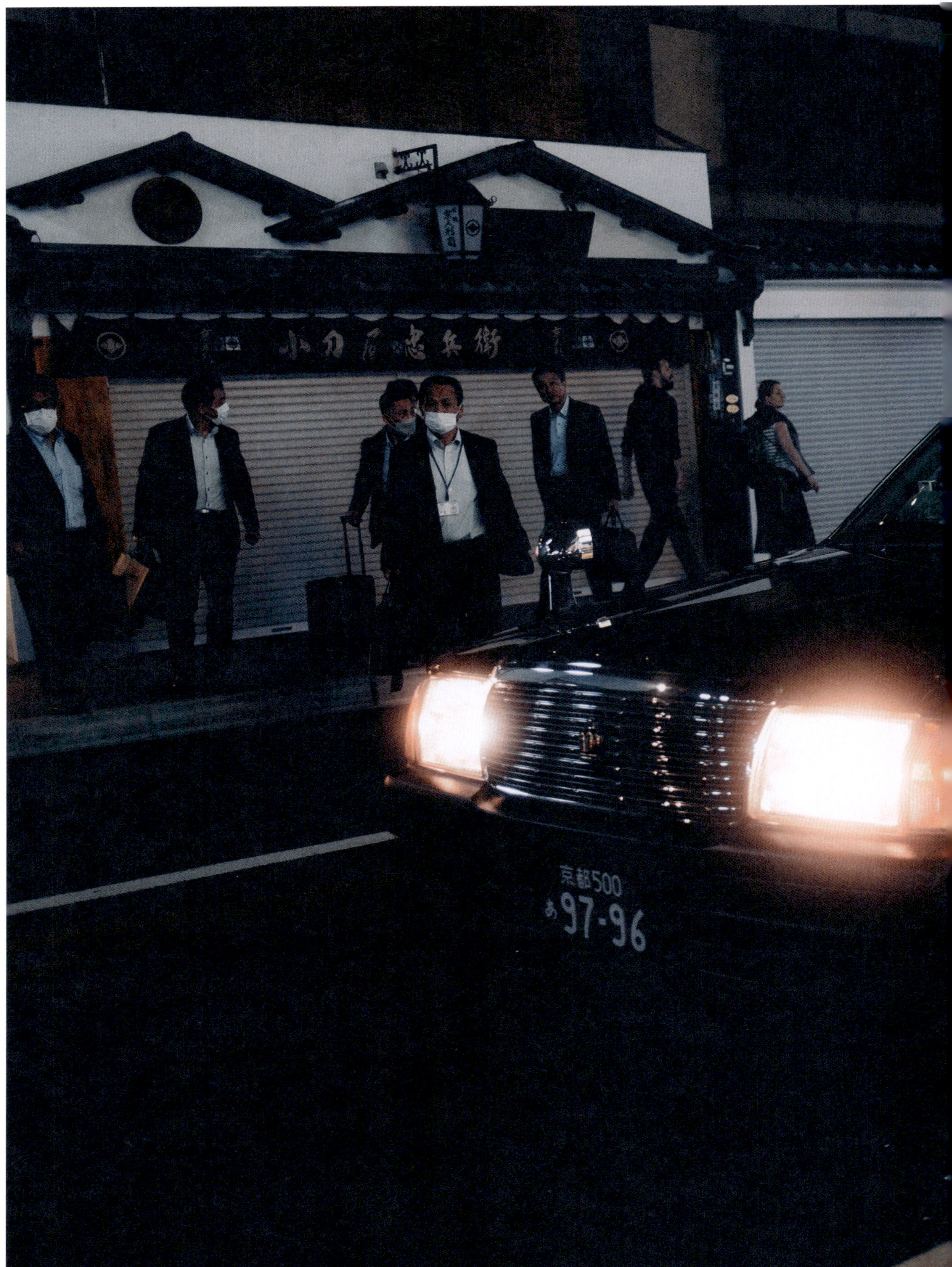
小刀屋忠兵衛
京都500
あ 97-96

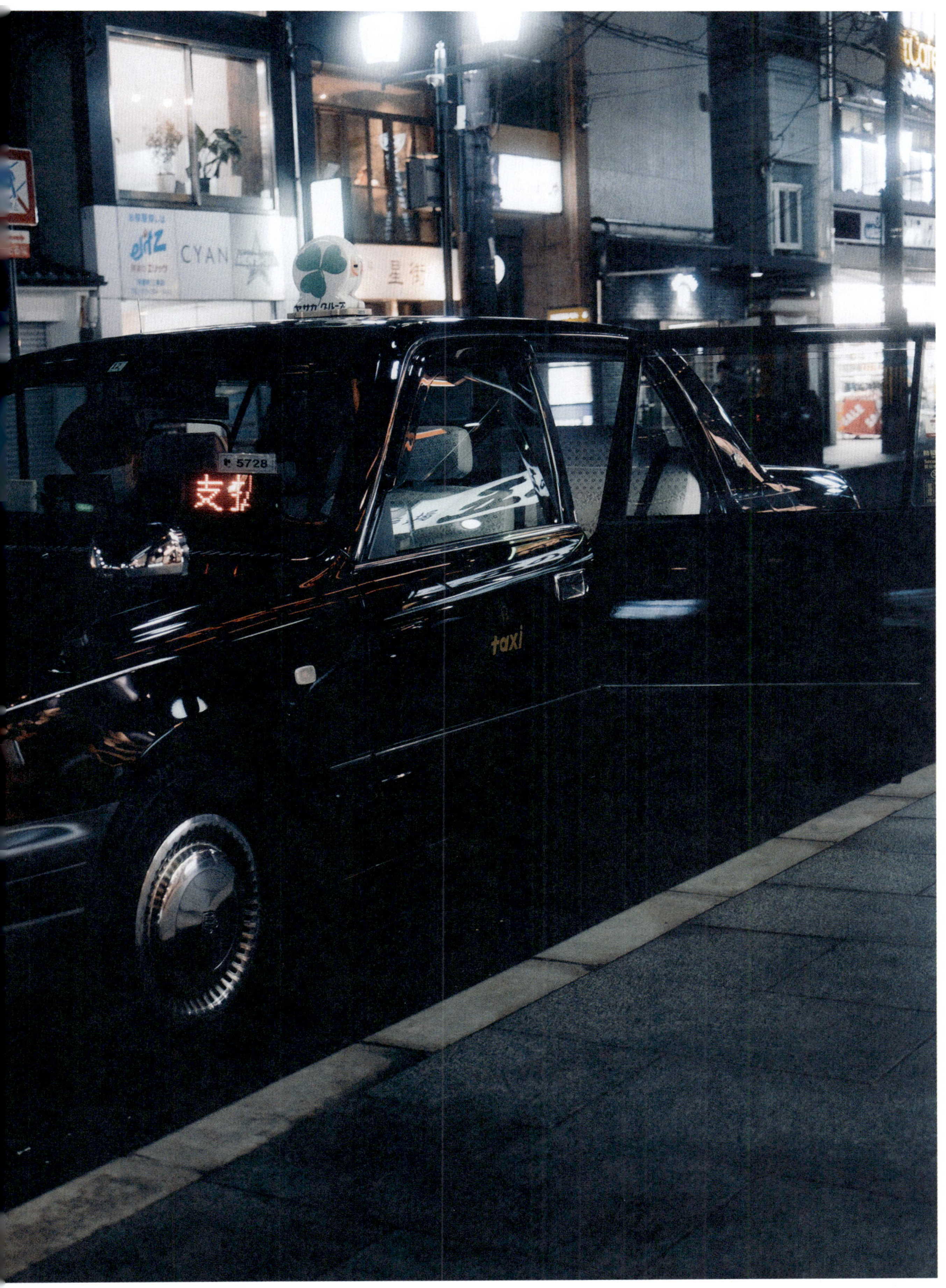
CYAN
ヤサカグループ
5728
支払
taxi

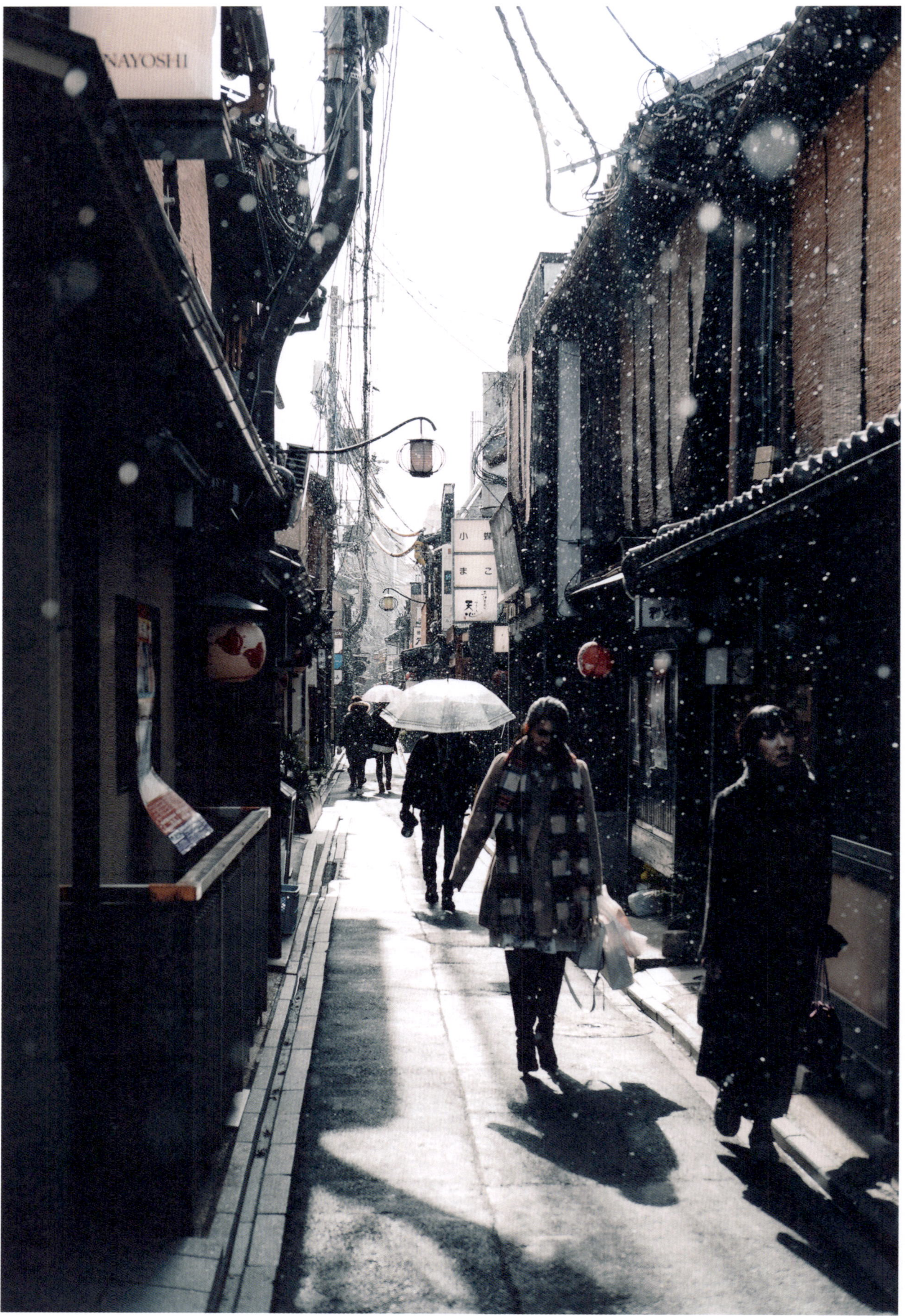
NAYOSHI

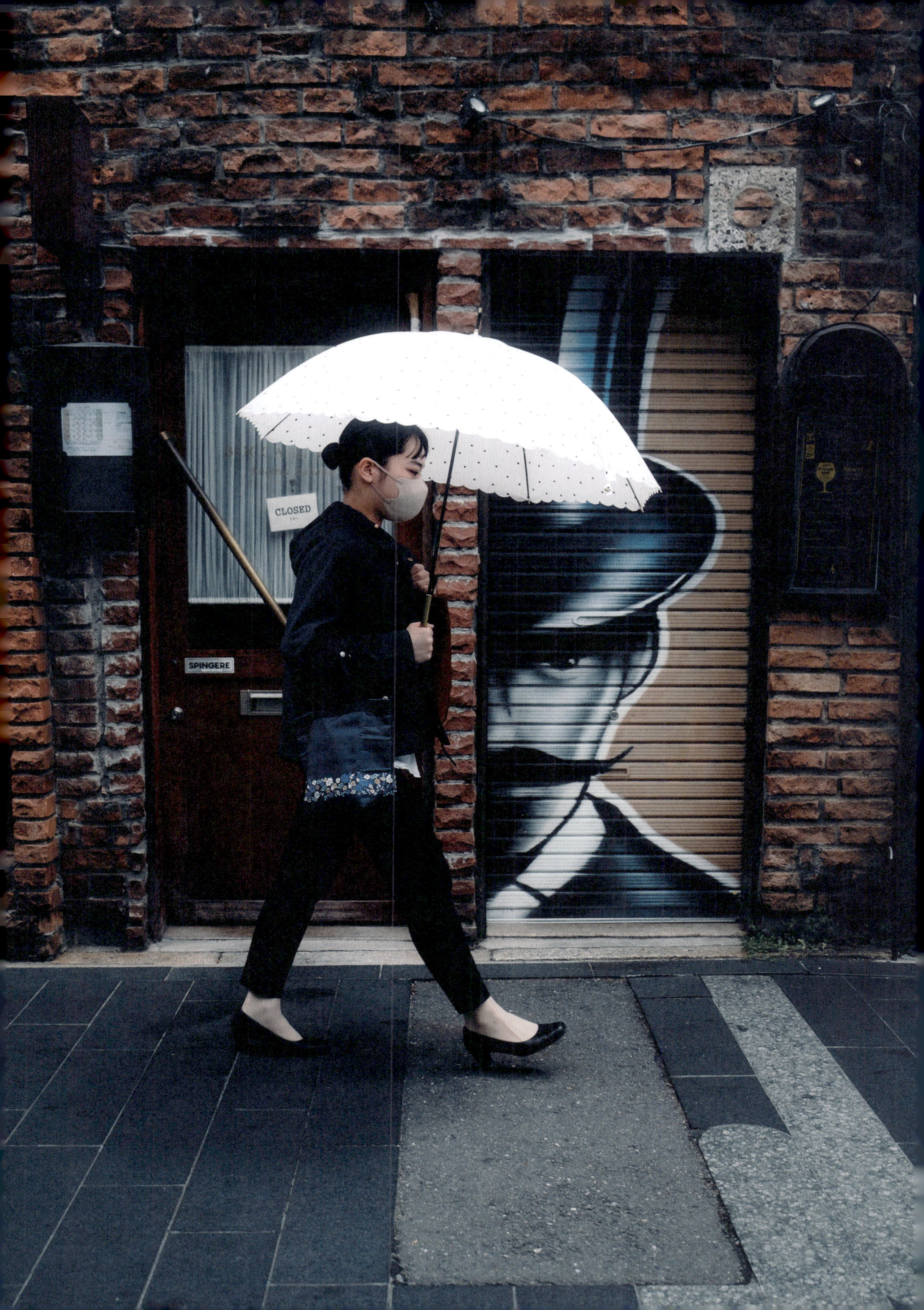
CLOSED
SPINGERE

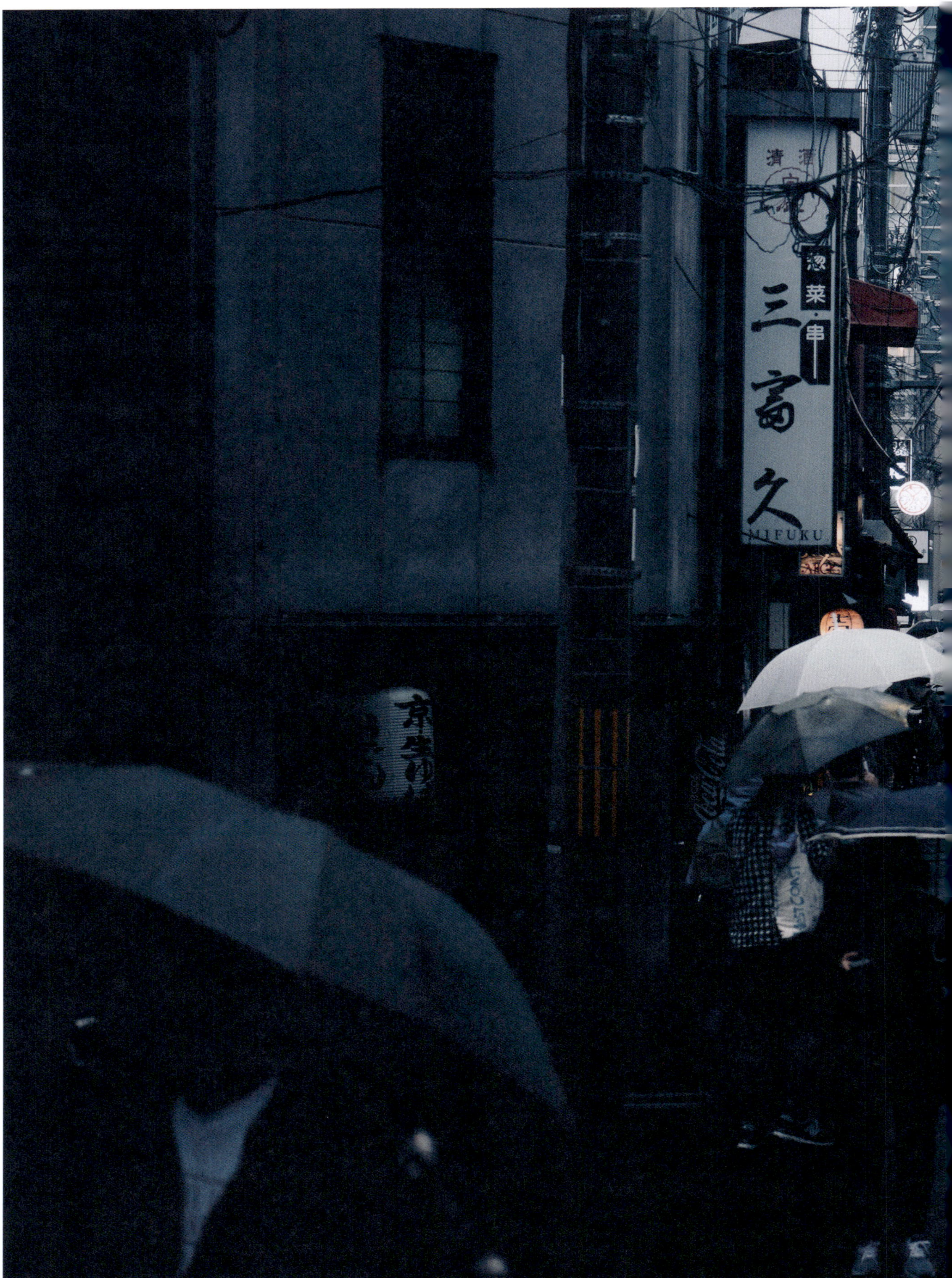
惣菜・串
三富久
MIFUKU

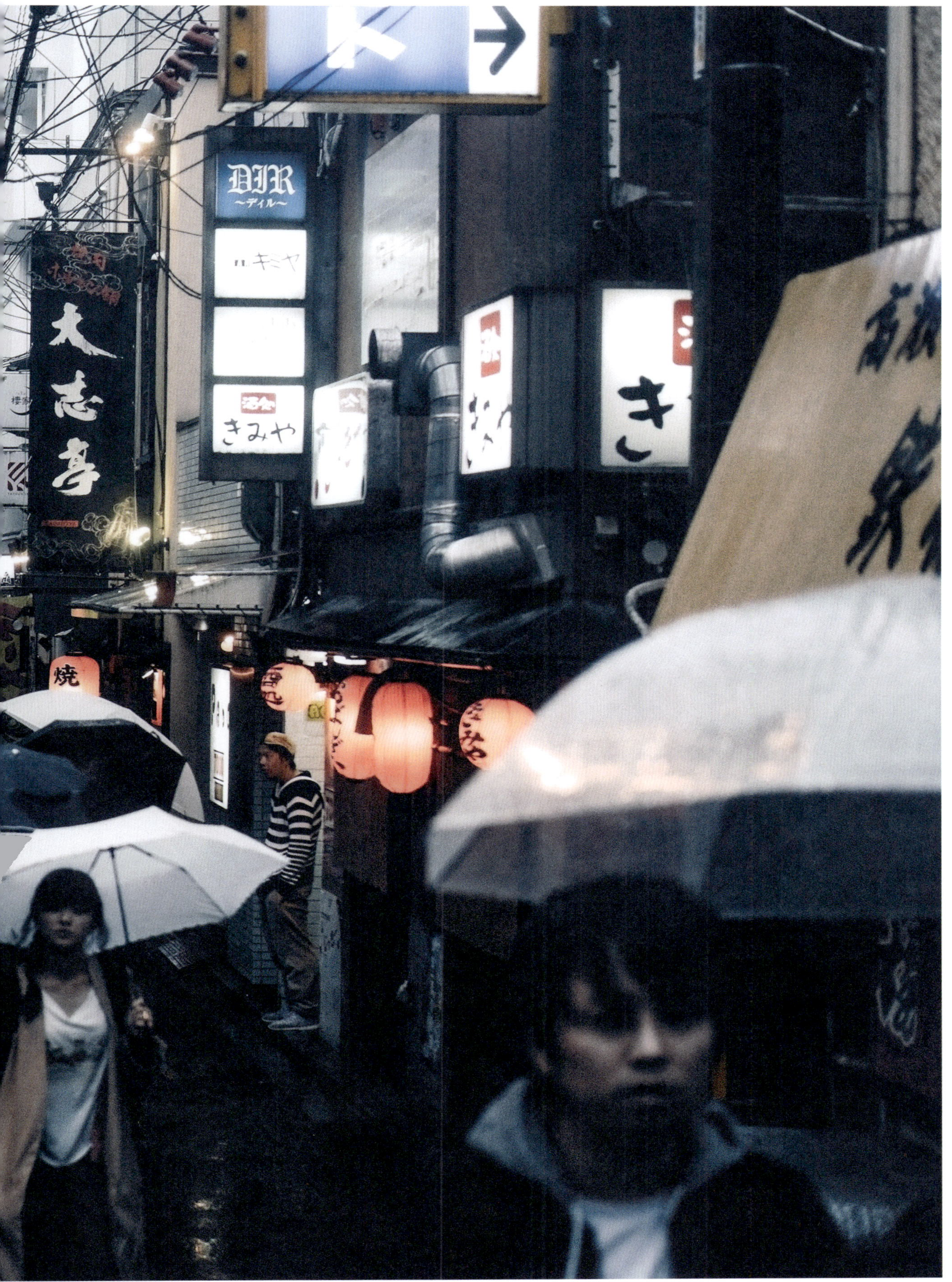
DIR
～ディル～
キミヤ
きみや
大志亭
焼

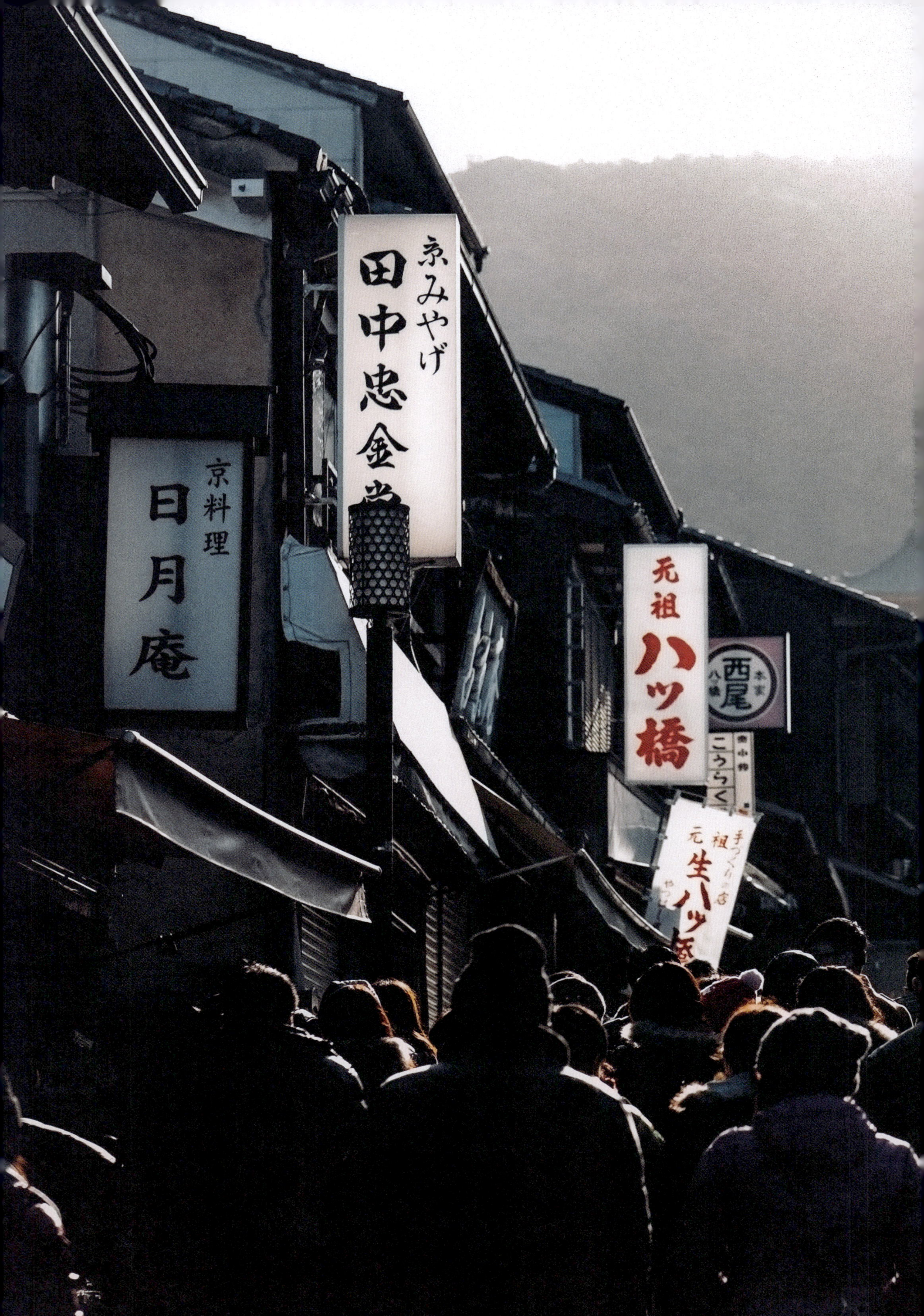

京みやげ
京料理
日月庵
元祖
ハツ橋
西尾

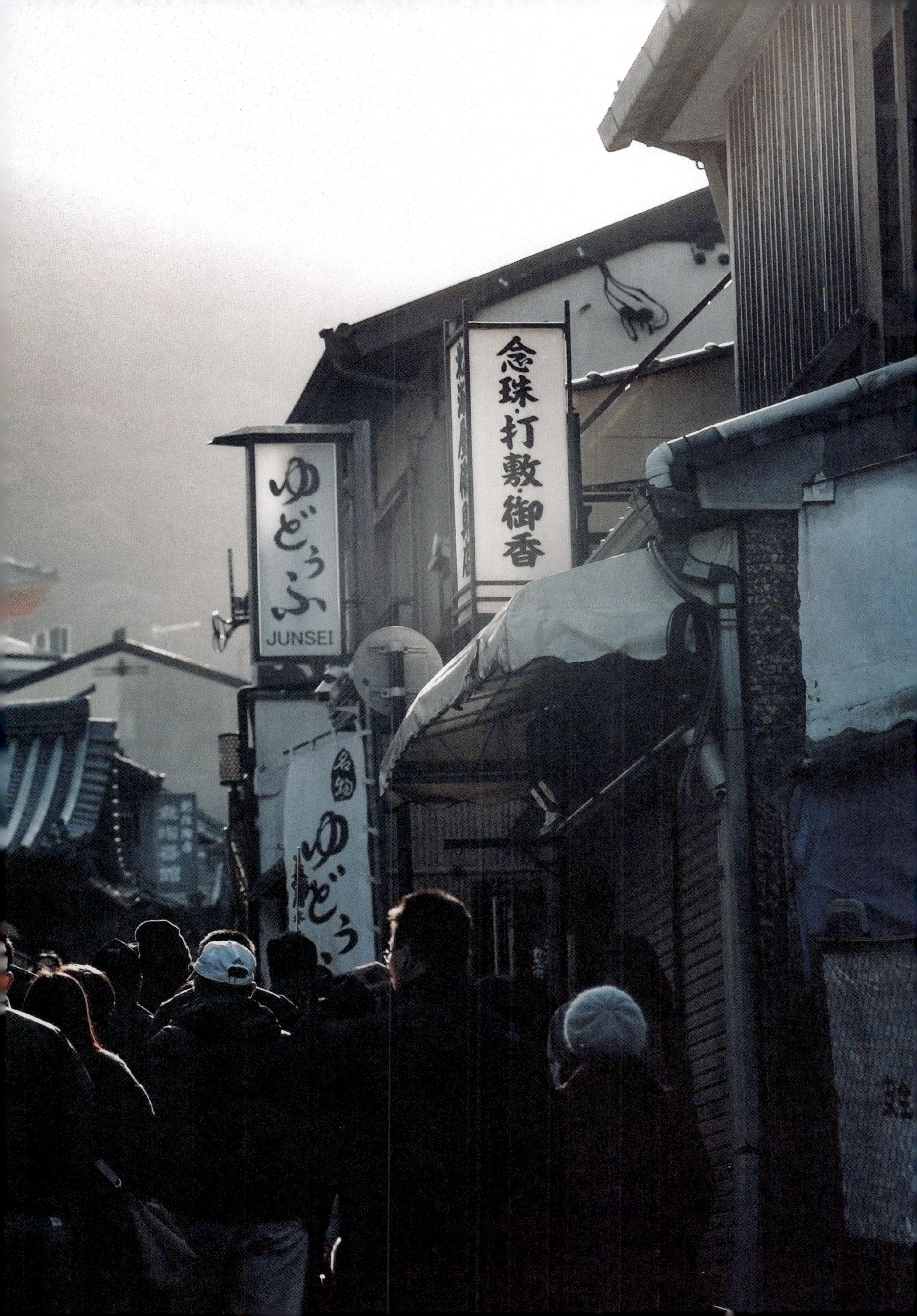
念珠·打敷·御香
ゆどうふ
JUNSEI
名物
ゆどう

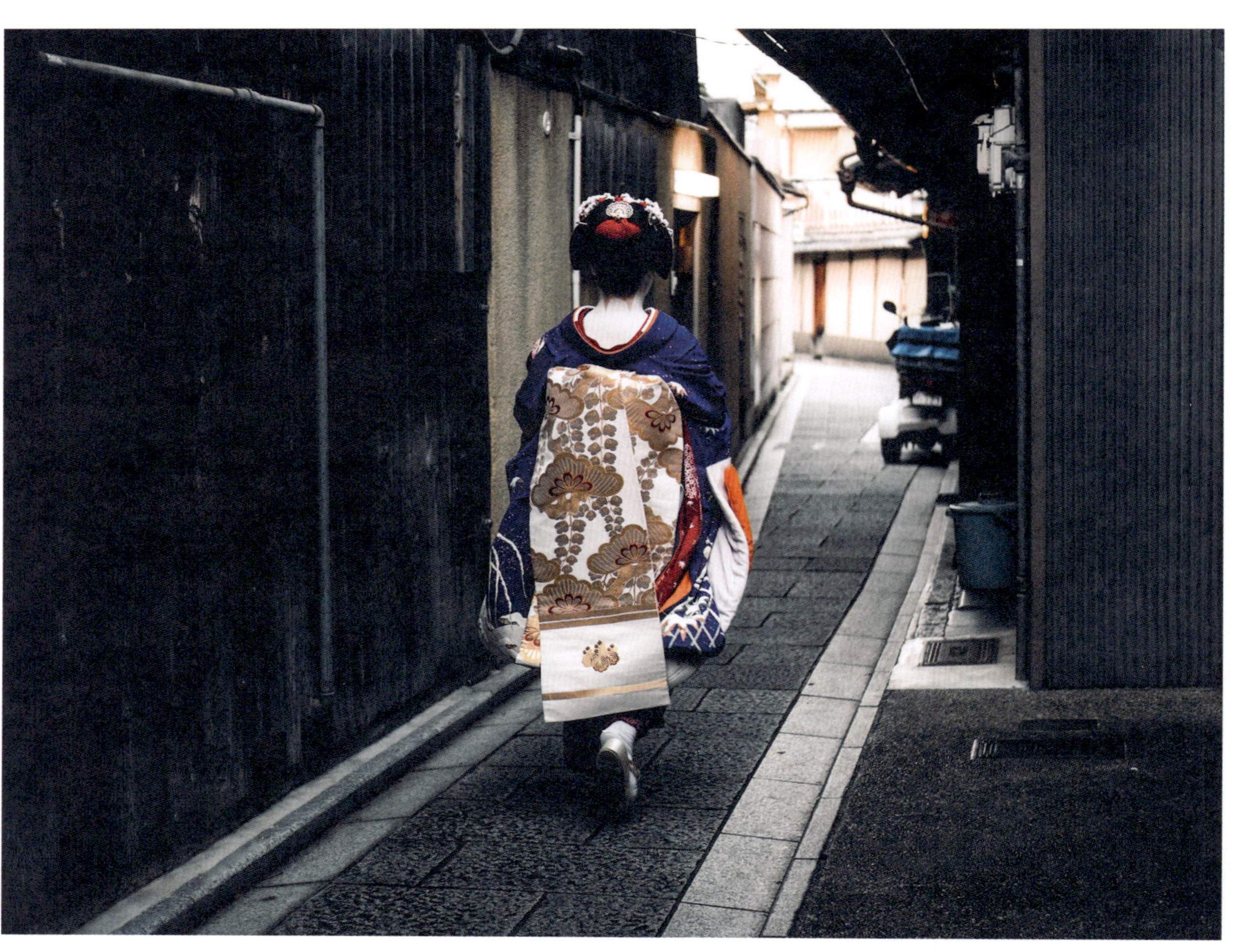

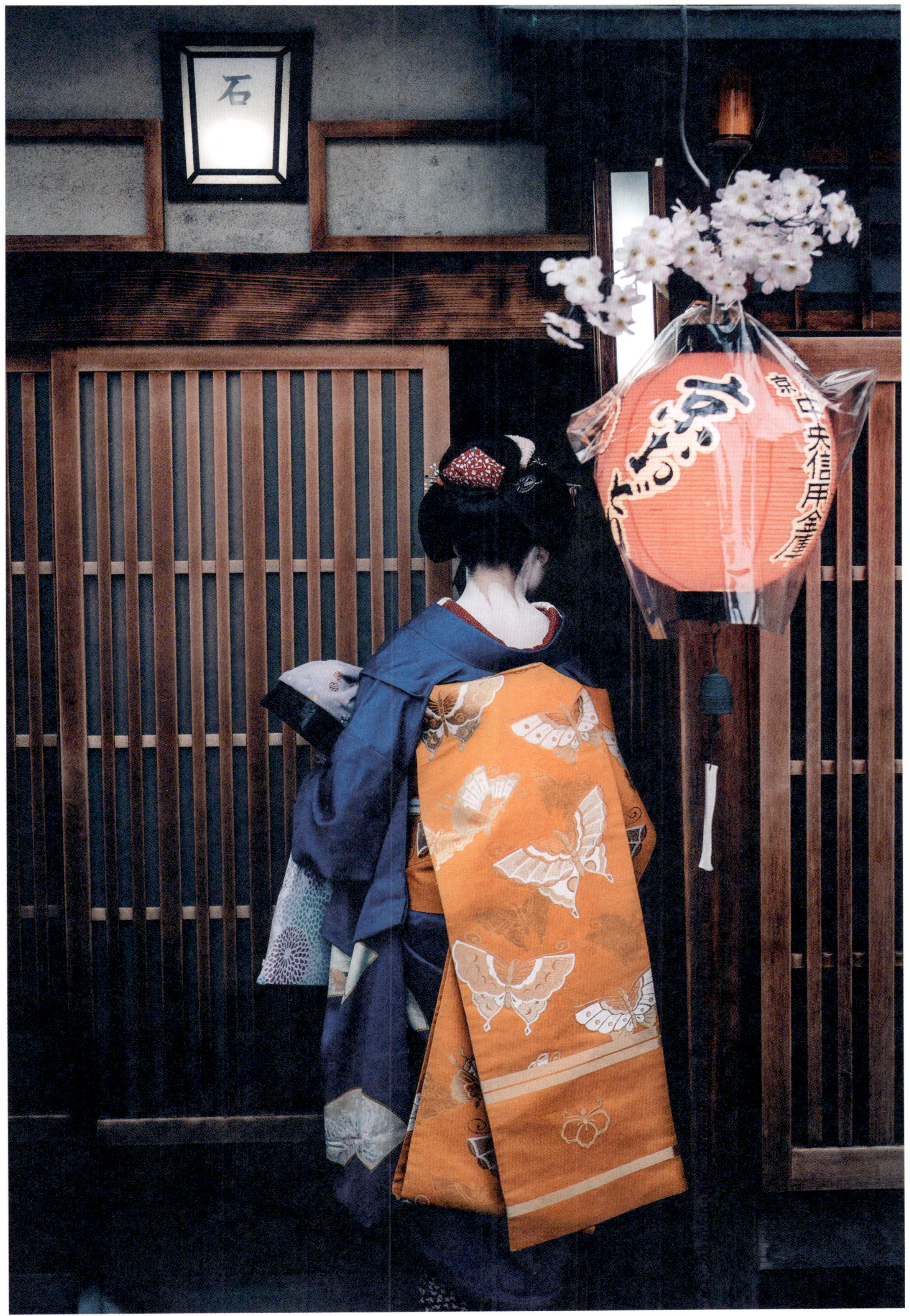
石
中央信用金庫

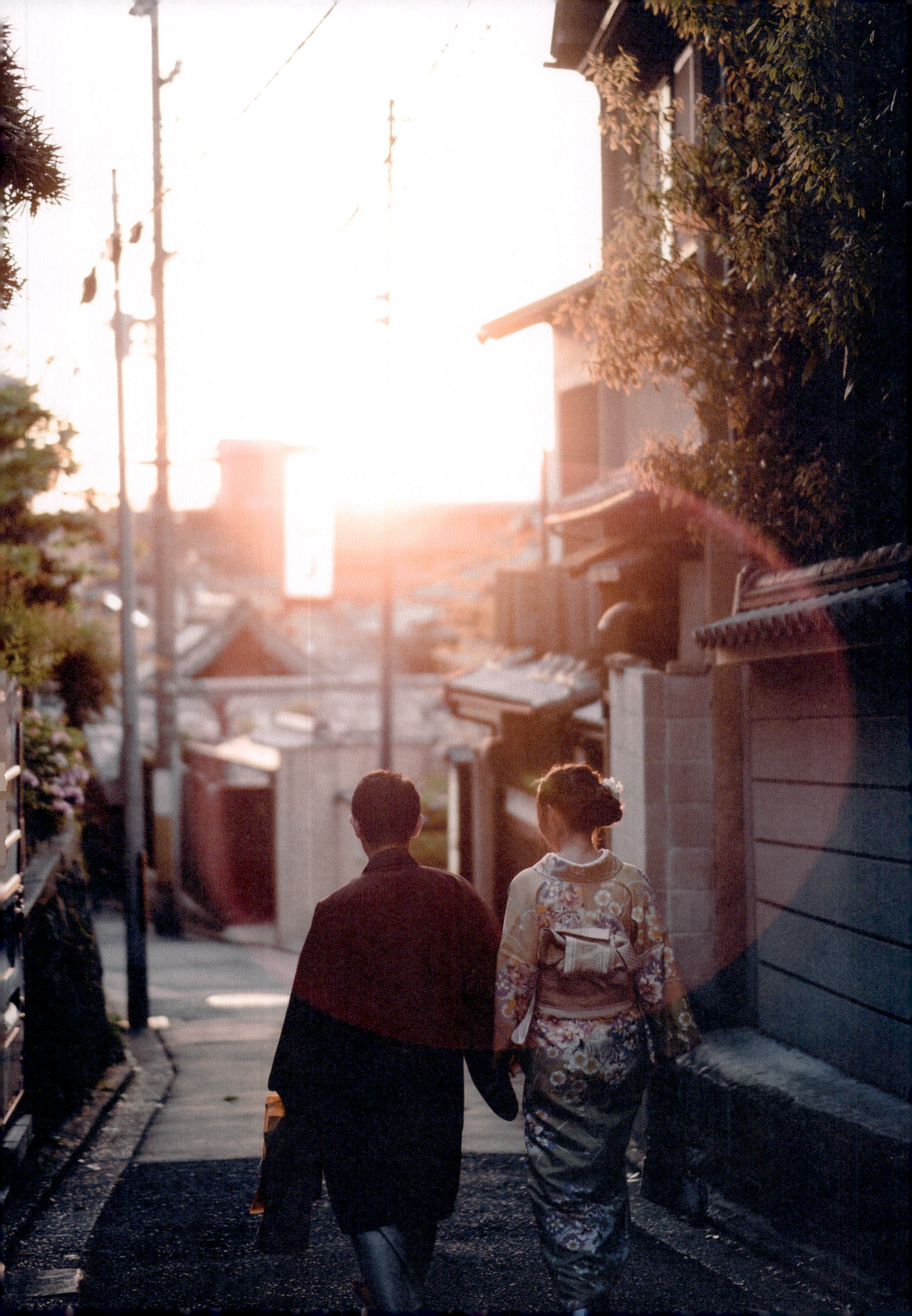

京にても
京なつかしや
ほとゝぎす

松尾　芭蕉

Now I am in the Capital

It seems so dear to me,

O, cuckoo.

Bashō

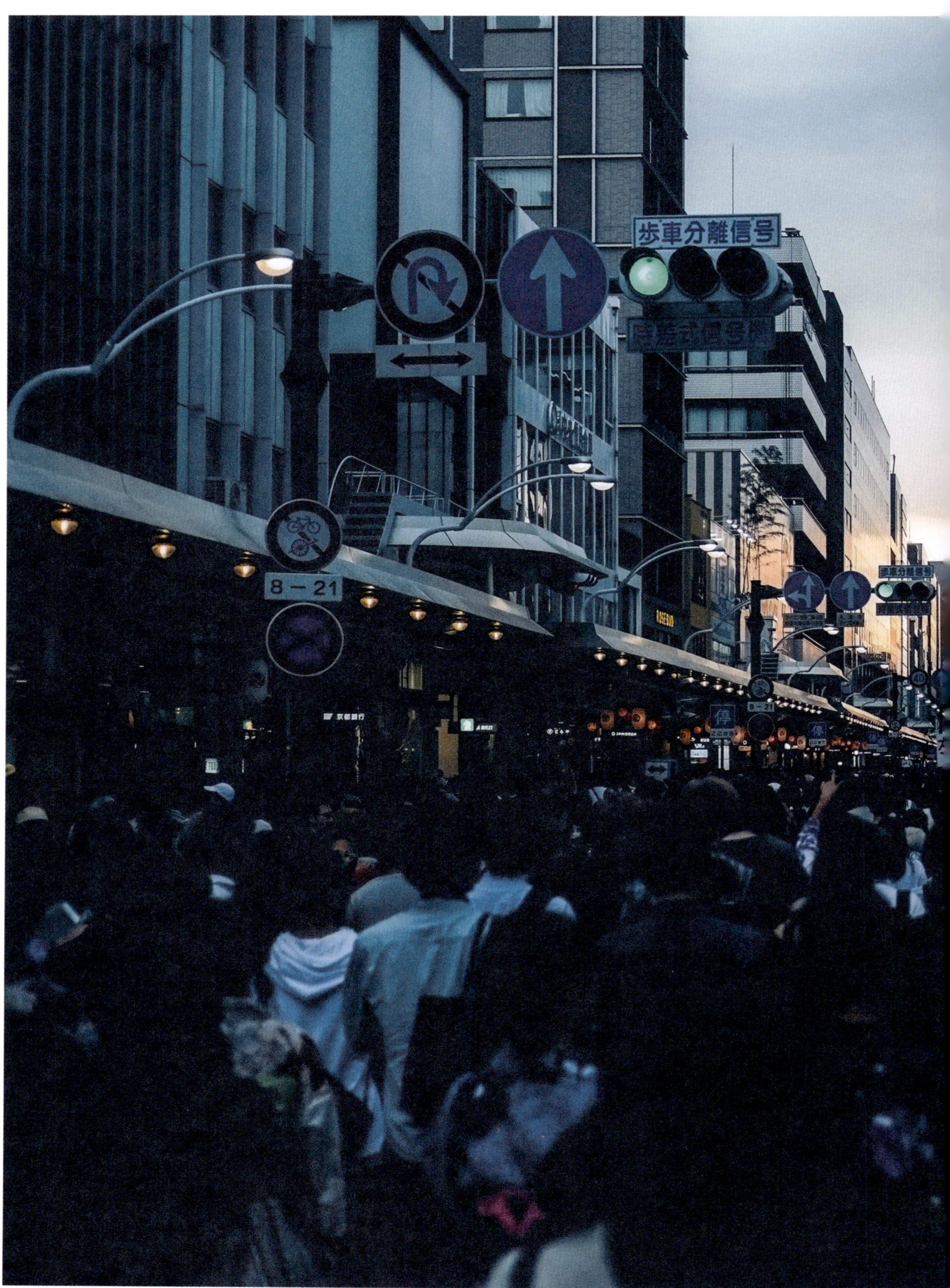
歩車分離信号
8－21

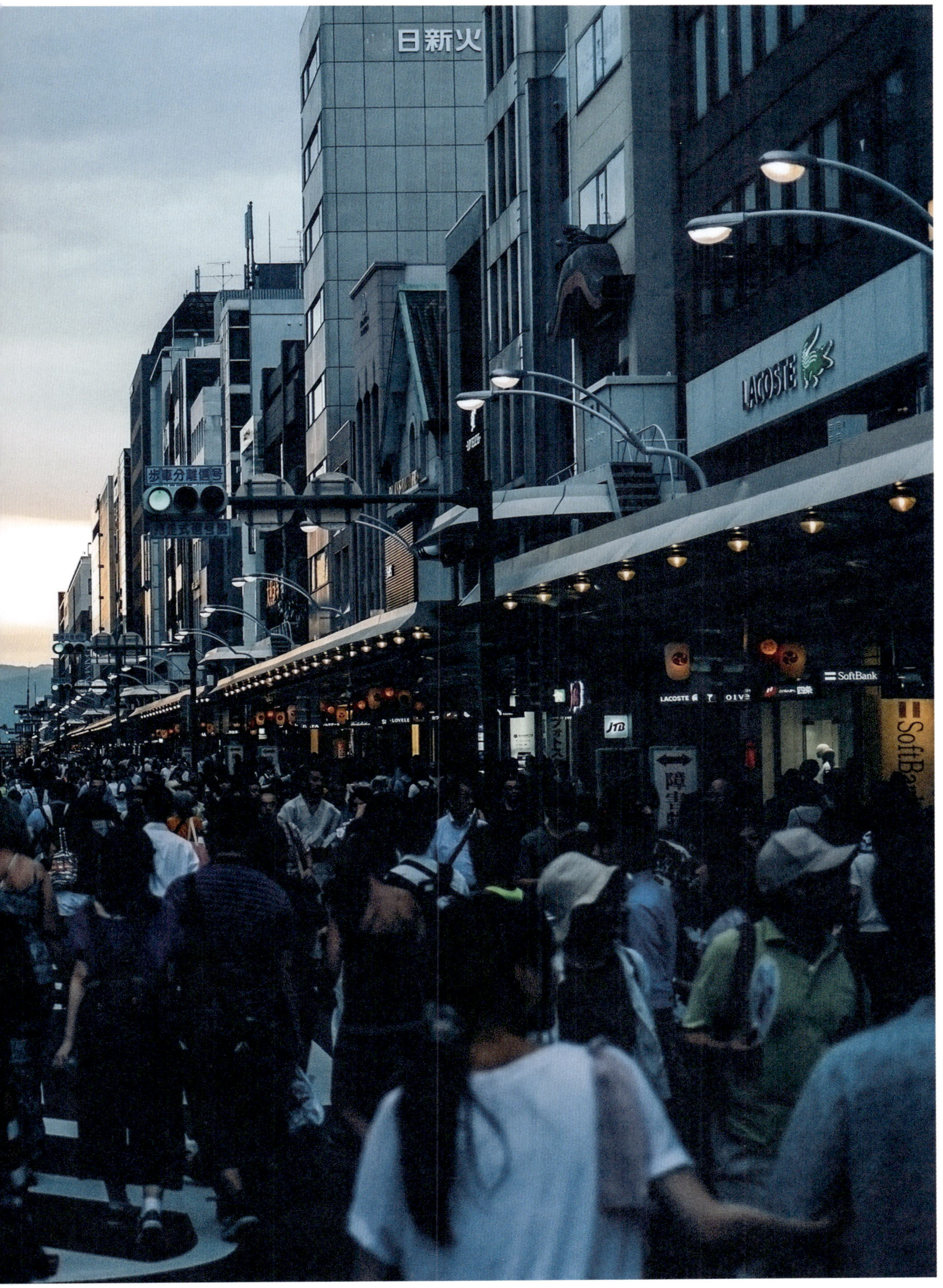
日新火
歩車分離信号
LACOSTE
SoftBank
JTB
SoftBank

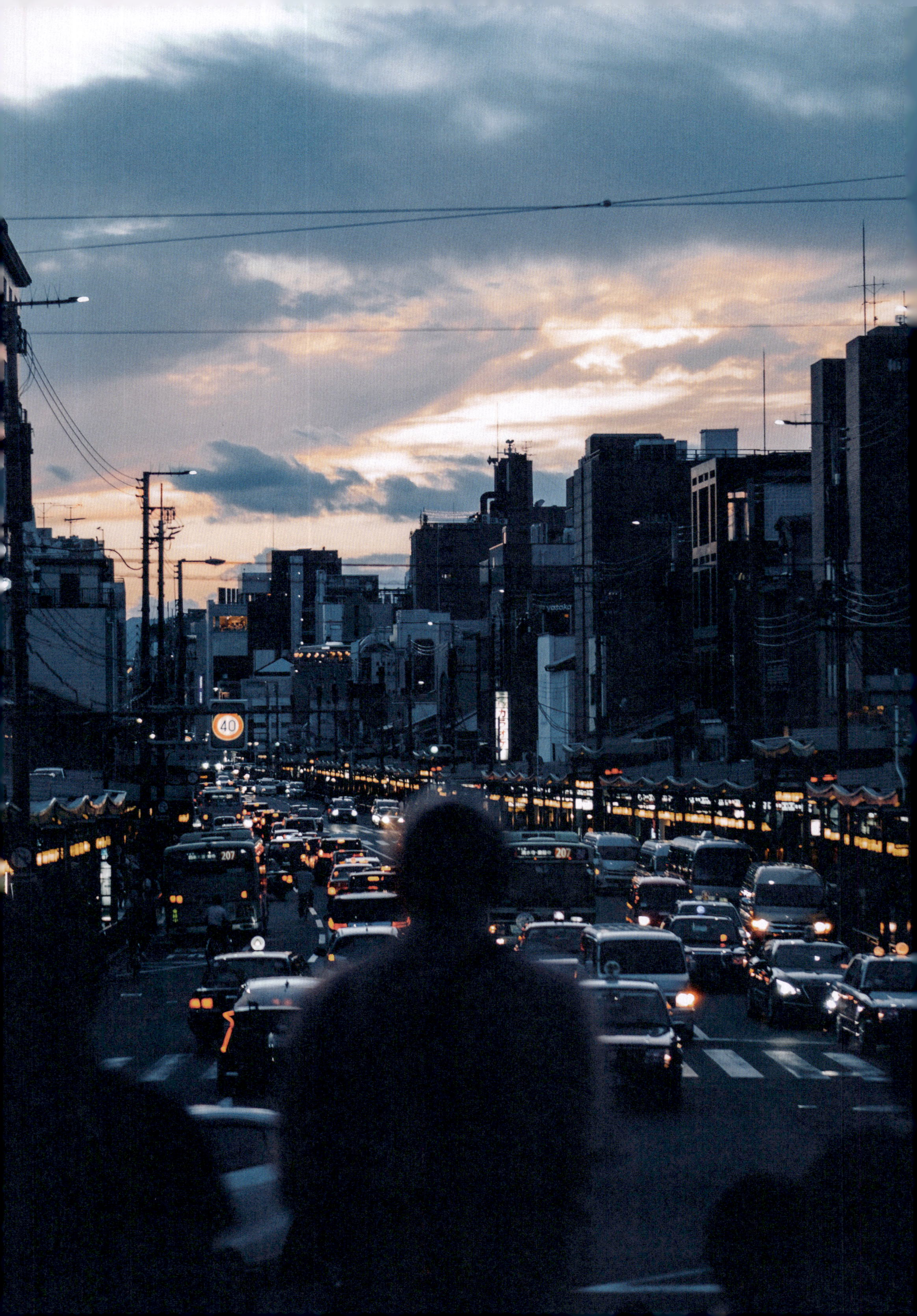
yasaka
40
207
207

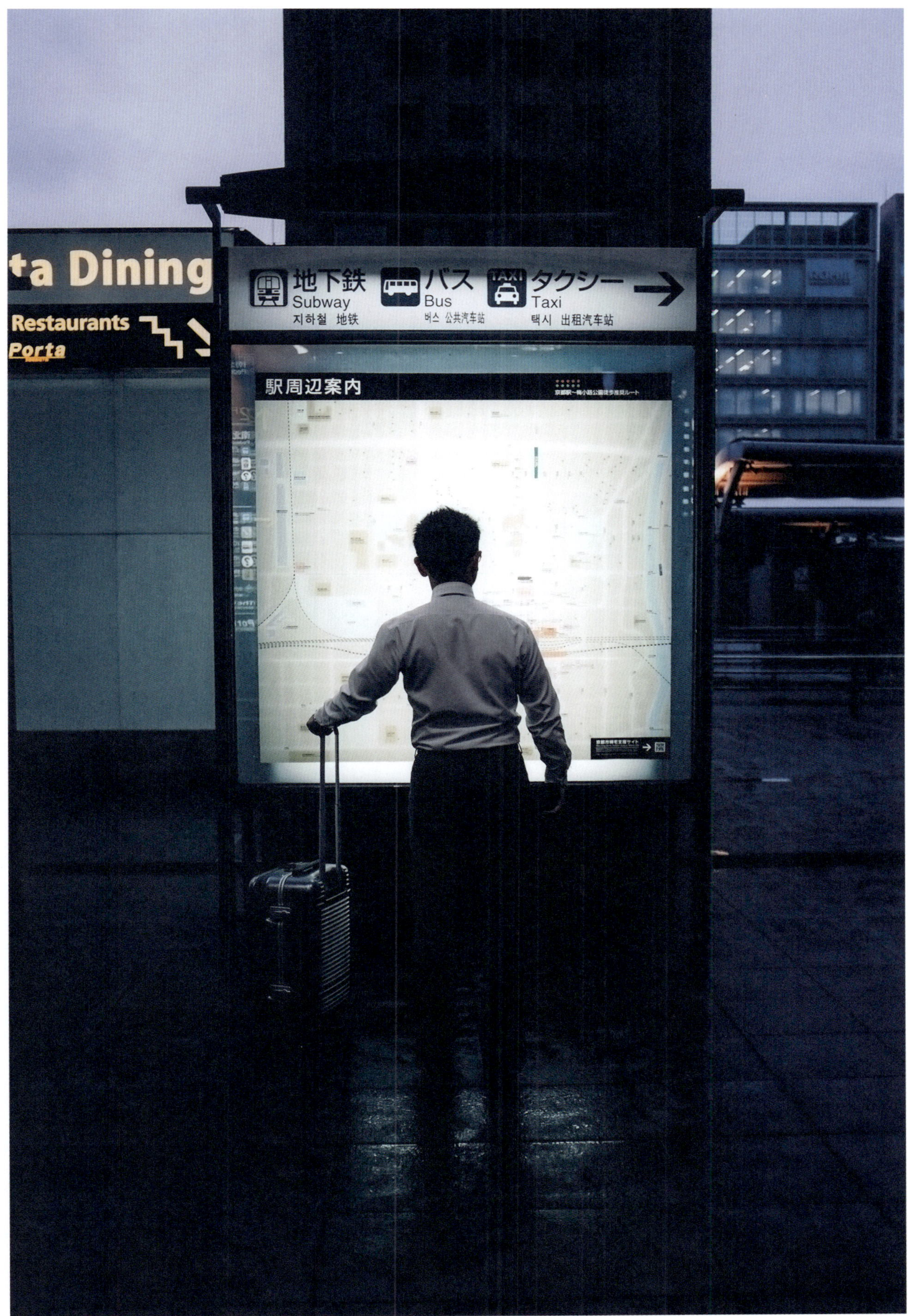
ta Dining
Restaurants
Porta
地下鉄
Subway
지하철 地铁
バス
Bus
버스 公共汽车站
TAXI
タクシー
Taxi
택시 出租汽车站
駅周辺案内

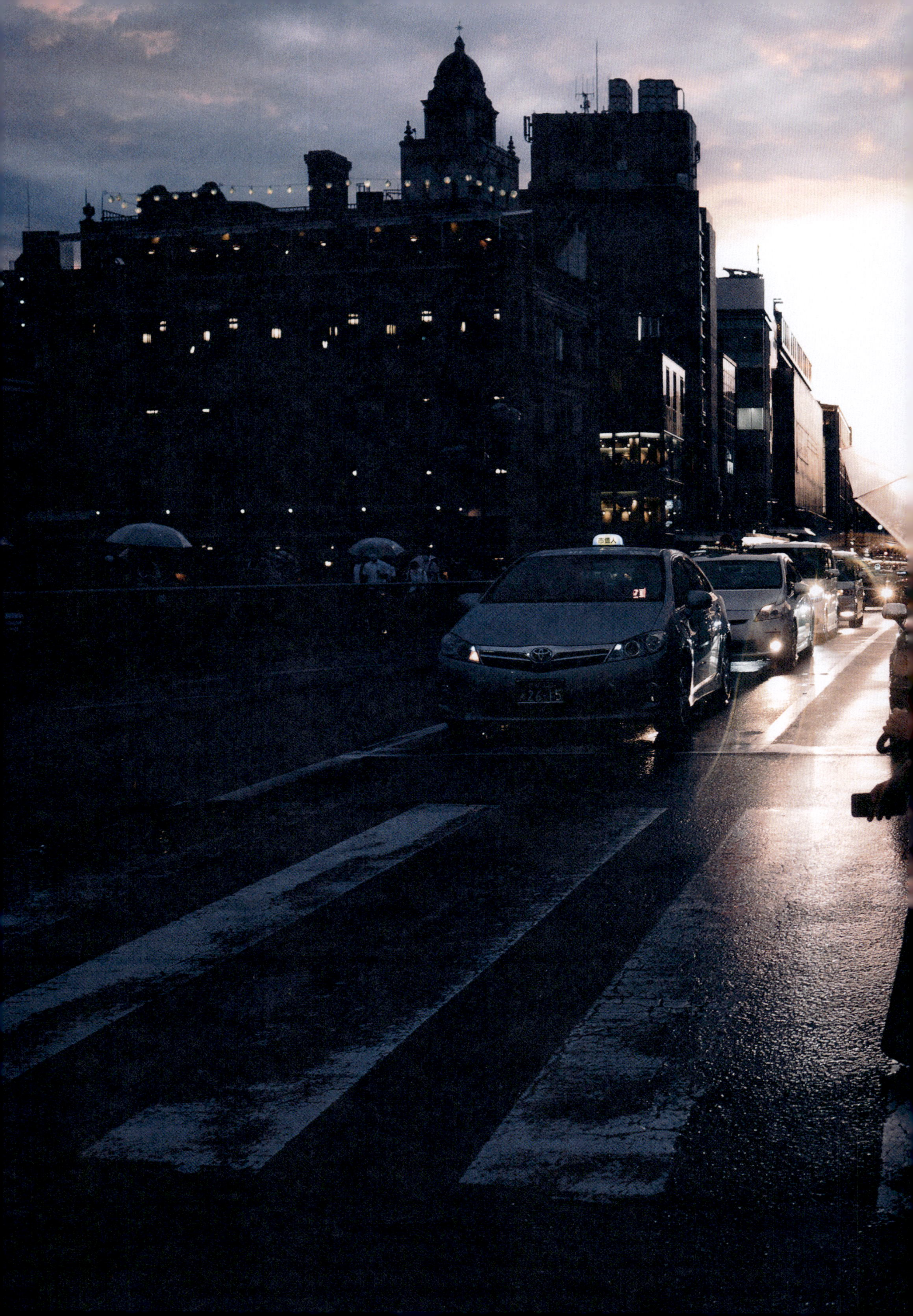

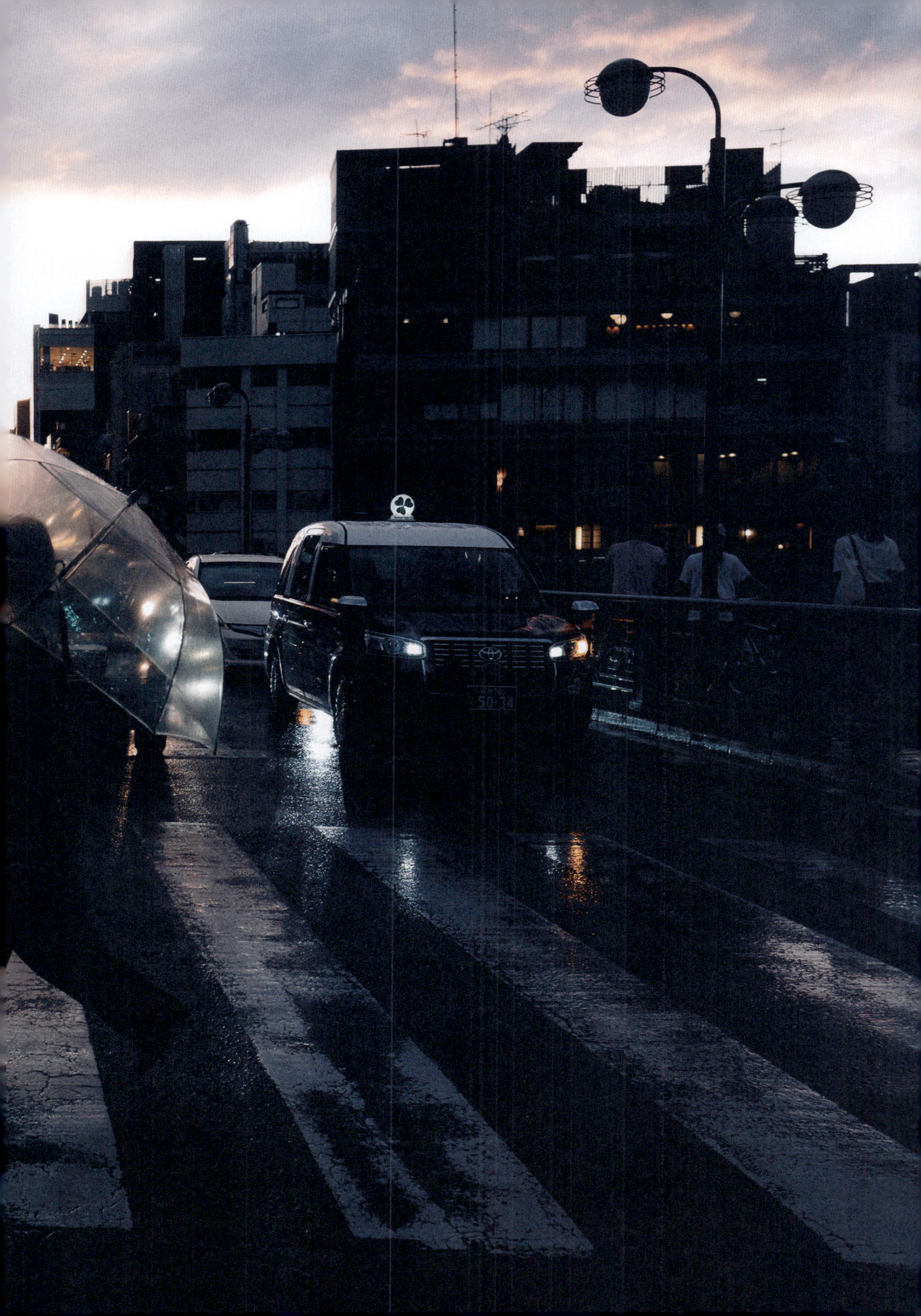
50-34

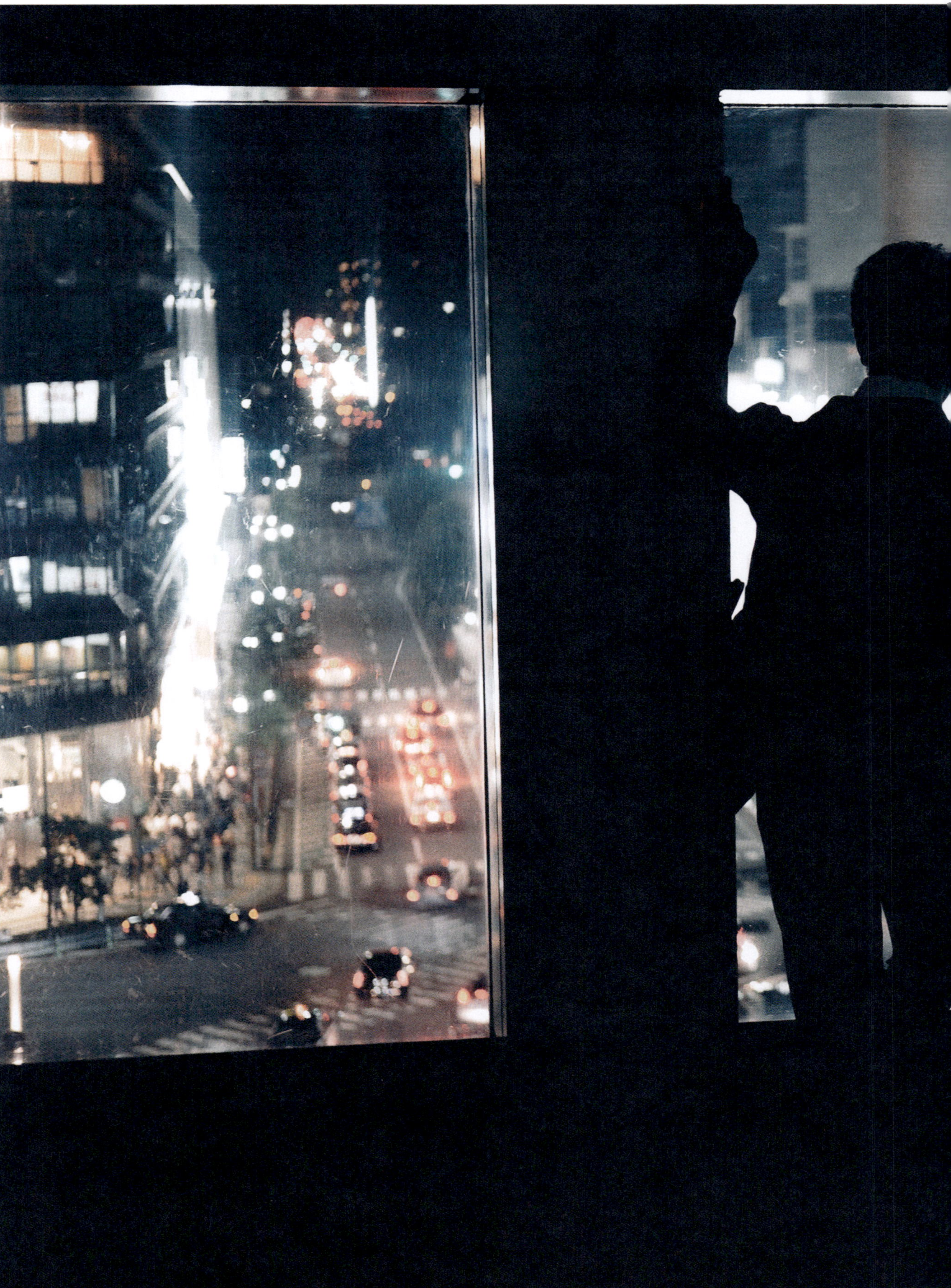

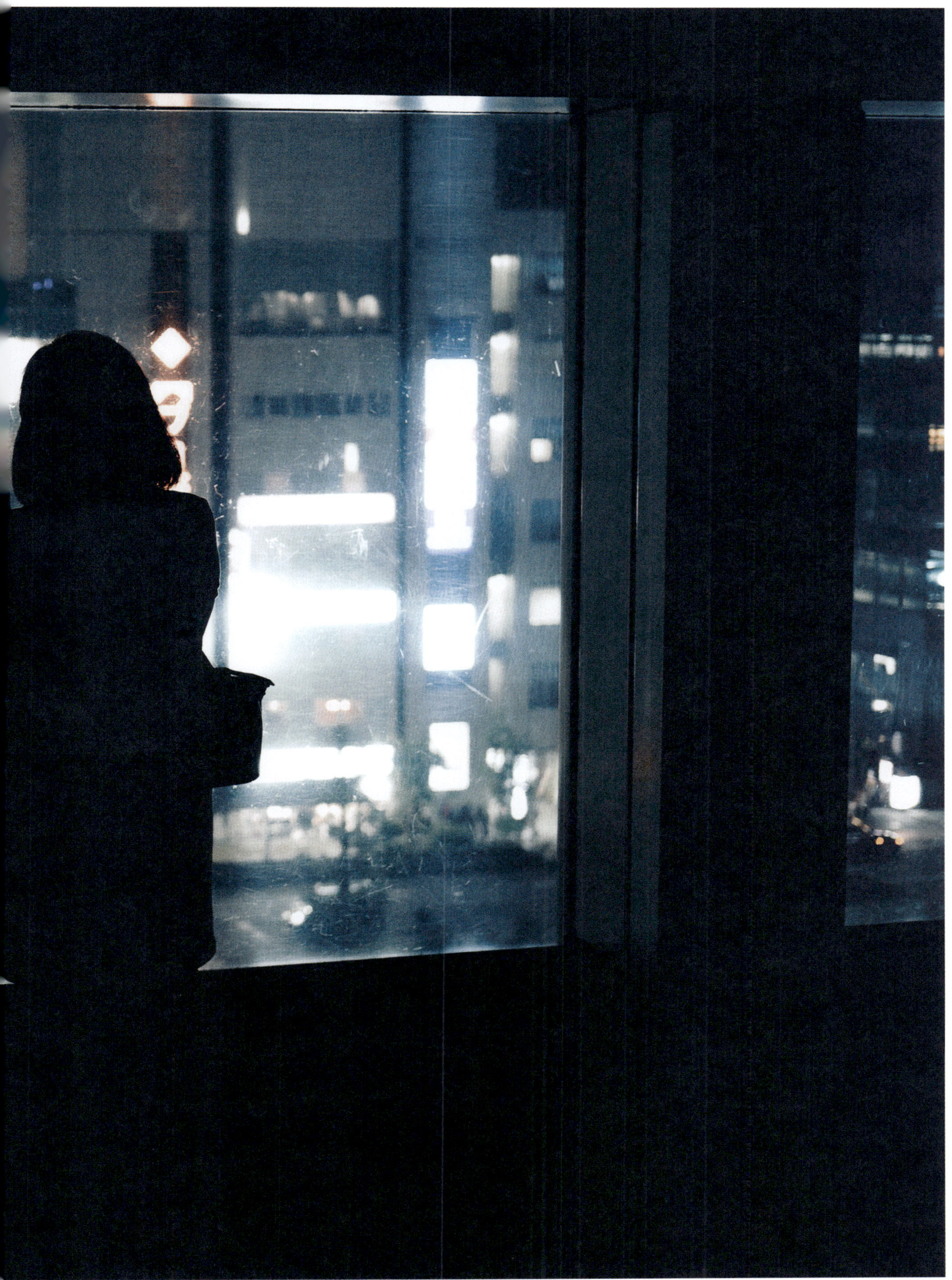

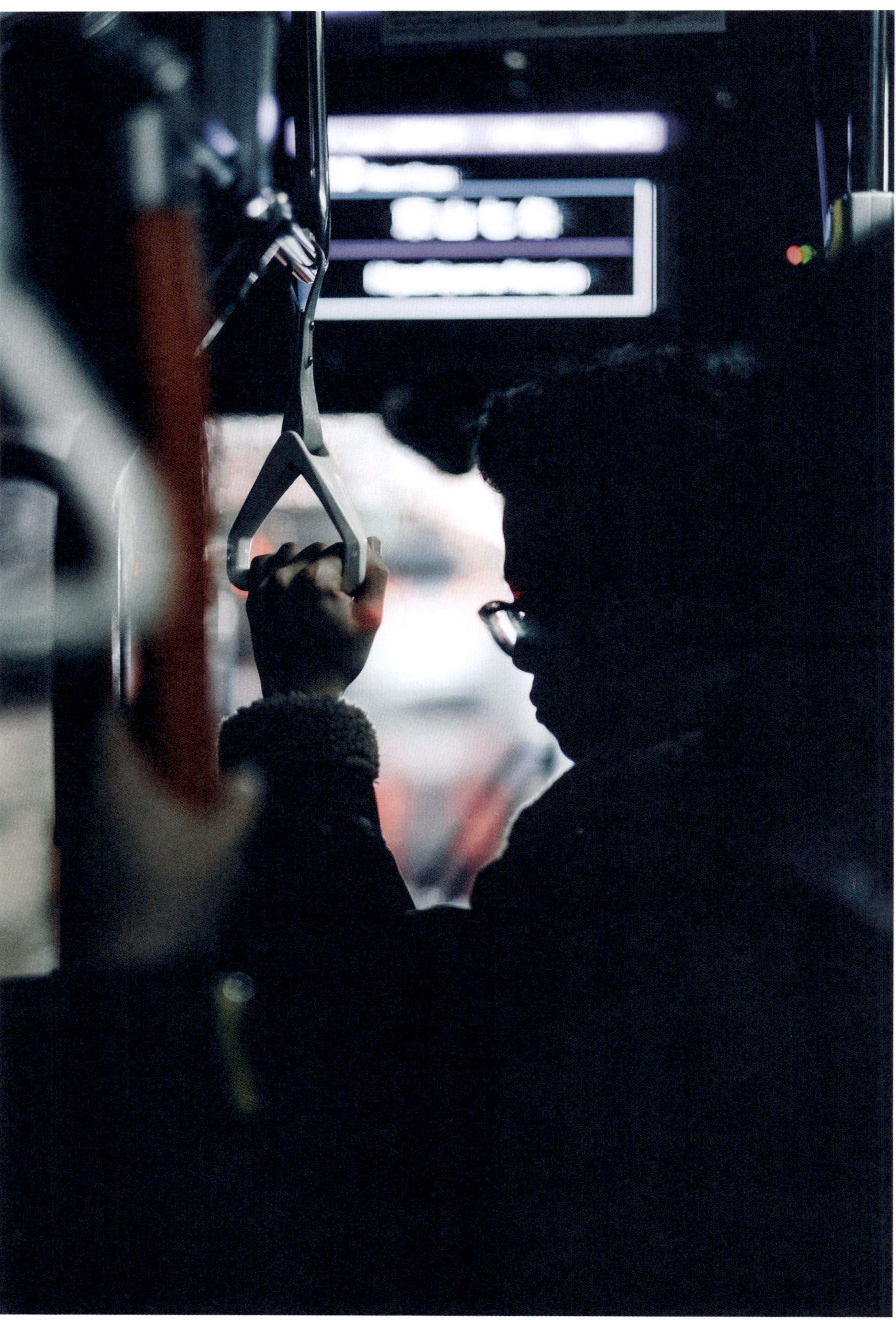

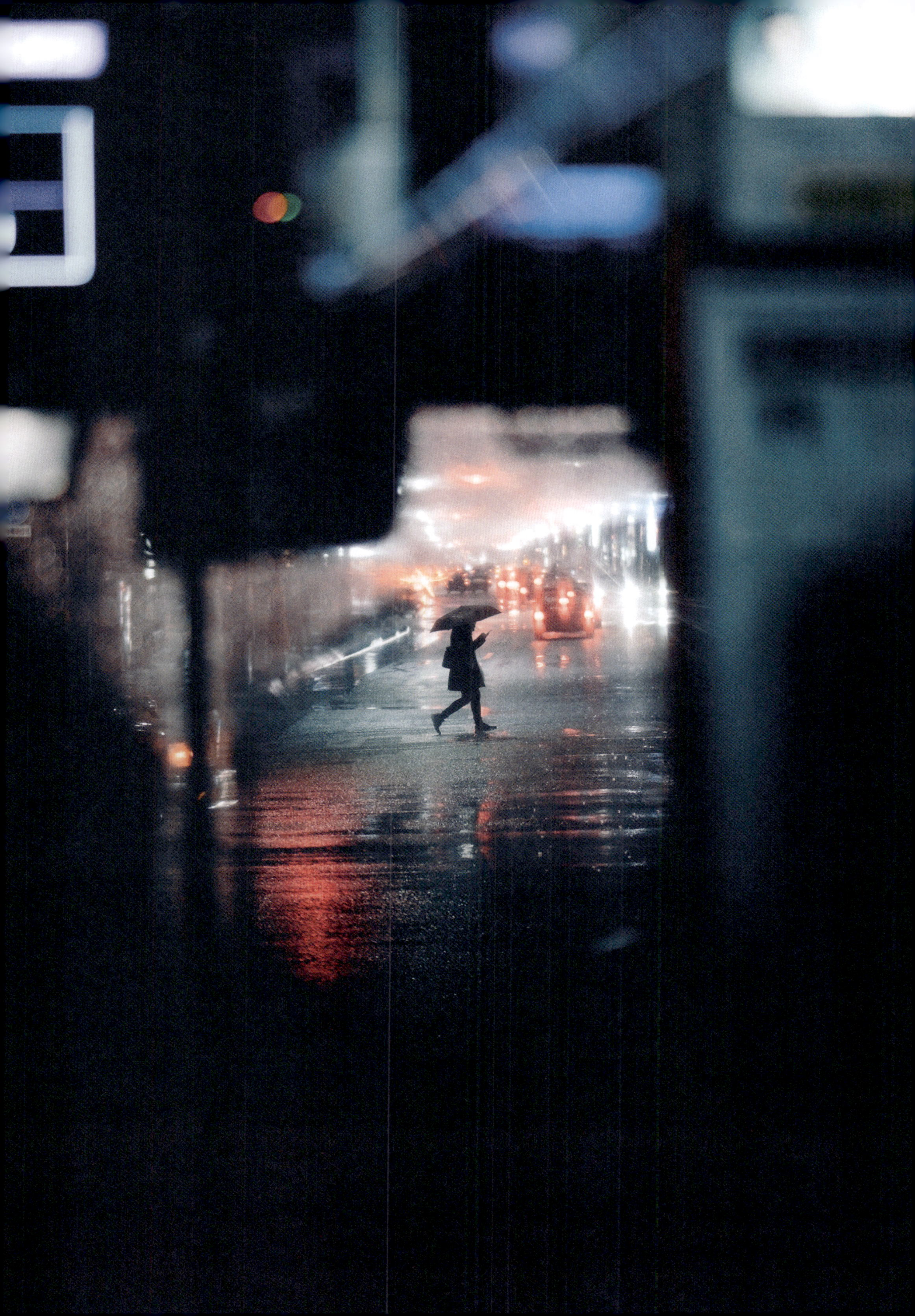

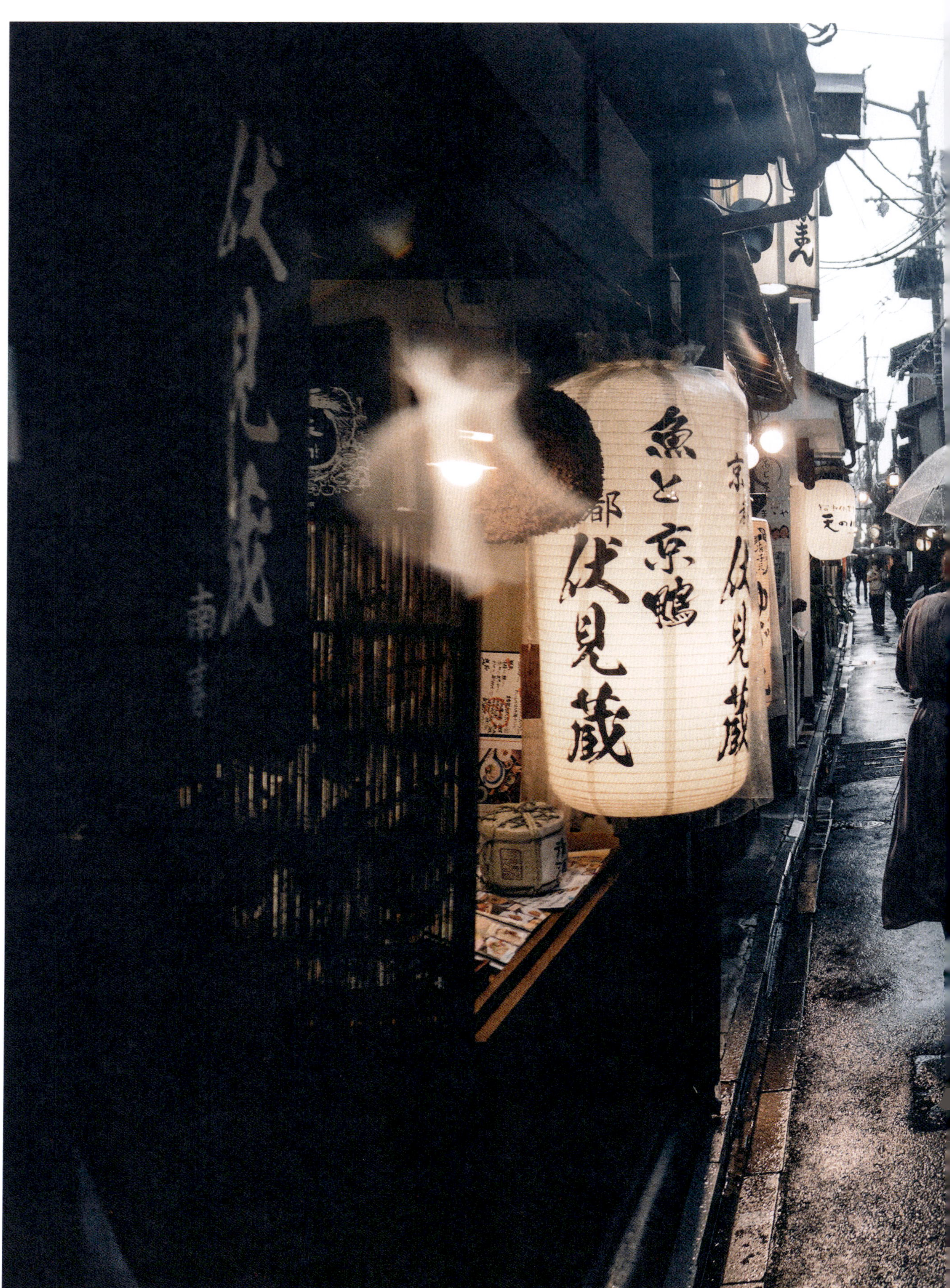
伏見蔵
魚と京鴨
都伏見蔵
伏見蔵

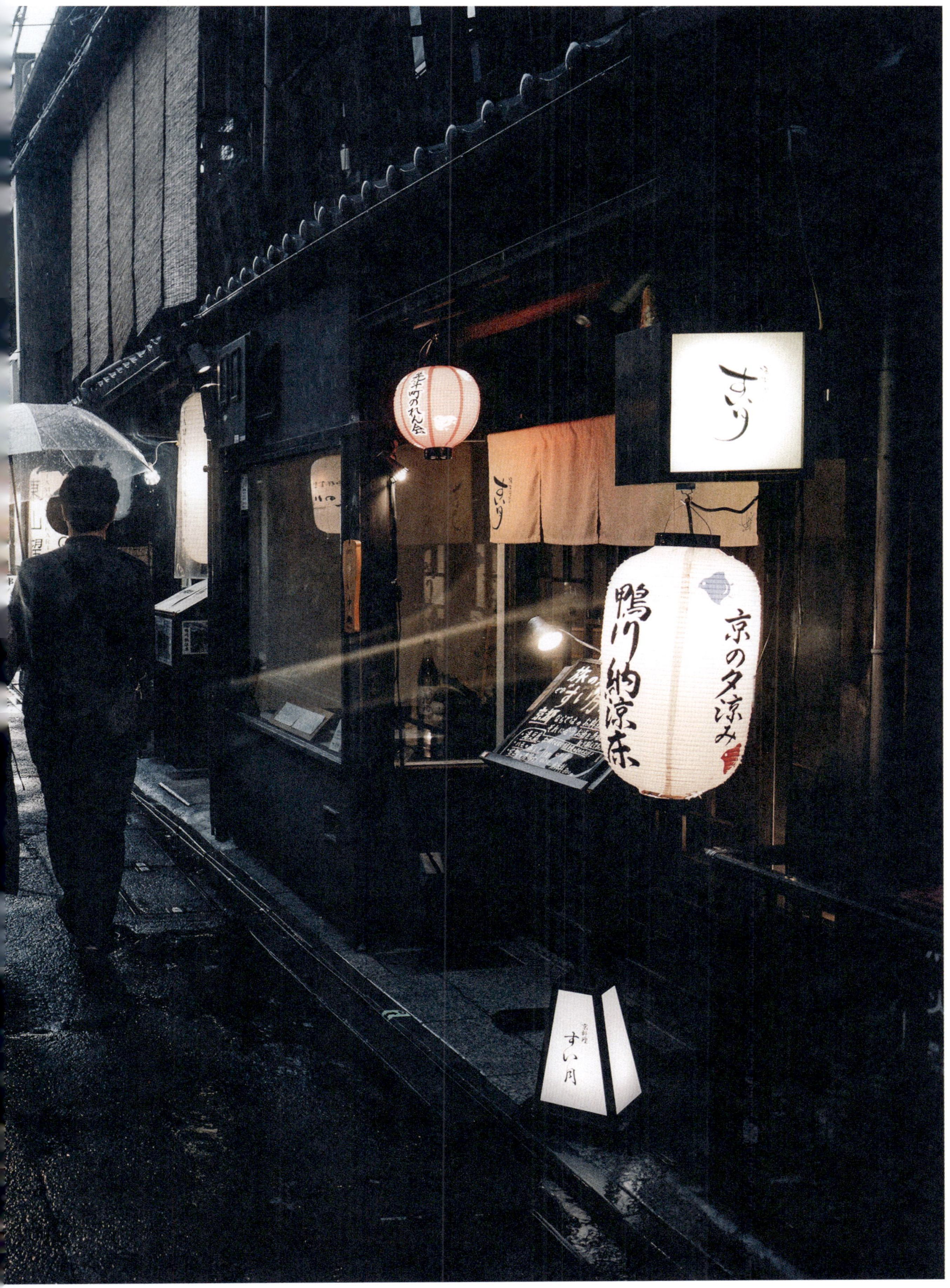
鴨川納涼床
京の夕涼み
すい月

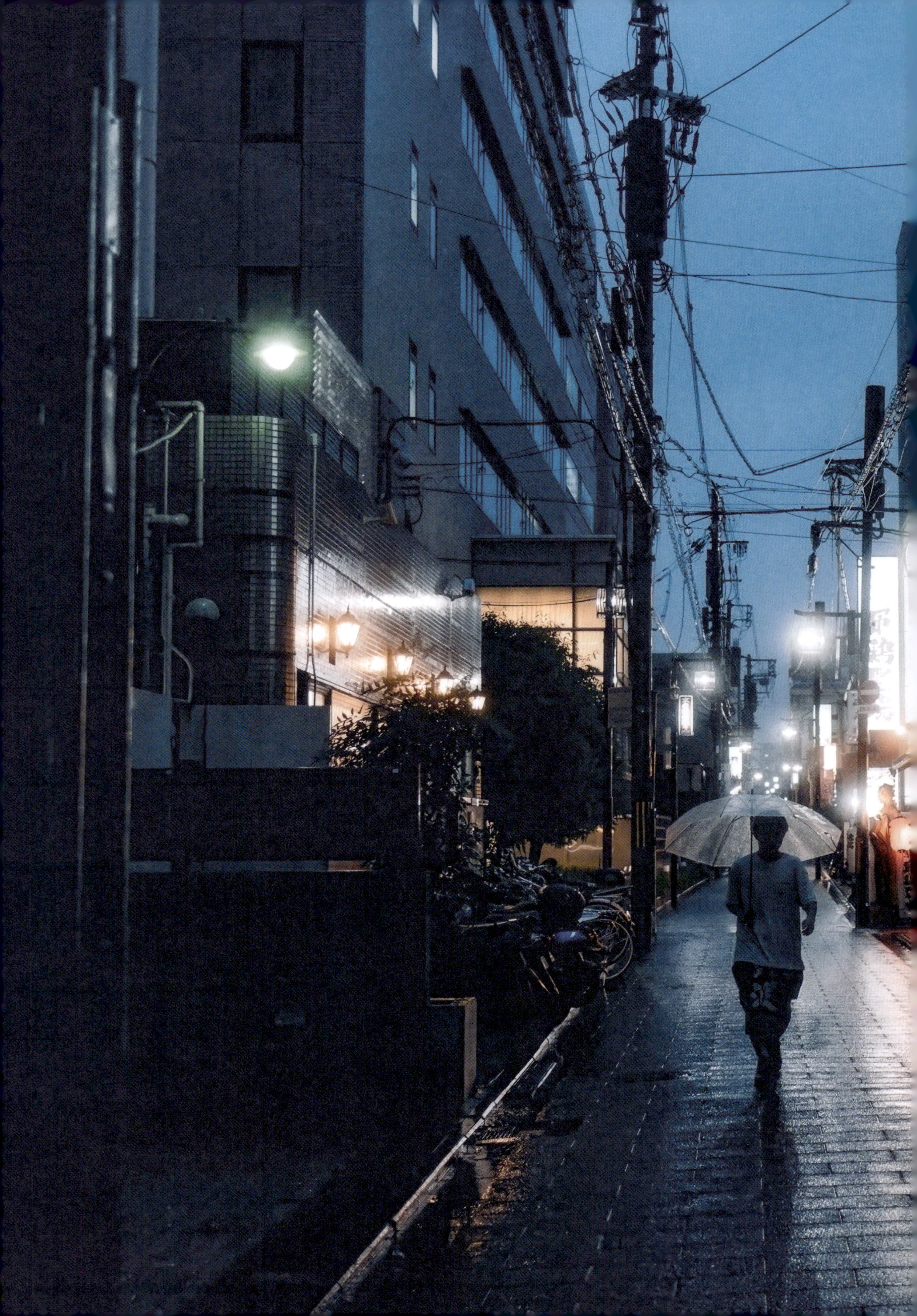

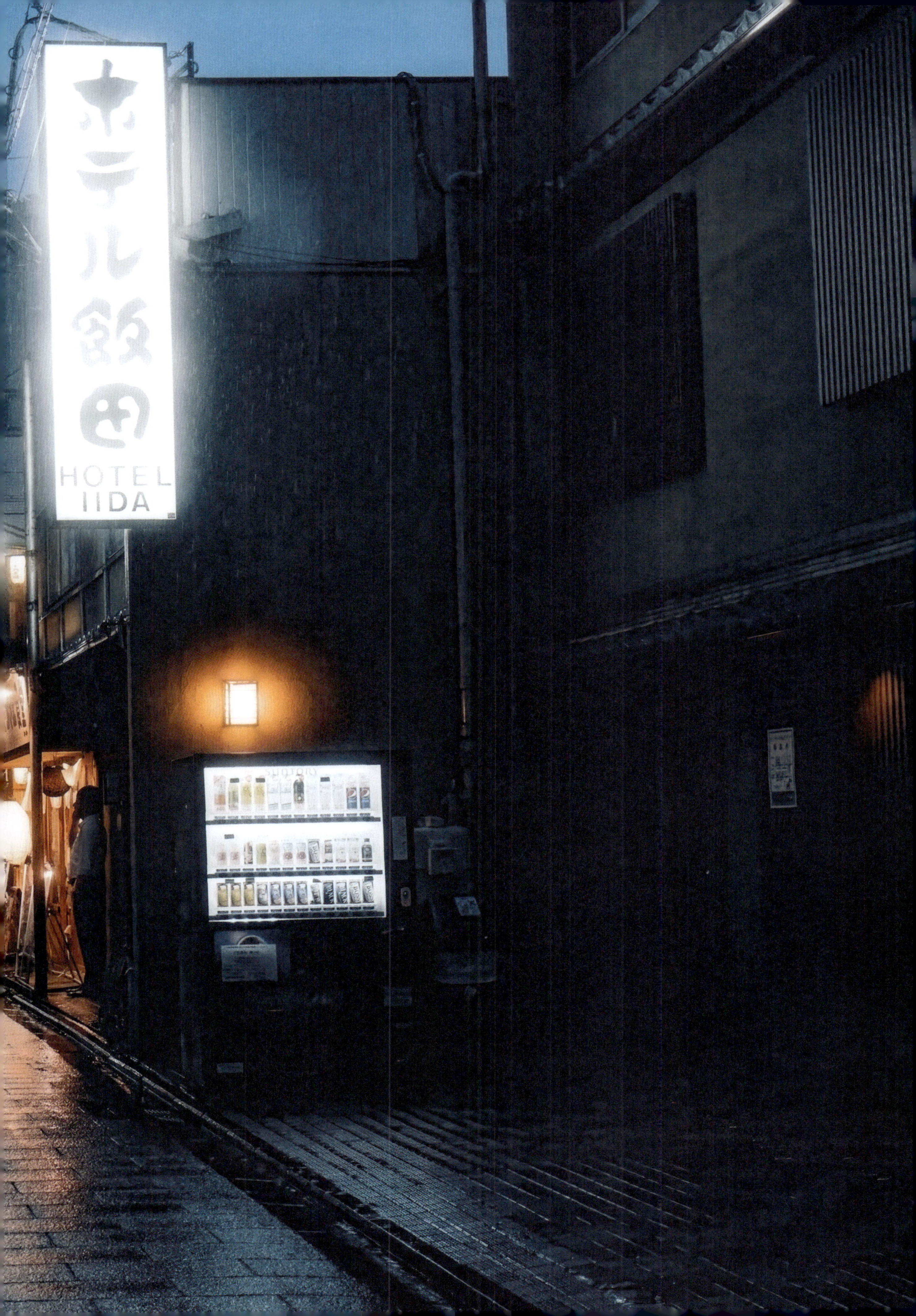
ホテル飯田
HOTEL
IIDA

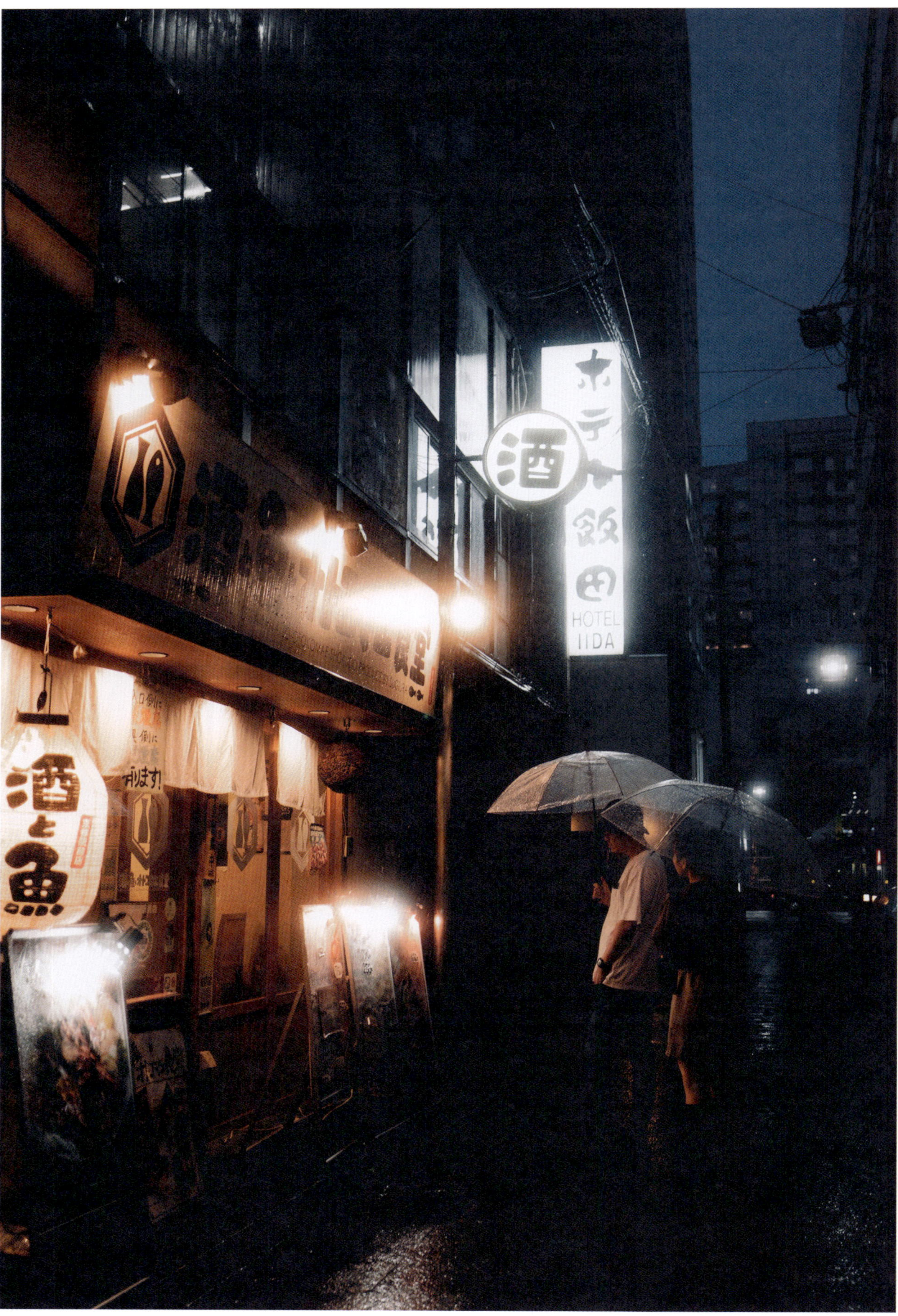
酒
飯田
HOTEL
IIDA
酒と魚

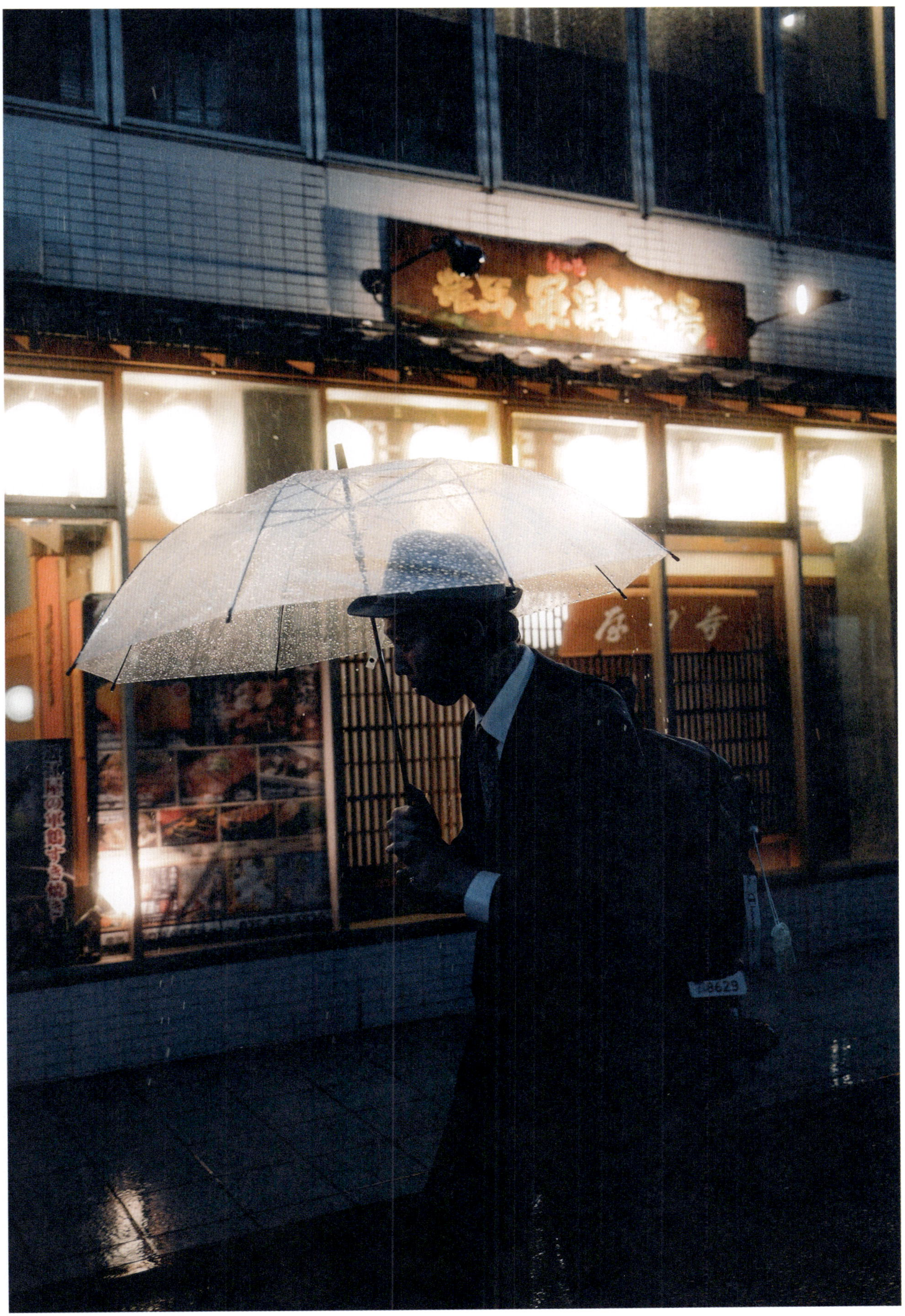

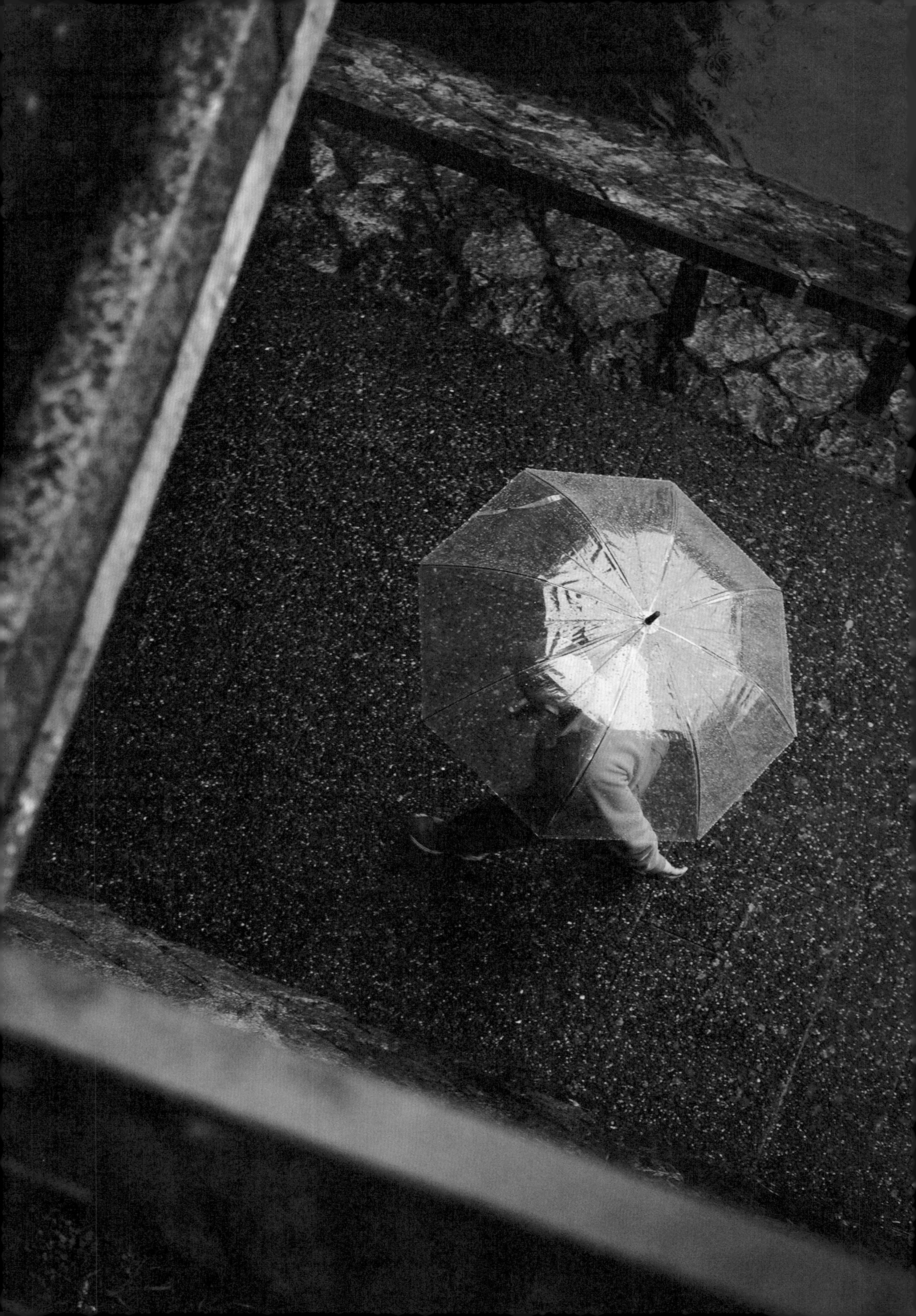

傘の雫も
かすむ
都哉

小林一茶

Paper umbrellas

dripping . . .

misty Kyoto

Kobayashi Issa

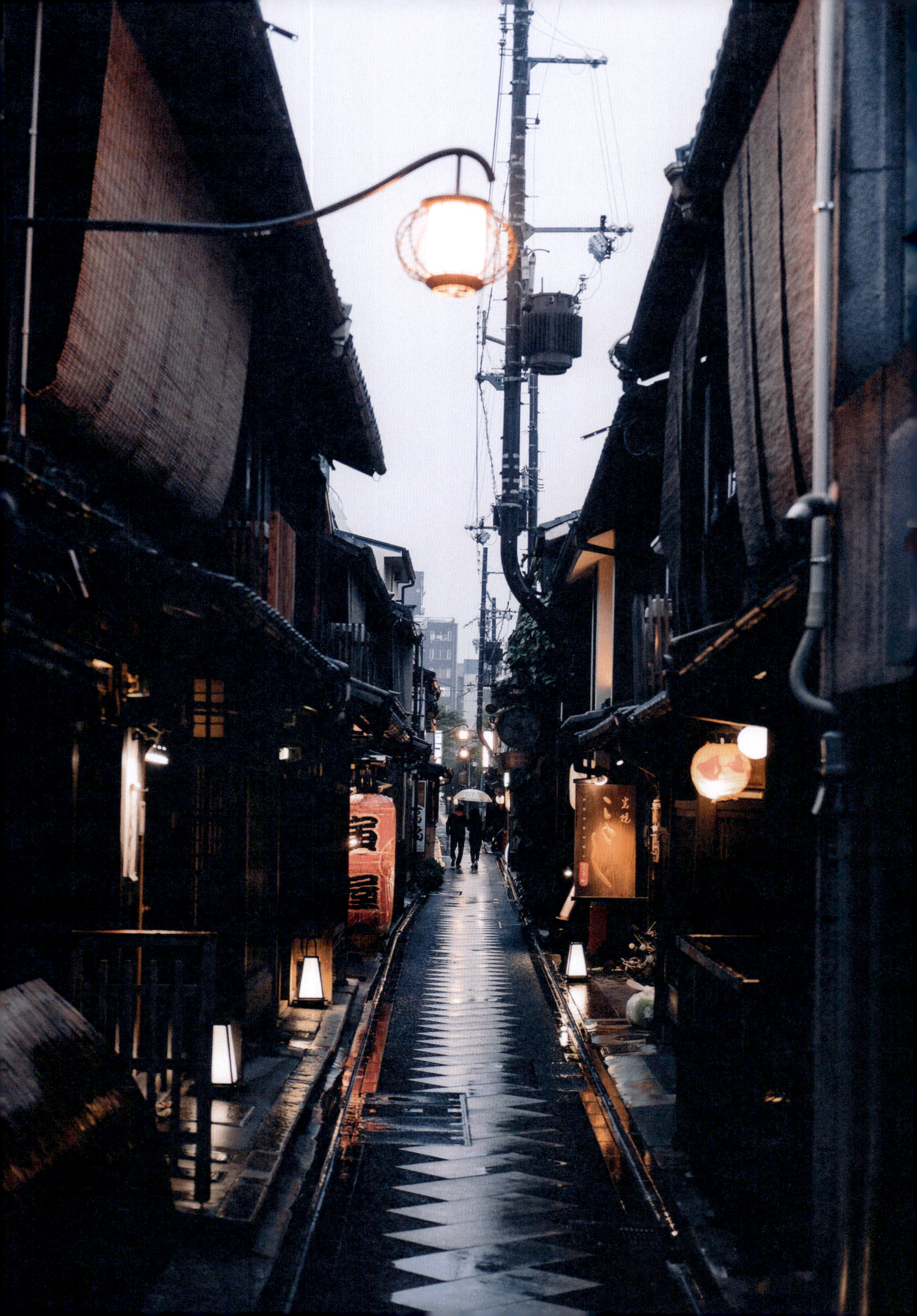

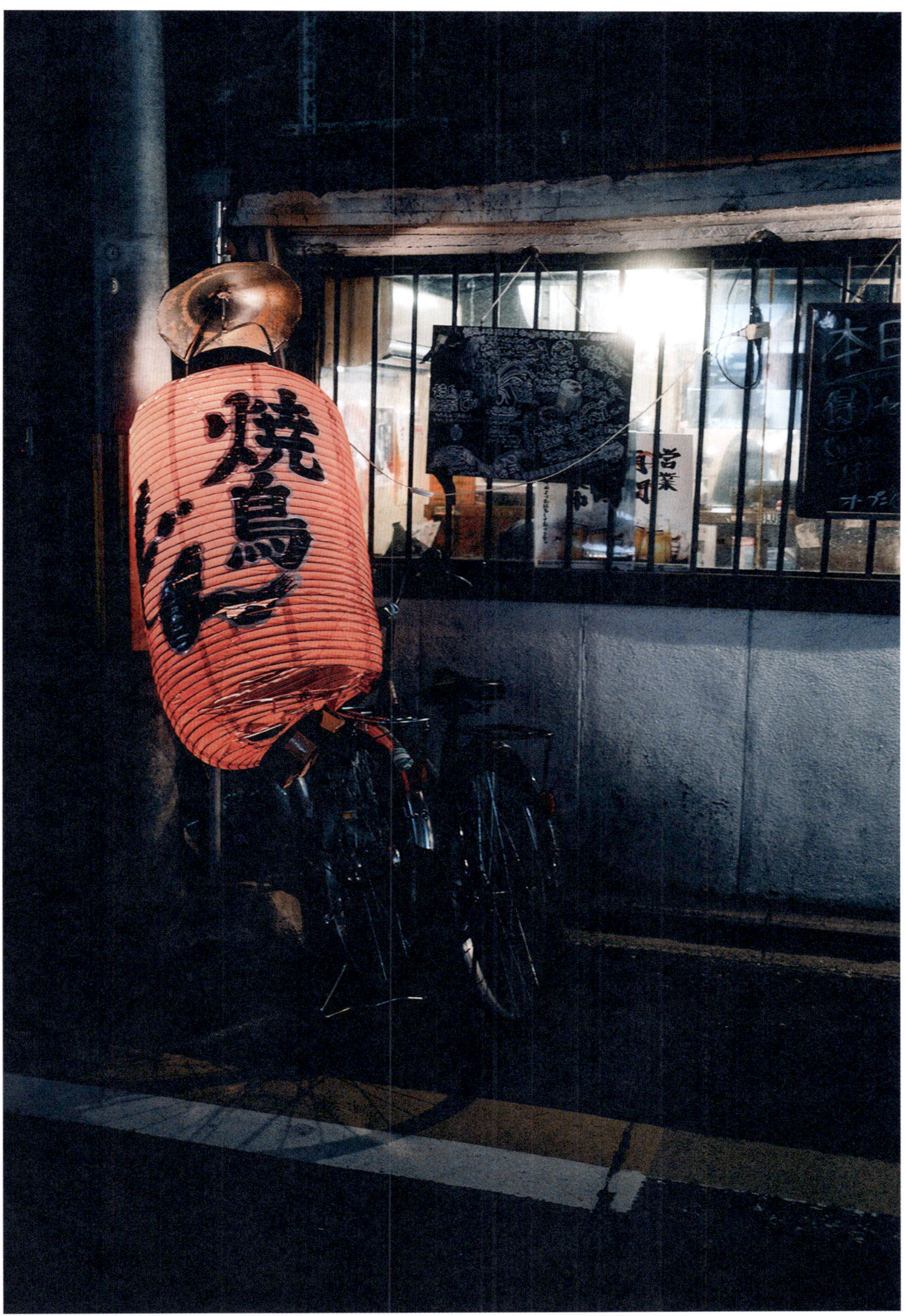
焼鳥
本日

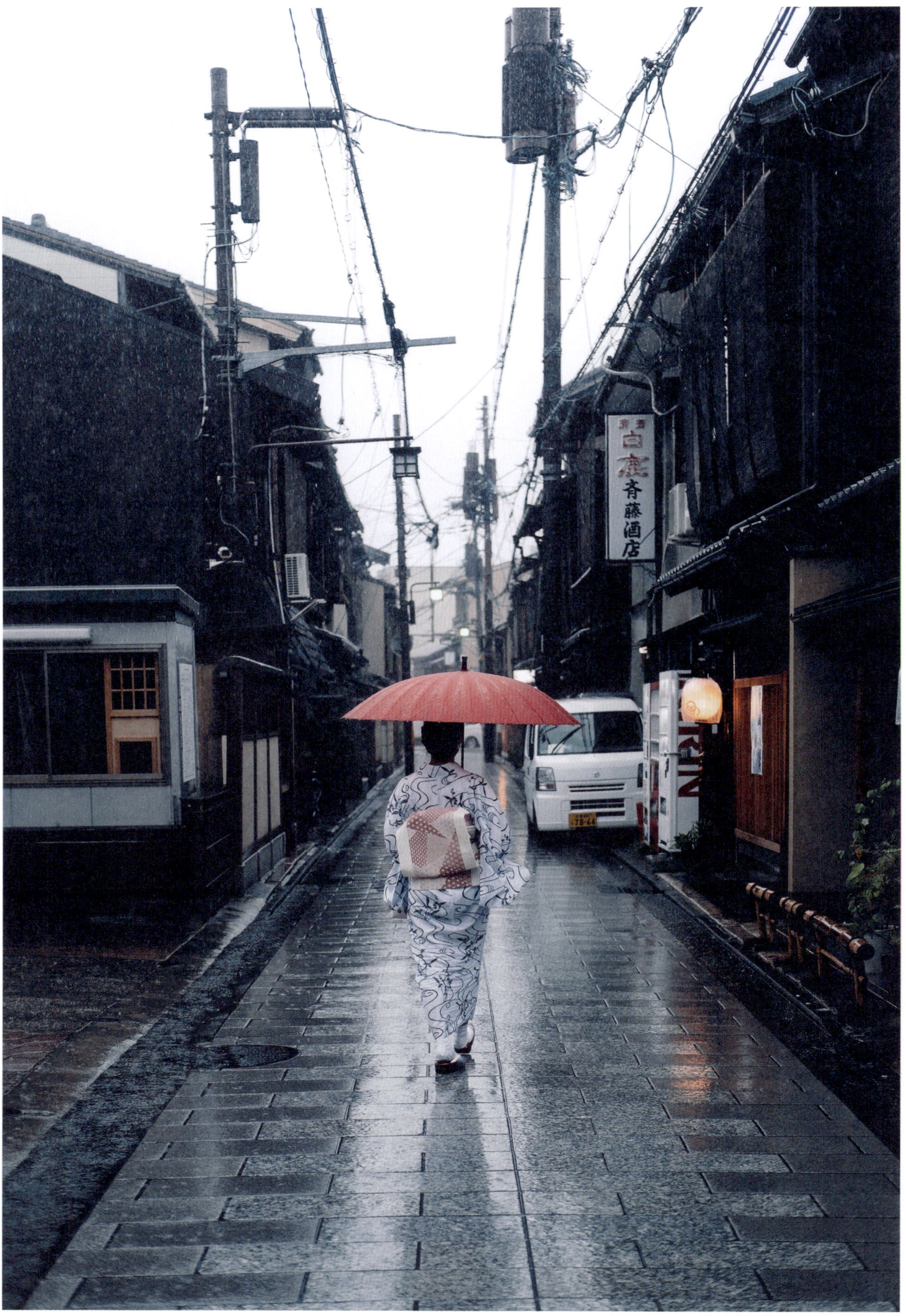
白鹿
斉藤酒店

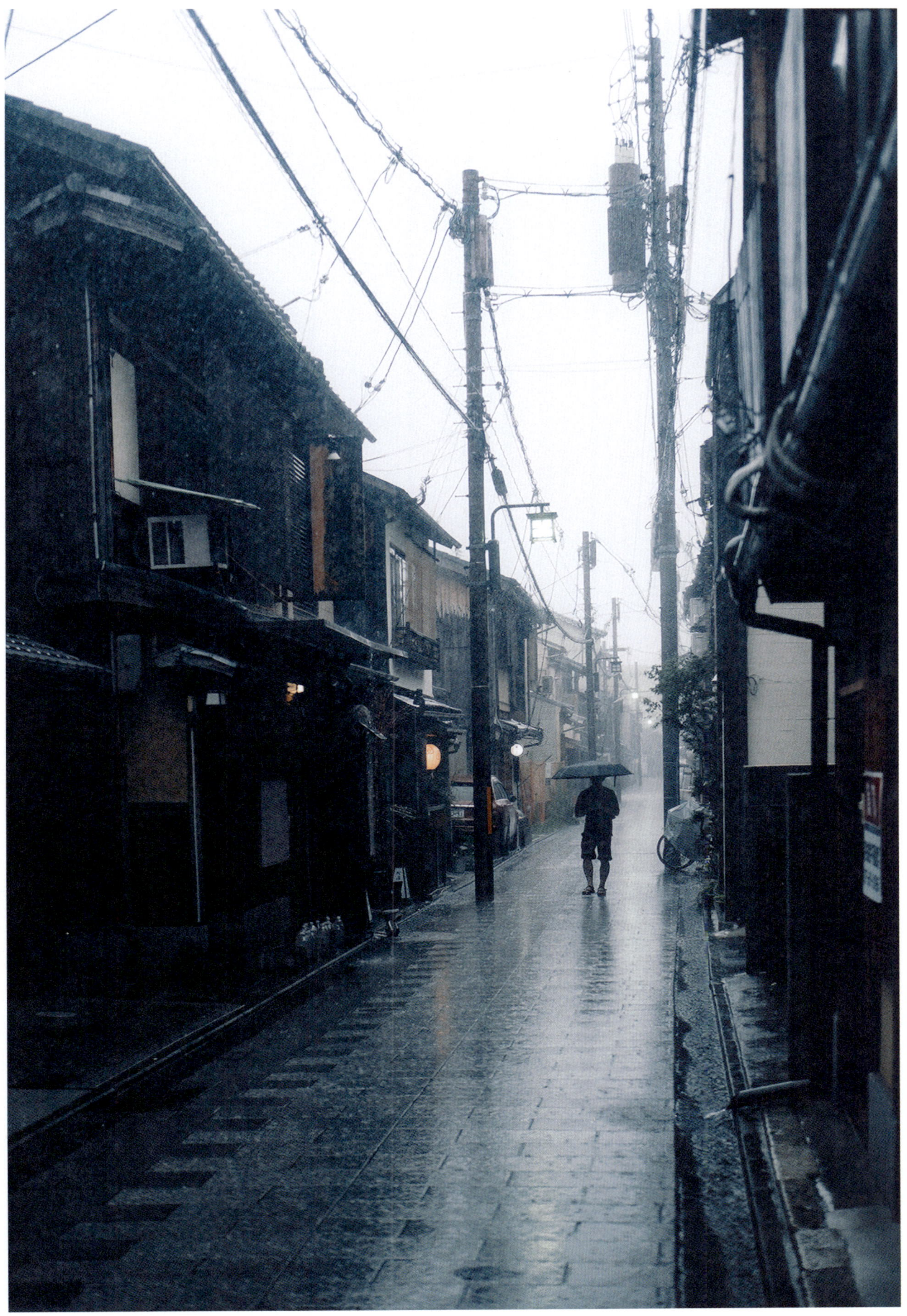

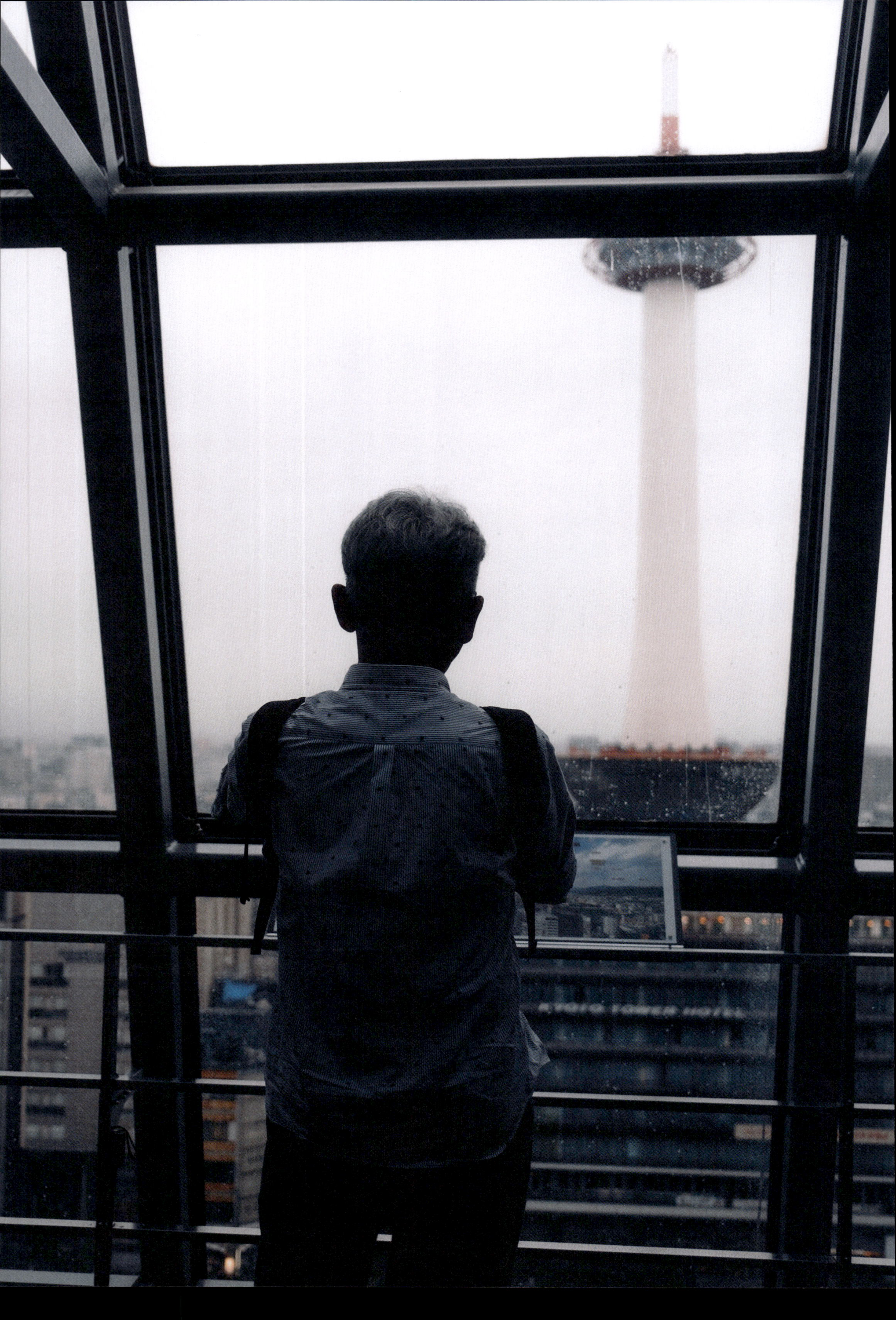

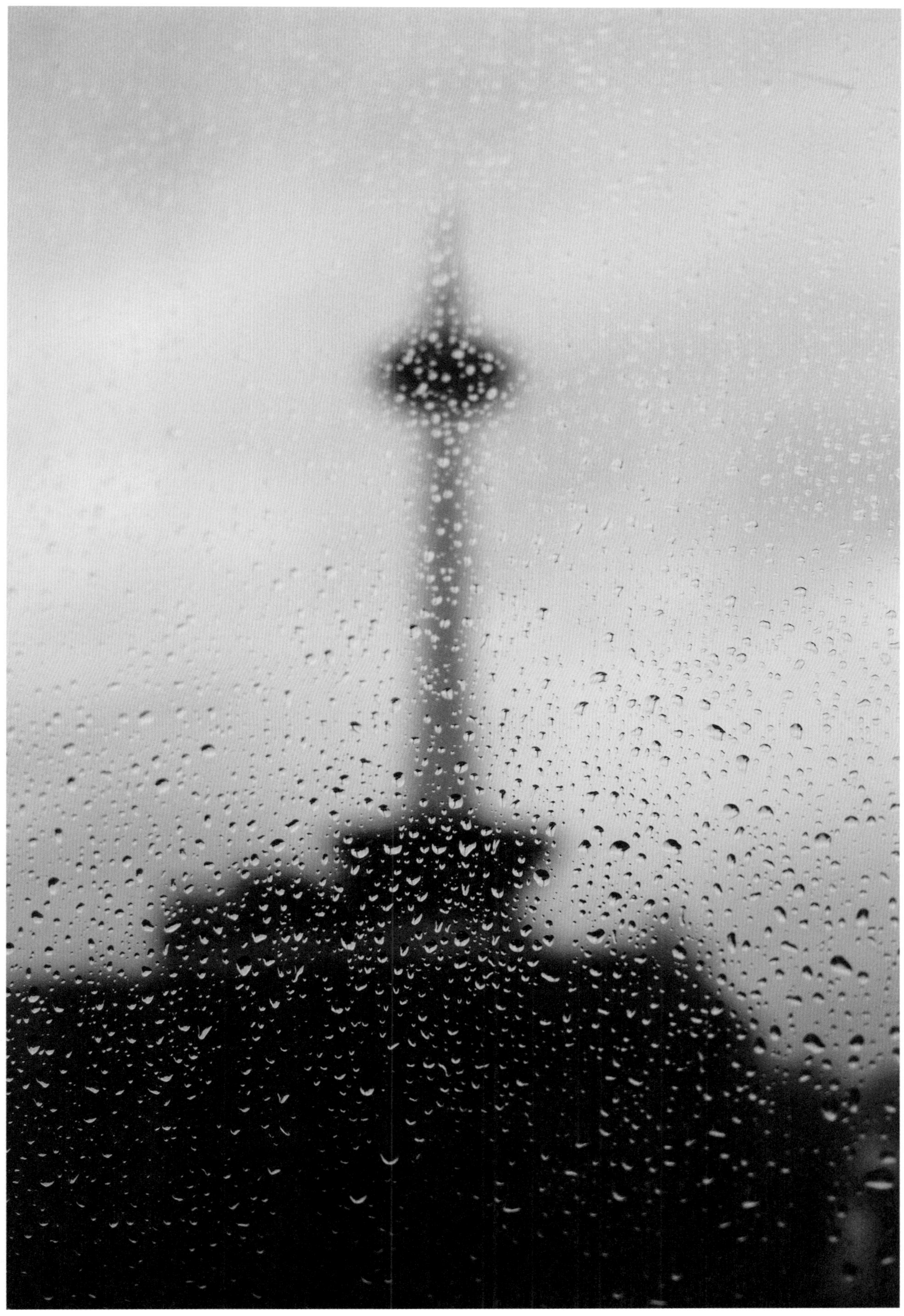

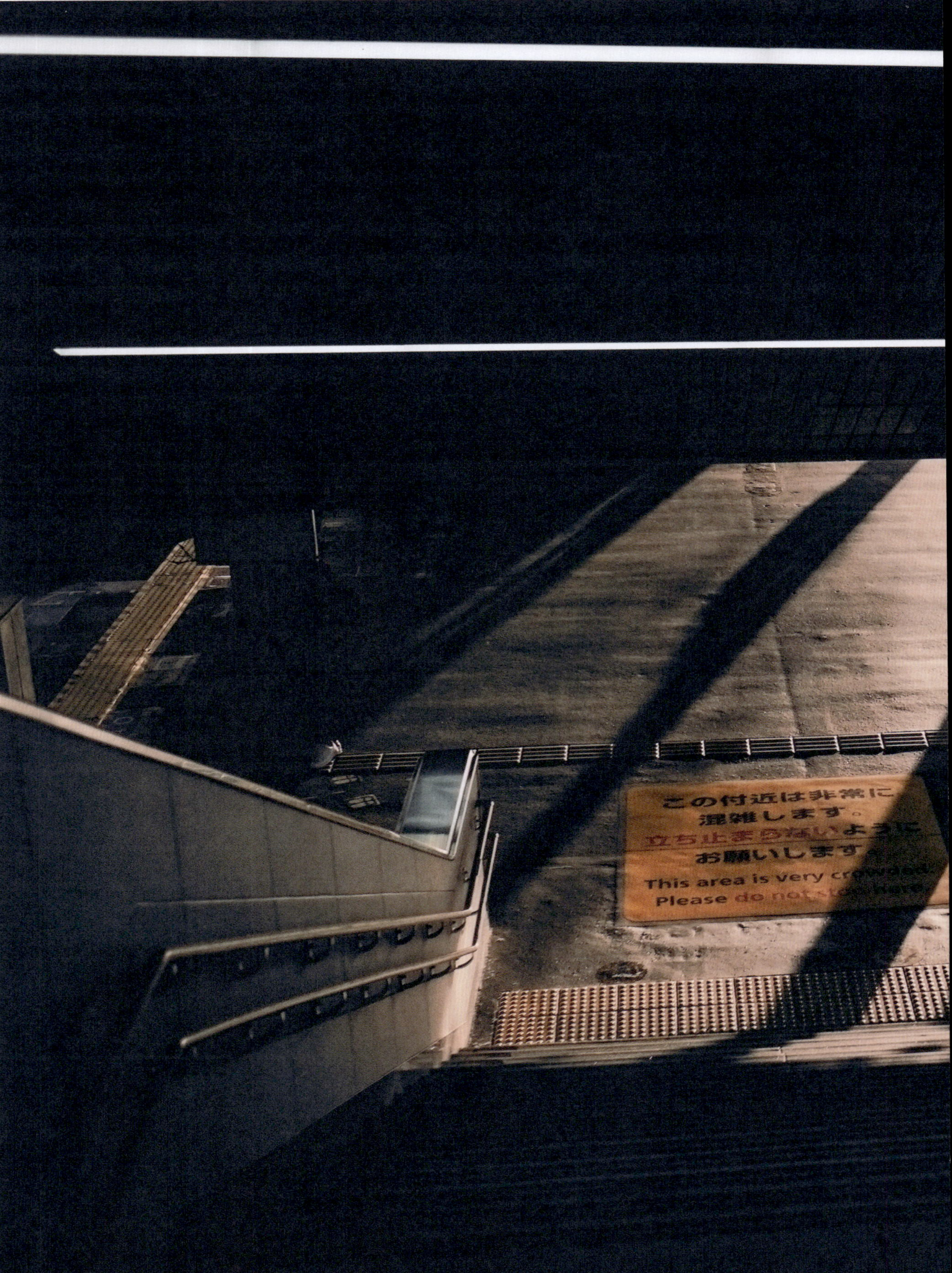
この付近は非常に
混雑します。
立ち止まらないように
お願いします。
This area is very crowded.
Please do not

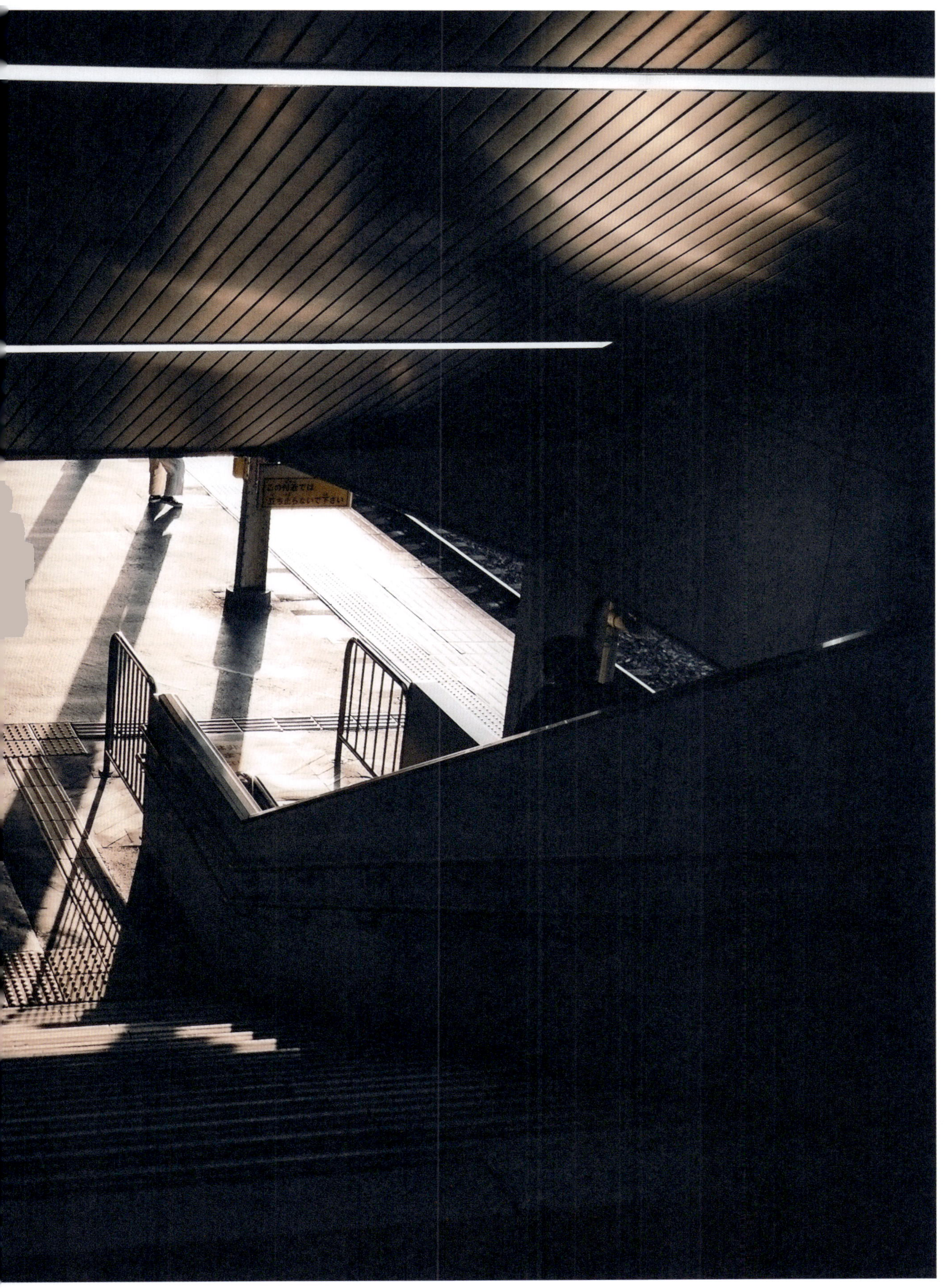

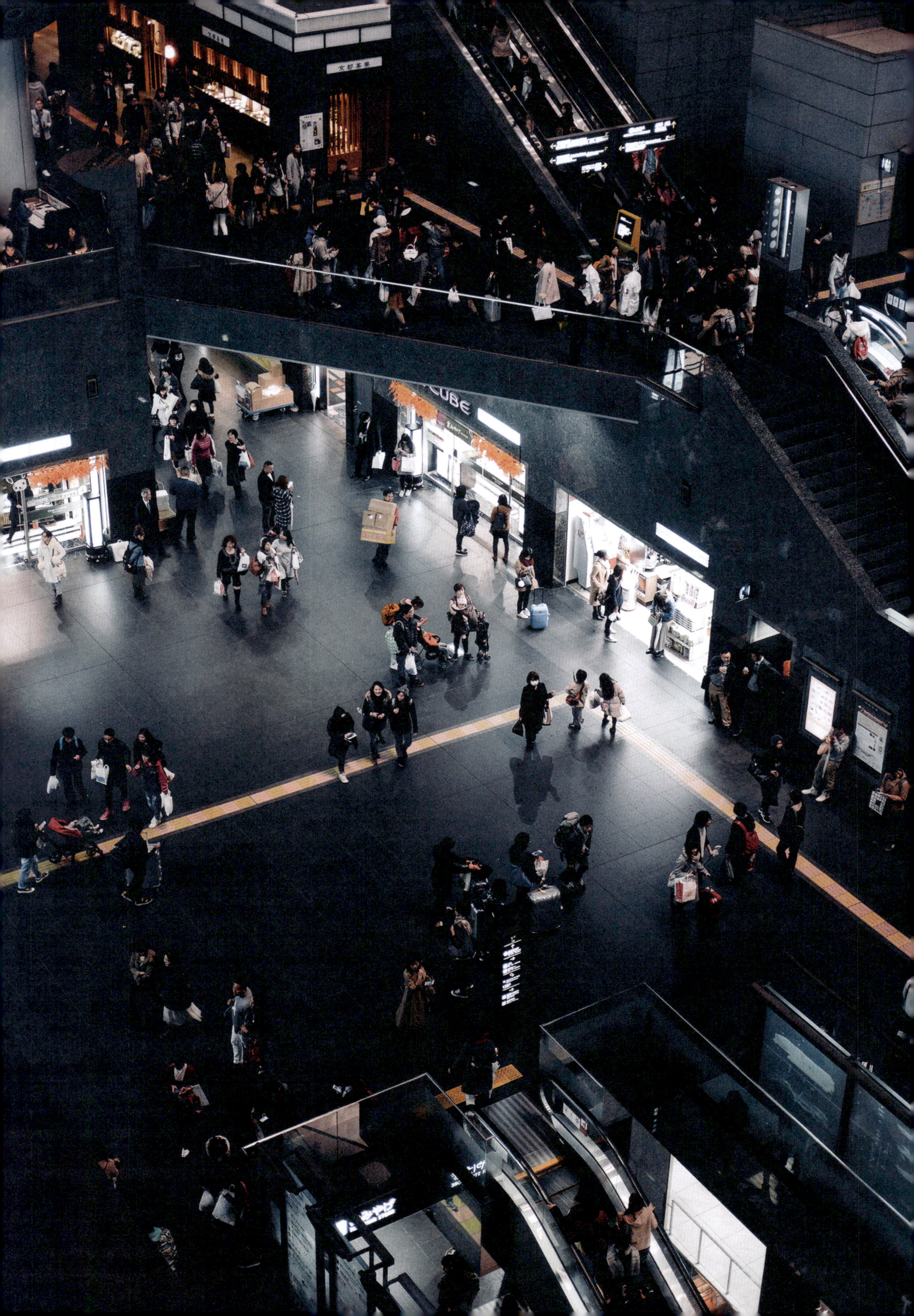

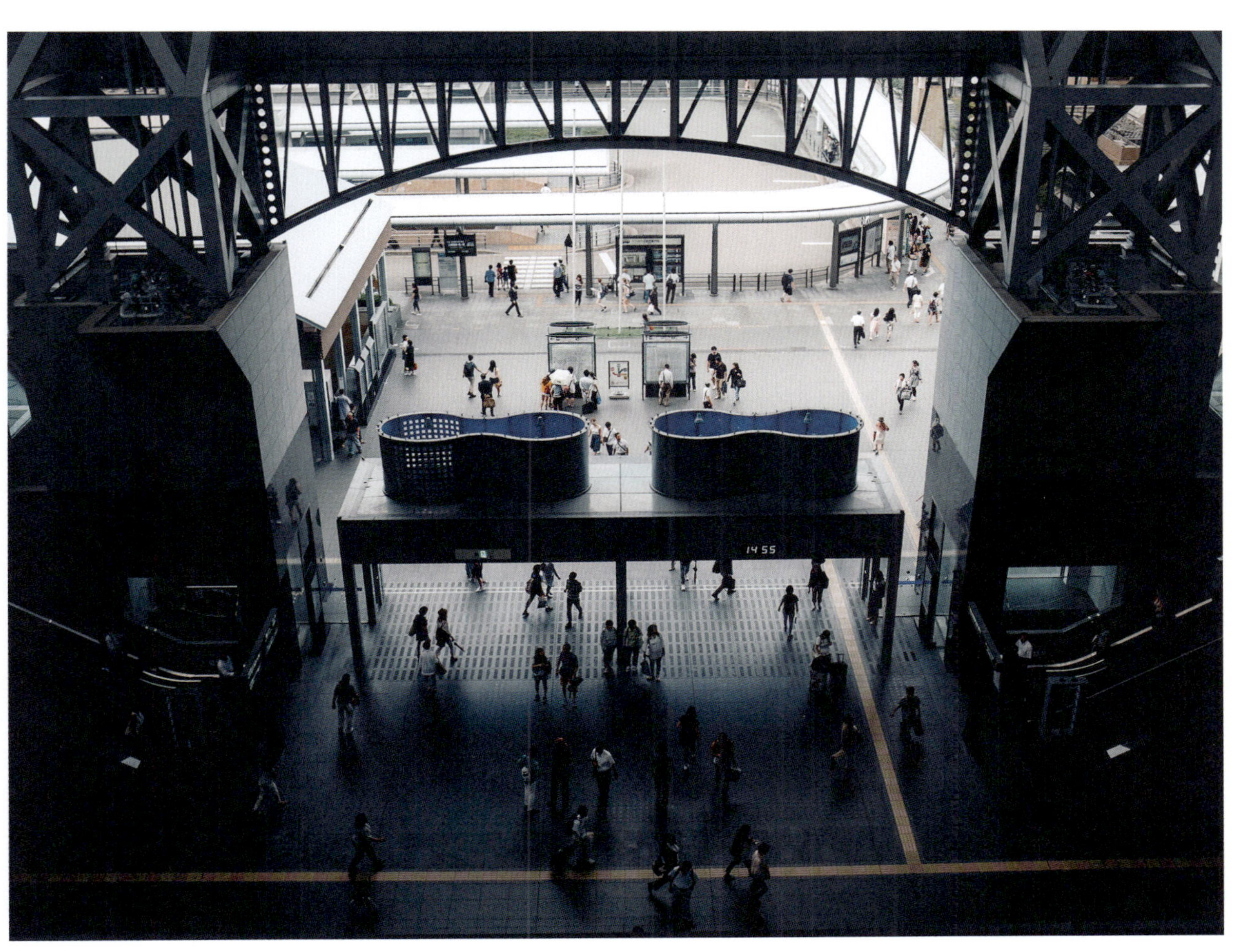
14 55

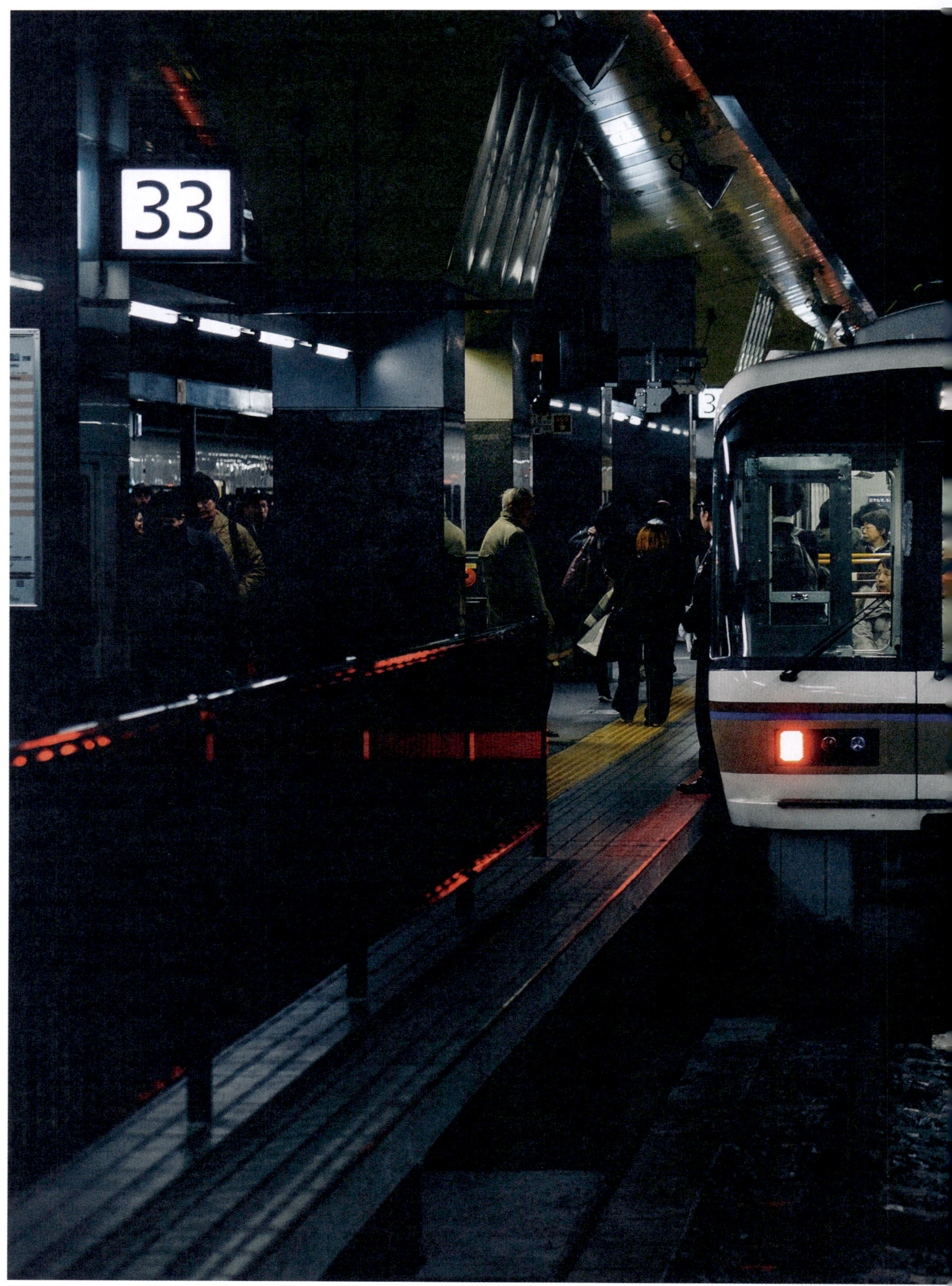
33

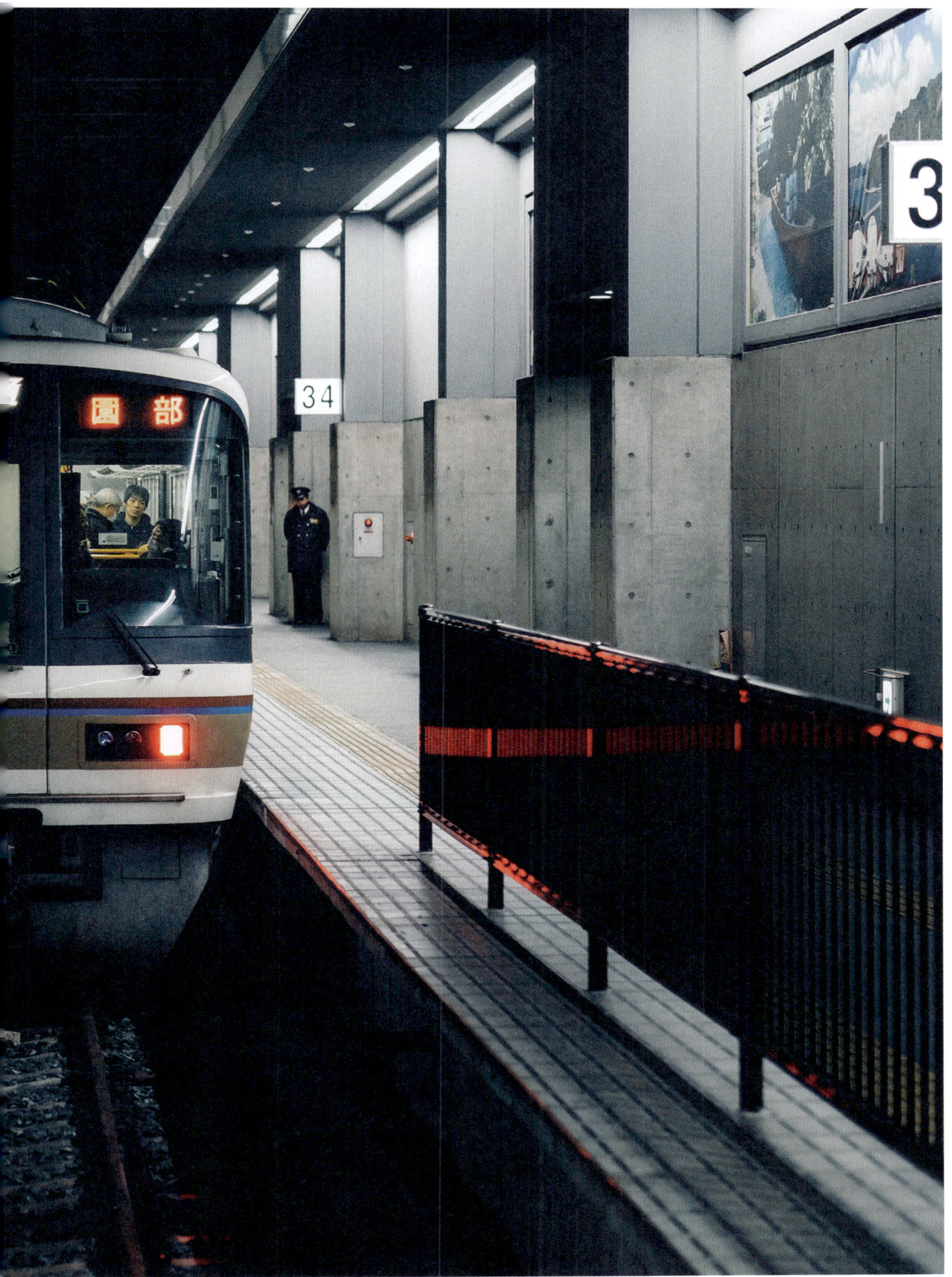
園 部
34
3

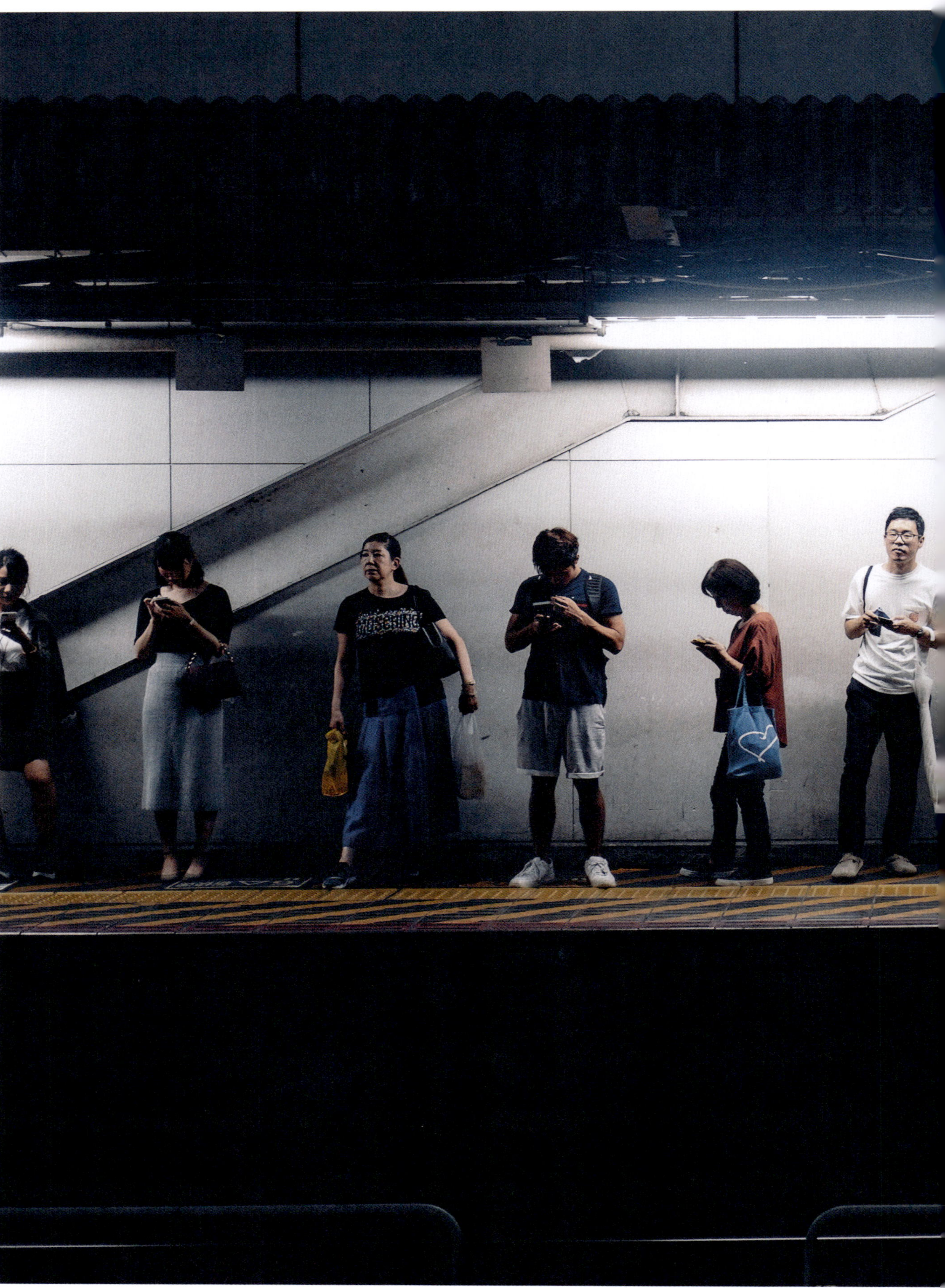

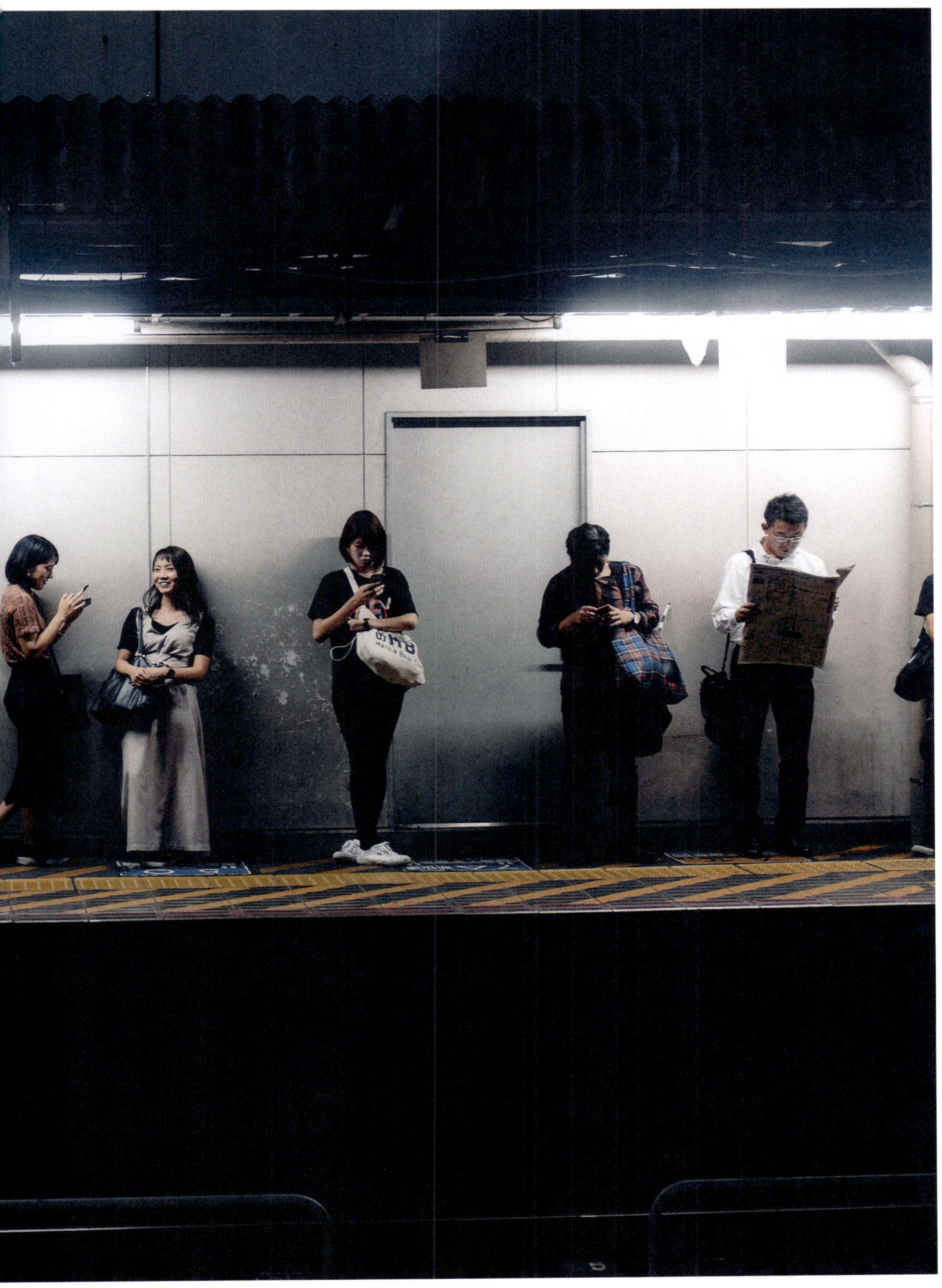

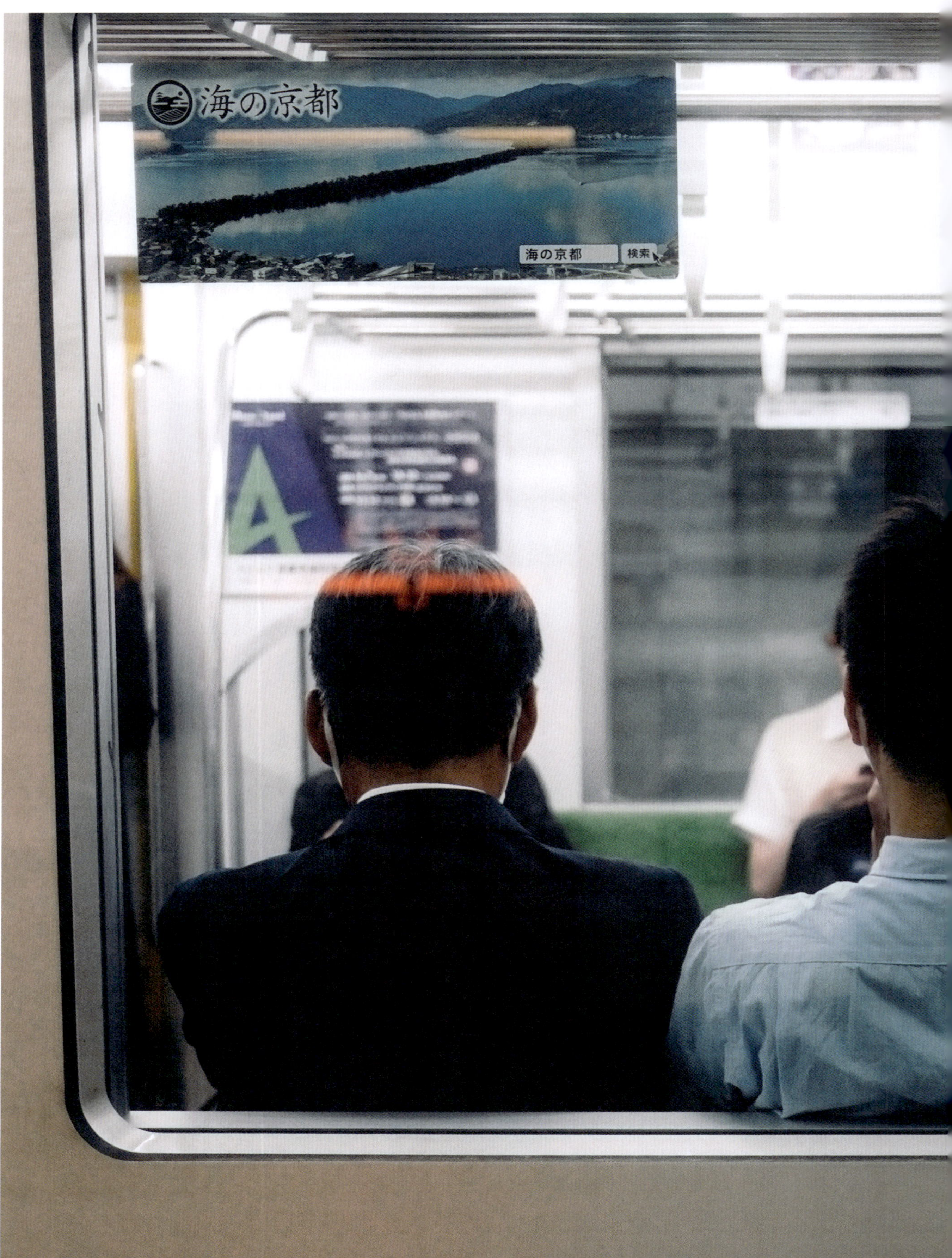
海の京都
海の京都
検索

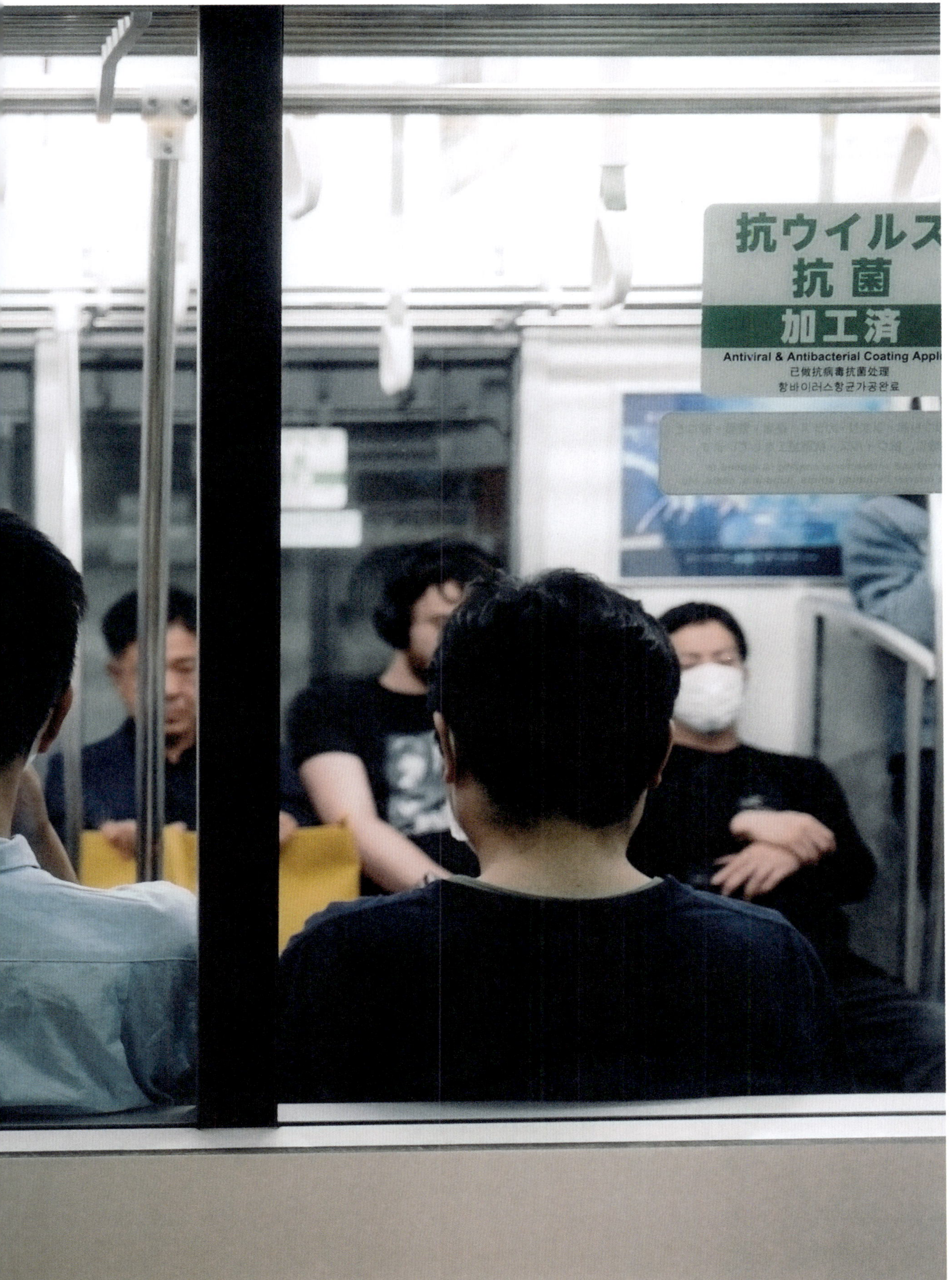
抗ウイルス
抗菌
加工済
Antiviral & Antibacterial Coating Appli
已做抗病毒抗菌处理
항바이러스항균가공완료

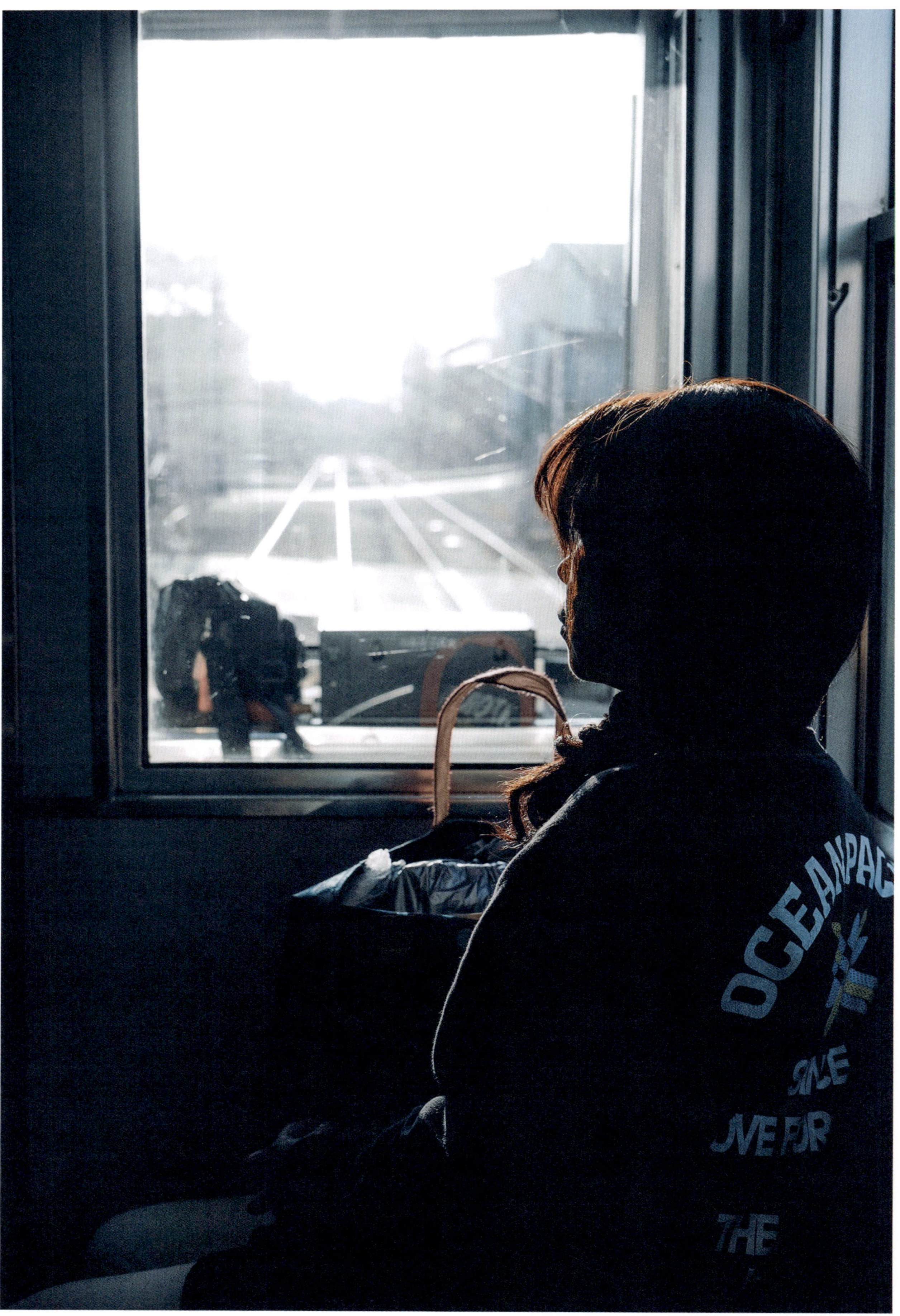
OCEANPAC
THE

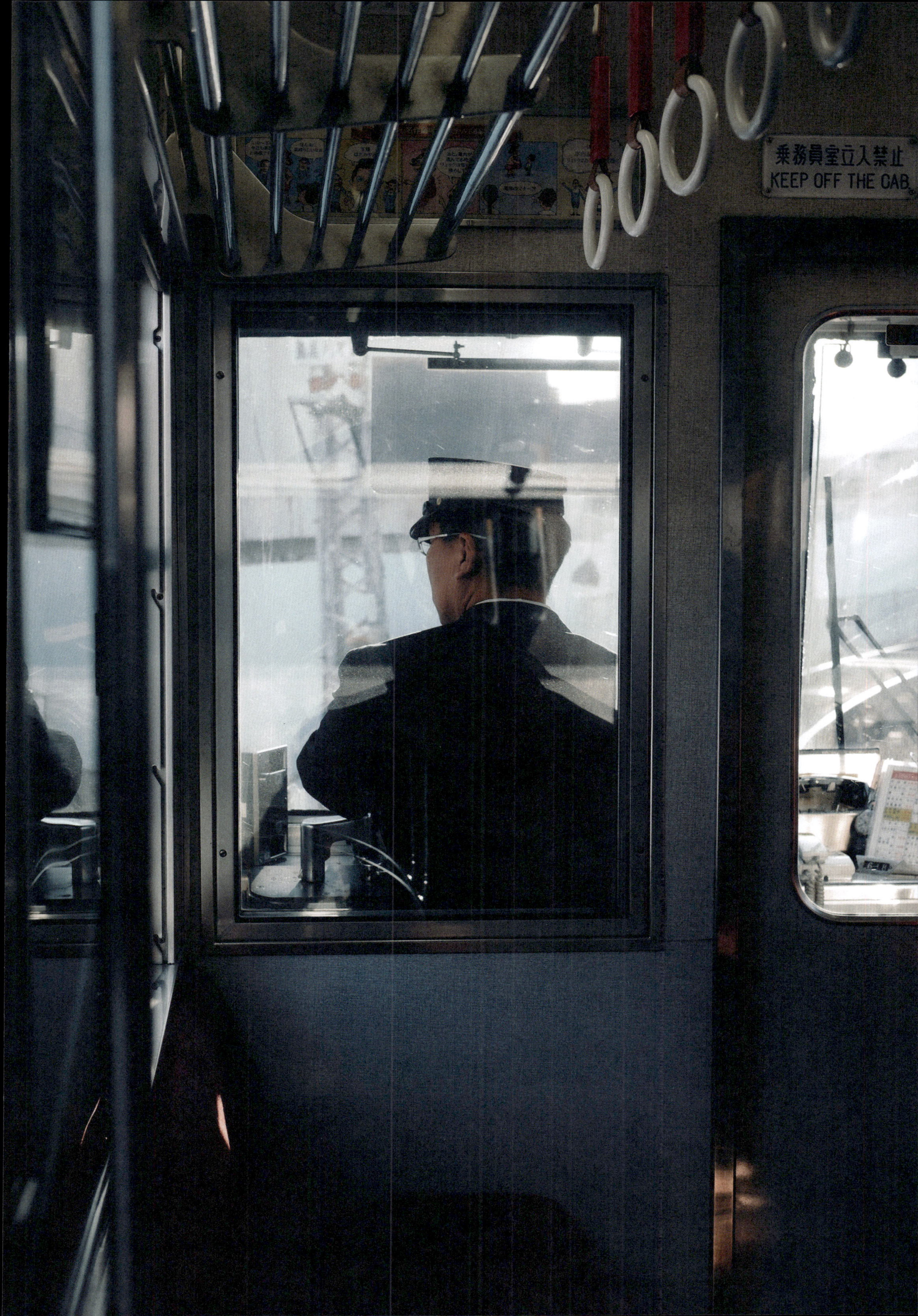
乗務員室立入禁止
KEEP OFF THE CAB

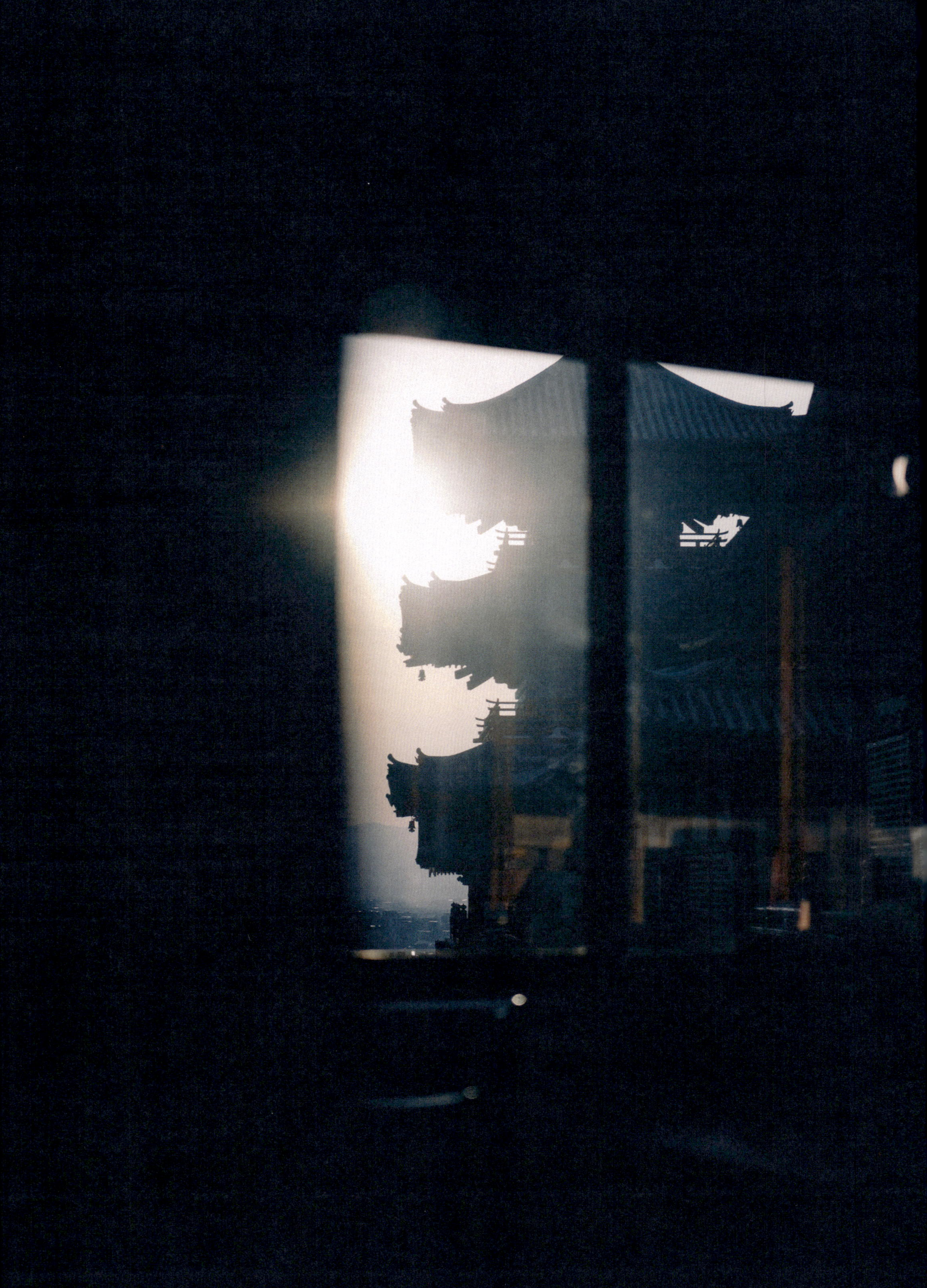

時鳥
鳴きつるかたを
ながむれば
たゞ有明の
月ぞのこれる
藤原実定

A cuckoo
Calls from yonder —
Gazing there,
Only the daybreak
Moon remains.

Fujiwara no Sanesada

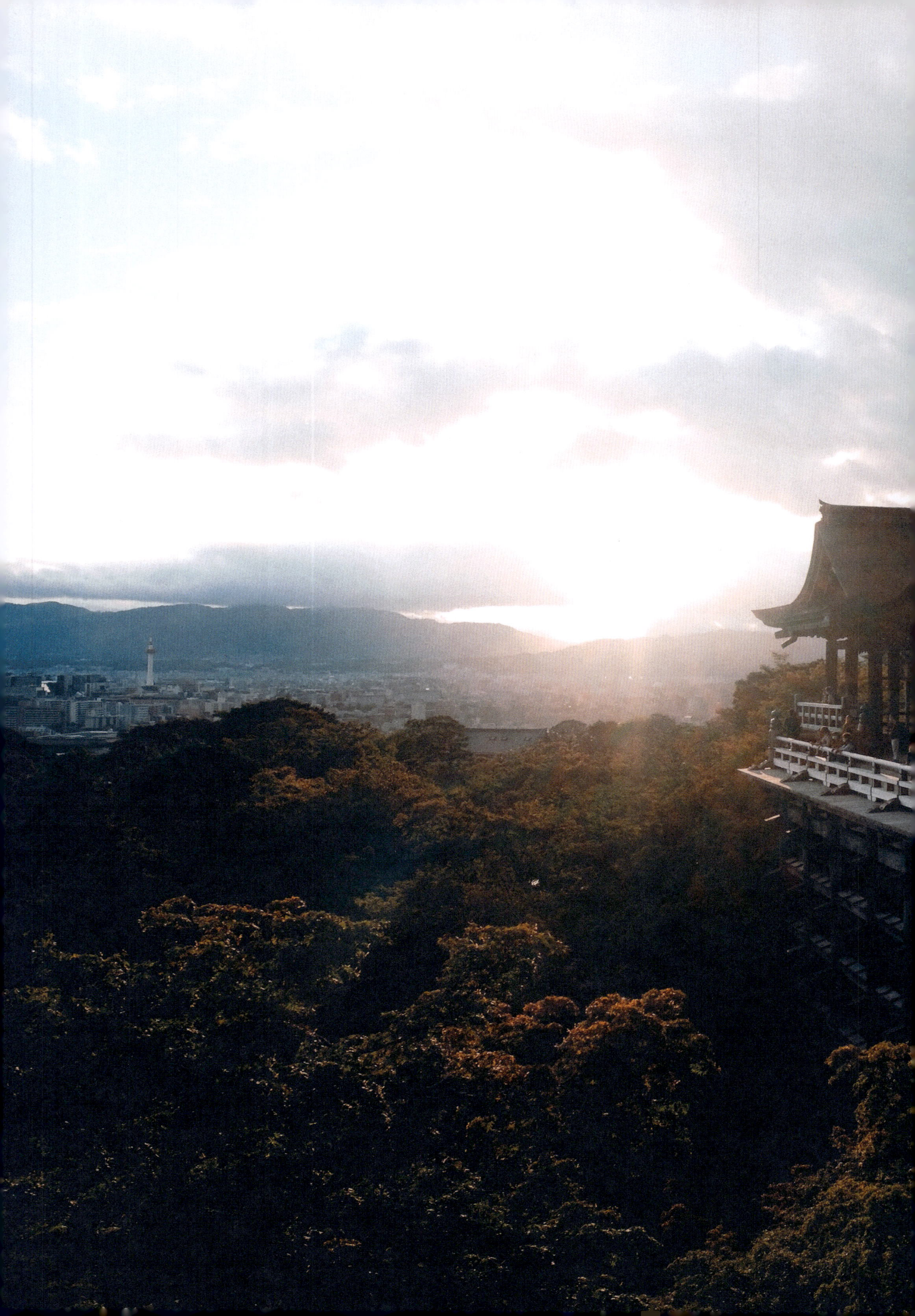

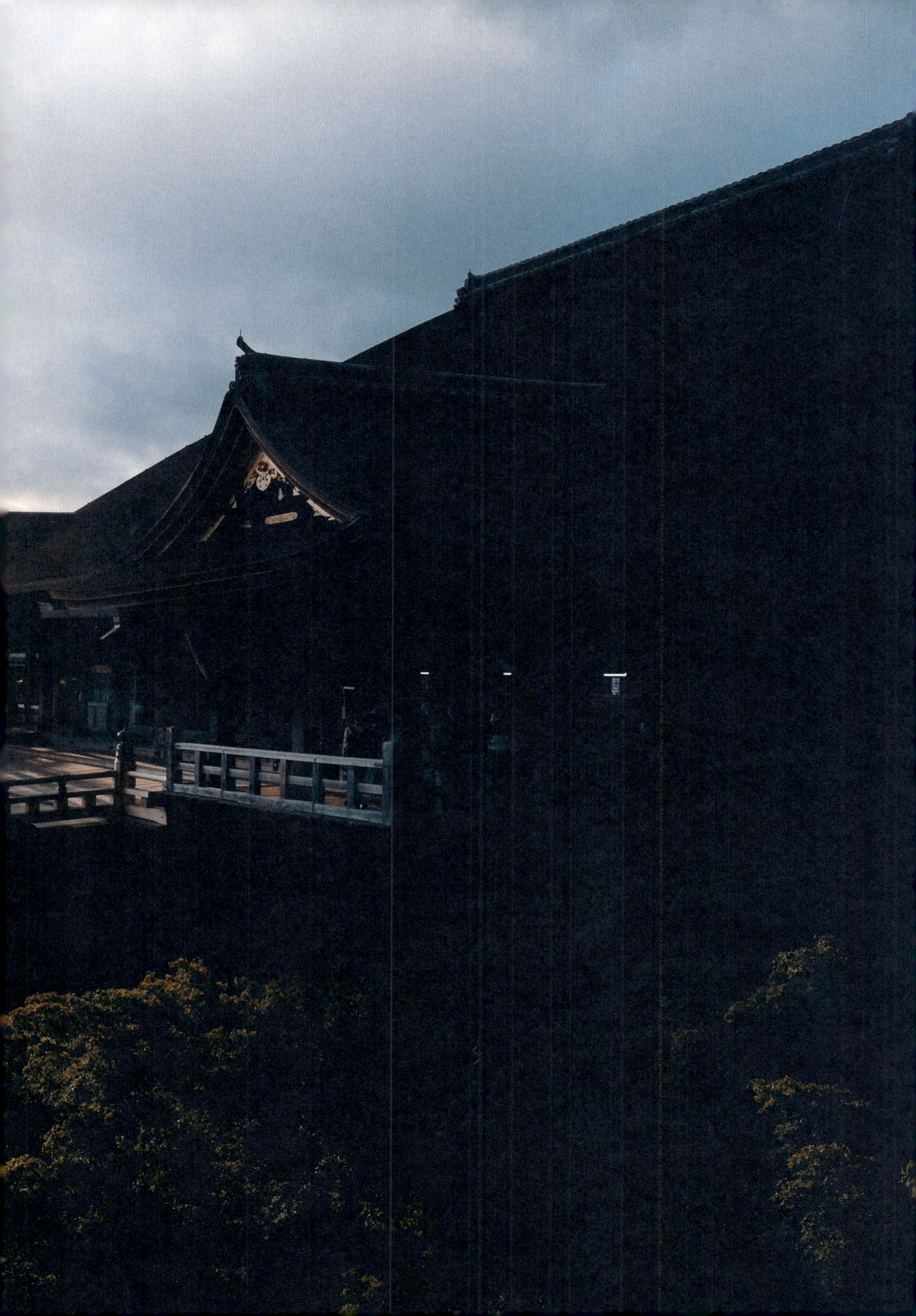

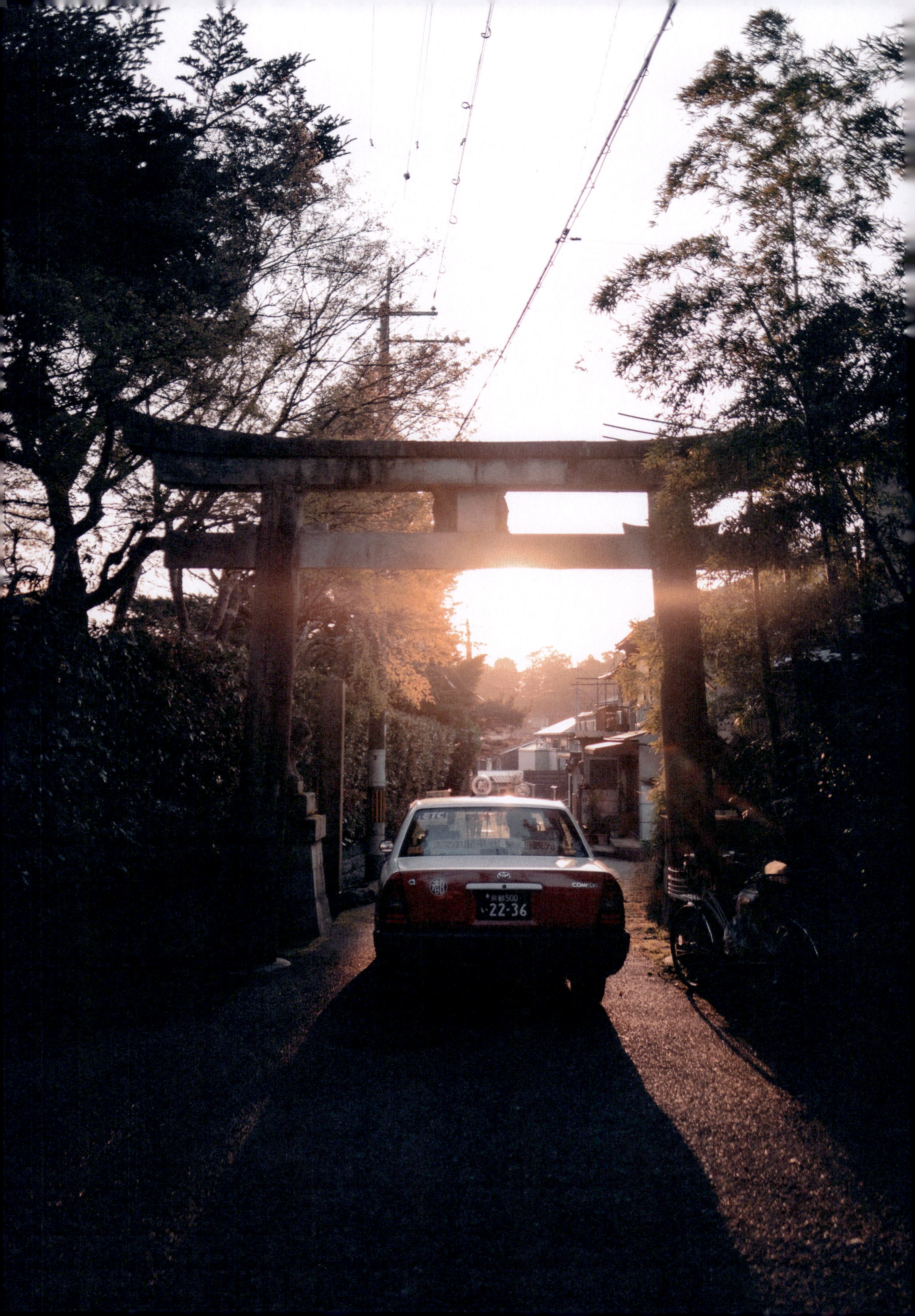
ETC
都
京都500
い 22-36

TARO MOBERLY

Taro Moberly is a street and travel photographer currently based in the Bay Area. His passion for photography started when he moved to Kyoto, Japan from his native California in 2015. Originally just a way to share his life with friends and family back home, his photography practice quickly became a source of curiosity and an opportunity to explore the world around him. Today, he's interested in using photography to share how he sees the world, its cultures, and its people. He hopes to inspire others to seek out the beauty that surrounds them.

ACKNOWLEDGMENTS

To my family—thank you for all of your love and care and for always encouraging me to cultivate my passions and dreams, no matter how varied they may be.

To all of the other artists I've had the privilege of befriending during my time in Japan—thank you for inspiring me with all your work and spirit and for welcoming me into this vibrant community.

To everyone at the Trope family—thank you for believing in my work from so early on and putting your dedication and effort into this beautiful project that I am proud to show the world.

And to you, the reader—thank you for joining me on this journey. To be able to share it with you is meaningful beyond what words can express, and I am deeply grateful.

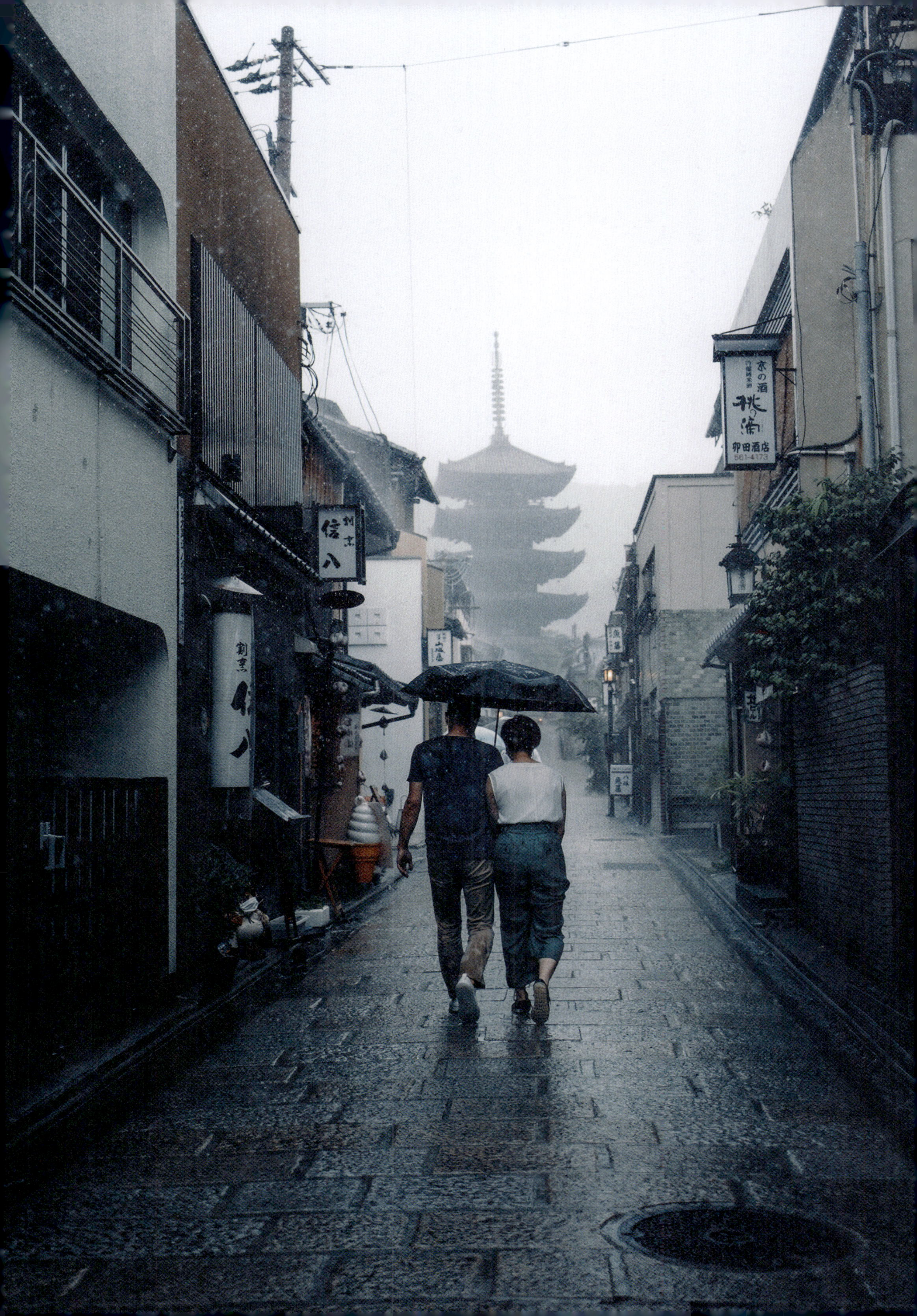
割烹
信八
京の酒
桃の滴
卯田酒店
561-4173

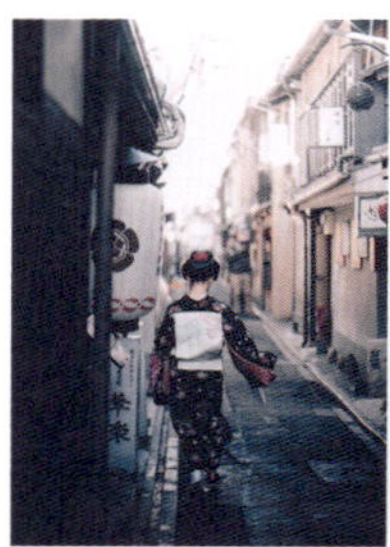

Cover Pontochō Alley

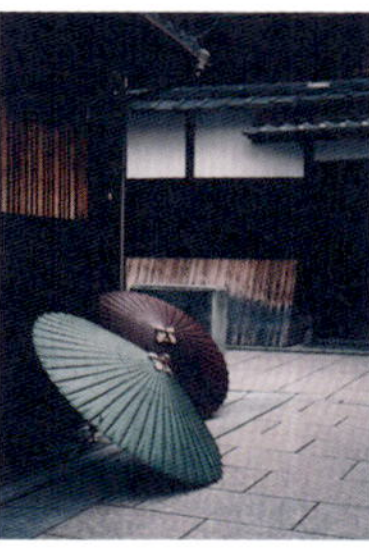

2 Gion

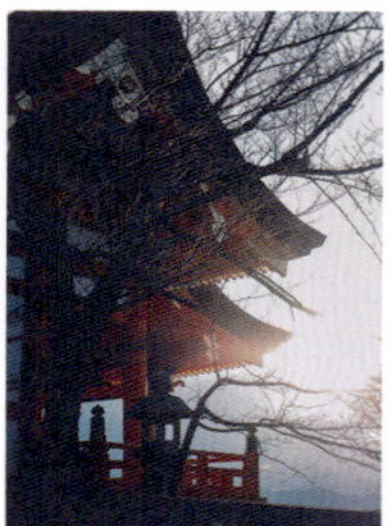

4 Kiyomizu-dera

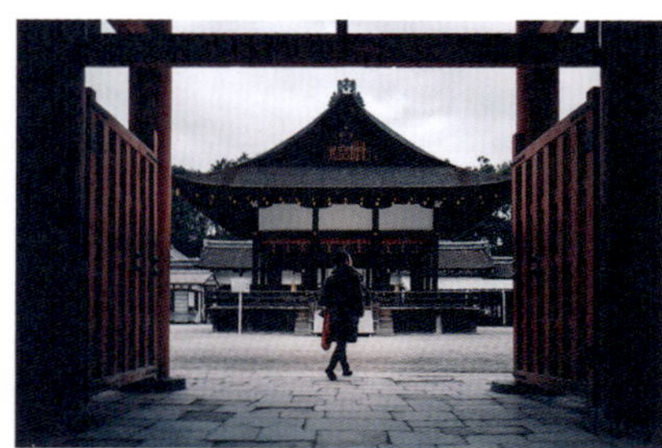

6-7 Shimogamo-jinja

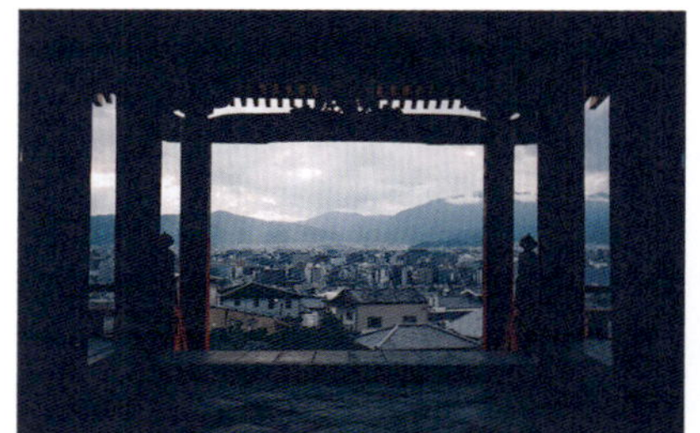

8-9 Kiyomizu-dera

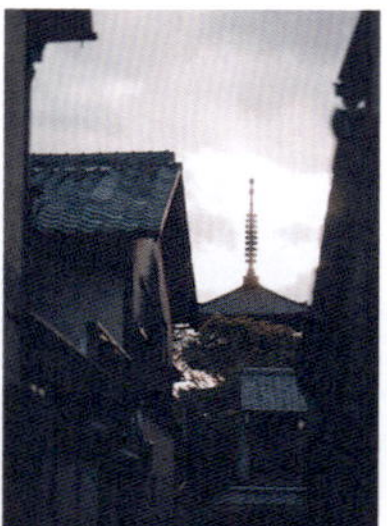

10 Ninenzaka

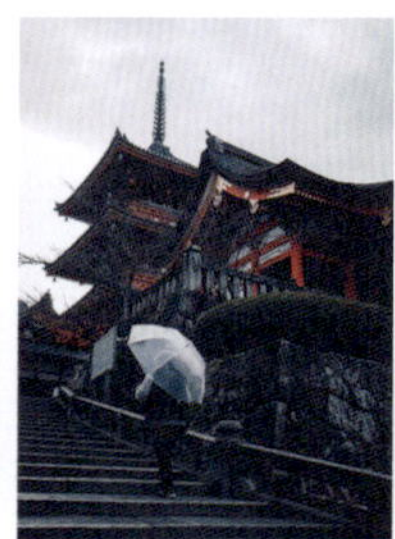

11 Kiyomizu-dera

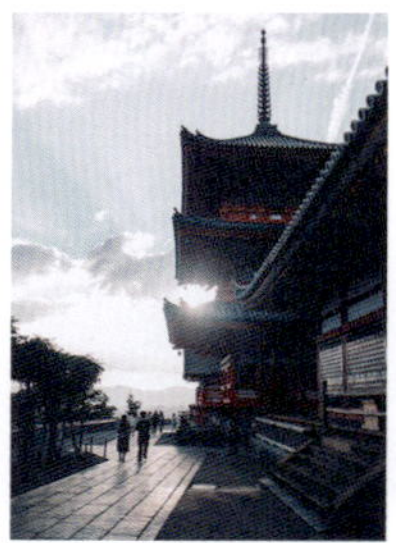

12 Kiyomizu-dera

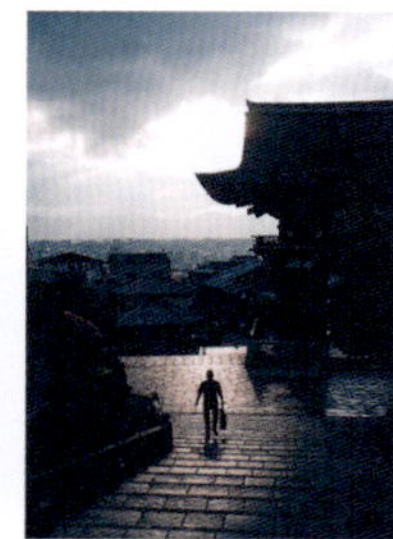

13 Kiyomizu-dera

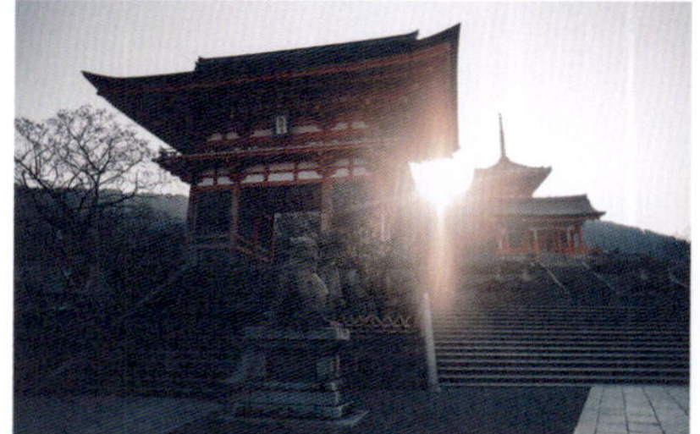

14-15 Kiyomizu-dera

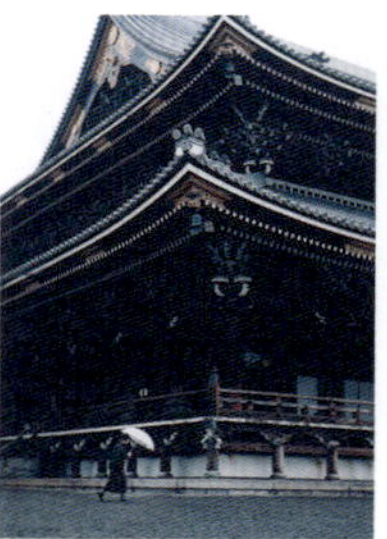

16 Higashi Hongan-ji

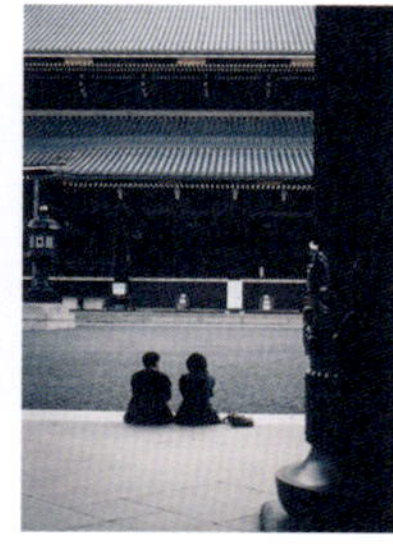

17 Higashi Hongan-ji

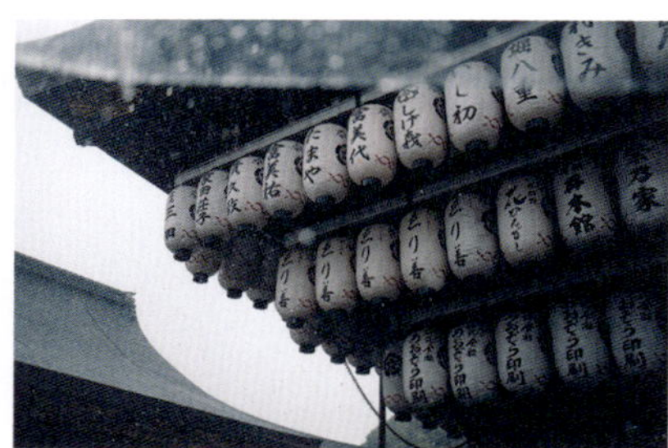

18-19 Yasaka-jinja

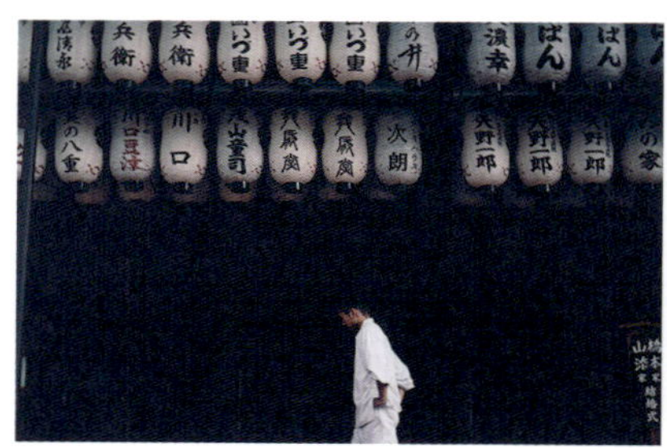

20 Yasaka-jinja

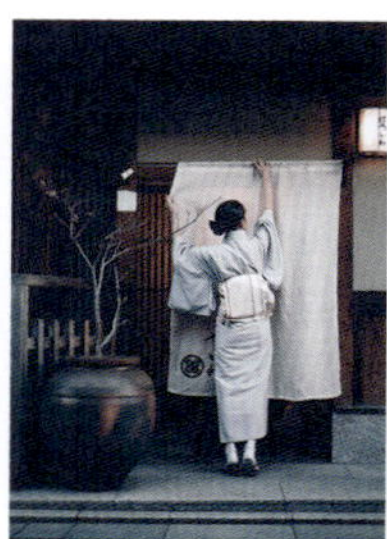

21 Gion

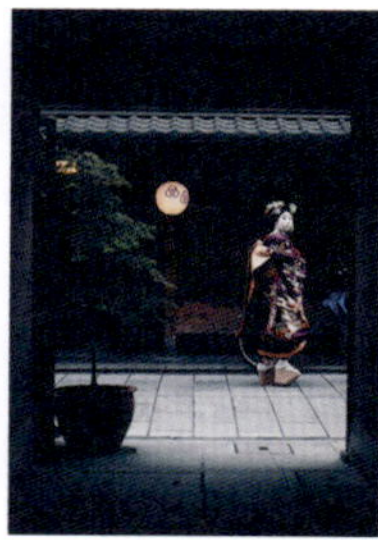

22 Miyakawa-cho

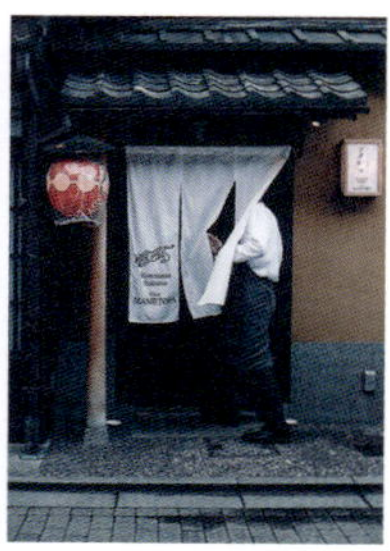

23 Gion

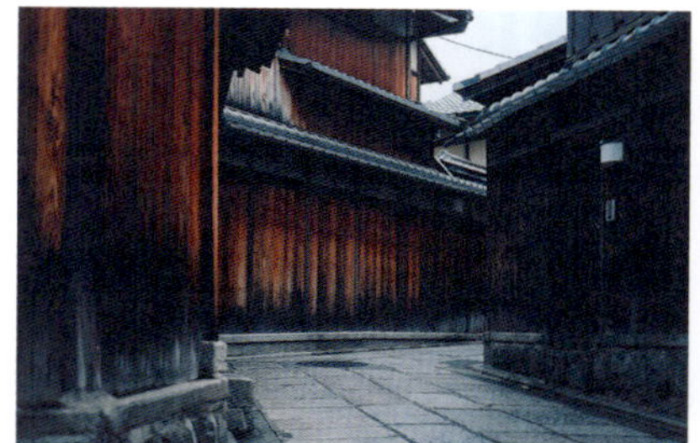

24-25 Ishibe-koji

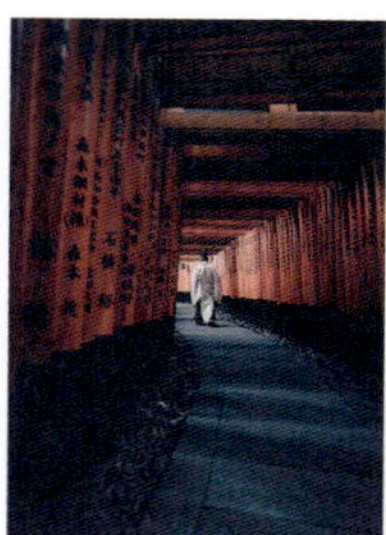

26 Fushimi Inari

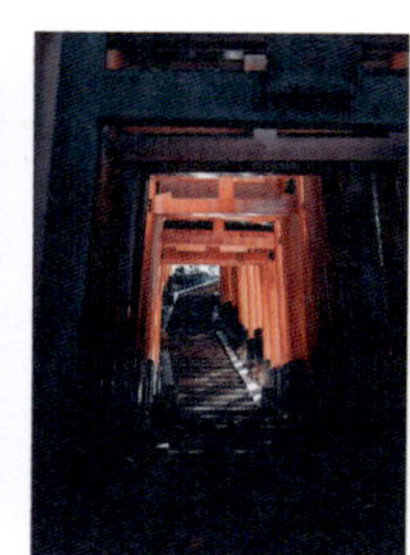

27 Fushimi Inari

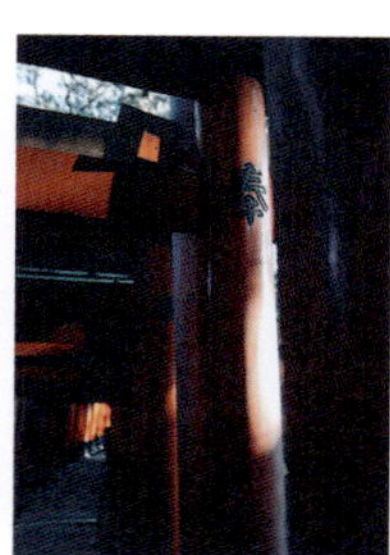

29 Fushimi Inari

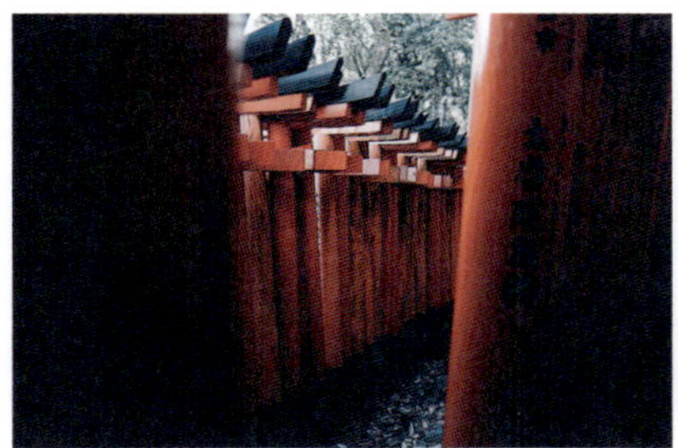
30-31 Fushimi Inari

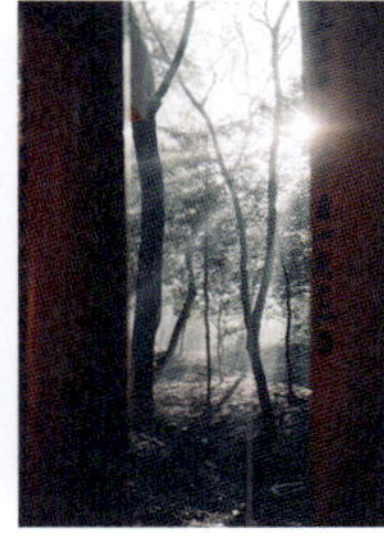
32 Fushimi Inari

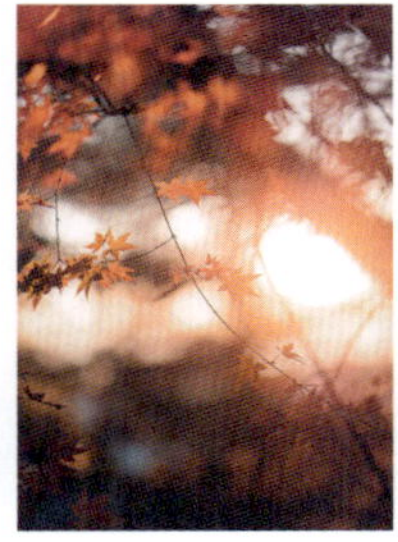
33 Arashiyama

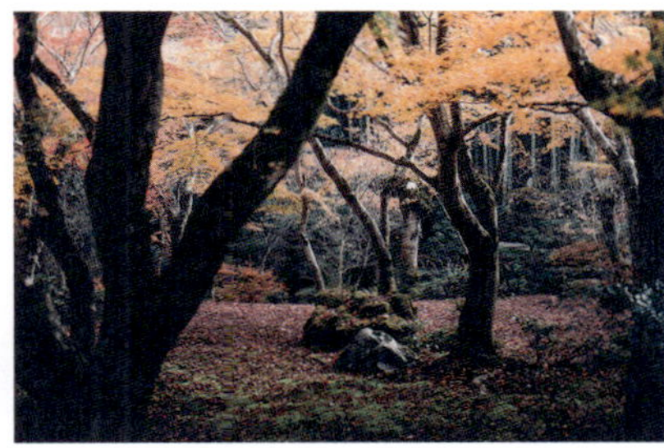
34-35 Enkō-ji

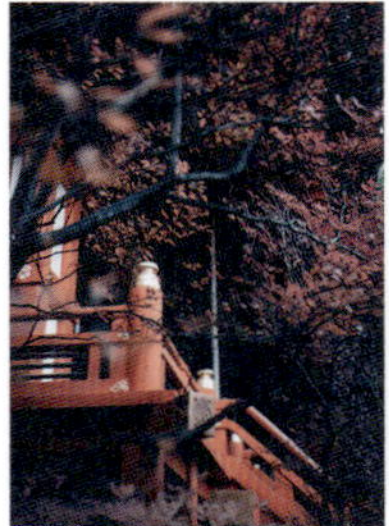
36 Bishamondō

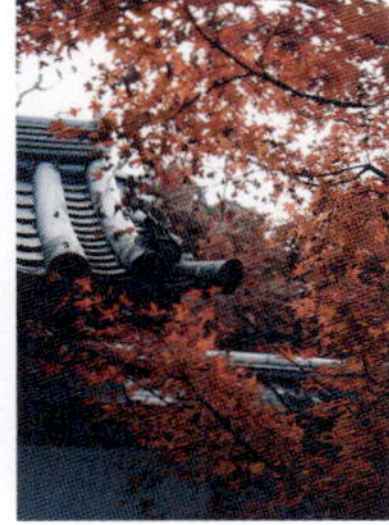
37 Enkō-ji

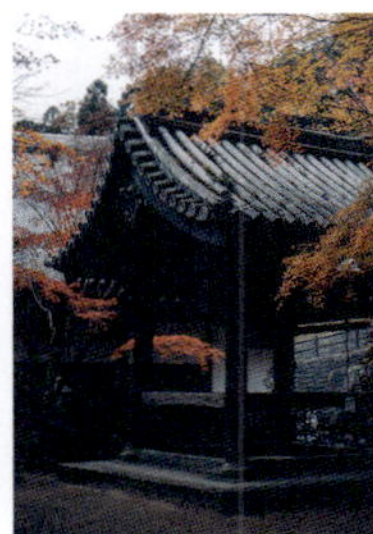
38 Enkō-ji

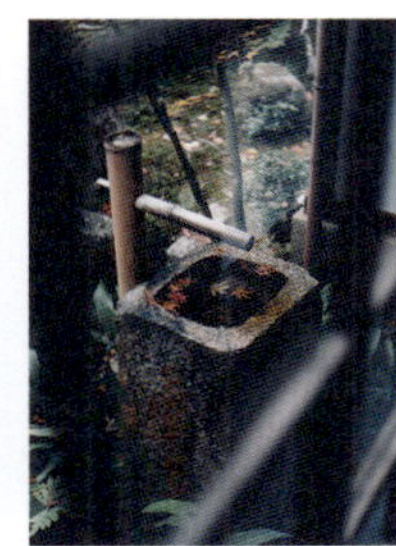
39 Enkō-ji

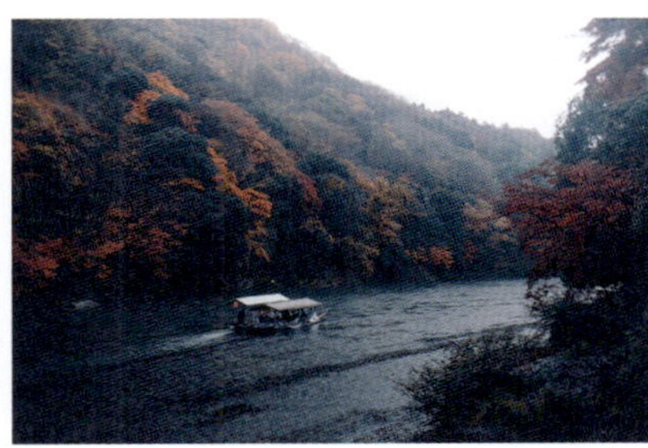
40-41 Hozugawa

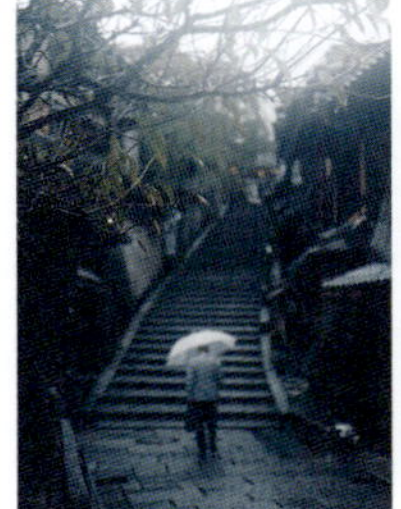
42 Sannenzaka

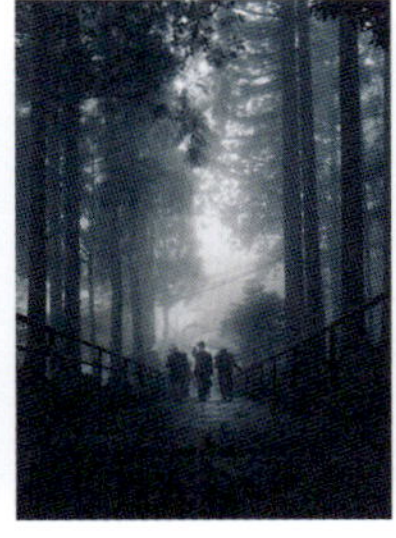
43 Hiei-zan

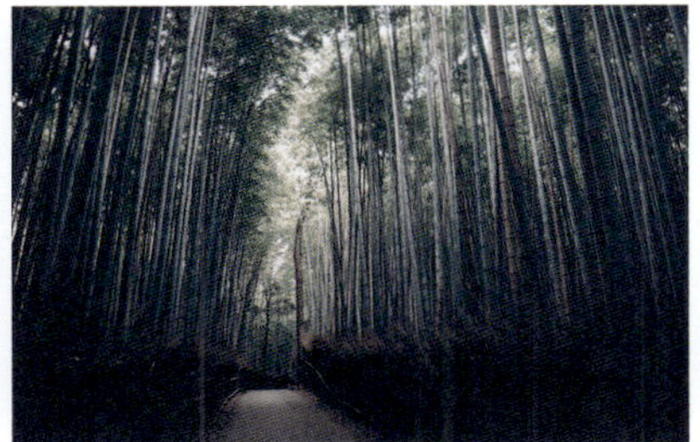
44-45 Arashiyama

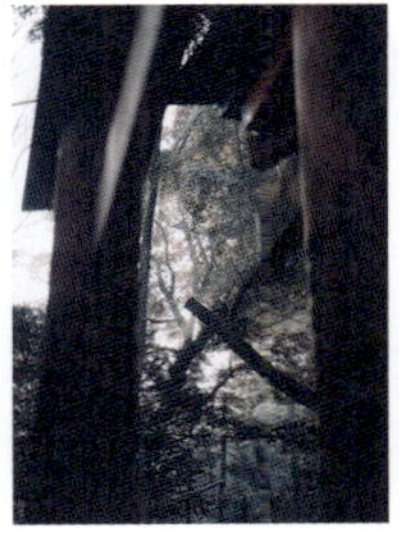
46 Fushimi Inari

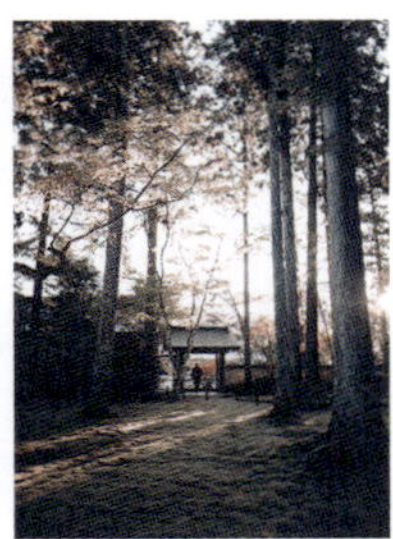
47 Ohara

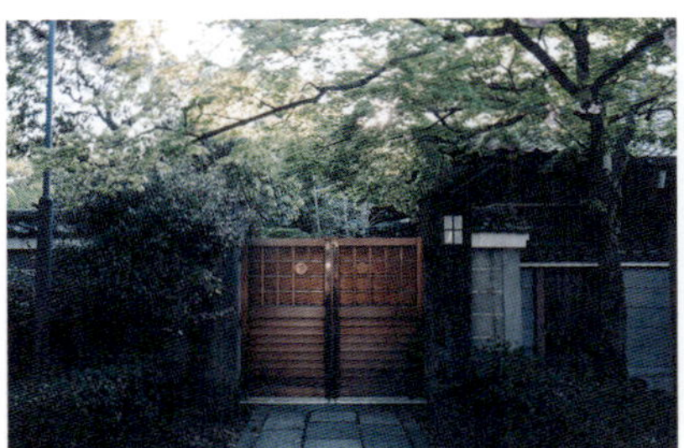
48-49 Yasaka-jinja

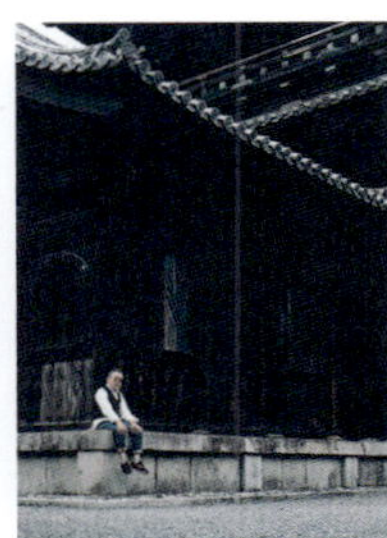
50 Chionin

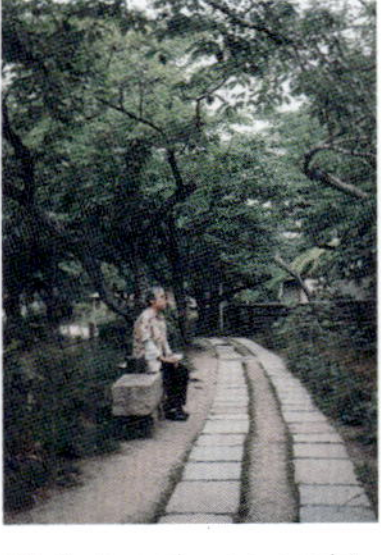
51 Tetsugaku-no-michi

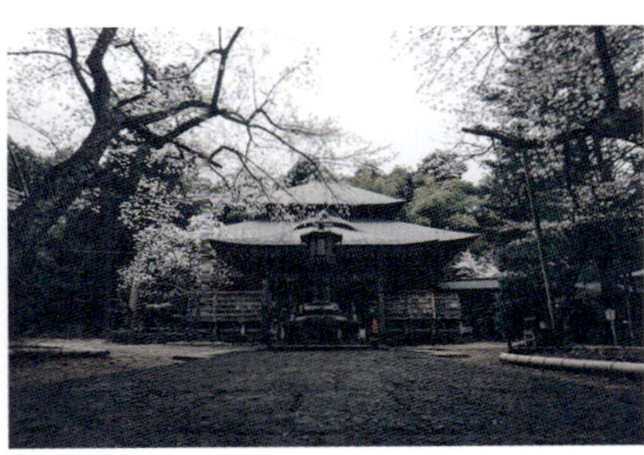
52-53 Ohara

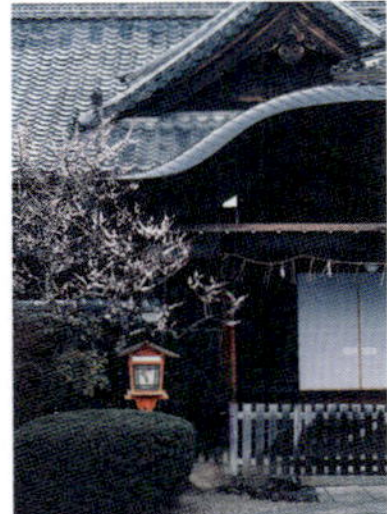
54 Yasaka-jinja

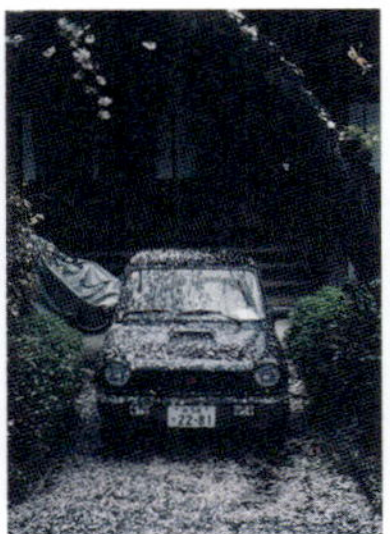
55 Nakagyō-ku

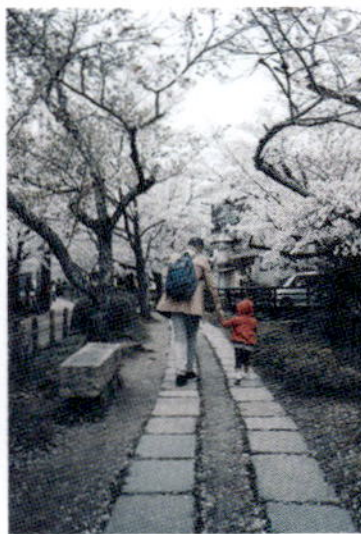
57 Tetsugaku-no-michi

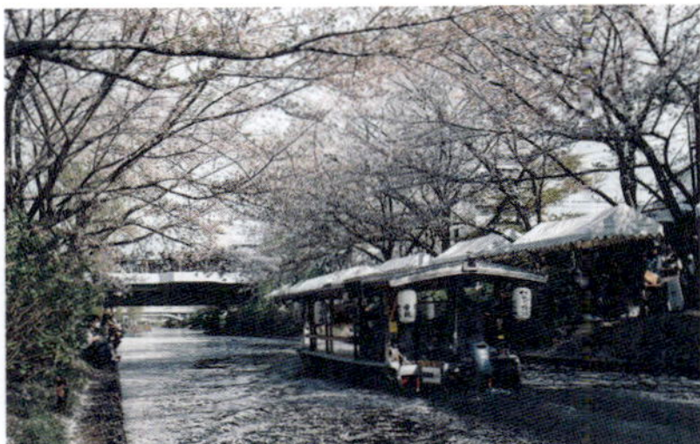
58-59 Fushimi-ku

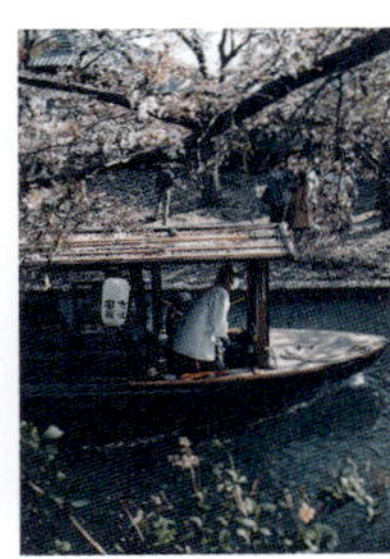
60 Fushimi-ku

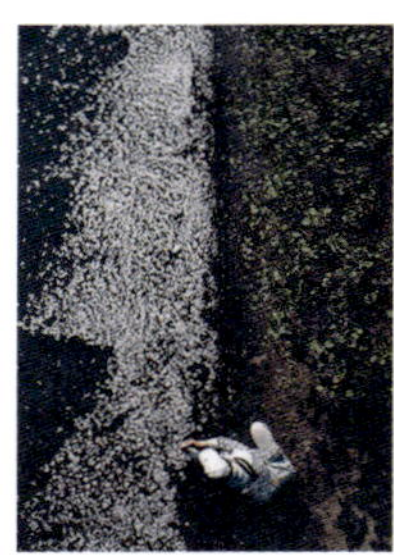
61 Fushimi-ku

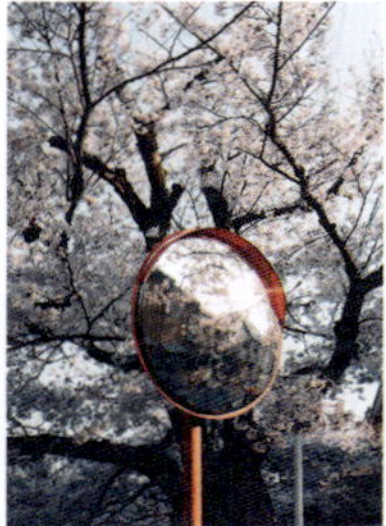
62 Tetsugaku-no-michi

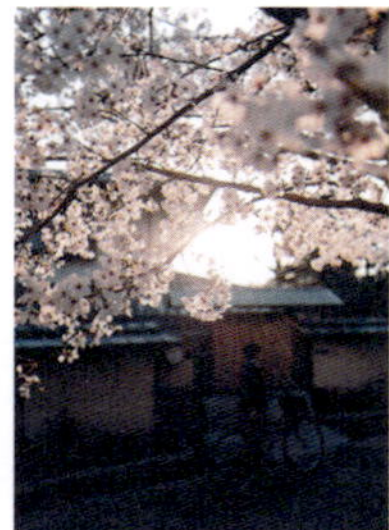
63 Tetsugaku-no-michi

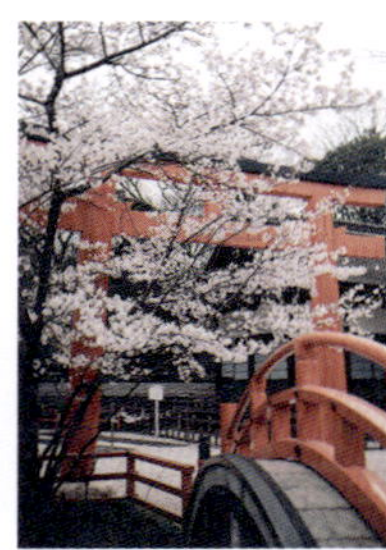
64 Shimogamo-jinja

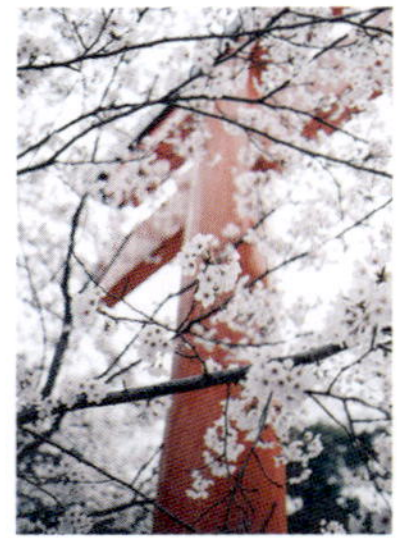
65 Shimogamo-jinja

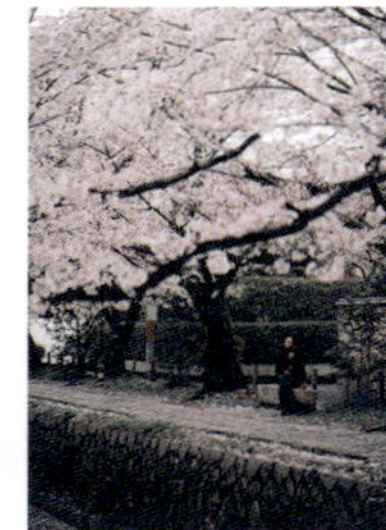
66 Tetsugaku-no-michi

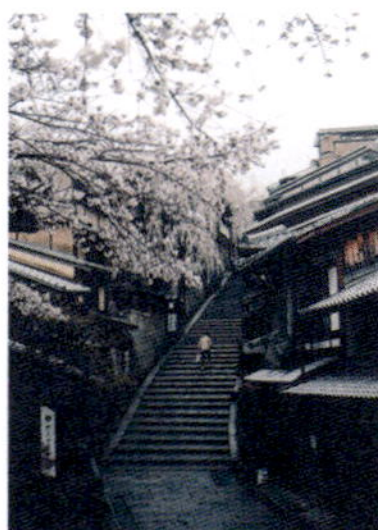
67 Sannenzaka

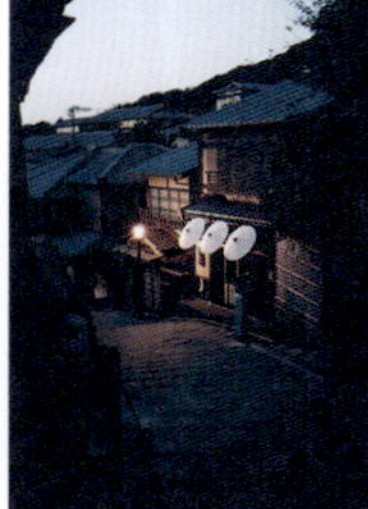
68 Ninenzaka

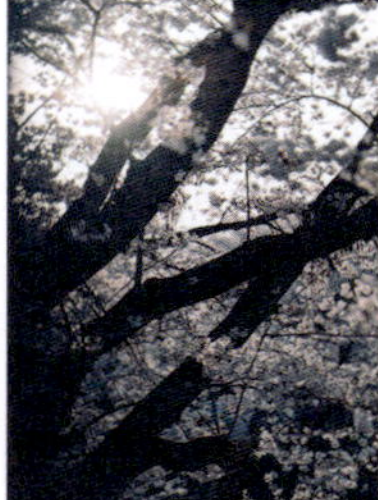
69 Sewaritei

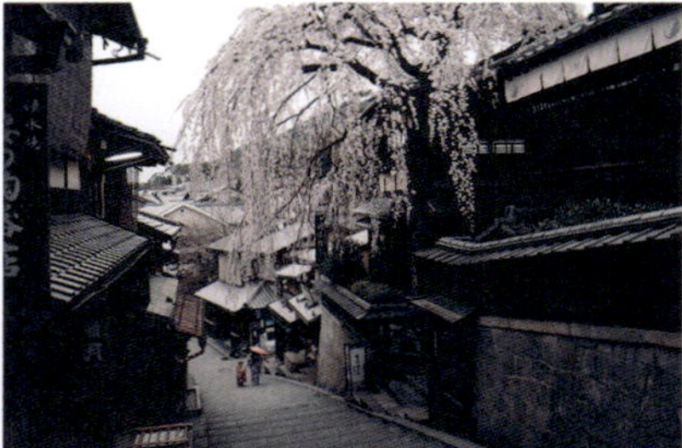
70-71 Sannenzaka

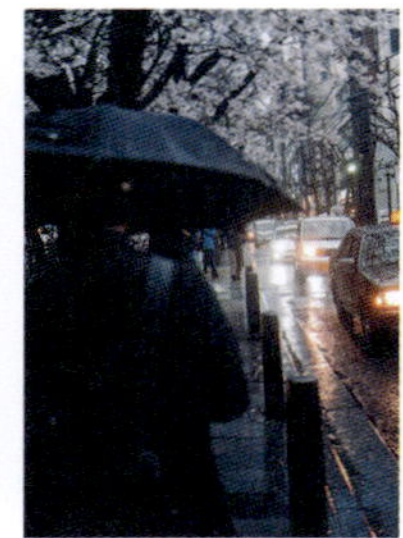
72 Kiyamachi-dōri

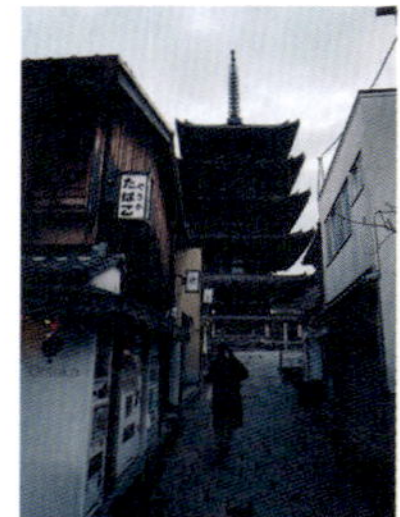
73 Yasaka-dōri

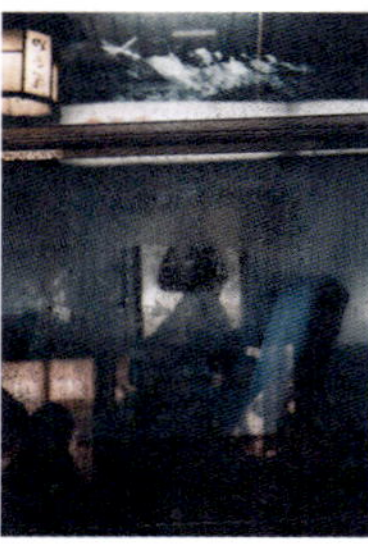
74 Shijō-dōri

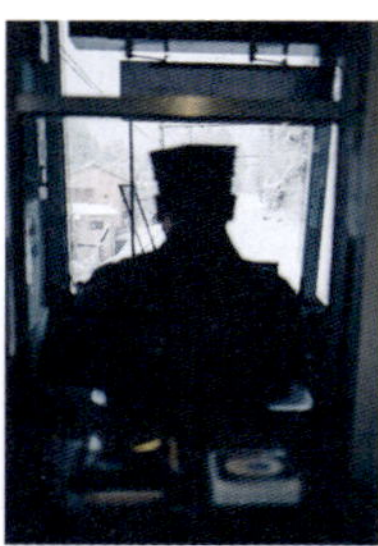
76 Kifune

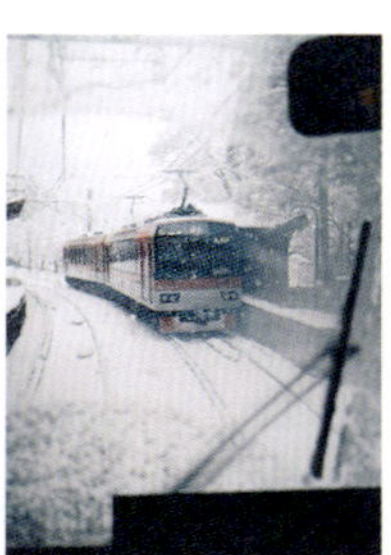
77 Kifune

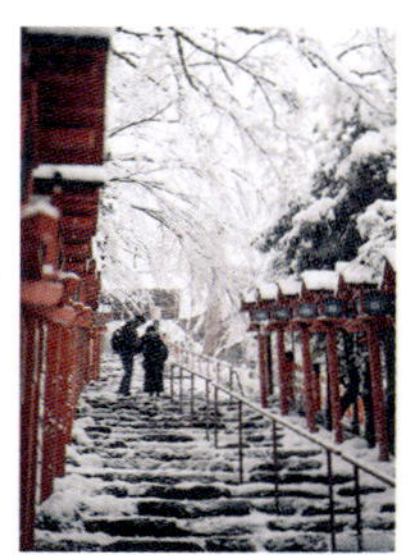
78 Kifune-jinja

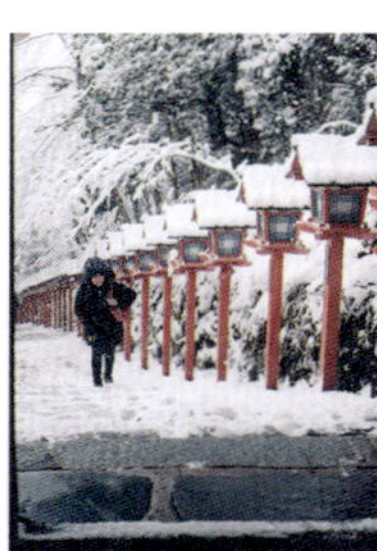
79 Kifune-jinja

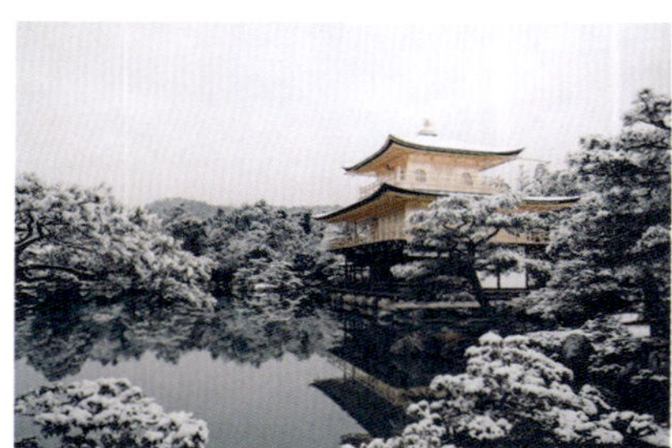
80-81 Kinkaku-ji

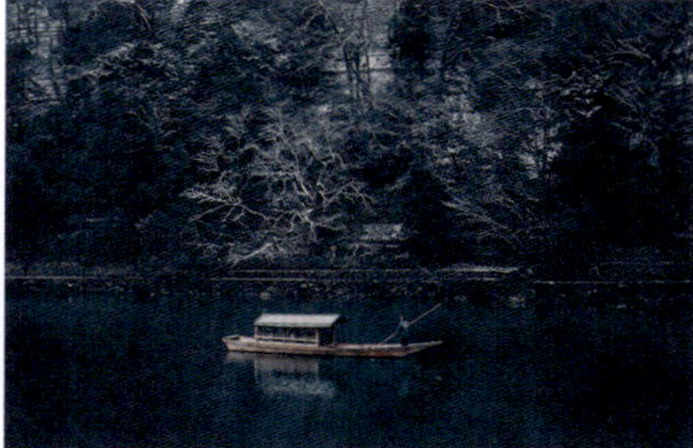
82-83 Hozugawa

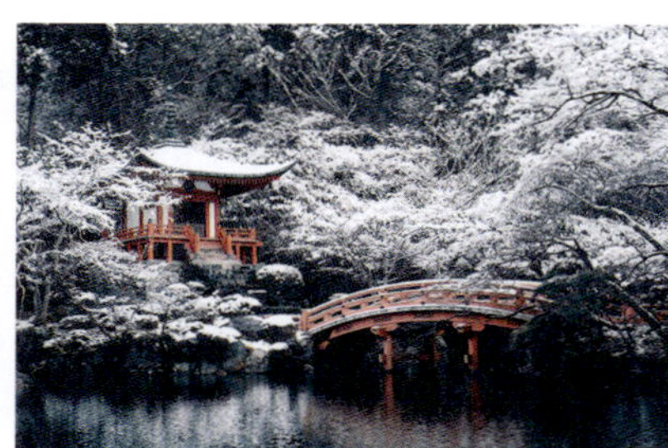
84-85 Daigo-ji

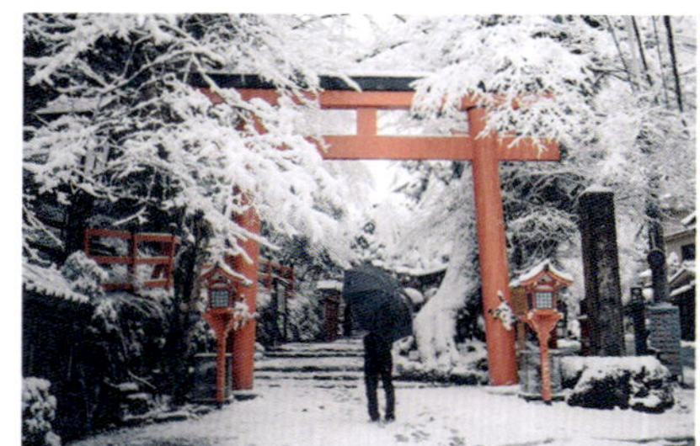
86-87 Kifune

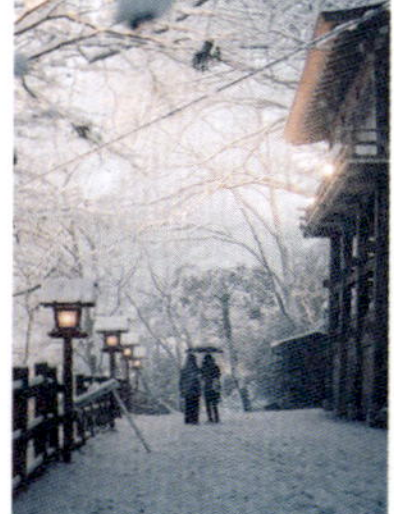
88 Kifune

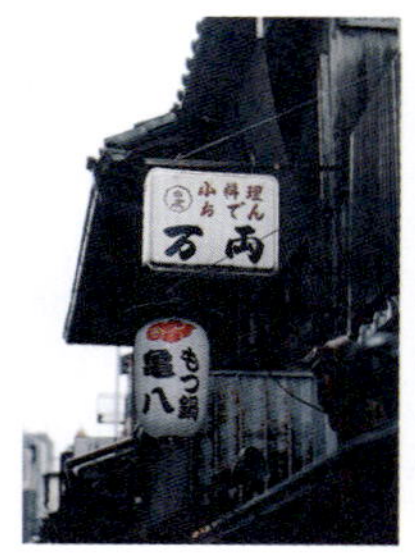

90 Gion

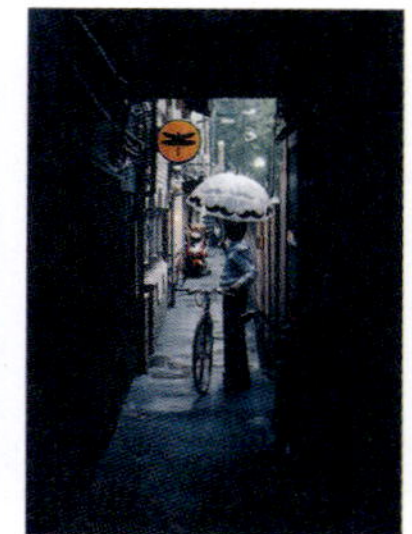
91 Pontochō Alley

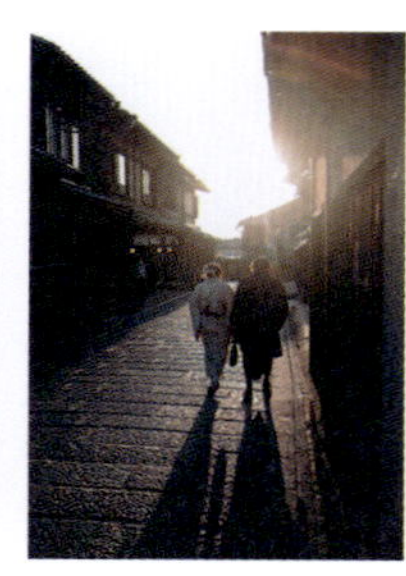
92 Yasaka-jinja

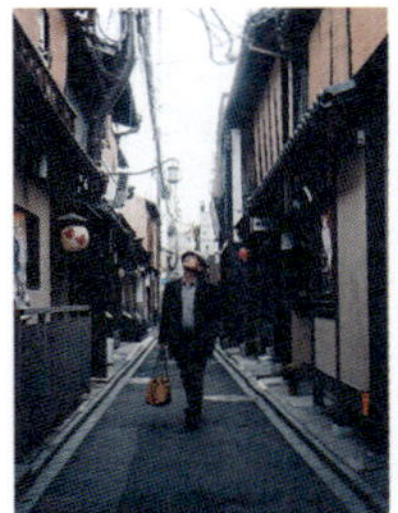

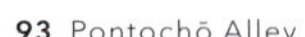

93 Pontochō Alley

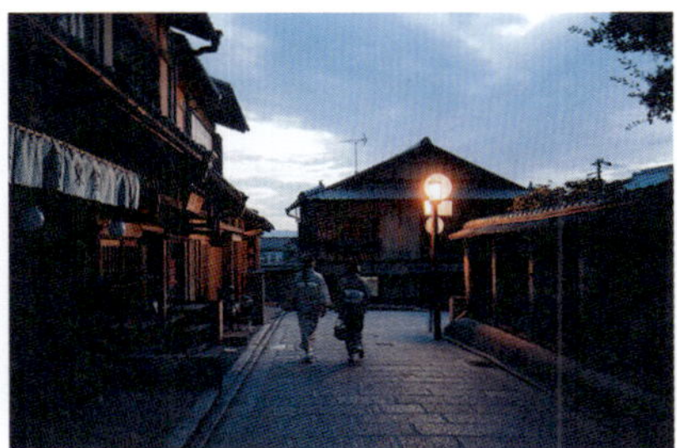

94-95 Yasaka-dori

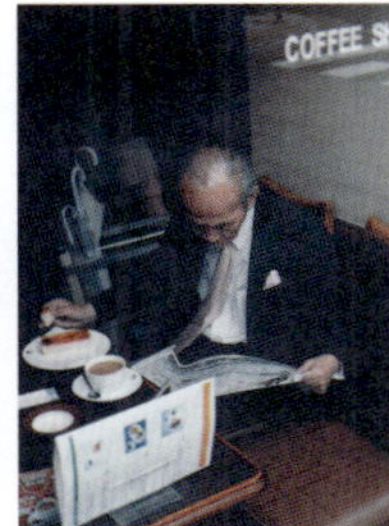

96 Hanamikoji

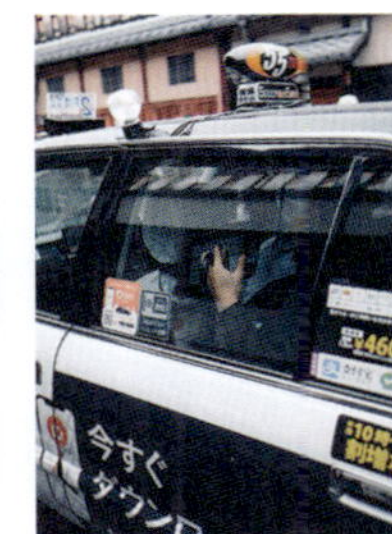

97 Hanamikoji

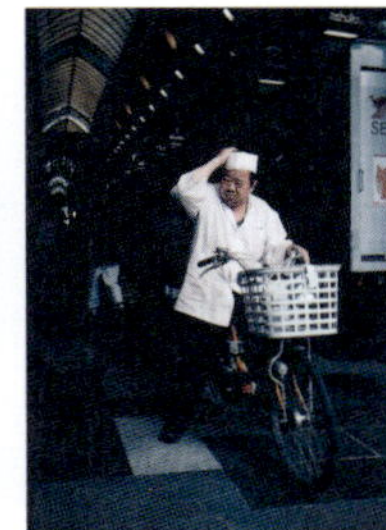

98 Fushimi-ku

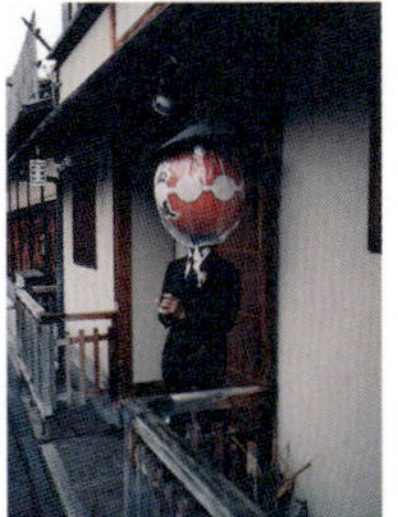

99 Hanamikoji

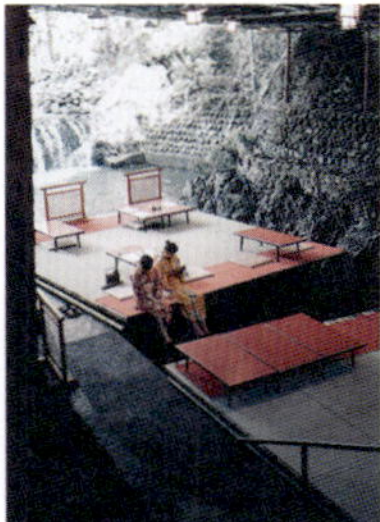

100 Kifune

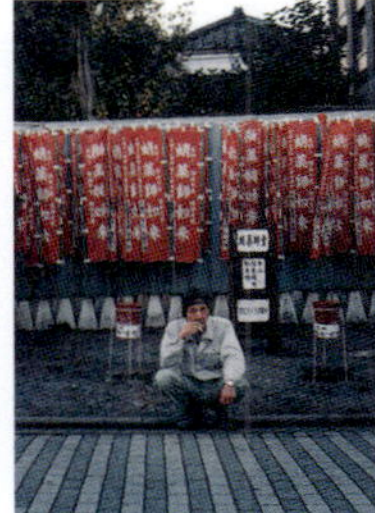

101 Teramachi

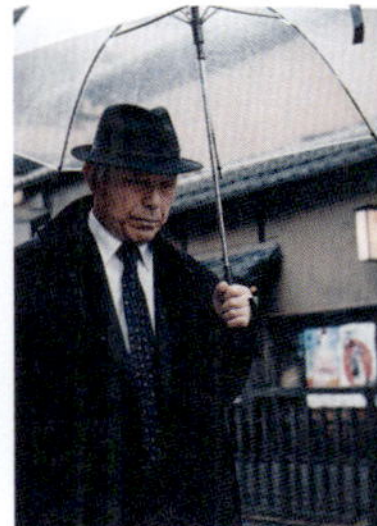

102 Hanamikoji

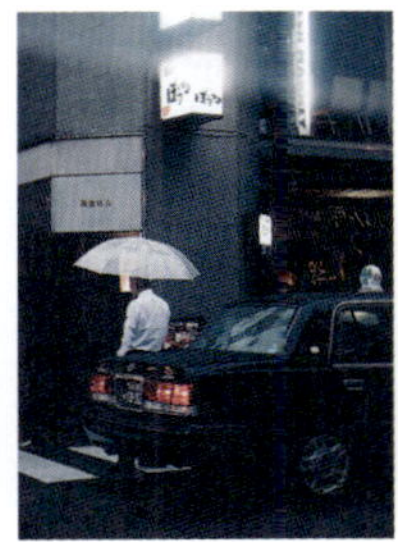

103 Gion

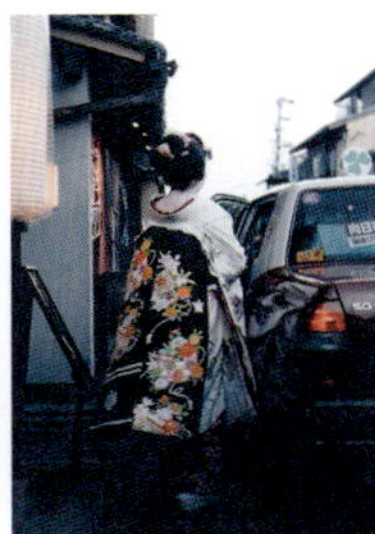

104 Gion

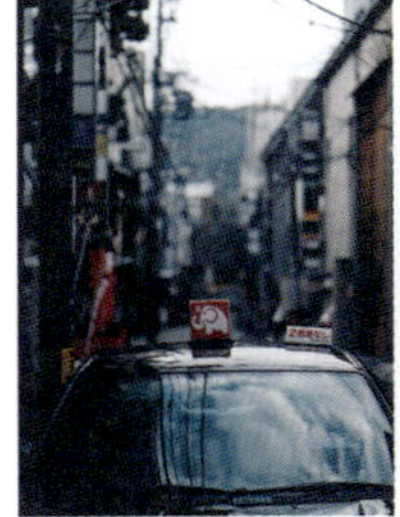

105 Gion

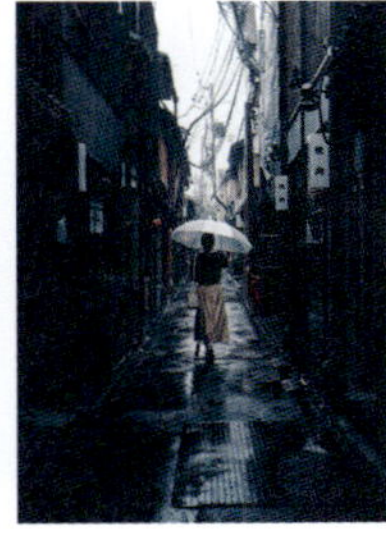

106 Pontochō Alley

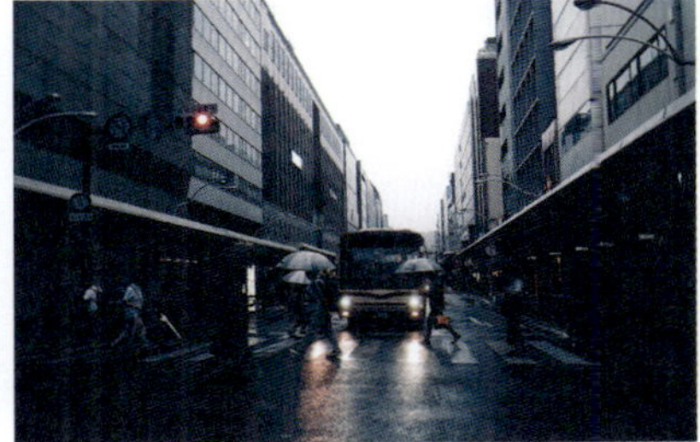

108-109 Shijō-dōri

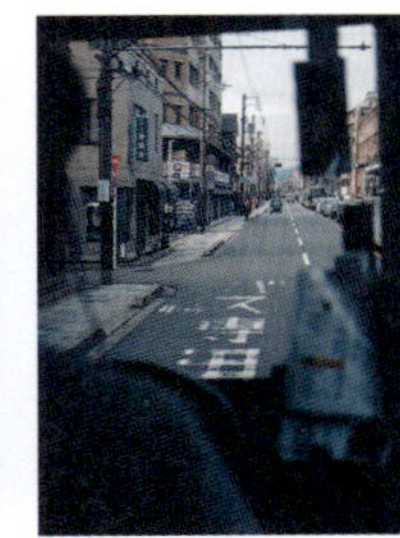

110 Kamigyō-ku

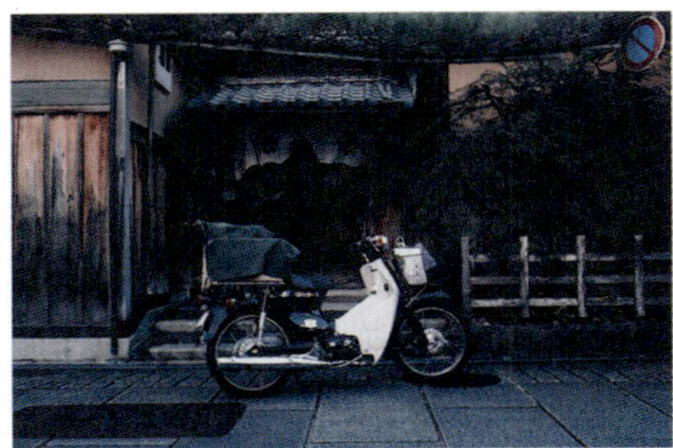

111 Higashiyama-ku

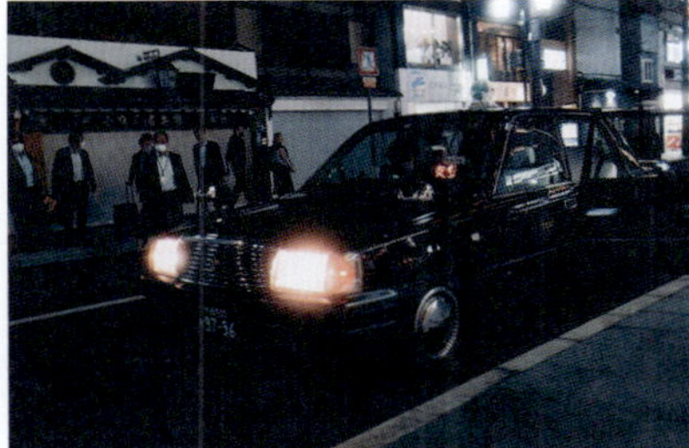

112-113 Nakagyō-ku

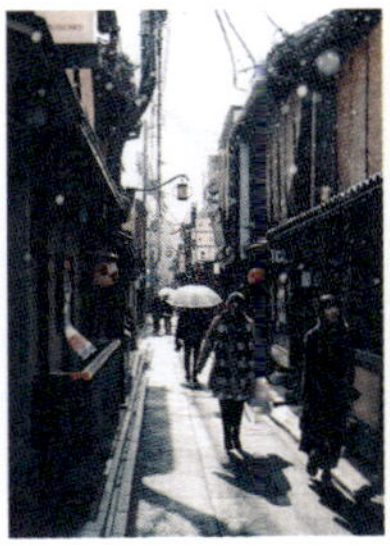

114 Pontochō A ley

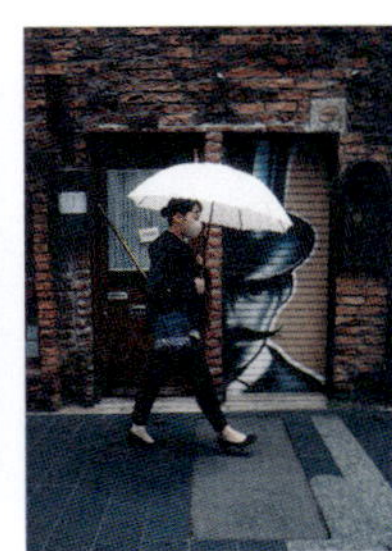

115 Nakagyō-ku

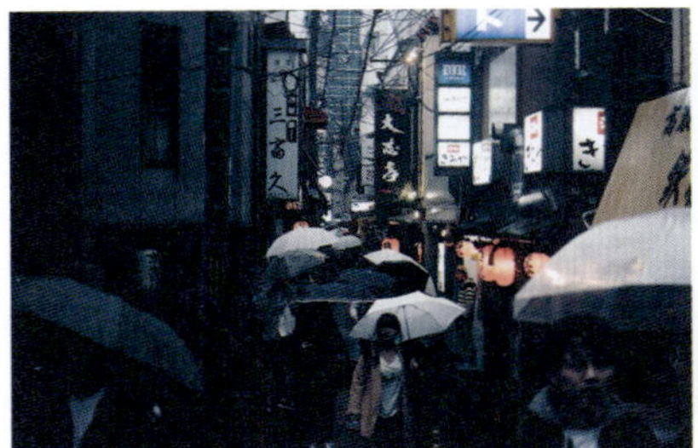

116-117 Kiyamachi

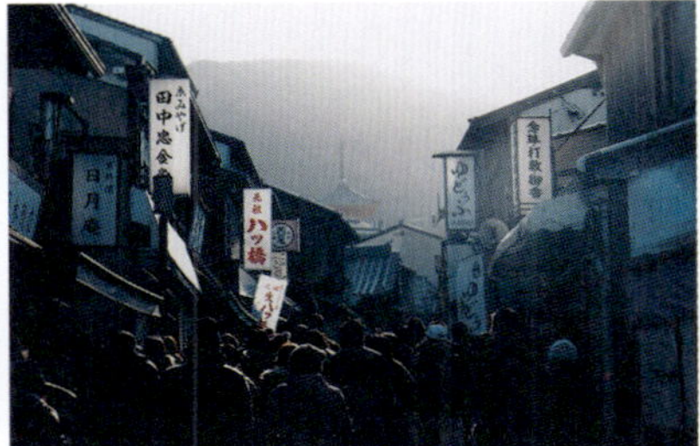

118-119 Sannenzaka

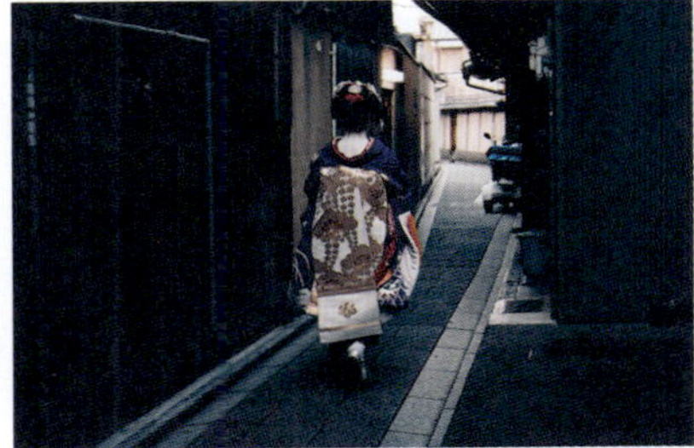

120 Gion

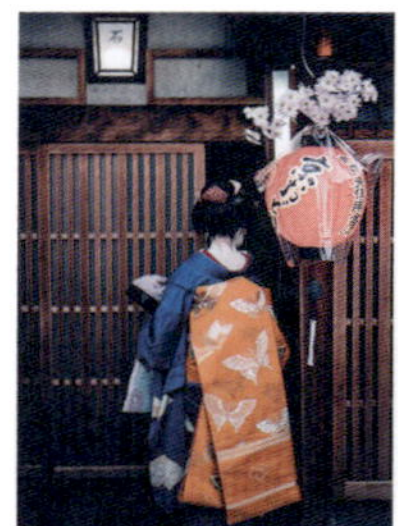

121 Miyagawa-chō

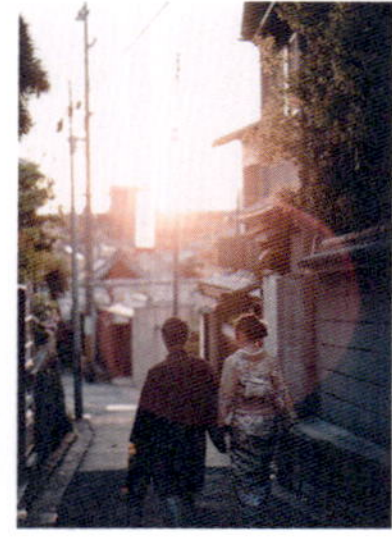

122 Higashiyama-ku

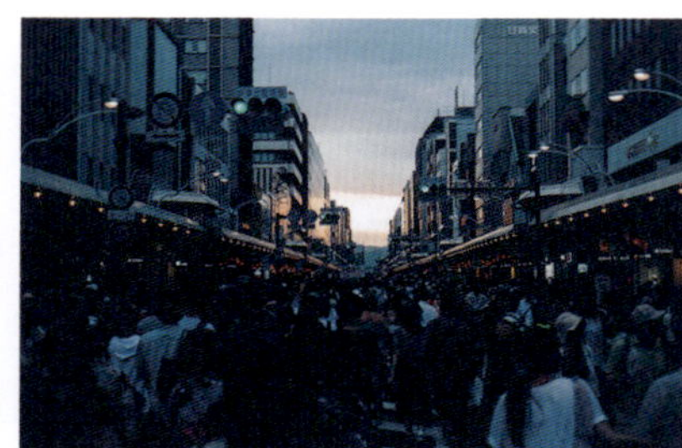

124-125 Shijō-dōri

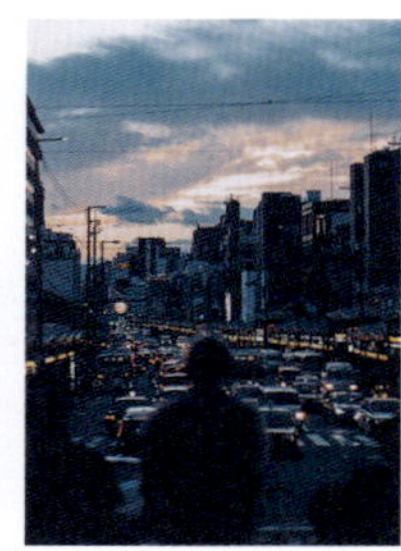

126 Yasaka-jinja

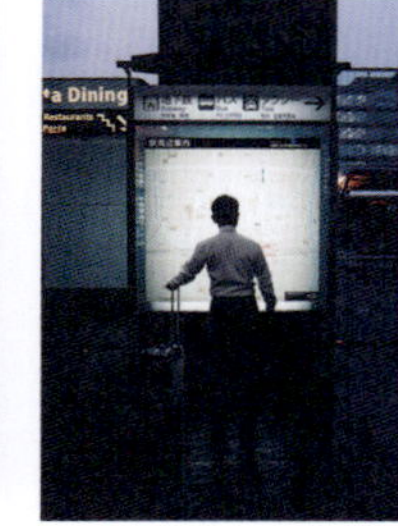

127 Kyoto Station

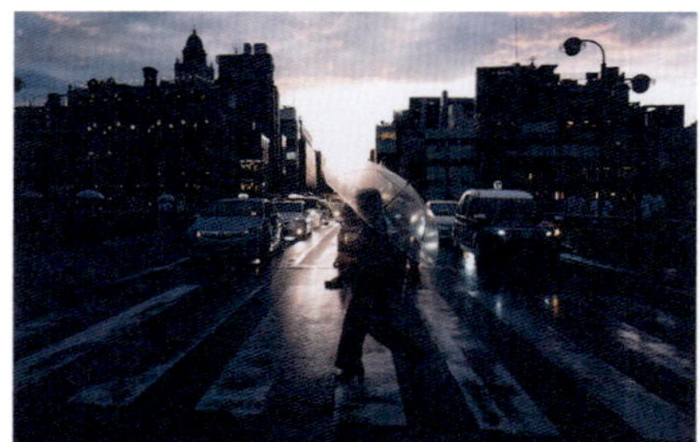

128-129 Shijō-dōri

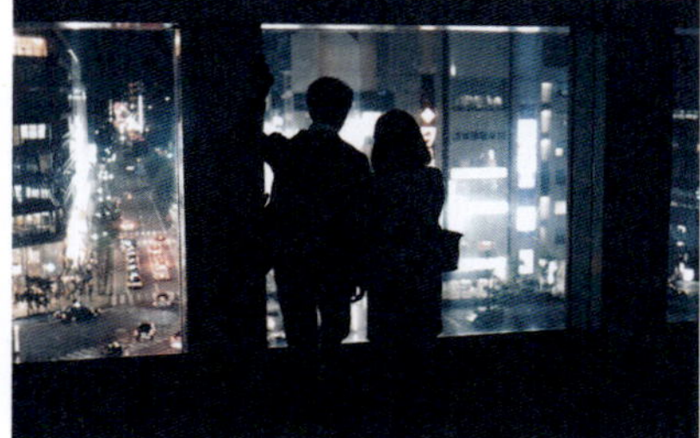

130-131 Kyoto Station

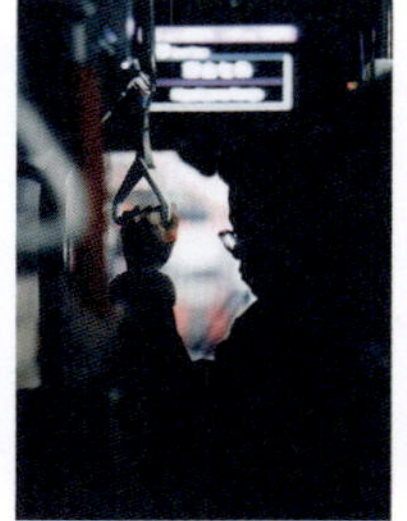

132 Kamigyō-ku

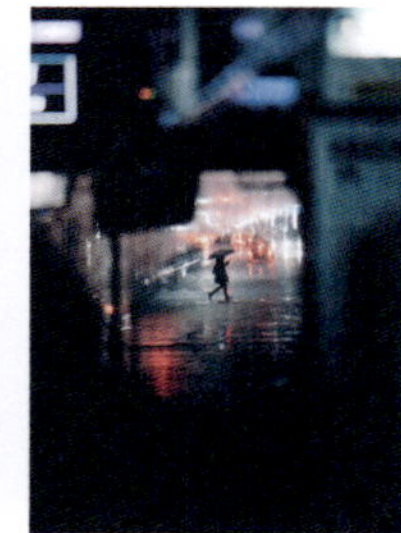

133 Kamigyō-ku

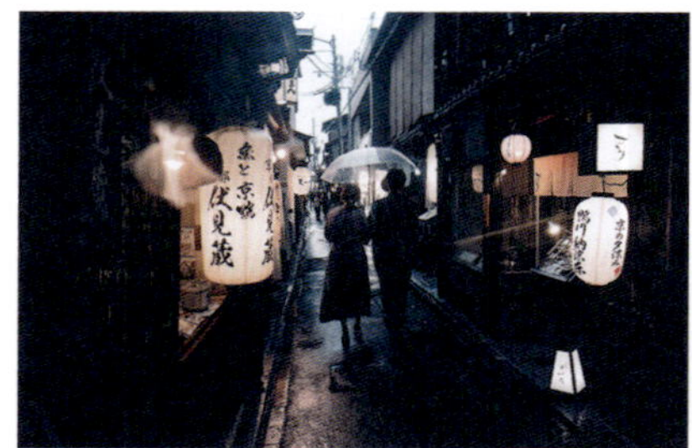

134-135 Pontochō Alley

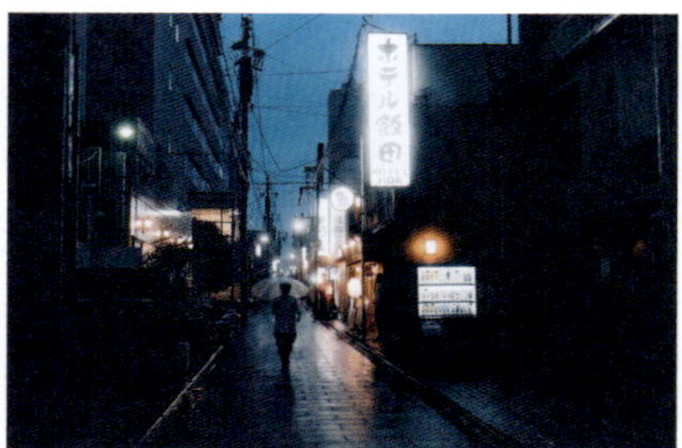

136-137 Shimogyō-ku

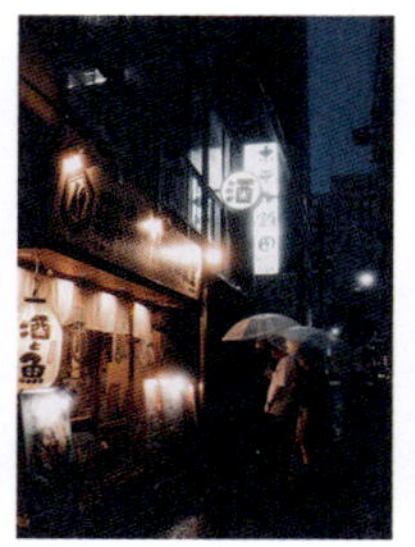

138 Shimogyō-ku

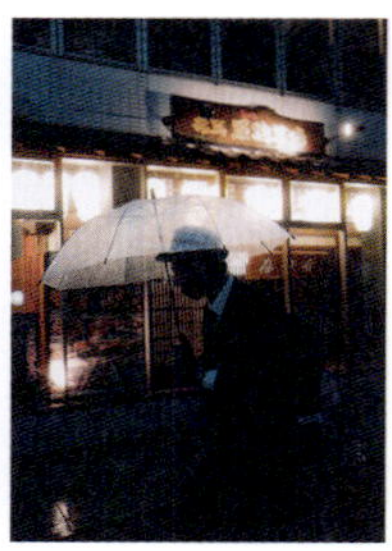

139 Shimogyō-ku

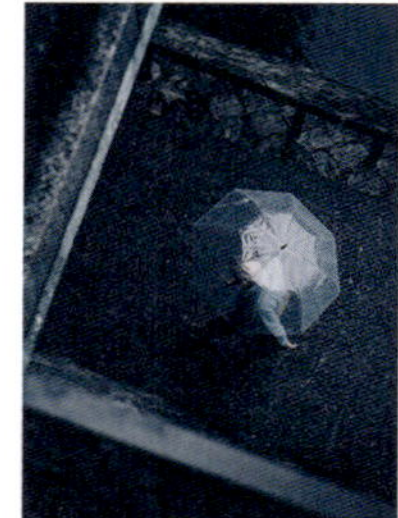

140 Shijō-dōri

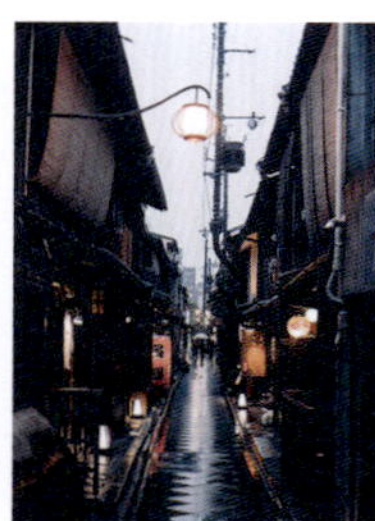

142 Pontochō Alley

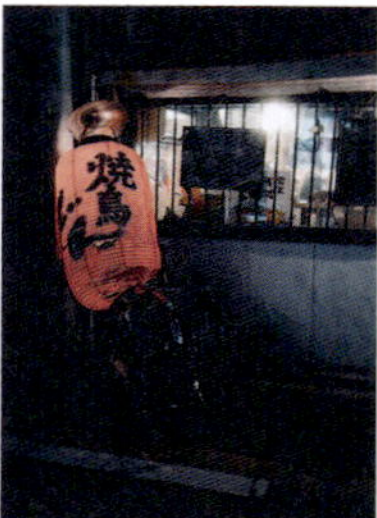

143 Nakagyō-ku

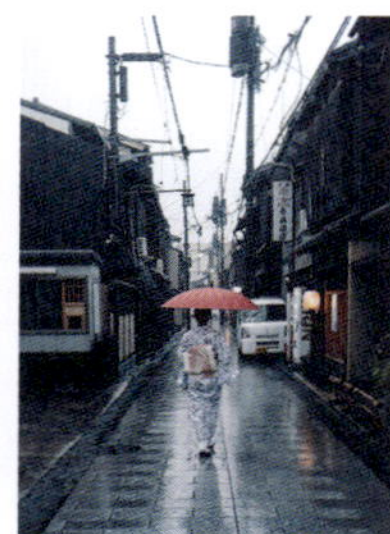

144 Miyagawa-chō

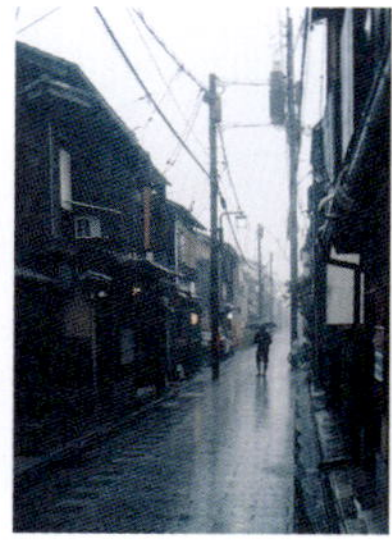

145 Miyagawa-chō

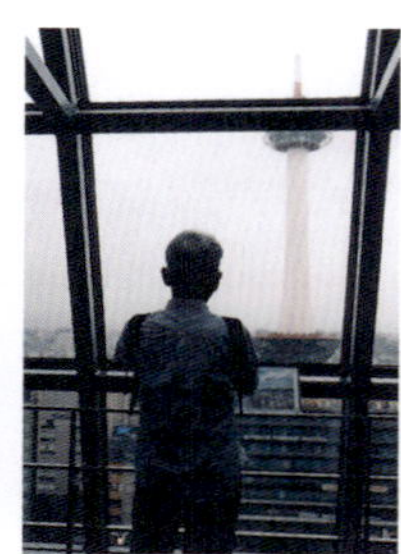

146 Kyoto Station

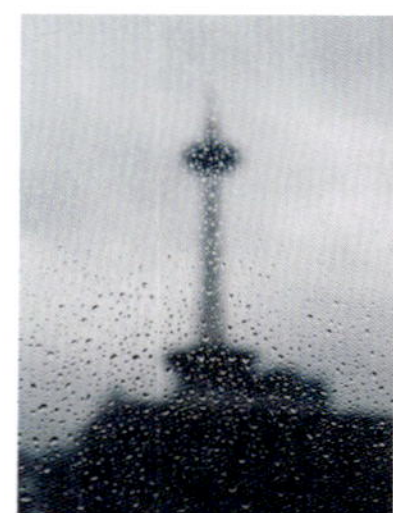

147 Kyoto Tower

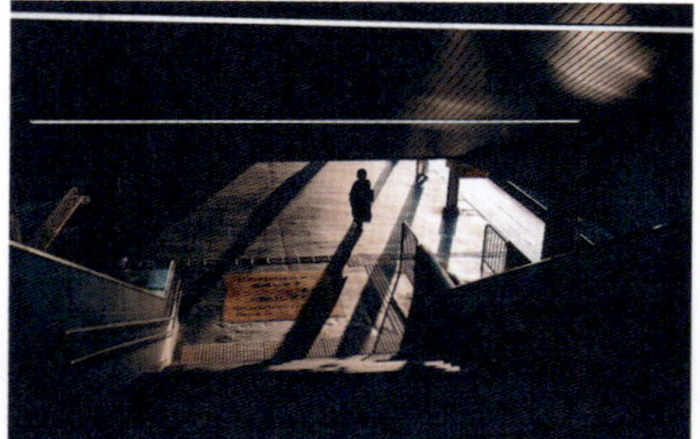

148-149 Kyoto Station

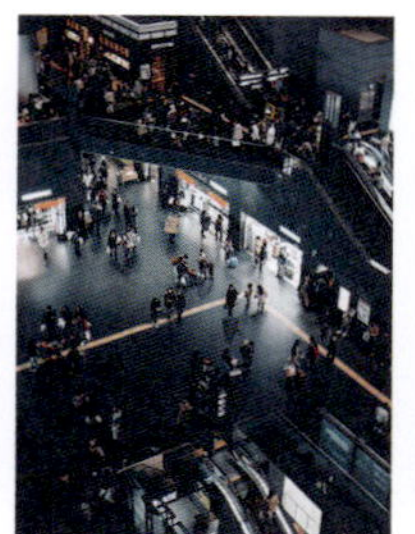

150 Kyoto Station

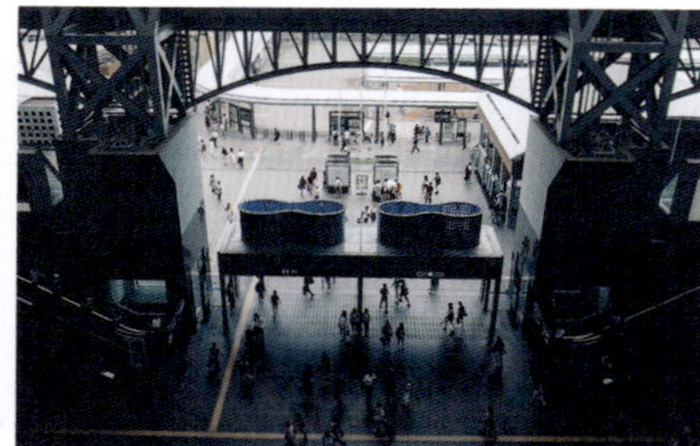

151 Kyoto Station

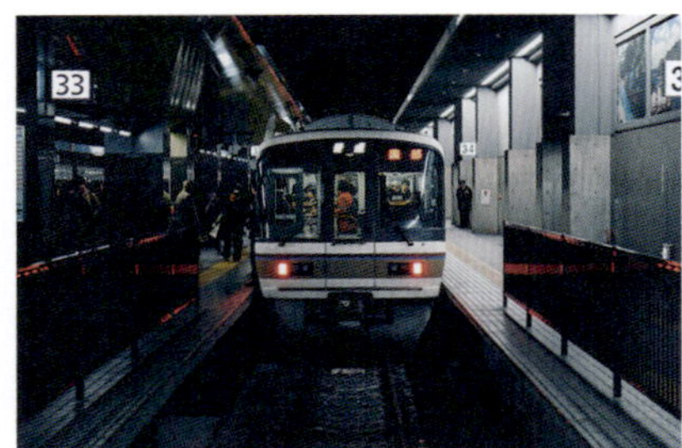

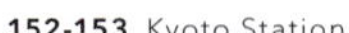

152-153 Kyoto Station

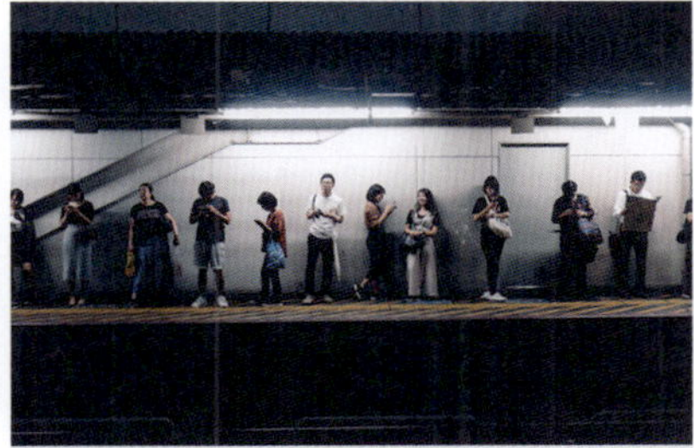

154-155 Kyoto Station

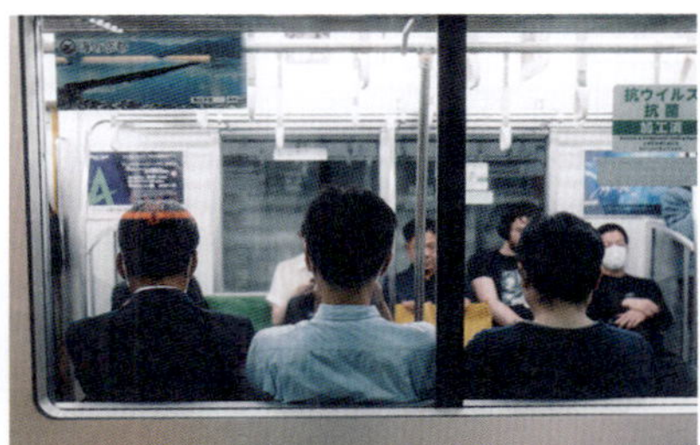

156-157 Gojō Station

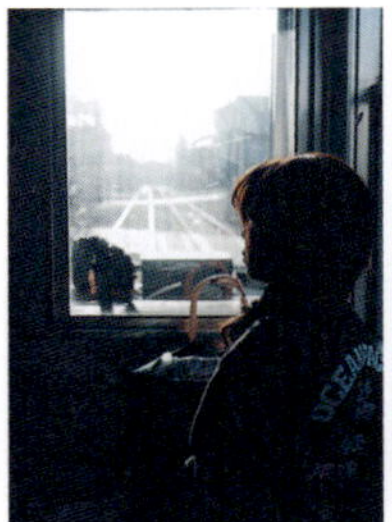

158 Yamashina-ku

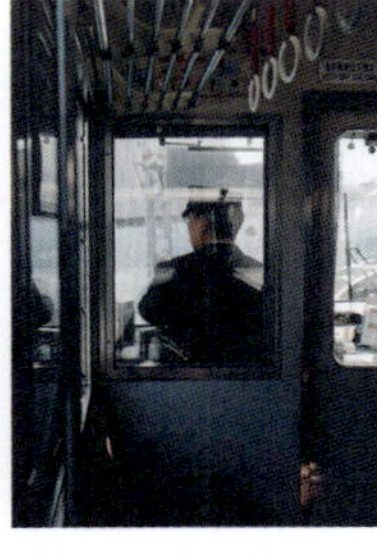

159 Yamashina-ku

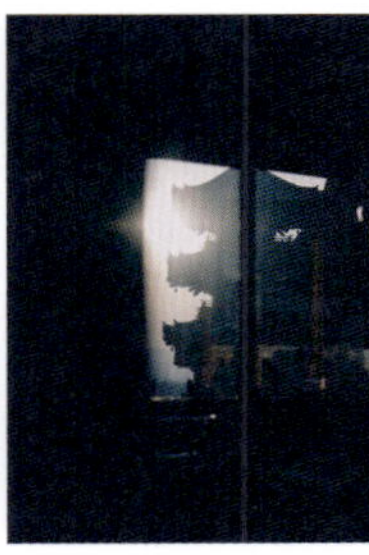

160 Kiyomizu-dera

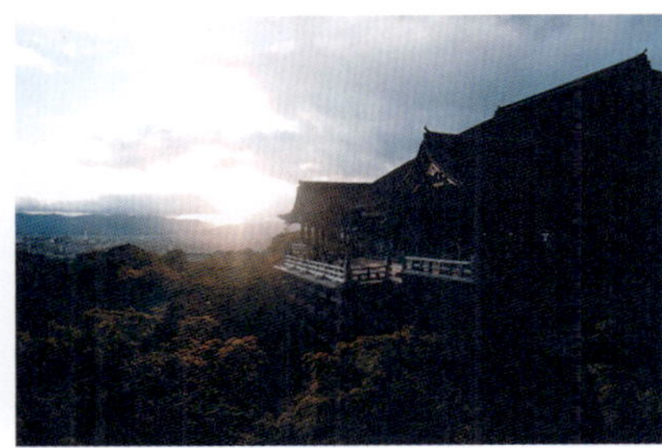

162-163 Kiyomizu-dera

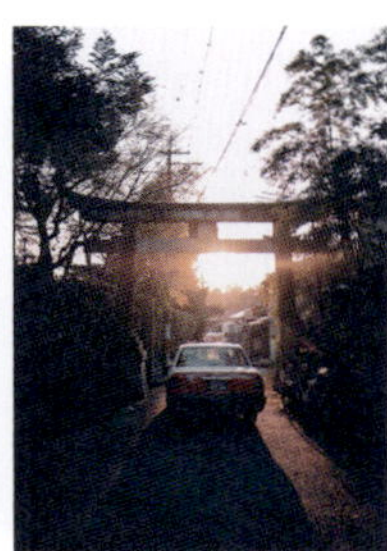

164 Tetsugaku-no-michi

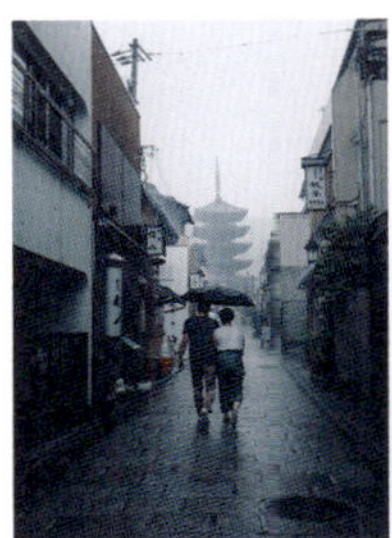

167 Yasaka-dōri

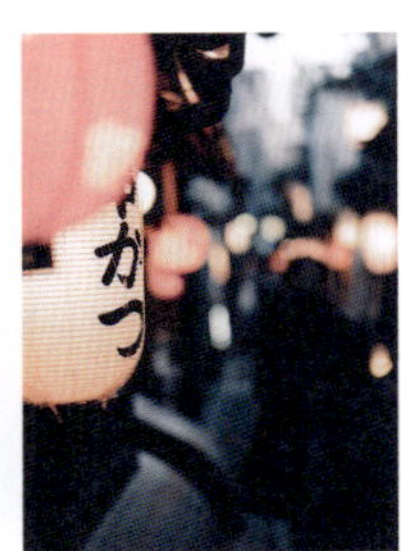

175 Pontochō Alley

LCCN: 2025940174
ISBN: 978-1-951963-52-1

Printed and bound in China
First printing, 2025

Trope Publishing Co.

Taro Moberly's photographs are available
for purchase. For inquires, go to trope.com
or email the gallery at info@trope.com

English translations reprinted with permission:

Pages 28, 75, 89, 107, 123, and 161:
From wakapoetry.net, trans. T.E. McAuley

Page 56:
From *Kyoto: A Literary Guide*, Camphor Press, 2020;
camphorpress.com/books/kyoto-literary-guide/

Page 141: From haikuguy.com/issa,
trans. David G. Lanoue

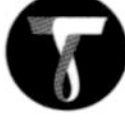

+ INFORMATION:
For additional information
on our books and prints,
visit trope.com

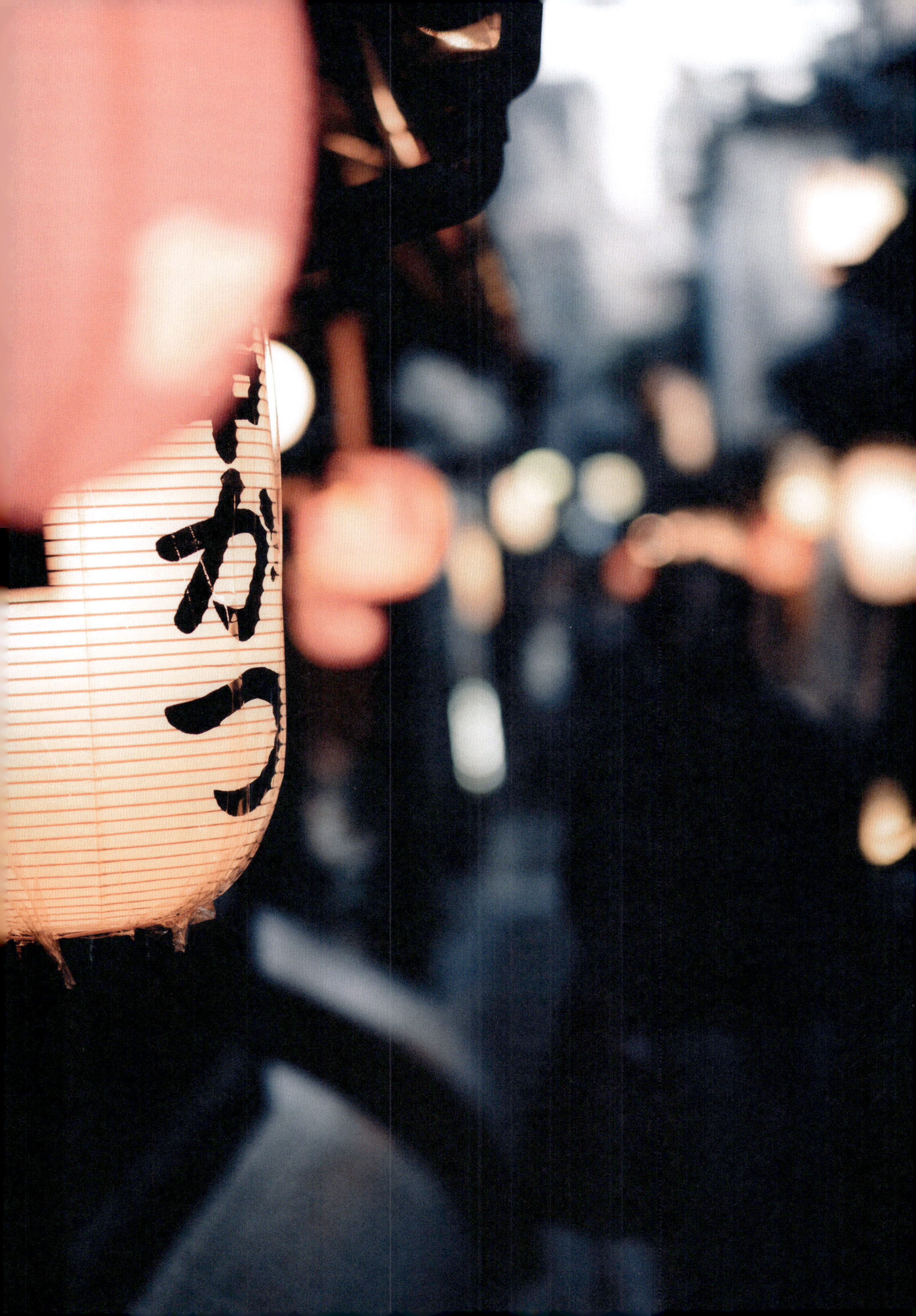
かつ

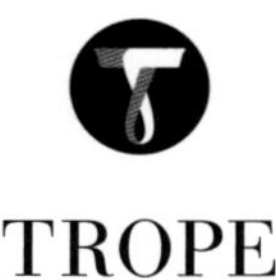

TROPE PUBLISHING Co.

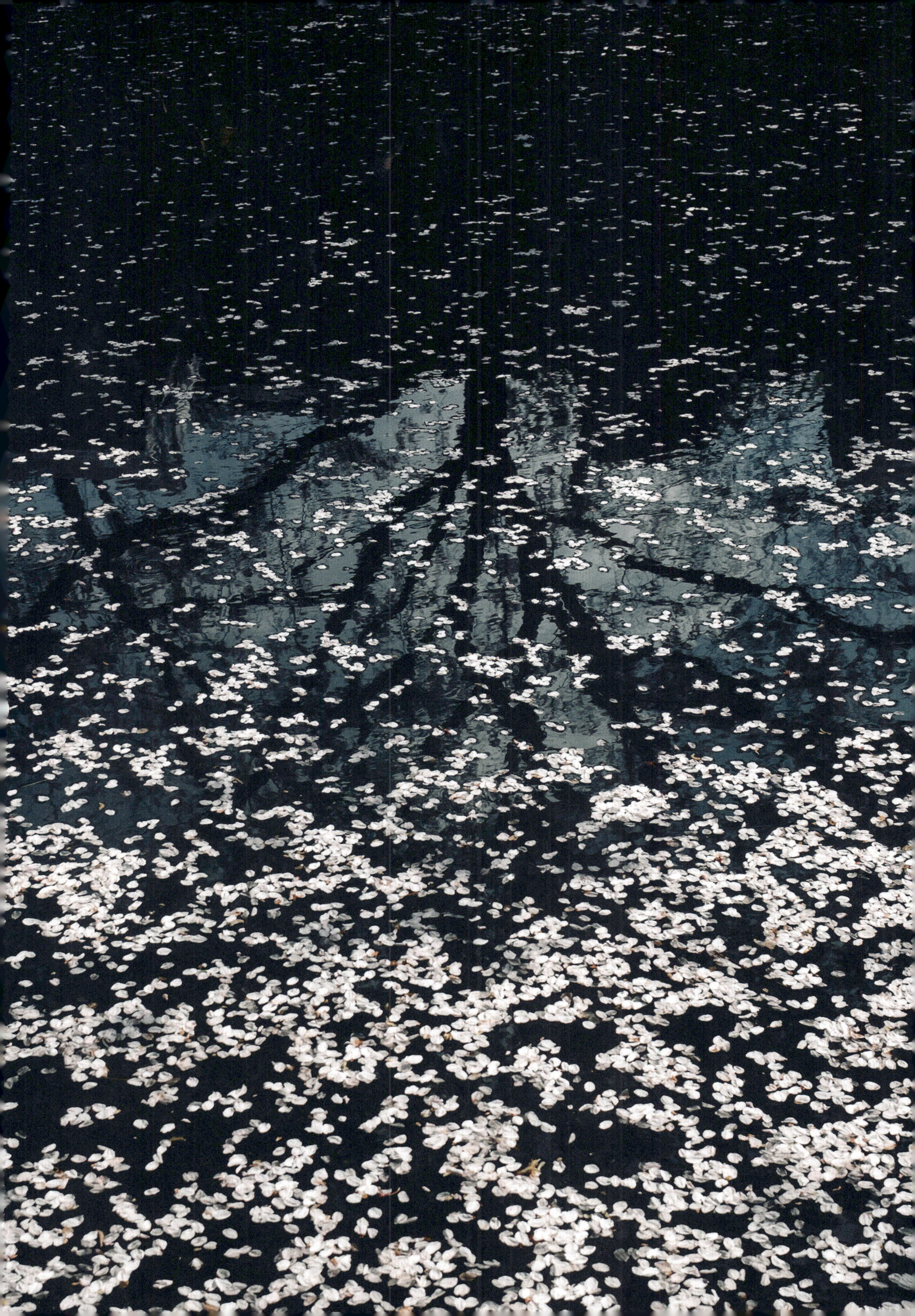

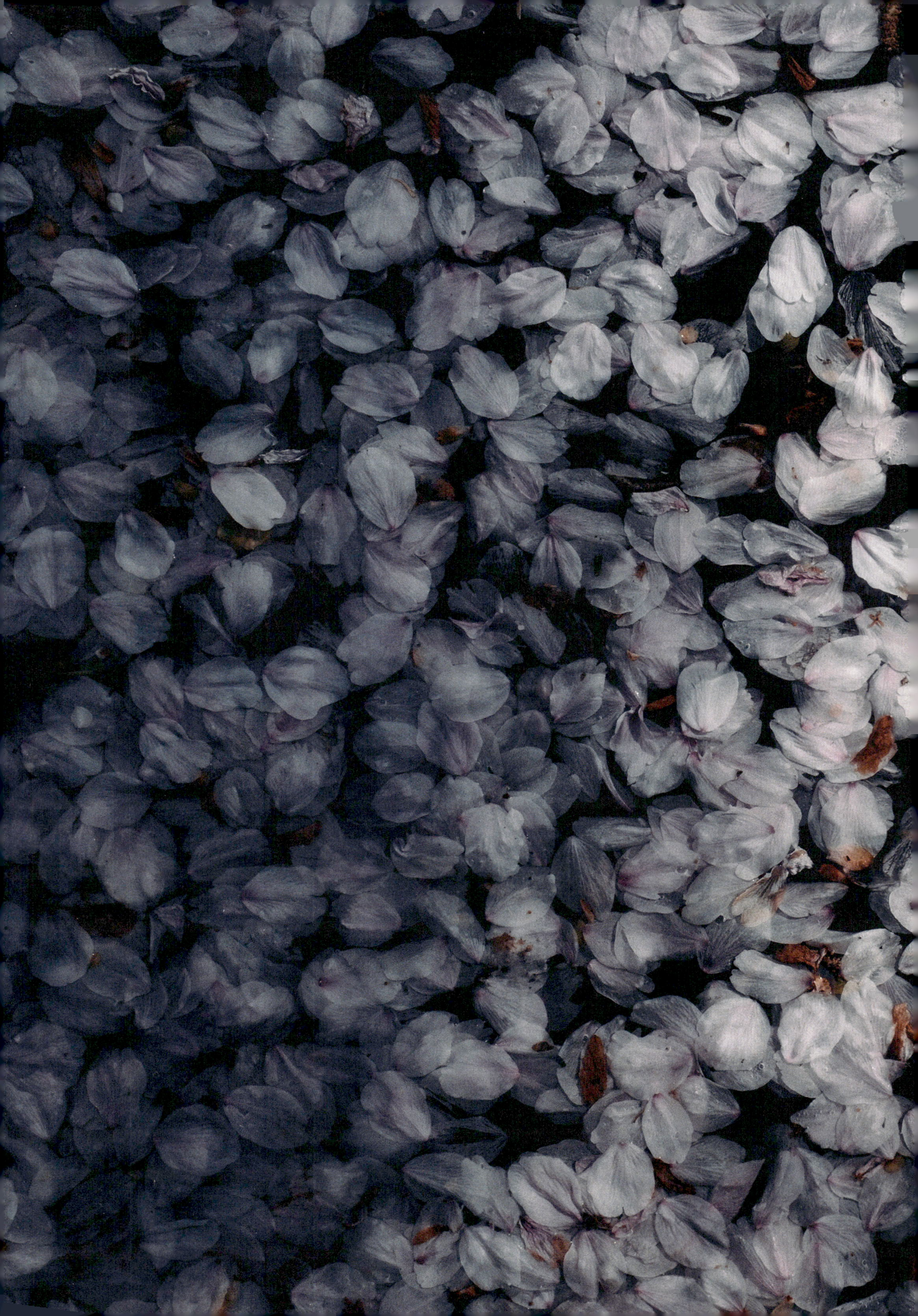